THE WEALTH OF NATIONS

ADAM SMITH was born at Kirkcaldy, on the east coast of Scotland, in 1723, and received his early education at the local burgh school. He subsequently attended Glasgow University (1737–40), where he studied under Francis Hutcheson, and Balliol College, Oxford (1740–46). Two years after his return to Scotland, Smith moved to Edinburgh, where he delivered lectures on Rhetoric which did much to establish his early reputation. In 1751 Smith was appointed Professor of Logic at Glasgow, but was translated to Hutcheson's old chair of Moral Philosophy in 1752. He held this appointment until 1763, during which tenure he published, in 1759, *The Theory of the Moral Sentiments*. In 1764 Smith resigned his professorship to become tutor to the young Duke of Buccleuch, at the invitation of Charles Townshend. This office took him to France, where he travelled extensively, meeting many of the leading thinkers of the day, including Voltaire, Quesnai, Turgot, and Helvetius. Smith began writing *The Wealth of Nations* in France, and continued his researches after his return to Britain in 1766. The book was published in 1776, the same year as the Declaration of Independence. In 1777 Smith became resident in Edinburgh, on his appointment as Commissioner of Customs, and remained there until his death in 1790. He was elected Lord Rector of Glasgow University in 1787, in succession to his friend, Edmund Burke. Smith's life was relatively uneventful and his disposition absent-minded and retiring. Yet he wrote with vigour and did not lack personal courage; a fact attested by his defence of the character of the alleged atheist, David Hume, after the latter's death.

ANDREW SKINNER was educated at Glasgow University and on graduation spent some time at Cornell, Ithaca, N.Y. He received his first academic appointment in 1959, at Queen's University, Belfast, moving in 1962 to the then Queen's College, Dundee, of the University of St Andrews. He taught the history of political theory until 1964. He is now Reader in Political Economy. Mr Skinner has published an edition of Sir James Steuart's *Principles* (1767) and is at present working on studies of Steuart and Adam Smith.

ADAM SMITH

THE
WEALTH OF NATIONS

BOOKS I-III

WITH AN INTRODUCTION BY
ANDREW SKINNER

PENGUIN BOOKS

Penguin Books Ltd, Harmondsworth, Middlesex, England
Penguin Books, 625 Madison Avenue, New York, New York 10022, U.S.A.
Penguin Books Australia Ltd, Ringwood, Victoria, Australia
Penguin Books Canada Ltd, 41 Steelcase Road West, Markham, Ontario, Canada
Penguin Books (N.Z.) Ltd, 182–190 Wairau Road, Auckland 10, New Zealand

—

First published 1776
Published in Pelican Books 1970
Reprinted 1973
Reprinted with revisions 1974
Reprinted 1976, 1977

—

Introduction copyright © Andrew Skinner, 1970, 1974

—

Made and printed in Great Britain
by Richard Clay (The Chaucer Press) Ltd
Bungay, Suffolk
Set in Linotype Granjon

CONTENTS

PREFACE

THE problem of size dictated that the whole of Smith's *The Wealth of Nations* could not be printed in the present series. Accordingly, it was decided to print Books 1 and 2 of the original work entire, thus presenting a volume which is solely concerned with Smith's contribution to the principles of economics. It would probably be agreed that the first two books contain the central part of Smith's work as a theoretical economist, and the real basis of a profoundly influential system of thought. Since the whole text is not printed anew, note references throughout the introduction are to the Cannan edition (Modern Library) with page references to the present volume placed in brackets where appropriate. The text followed is that of the 1789 edition, and Book Three has also been included in order to make the maximum use of the available space.

The nature of the introduction is, of course, dictated by the choice of text, and the argument is presented in a skeletal form which, it is hoped, will assist the reader to find his way through those parts of the original work which are here reprinted. However, since Smith was much more than an *economist* (in the modern sense of the term), some attempt has been made to place the discussion of 'principles' within the broader framework of his philosophical and historical thought. In each case, the argument is presented in a form which may be helpful to the student of Smithian *economics*, and not as an attempt to provide a complete and rounded account of Smith's contribution to philosophy, broadly defined.

I must acknowledge the kind assistance given me by my wife, who has acted the part of 'general reader' throughout with quite remarkable patience and forbearance. I am also indebted to certain of my colleagues in the Department of Political Economy, who have read and commented on the manuscript;

more especially Professor Thomas Wilson, Miss Diane Dawson, and Mr Malcolm MacLennan. As usual, my greatest debt is to Professor A. L. Macfie, who has examined the introduction at every stage, and given me the great benefit of his comment and criticism. None of the above named is in any way responsible for such inadequacies as may remain.

Glasgow University
Spring 1969   *Andrew S. Skinner*

For this second reprint, I have been given the opportunity of effecting a number of small changes, principally with regard to the reading list. I have also taken the opportunity of altering the last ten pages of the introduction with a view to clarification of the doctrines there reviewed.

June 1974   *Andrew S. Skinner*

ADAM SMITH

Born Kirkcaldy, on the east coast of Scotland, in 1723. Educated at Kirkcaldy Burgh School (1730–37); Glasgow University (1737–40), and Balliol College, Oxford (1740–46). Delivered lectures on Rhetoric and Belles Lettres in Edinburgh, 1748–51. Appointed to the Chair of Logic in Glasgow (1751); Professor of Moral Philosophy (1752–64). Travelled on the Continent as tutor to the Duke of Buccleugh (1764–6). 1777 appointed Commissioner of the Customs and Salt Duties in Scotland, resident in Edinburgh. Lord Rector of Glasgow University, 1787–9, died 1790.

MAJOR PUBLICATIONS

The Theory of Moral Sentiments. First edition, London, 1759; second edition 1761; third edition 1767 with the addition of the *Dissertation on the Origin of Languages*. Fourth edition 1774, fifth 1781, and the sixth (with considerable additions), 1790.

An Inquiry into the Nature and Causes of the Wealth of Nations. First edition, London, 1776, second edition 1778. Third edition with major additions), 1784, fourth edition 1786, and fifth edition 1789.

Essays on Philosophical Subjects. Edited by Joseph Black and James Hutton, Edinburgh, 1795.

LECTURE NOTES

Lectures on Justice, Police, Revenue and Arms. Delivered in the University of Glasgow by Adam Smith. Reported by a student in 1763. Edited by Edwin Cannan, Oxford, 1896.

Lectures on Rhetoric and Belles Lettres. Delivered in the University of Glasgow by Adam Smith. Reported by a student in 1762–3. Edited by John M. Lothian, Edinburgh, 1963.

FURTHER READING

While there is a vast literature on Smith, the reader with a general interest in this subject may find the following books particularly helpful:

Blaug, M. *Economic Theory in Retrospect* (1961).
Cannan, E. Introductions to Smith's *Lectures on Justice* etc. (1896), and *The Wealth of Nations* (1904).
Fay, C. R. *Adam Smith and the Scotland of his Day* (1956).
Higgs, H. *The Physiocrats* (1898).
Hollander, J. (ed.) *Adam Smith, 1776–1926* (1928).
Hume, David *Writings on Economics*, ed. E. Rotwein (1955).
Lehmann, W. C. *John Millar of Glasgow* (1960).
Letwin, W. *The Origins of Scientific Economics* (1963).
Macfie, A. L. *The Individual in Society: Papers on Adam Smith* (1967).
Meek, R. L. *Economics and Ideology and Other Essays* (1967); *The Economics of Physiocracy* (1962).
Morrow, G. *The Ethical and Economic Theories of Adam Smith* (1923).
Rae, John *Life of Adam Smith* (1895). Reprinted and with an introduction: *Guide to John Rae's Life of Adam Smith*, by Jacob Viner (1965).
Schumpeter, J. *A History of Economic Analysis* (1954); *Economic Doctrine and Method* (1954).
Scott, W. R. *Adam Smith as Student and Professor* (1937).
Stewart, D. 'Biographical Memoir of Adam Smith' in *Collected Works*, ed. Sir W. Hamilton, vol. 10 (1858).
Turgot, A. J. *Reflexions sur la Formation et la Distribution des Richesses* (1766) ed. and trans. Ashley (1898).

Since the first publication of this volume a number of works have been published which deal with Adam Smith. The most notable are:

T. D. Campbell, *Adam Smith's Science of Morals* (1971).
M. Bowley, *Studies in the History of Economic Theory Before 1870* (1973).
S. Hollander, *The Economics of Adam Smith* (1973).
J. R. Lindgren, *The Social Philosophy of Adam Smith* (1973).

In addition to the above, there are a number of useful general histories, for example: *The History of Economic Thought* by Eric Roll (1937); and a separate book with the same title by W. J. Barber (1967); Gide (C) and Rist (C) *History of Economic Doctrines* (1915); and L. Rogin, *The Meaning and Validity of Economic Theory* (1956). On the philosophical side, the reader might consult G. H. Sabine's *History of Political Theory* (1937), chapters 26–9, and C. Becker *The Heavenly City of the Eighteenth Century Philosophers* (1932).

INTRODUCTION

ADAM SMITH was undoubtedly the remarkable product of a remarkable age, and one whose writings clearly reflect the intellectual, social, and economic conditions of the period. Unlike some men of distinguished abilities, Smith's literary output brought him great fame during his own lifetime; a great reputation initially founded on *The Theory of Moral Sentiments* and firmly consolidated by his major work.

When *The Wealth of Nations* was first published in March 1776 David Hume wrote to his old friend in terms of the greatest praise, while qualifying his hopes by remarking that 'the reading of it necessarily requires so much attention, and the public is disposed to give so little, that I shall still doubt for some time of its being at first very popular'.[1] Strahan, Smith's publisher, wrote very much in the same vein when commenting that the sales of the book had been much more 'than I could have expected from a work that requires much thought and reflection (qualities that do not abound among modern readers) to peruse to any purpose'.[2] But despite the doubts of Smith's friends, the book sold well, not least because the general 'philosophy' which it contained was so thoroughly in accord with the aspirations and circumstances of the age. In a work which did not eschew the weapons of rhetoric and irony, Smith stated his famous theme of economic liberty with telling force, and in a manner which apparently caught and held the attention of his contemporaries. Indeed, the arguments of *The Wealth of Nations* seemed to lend a certain sanctity to the self-interested pursuit of gain, by showing that such activity was productive of benefit to society at large; by demonstrating that the enterprise of individuals was capable, when left free of regulation, of carrying the standard of material well-being to heights hitherto impossible and scarcely calculable. In the words of one (rather bitter) critic, Smith seemed to have provided a great 'masked battery',[3] whose fire could be used to support the pretensions of the emergent mercantile or manufacturing interests (whose motives Smith often doubted) and to sweep away those institutional obstacles to which every society or economy in a process of transition is inevitably subject. To many contemporaries Smith's message was both powerful and attractive, while to us, armed with the benefit of hindsight, he appears as the herald if not the prophet of a new order.

Yet Hume was undoubtedly correct in stating that the book requires 'great thought', the reason being that *The Wealth of Nations*, which so frequently has the air of a tract for the times, is in reality a great analytical performance. The 'analytics' are contained in the first two books and would appear to be particularly worthy of our attention for a number of reasons, few of which in all probability explain the immediate impact of the work, although they may explain its continuing importance.

Smith was concerned with a type of economy recognizably 'capitalist' in outline, and his purpose was to expose the basic laws of motion which govern its operation. In successfully undertaking this revolutionary task, Smith left us a book of lasting relevance: a book which contains in effect a great system of thought, constructed by first analysing individual problems (such as the determinants of price, or distribution) before going on to demonstrate their mutual connexion and thus the interdependence of all economic phenomena. Looked at in this light, Smithian economics in fact provides the reader with the analytical means of understanding the *modus operandi* of a particular type of *economy*, and with a body of theory which falls exactly within his own definition of the nature and purposes of the intellectual system:

Systems in many respects resemble machines. A machine is a little system, created to perform, as well as to connect together, in reality, those different movements and effects which the artist has occasion for. A system is an imaginary machine, invented to connect together in the fancy those different movements and effects which are already in reality performed.[4]

It is probably no more than the truth to suggest that Smith's real sophistication is to be seen in the vast analytical system with which he provided us, rather than in his contribution to individual areas of economic analysis. It is certain that the systematic character of Smith's formal economics is of great historical importance, not merely because of the extent of his coverage but also because he in fact provided the foundation of a great edifice, which has been extended rather than destroyed by those who followed.

However, while the theoretical economist may be pardoned for concentrating on this aspect of Smith's work, it is to be remembered that his system building went well beyond the analytics of the major book. In this connexion it is instructive to recall that the source of Smith's initial fame was (social) philosophy, rather than economics, and that he himself regarded *The Moral Sentiments* and *The Wealth of Nations* as but parts of a single, greater whole; as the parts of a grand synthetic system which he hoped to complete with a published account of 'the general principles of law and government, and of the different revolutions they had undergone in the different ages and periods of society'.[5] The area of study just mentioned embraces a particular type of historical (and sociological) exercise and a discipline which is clearly distinct from philosophy and economics.[6] Smith himself appears to have viewed the areas of analysis just mentioned in exactly this light; a fact which constitutes a major part of his achievement and which makes it possible to examine any one section of his thought in isolation from the others. However, precisely because Smith viewed his philosophical, historical, and economic work as parts of a single whole, we should perhaps expect that a useful perspective on any one may be gained by paying at least *some* attention to the others. This judgement would appear to be particularly valid in the case of *The Wealth of Nations*, not least because the latter work, taken in conjunction with the two other relevant areas, demonstrates that Smith may be described not just as an economist but also as a social scientist in the broadest sense of the term.

Smith never lost sight of the fact that the study of economic phenomena involves the examination of one aspect of the activities of man in society. The modern economist would of course accept this view, although Smith's position may differ in the degree of attention given to the fact in question; a degree of attention which may reflect not only Smith's wide range of competence but also his interest in the economy as an entity. It is certainly true that the theoretical economics of *The Wealth of Nations* rests upon two assumptions of a broadly sociological character: first, that man is found in the social *state*, and second, that man will be found within a particular type of social *structure* wherever the exchange economy prevails. Both assumed conditions are verifiable in fact, but Smith went further than the simple empirical exercise in offering some explanation of the relevant phenomena, in the philosophical and historical works respectively. This point alone makes the theory of history, and *The Theory of the Moral Sentiments*, relevant for the student of Smithian economics, in the sense that both areas of analysis help to establish certain premises (sociological and psychological) of *The Wealth of Nations*. Moreover, the relationships between the parts of Smith's grand synthetic system are positively instructive not least because they enabled Smith to demonstrate that economic advance has sociological consequences which are not always of a beneficent tendency.

Accordingly, this introduction to Smithian economics will be divided into three sections. In the first we shall be concerned with the *Moral Sentiments*, and with Smith's analysis of man's disposition to, and fitness for, society. The argument is particularly relevant for our purposes in that it serves to expose the minimum conditions which must be satisfied before society can *subsist* together with the psychology employed in Smith's economics.

In the second part we shall consider Smith's views as to the form and historical origin of the particular type of social structure which is assumed in the economic *sections* of *The Wealth of Nations*.

Finally, we consider in broad outline the content and purpose of Smith's economics, placing most emphasis on the theme of interdependence, and on its broadly systematic character.

Throughout the present argument, an attempt is made to elucidate the interconnexions which exist between the formally separate *areas* of Smith's thought, at least by indicating that we may proceed from one to the other in a fairly clear and logical order. At the same time, it is hoped that an argument of this kind will demonstrate the truth that each of the relevant areas is linked by common doctrines, particularly as regards the psychology of man, and the manner in which human activities are controlled by, and help to create, certain social institutions.

SECTION I: THE SOCIAL PHILOSOPHY[1]

I

Adam Smith's *Theory of the Moral Sentiments* has much in common with the works of contemporaries, such as Hutcheson, Hume, George Turnbull, and Thomas Reid. Indeed, if we add the names of Henry Home (Lord Kames), Adam Ferguson, and Dugald Stewart to this list it may be said that such men comprised a distinctive School of Scottish Philosophy.[2]

The term 'school' is used advisedly in that the writings of its members disclose certain common elements; elements which appear in all areas of Smith's work.

First, the method employed was empirical rather than speculative, owing more to the example of the *Novum Organum* (1620) than to Descartes' *Discours de la Méthode* (1637). Bacon was almost as much admired as Montesquieu in Scottish intellectual circles, but unquestionably the main debt, in respect of method, was due to Sir Isaac Newton. Newton, as an exponent of the 'experimental method', was the author of a new synthesis, not least in that he effected a union between the inductive approach associated with Bacon and the more purely deductive tradition of which Descartes was the representative. Indeed, Newton himself had explicitly suggested that the 'experimental method' which he had used in natural philosophy could be profitably applied to moral philosophy itself.[3]

Secondly, the work of the School shows a concern with the nature of human behaviour and with the fact that man is generally found not in the isolated but in the social state. It was also clearly recognized that the scientific study of the nature of man was an essential prelude to the study of problems both sociological and philosophical in character, so that in this respect Hume's position commanded wide agreement: 'As the science of man is the only solid foundation for the other sciences, so the only solid foundation we can give to this science itself must be laid on observation and experience.'[4]

Thirdly, the philosophy of the School maintains that while observation, introspection, and reason enable us to establish the characteristics or 'propensities' of human nature, these propensities exist independently of our knowledge of them. The School in fact generally adopted the position that certain characteristics are implanted *in* man by the Author of Nature, thus providing the means by which a Rational Plan, whose purposes are not always known *to* man, is unfolded.

Fourthly, the members of the School shared a common interest in two questions which were considered to be of particular importance for the moral philosopher. First: 'By what means does it come to pass that the mind prefers one tenor of conduct to another?' And secondly: 'Wherein does virtue consist, or what is the tone and tenor of conduct which constitutes the excellent or praiseworthy character?'[5]

While our main interest here is in the content of Smith's social (as distinct from moral) philosophy, the two areas are so inter-connected as to be virtually indistinguishable, the reason being that the answers provided to the two questions above mentioned helped Smith to explain man's fitness for that social state in which he is generally found.

In demonstrating man's fitness for society, Smith's argument rests on certain judgements with respect to human nature. Specifically, he suggested that man is endowed (by the Author of Nature) with certain faculties (such as reason or imagination) together with particular propensities (such as self-love or fellow feeling);[6] propensities which at once incline man to the social state and at the same time prove potentially disruptive of it.

On Smith's argument, the existence of selfish (or at least self-regarding) propensities suggests that those facets of human nature which incline man to the social state cannot of themselves be sufficient to sustain it in any degree of harmony or order. In other words, certain sources of control are required over the self-regarding activities of individual men; sources of control such as the rules of justice and morality which must be known and observed by the members of any social group. Of itself, the point is perhaps unexceptional, but Smith's discussion of the necessity and origin of those general rules which guide the activities of men is of great importance, not least because it exposes one of the most characteristic features of his thought. Briefly stated, it may be said that some aspects of human nature require certain sources of control, while others ensure that they do in fact develop. Smith's argument thus suggests that social order becomes possible by virtue of the restraints which individuals impose upon *themselves*, thus unfolding at least part of a Divine Plan; a Plan which is given substantial expression by virtue of the activities of individuals who are quite unconscious of the end which these activities help to promote. In what follows we shall make some attempt to delineate the main elements of Smith's argument with a view to exposing the conditions which must be satisfied before orderly social existence is possible. Looking at the *Moral Sentiments* from this point of view, it will be convenient to start with the central concept of 'propriety'; that is, with Smith's account of the way in which the individual forms judgements (applied both to himself and others) concerning what is fit and proper to be done or avoided.

2

In Smith's view, the *process by which* we distinguish between objects of approval or disapproval involves a complex of abilities and propensities which include sympathy, imagination, reason, and reflection. To begin with, he stated, (following Hume) that man is possessed of a certain 'fellow feeling':

How selfish soever man may be supposed, there are evidently some principles in his nature which interest him in the fortune of others, and render their happiness necessary to him, though he derives nothing from it except the pleasure of seeing it.[7]

This 'fellow feeling', or interest in the situation of others, is important in that it permits man to feel joy or sorrow for the fortune or misfortune of others, and to look, as it were, with a sympathetic eye upon their circumstances. The same disposition also enables us to judge as to the nature of the situation in which others find themselves; for example, as to whether or not this situation contributes to the happiness or unhappiness of the individual. In doing this, we stand in the relation of bystander or spectator, and Smith was careful to argue that, 'As we have no immediate experience of what other men feel, we can form no idea of the manner in which they are affected, but by conceiving what we ourselves should feel in a like situation.'[8] An expression of sympathy (broadly defined) for others thus involves an act of *reflection* and *imagination* in the sense that in observing the situation of another we can only form an opinion 'by changing places in fancy' with him.

Having established these basic principles as regards the way we judge others, Smith went on to apply them to the explanation of our sense of propriety.

The question of *propriety* becomes relevant when we go beyond the consideration of the circumstances facing the subject, to examine the extent to which his actions or 'affections' are appropriate to the conditions under which they take place, or the objects which they seek to attain. Smith thus defined propriety or impropriety to consist in 'the suitableness or unsuitableness, in the proportion or disproportion, which the affection seems to bear to the cause or object which excites it'.[9]

Given the principles so far established, it follows that where the *spectator* of another man's actions seeks to form an opinion as to its propriety, he must 'bring home to himself' both the circumstances and the actions of the person judged. As before, Smith argued that an act of judgement on the part of the spectator must involve an effort of imagination and comparison, since, 'When we judge . . . of any affection as proportioned or disproportioned to the cause which excites it, it is scarce possible that we should make use of any other rule or canon but the correspondent affection in ourselves.'[10] The same basic principles also apply, Smith argued, when the individual seeks to form an opinion as to the propriety of his *own* conduct. In this case we act not as the spectator of another's conduct but rather seek to judge our own by visualizing the manner in which the real or supposed spectator might react to it:

We can never survey our own sentiments and motives, we can never form any judgement concerning them, unless we remove ourselves, as it were, from our own natural station, and endeavour to view them as at a certain distance from us. But we can do this in no other way than by endeavouring to view them with the eyes of other people, or as other people are likely to view them.[11]

Now this argument means that the actions of men are always judged by some agency regarded as external to themselves; that is, by either the real or supposed spectators of their conduct. This in turn indicates that the actions of the person judged will be considered proper or improper, worthy of approval or disapproval, according to the degree to which *the spectator* can agree or sympathize with them. As Smith put it: 'To approve of the passions of another . . . as suitable to their objects, is the same thing as to observe that we entirely sympathize with them.'[12] He added: 'When the original passions of the persons principally concerned are in perfect concord with the sympathetic emotions of the spectator, they necessarily appear to this last just and proper.'[13] This argument raises two distinct but connected problems affecting the person judged, and the person judging. In the first place, it is evident that the spectator can only 'enter into' the situation of another to a limited degree; the problem being that we have 'no immediate experience of what other men feel'. As Smith pointed out: 'Mankind, though naturally sympathetic, never conceives for what has befallen another, that degree of passion which animates the person principally concerned.'[14] In recognition of this point, Smith went on to argue that the *degree to which* the spectator can enter into the situation of another may involve a virtue, the 'soft and amiable virtue of sensibility or humanity'. Secondly, it is evident that if the reactions of the spectator provide the means by which the conduct of others is judged, and if the spectator has no immediate experience of what 'other men feel', then it follows that an action considered proper by the spectator must involve an element of restraint on the part of the agent. In other words, the person judged of can only attain the agreement and thus the approval of the spectator 'by lowering his passion to that pitch in which the spectators are capable of going along with him. He must flatten, if I may be allowed to say so, the sharpness of its natural tone, in order to reduce it to harmony and concord with the emotions of those who are about him.'[15]

It thus follows that before the action taken, or feelings expressed, by the agent can be approved of by the spectator, there must be a certain 'mediocrity' in expression; an element of self-control with which Smith associated the 'awful and respectable virtue' of self-command.

The argument so far establishes two important results. First, it suggests that man has the ability to judge the actions both of himself and others by virtue of his powers of fellow-feeling, reflection, and imagination. Secondly, the argument suggests that before the spectator can approve the actions or feelings of others as suitable to their objects, there must be a certain restraint on the part of the agent. It will be observed that neither the ability to judge nor the recognition of the nature of a sense of propriety is sufficient to ensure that the individual will impose any restraint on his actions, feelings, or affections. We may, for example, deplore our own practices, and happily spend the proceeds; we may recognize that others deplore our activities and conveniently ignore them. In Smith's model the logical problem thus raised is at least partially solved by the argument that man is naturally disposed to seek the *approval of his fellows*, and also to be *worthy of approval* :

Nature, when she formed man for society, endowed him with an original desire to please, and an original aversion to offend his brethren. She taught him to feel pleasure in their favourable, and pain in their unfavourable regard. She rendered their approbation most flattering to him for its own sake, and their disapprobation most mortifying and most offensive.[16]

It is precisely because the individual regards the opinions of the spectator as important, and because he seeks approval, that he imposes *upon himself* a degree of restraint or self-command. However, Smith went on to suggest that :

This desire of the approbation, and this aversion to the disapprobation of his brethren, would not alone have rendered him fit for that society for which he was made. Nature, accordingly, has endowed him with a desire not only of being approved of, but with a desire of being what ought to be approved of, or of being what he himself approves of in other men.[17]

The individual is thus, on Smith's argument, subject to two

types of jurisdiction, both of which serve to control his feelings and actions; the jurisdiction of the actual spectator and that of his own conscience – the jurisdiction of what Smith called the 'man without' and the 'man within' the 'great judge and arbiter' of our conduct.[18]

3

As the statements just quoted serve to indicate, one purpose of Smith's argument was to demonstrate man's disposition to, and fitness for, society. It will be evident that this analysis depends in large measure on the existence of certain propensities in human nature which incline man to society; propensities such as fellow feeling and the desire to attain the approval of his brethren.

However, as we observed earlier, Smith criticized Hutcheson for failing to give due weight to man's selfish propensities, and to the fact that: 'Every man ... is much more deeply interested in whatever immediately concerns himself, than in what concerns every other man.'[19] Recognition of this fact presented Smith with two problems. In the first place, he noted that because man tends to be more conscious of himself than others, a general *disposition* to gain the approval of his fellows may be inadequate to ensure control over his actions and passions. In the second place, he observed that because men actively pursue certain objectives with the object of bettering their material or social position, the individual may act in ways which have hurtful consequences for others. We may take these problems in turn.

1. As we have already noted, the individual who seeks to form a judgement as to the propriety of his own actions 'can do this in no other way than by endeavouring to view them with eyes of other people'.[20] Now on Smith's argument, there are two occasions on which we are likely to examine our own conduct, and when we 'endeavour to view it in the light in which the impartial spectator would view it. First when we are about to act, and secondly, after we have acted.'

In both cases Smith suggested that our judgements were likely to be partial, that is, less objective than would be required to form an accurate assessment. With respect to the first of these occasions, Smith pointed out: 'When we are about to act, the eagerness of passion will seldom allow us to consider what we are doing with the candour of an indifferent person.'[21] As regards the second, he observed: 'It is so disagreeable to think ill of ourselves that we purposely turn away from those circumstances which might render judgement unfavourable.'[22] In short, we suffer from the real danger of self-delusion or self-deceit, and Smith went on in a manner echoed by Robert Burns to argue:

This self deceit, this fatal weakness of mankind, is the source of half the disorders of human life. If we saw ourselves in the light in which others see us, or in which they would see us if they knew all, a reformation would generally be unavoidable.[23]

It is obvious, given the existence of this 'fatal weakness', that in particular instances a general disposition to seek the approval of our fellows may be an inadequate source of control. However, in Smith's model the resulting problem was partially solved by introducing the concept of 'general rules' of morality or behaviour. These rules Smith regarded as being 'of great use in correcting the misrepresentations of self love', going on to argue that without them 'there is no man whose conduct can be much depended upon'. Such rules provide us with an idea of 'what is fit and proper to be done or to be avoided' and thus provide the individual with a guide or yardstick against which he can at all times measure the propriety of his own behaviour.

It may be observed that Smith's explanation of the origin of these general rules does not involve any principle in addition to those we have already considered. As we have noted, man is able to form judgements in particular cases by virtue of his powers of fellow feeling, reflection, and imagination. Smith simply argued on this basis that the general rules 'concerning what is fit and proper' are the result of our 'continual observations upon the conduct of others'.[24] Specifically, Smith argued that a knowledge of particular cases enables man, by using his faculty of reason and the technique of induction, to frame general rules of justice and (positive) morality; rules which serve to guide or control his behaviour:

It is thus that the general rules of morality are formed. They are ultimately founded upon experience of what, in particular instances,

our moral faculties, our natural sense of merit and propriety, approve
or disapprove of. We do not *originally* approve or condemn particular
actions because, upon examination, they appear to be agreeable or
consistent with a general rule. The general rule, on the contrary, is
formed by finding from experience that all actions of a certain kind,
or circumstanced in a certain manner, are approved or disapproved
of.[25]

It is also worth observing that a regard to these general principles is *normally* ensured, on Smith's argument, by man's
desire to be worthy of approval, by the voice of the 'man within
the breast', allied to an opinion 'first impressed by nature and
afterwards confirmed by reasoning and philosophy, that these
important rules of morality are the commands and laws of the
Deity'.[26]

2. The second main problem is presented by the fact that man
is an *active* being; that is, one disposed actively to pursue objectives which will command the admiration of his fellows: 'What
are the advantages we propose by that great purpose of human
life which we call bettering our condition? To be observed, to
be attended to, to be taken notice of ... are all the advantages
we can propose from it.'[27] While Smith was able to regard
such objects with the detachment of the philosopher, he recognized that they were natural to man and indirectly productive
of benefit to society at large; productive of benefit in that the
drive to better our condition brings in its train the development
of productive forces in an economic sense. There was, he felt, a
deception involved in this process, since the conveniences which
we imagine wealth and rank will bring us are rarely realized,
but he added that:

... it is well that nature imposes upon us in this manner. It is this
deception which rouses and keeps in continual motion the industry
of mankind. It is this which first prompted them to cultivate the
ground, to build houses, to found cities and commonwealths, and to
invent and improve all the sciences and arts which ennoble and
embellish human life, which have entirely changed the whole face
of the globe, have turned the rude forests of nature into agreeable
and fertile plains, and made the trackless and barren ocean a new
fund of subsistence and the great highroad of communication to
the different nations of the earth.[28]

This is an important argument not only because it indicates that
the objectives of self-interested action have a social reference but
also because it is directly relevant to Smith's treatment of
economics and his analysis of man's 'gradual progress' from the
'rude' to the civilized state. However, for our present purpose,
the argument is chiefly important because it enabled Smith to
point out that the self-interested pursuits of individuals were a
fertile source of civil discord :

Place, that great object which divides the wives of aldermen is the
end of half the labours of human life, and is the cause of all the
tumult and bustle, all the rapine and injustice which avarice and
ambition have introduced into this world.[29]

Given that man is an active being, disposed to pursue objectives
which involve benefit to himself, two kinds of problem arise.
First, it is possible that while men in general may pay due
regard to the interests of others, particular men may not.
Secondly, it is possible that even in cases where the individual
generally recognizes the need to 'humble the arrogance of his
self love', he may in particular instances fail to do so. These two
possibilities yield two distinct, but related cases. On the one
hand, particular individuals may commit actions which lack
'propriety', but which do not affect the well-being of others.
In this case there would be a breach of the rules of (positive)
morality; rules which are *not* strictly enforceable, and whose
observance depends entirely on the restraint which individuals impose upon themselves. On the other hand, particular men
may commit actions which lack 'propriety' and also have 'hurtful consequences' as far as other men are concerned. In such
cases there would be a breach of the rules of *justice;* rules which
depend in part on the restraint which individuals impose upon
themselves, but whose observance is secured by the fact that
they are enforceable. We may take these issues in turn :

In Smith's argument, our general disposition to observe the
rules of justice is based upon 'the general fellow feeling which
we have with every man merely because he is our fellow
creature'.[30] As we have already seen, 'fellow feeling' is basic to
the sympathetic 'emotions' of the spectator. Given this, Smith
argued that the sympathy we feel for the person who suffers

naturally causes us to resent the actions of those responsible. Thus the individual

... in the race for wealth and honours and preferments ... may run as hard as he can, and strain every nerve and muscle, in order to outstrip all his competitors. But if he should justle or throw down any of them, the indulgence of the spectators is entirely at an end. It is a violation of fair play, which they cannot admit of.[31]

However, Smith was careful to argue that knowledge of the spectator's *resentment* may not be sufficient of itself to effectively control the actions of individuals. Certain sanctions are required; sanctions which, on Smith's argument, are of three main types.

First, Smith argued that acts of injustice, that is, acts which have a hurtful tendency, generally involve remorse on the part of the person who commits them; a feeling which 'is made up of shame from the sense of impropriety of past conduct, of grief for the effects of it, of pity for those who suffer by it, and from dread ... of the justly provoked resentment of all rational creatures'.[32]

Secondly, Smith suggested that actions of an unjust tendency, and especially those which affect the lives, liberty or property of others, are likely to be affected by man's natural fear of punishment in after life. Smith suggested that this type of conviction was natural to man, going some way towards explaining the fact that: 'In every religion, and in every superstition that the world has ever beheld ... there has been a Tartarus as well as an Elysium – a place provided for the punishment of the wicked, as well as one for the reward of the just.'[33]

It will be evident of course that while these sanctions may provide important sources of control, neither may be sufficient to ensure control. Smith thus added a third source, in arguing that our natural feelings of resentment for acts of injustice bring with them the equally natural approval of punishment: 'All men, even the most stupid and unthinking, abhor fraud, perfidy and injustice, and delight to see them punished.'[34] In this world at least, it is our disposition to, and approval of, *punishment* which serves to prevent us from committing acts of injustice – although once again this emerges as a necessary rather than a sufficient condition to maintain the social state.

The final condition required, as Smith noted, is a system of 'positive law' embodying our conception of the rules of justice and administered by some system of government or magistracy:

> As the violation of justice is what men will never submit to from one another, the public magistrate is under the necessity of employing the power of the commonwealth to enforce the practice of this virtue. Without this precaution, civil society would become a scene of violence and bloodshed, every man revenging himself at his own hand whenever he fancied he was injured.[35]

With this addition, Smith's basic model is apparently complete.

4

It will now be evident that Smith's argument does tell us something of importance as regards our understanding of man in society. In this connexion we may note some points, which are of relevance in respect of our three major areas of interest.

(1.) As we have seen, Smith worked in terms of two sets of human 'propensities' those which are 'selfish' in character and those which are 'social'. It is also apparent from Smith's argument that propensities of the latter kind, such as fellow feeling and the desire to be approved of, dispose man to society without however being sufficient to sustain it. As we have observed, the main problem is presented by the existence of selfish propensities; propensities which make it necessary to establish sources of control such as the rules of justice and morality.

(2.) The rules above mentioned thus emerge as being *useful* in the sense that without the rules of morality there would be 'no man whose behaviour could be much depended upon', while in the absence of justice there would be no restraint on injury. However, Smith was careful to argue that these rules did not come into being *because* men grasp their utility; on the contrary, he insisted that they gradually develop as the result of natural responses to natural problems. Thus, for example, Smith pointed out that the rules of justice basically reflect man's *fellow feeling* rather than any recognition of *their utility*, while observing:

> When by *natural principles* we are led to advance those ends which

a refined and enlightened reason would recommend to us, we are
very apt to impute to that reason, as to their efficient cause, the
sentiments and actions by which we advance those ends, and to
imagine that to be the wisdom of man which is in reality the
wisdom of God.[36]

The same point appears in the discussion of the rules of (positive) morality, in that '*by acting according to the dictates of our
moral faculties*, we necessarily pursue the most effectual means
of promoting the happiness of mankind, and may therefore be
said in some sense to co-operate with the Deity and to advance,
as far as in our power, the Plan of Providence'.[37]

These statements illustrate one of Smith's most characteristic
theses; the view that man is led as if by an Invisible Hand to
promote ends which were not part of his original intention.[38]

3. Since the rules of justice and morality are the expressions of
man's nature, and only in part the results of his conscious intention, it follows that there is a certain similarity between
them. However, Smith clearly regarded the two sets of rules as
different in that they refer to two different types and standards
of behaviour. The rules of justice for example, only hinder us
'from hurting our neighbour'; they only involve restraint from
damage and may thus be fulfilled by 'sitting still and doing
nothing',[39] while the rules of morality embody a more positive
and comprehensive guide. The essential difference between
them thus emerges as the difference between the negative and
the positive virtues of justice and beneficence. As Smith put
it :

The rules of justice may be compared to the rules of grammar; the
rules of the other virtues, to the rules which critics lay down for the
attainment of what is sublime and elegant in composition. The one
are precise, accurate and indispensable. The other are loose, vague
and indeterminate, and present us with a general idea of the perfection we ought to aim at, than afford us any certain and infallible
directions for acquiring it.[40]

4. It now appears that while both sets of rules are useful to
society, they must each, taken separately, be compatible with
different levels of social experience. For example, Smith argued
that where men act with an eye to the positive rules of morality,

and where their behaviour is characterized by 'beneficence' rather than justice, then the society 'flourishes and is happy'. Where, on the contrary, only the negative virtue of justice is observed, then life in society can be characterized by nothing more than 'a mercenary exchange of good offices according to an agreed valuation'.[41] Smith plainly regarded the first situation as compatible with a higher level of human achievement than the second, but he was in no doubt from the point of view of *analysis* as to which rules were the more essential for the maintenance of the social state. The rules of positive morality clearly emerge as 'the ornament which embellishes' while 'Justice, on the contrary, is the main pillar that upholds the whole edifice. If it is removed, the great, the immense fabric of human society . . . must in a moment crumble into atoms'.[42] The conclusion just mentioned is of particular importance since a system embodying the rules of justice (including equity) emerges as the minimum condition which must be satisfied before society can subsist and is *all that is necessary* for the purposes of Smith's *economic*, if not his philosophical work.[43]

5. One further point remains to be noticed. It will be observed that Smith relies on certain judgements with respect to the psychology of man in explaining the origin and nature of those conditions which must be satisfied before social life is possible. The argument, in short, is designed to explain the phenomenon of social existence and thus applies to *all* forms of society, the necessary condition being that human nature can be regarded as a constant. Moreover, it will be observed that while Smith demonstrates that the existence and observance of general rules are necessary to sustain the social state, yet at no time does the argument of the *Moral Sentiments* suggest that these rules have a *specific* content which is universally valid.[44] While Hume would have approved, the point may simply reflect Smith's awareness of the fact that conceptions as to what is fit and proper 'to be done or to be avoided' vary between different societies at the same point in time, and also within the same society at different points in time. Awareness of the former point is perhaps only to be expected in an age profoundly influenced by the teaching of Montesquieu; awareness of the latter, may reflect Smith's own early interest in the dynamics of historical change.[45]

It is to the theory of history that we now turn; a theory which may be represented as taking up problems raised by the *Moral Sentiments*, and which formally explains the nature of the specific type of social structure which is assumed in the analysis of a specific type of economic organization. Although Smith did not live to complete his projected history of government and society, the main elements of the theory are in fact to be found both in *Lectures* and *The Wealth of Nations* itself.

SECTION 2: THE HISTORY OF CIVIL SOCIETY

I

In this field Adam Smith may be regarded as the founder of a school which included Adam Ferguson, Lord Kames, and John Millar.[1] The distinctive contribution of the School was to a *type* of inquiry now known as 'philosophical' history, and more usually associated with Hegel, Herder, and Marx. Although the first major eighteenth-century exercise in philosophical history was G. Vico's *New Science*,[2] the approach used by the Scottish Historians was considered to be novel; a quality which led Dugald Stewart to describe it as 'natural' or 'theoretical' history, as distinct from the orthodox or 'vulgar'.[3] The terms used convey something of the essence of a study which was 'philosophical' or 'theoretical' in that it featured an analytical purpose, and 'natural' in that it was concerned with the process of development from the 'rude' to the 'civilized' state.

The technique found applications in a wide number of areas, and indeed Smith himself had at one time two separate works 'upon the anvil': 'the one is a sort of philosophical history of all the different branches of literature, of philosophy, poetry and eloquence; the other is a sort of history of law and government.'[4] Others besides Smith undertook a similar range of studies, but perhaps the most important contribution of the School is to be found in the attention given to the natural history of civil society; a field which embraced to a large extent the separate inquiries above mentioned.

In fulfilling what David Hume had shown to be the His-

torian's 'nobler duty as delineator of the state of society'[5], the
members of the School both found precedents and acknowledged debts. Apart from classical sources, the work of Rousseau is of some significance,[6] while Voltaire had already announced that his object as a historian was to examine 'the
manners of a people and to study the human mind; I shall
regard the order and succession of kings and chronology as
my guide, but not as the subject of my work'.[7] This statement
also typifies the objectives of the Scottish Historians, although it
was Montesquieu rather than Voltaire who provided the most
important impetus to their studies. Montesquieu was widely
regarded as the 'greatest genius of the present age'[8] and his
Esprit de Lois[9] came to enjoy a considerable vogue in the circle
of Smith's friends.

But while Montesquieu's work provided an important
stimulus, the Historians in general, and Smith in particular,
went well beyond the teaching of the master. In the words of
one of their number: 'The great Montesquieu pointed out the
road. He was the Lord Bacon of this branch of philosophy. Dr
Smith is the Newton.'[10] An important difference between the
work done by Smith and Montesquieu is to be found in the fact
that the former produced a more systematic analysis. To some
extent, the contrast reflects a difference in temperament, but in
the present context the difference stems basically from the fact
that Smith rejected the casual role which Montesquieu assigned
to soil and climate, in favour of a heavier reliance on economic
forces.[11]

Following Smith's lead, the Historians as a group emphasized the importance of economic forces in three characteristic ways. First, the process of change and development,
starting from the primitive society as the first in time, was explained in terms of the hypothesis that man is an active being,
disposed to improve the material conditions of life. The typical
argument was that man is subject to certain 'natural' and 'insati-
able wants'; wants which, as we observed in the previous
section, serve to 'rouse and keep in continual motion the
industry of mankind'.[12] Where this force is released, the result
must be the development of productive forces (such as agriculture or manufacture), leading to an escape from the primitive

state and a gradual improvement in the (material) standard of life.

Secondly, the Historians suggested that contemporary and historical experience disclosed the existence of four stages of economic growth. These stages were held to be qualitatively distinct in that they featured different types of productive activity, different modes of earning subsistence, and different forms and arrangements of property. As Smith put it in a typical passage : 'The four stages of society are hunting, pasturage, farming, and commerce.'[13] Moreover, it was argued not only that such distinct stages exist and had existed, but also that each society would *tend* to pass through them in *sequence*. In the words of Lord Kames: 'These progressive changes in the order now mentioned may be traced in all societies.'[14] Thirdly, the Historians suggested that the four types of economic organization served to explain the existence of four recognizably different types of social structure; a phenomenon which was again verifiable from contemporary and historical experience. In modern terms, the Historians sought to demonstrate a relationship between the (economic) substructure and the (social) superstructure, so that the characteristic argument was aptly stated by William Robertson when he remarked: 'In every inquiry concerning the operations of men when united together in society, the first object of attention should be their mode of subsistence. Accordingly as that varies, their laws and policy must be different.'[15]

The doctrines we have just reviewed may be said to be typical of the Scottish Historians, and as such they serve to expose the leading features of their thought. For example, we find an emphasis on change in all its manifestations; an emphasis which helps to explain why Adam Ferguson chose the 'passing stream' rather than the 'stagnant pool' as the emblem of mankind. Furthermore, we find an attempt to explain the phenomenon of change and development, in the form of an argument which set out to analyse the nature of the four stages of man's progress, and to show the causes of transition between them.

In what follows we shall mainly be concerned with Smith's handling of the four stages of man's progress, placing most emphasis on the links established between the mode of earning subsistence and the patterns of authority and subordination generated as a result.[16] In dealing with this aspect of Smith's thought we will use the first two stages (of hunting and pasture) to establish some basic principles, and then illustrate the working of these principles by reference to the subsequent periods.

2

Smith defined the first economic and social stage as 'the lowest and rudest state of society, such as we find it among the native tribes of North America'.[17] The second stage, that of pasture, he defined as 'a more advanced state of society, such as we find it among the Tartars and Arabs'.[18] An obvious difference between these two situations is to be found in the fact that in each there is a distinct type of activity. In the first, men acquire the means of subsistence through gathering the 'spontaneous fruits of the soil', or by hunting, while in the second they do so by virtue of the domestication of animals. The contrast must have, as Smith suggested, certain sociological consequences; thus for example, he insisted that in the stage of hunting, communities must be small in size, being based on the family or extended family unit.[19] In the second case, Smith argued that the mode of earning subsistence would be compatible with larger groupings and must necessarily imply a nomadic existence: 'Such nations have commonly no fixed habitation, but live, either in tents or in a sort of covered waggons which are easily transported from place to place.'[20]

From the point of view of the type of social structure which may be expected to prevail in the two situations, it is however more important to observe that in the case of hunting, private property must be relatively insignificant, while in the case of pasture, we find a distinct form of property (cattle) which can be accumulated.[21] It is thus in the period of pasture that inequality first becomes significant, leading to a new source of social tension which Smith ascribed to ambition in the rich, and to envy and hatred of labour in the poor; passions which were, he thought, 'steady in their operation' and 'fairly universal in their influence'.[22] It thus follows that in this situation civil government becomes particularly necessary:

The acquisition of valuable and extensive property, therefore, necessarily requires the establishment of civil government. Where there is no property, or at least none that exceeds the value of two or three days labour, civil government is not so necessary.[23]

He added:

Civil government, so far as it is instituted for the security of property, is in reality instituted for the defence of the rich against the poor, or of those who have some property against those who have none at all.[24]

Smith went on to argue that the appearance of property divisions must bring with them not only the necessity of government, but also certain relationships of authority and subordination in society. Thus, for example, he suggested that wealth must bring power, and added, with reference to the state of pasture, that 'The authority of riches, however, though great in every age of society, is perhaps greatest in the rudest age of society which admits of any considerable inequality of fortune'.[25] Smith contrasted this situation with that prevailing in the previous period, where 'universal poverty establishes universal equality', from which it follows that in the first stage of society 'the superiority either of age, or of personal qualities, are the feeble, but the sole foundations of authority and subordination'.[26] Smith also suggested, following on from the previous argument, that the authority of particular *families* would tend to be greater in the second period, the reason being that wealth once accumulated can be transmitted from one generation to another. Thus, in speaking of the period of hunting, we find Smith remarking that 'The distinction of birth, being subsequent to the inequality of fortune, can have no place in nations of hunters, among whom, all men being equal in fortune, must likewise be very nearly equal in birth'.[27] But in the shepherd state, it was suggested that inequality of fortune and thus birth, must be of particular importance, and indeed that these were 'the principal causes which naturally establish authority and subordination among men'.[28]

Now this argument, simple as it is, enables us to state one or two important principles. As we have seen, the stage of hunting features a form of economic activity which precludes the

appearance of private property on any significant scale. On the
other hand, it is argued that in the second period the relevant
type of activity makes the acquisition, accumulation, and trans-
mission of property possible. In this connexion it is noteworthy
that Smith equates the exercise of power with the possession of
'riches', and argues that where there is inequality a pattern of
subordination and authority must be generated as a result; a
pattern which first appears in the second stage and 'which could
not possibly exist before'. These arguments are employed
throughout Smith's analysis, although as we shall see he recognized that in the periods succeeding the age of pasture, the
source of authority (wealth) must alter, and the associated
patterns of subordination and dependence with them.

3

While Smith did work in terms of a sequence of four stages, he
did not regard advance beyond the period of pasture as inevitable, and indeed observed that all the inland parts of Africa,
together with 'the modern Tartary and Siberia, seem in all ages
of the world to have been in the same barbarous and uncivilized
state in which we find them at present'.[29] The reasons, he suggested, lay in the fact that such areas were not susceptible to
'improvement' while in addition they lacked natural means of
transport and communication. It was thus that progress beyond
the second period had first taken place in Attica, and then in
Europe; areas which 'are divided by rivers and branches of the
sea, and are naturally fit for the cultivation of the soil and other
arts'.[30]

In terms of European history, Smith illustrated the nature of
the third (agrarian) stage, by reference to that period which
followed the fall of the Roman Empire and which witnessed the
dominance of the German and Scythian nations[31]; a period in
which all lands 'were engrossed, and the greater part by a few
great proprietors'.[32]

In contrast to the previous stage, the agrarian period features
a settled abode, rather than a nomadic existence. There are of
course further (inevitable) differences, most obviously in that
tillage is the dominant form of activity, while land becomes the

major form of property. In this situation we thus find a continuing emphasis on paternity and the law of primogeniture, while
in addition the phenomenon of property in land brings with it
the use of entails, designed to preserve a certain lineal succession. Smith was later to criticize such property arrangements,
but he did consider them to be not unreasonable *at that point in
time* when 'great landed estates were a sort of principalities'.[33]

As before, Smith explained the existence of patterns of
authority and subordination in terms of inequalities of wealth
and thus birth, although at this stage of the argument he
offered a more complete explanation as to the basis on which
authority must rest. In this connexion three important points
arise.

First, Smith pointed out that where landed estates were a
'sort of principalities', individual owners would require to
maintain a military establishment in order to protect themselves
against their neighbours. Secondly, he suggested that those who
possess the land and its products could have no means of ex-
pending their wealth save in the form of 'rustic hospitality' and
the maintenance of servants.[34] Thirdly, it was argued that those
who lacked the means of subsistence (land and its products)
could only acquire it through the exchange of personal service.

It thus follows that, in this period, the proprietor of land

... is at all times ... surrounded with a multitude of retainers or dependents, who, having no equivalent to give in return for their
maintenance, but being fed entirely by his bounty, must obey him,
for the same reason that soldiers must obey the prince who pays
them.[35]

In this situation, it is to be expected that the lower orders,
including the occupiers of land, will be in a highly subordinate
position to the proprietors; a fact which derives from the prevailing mode of earning subsistence. On the other hand, the
same mode of earning subsistence serves to explain the (historically) great authority of the proprietors; an authority which
could be illustrated in terms of the lack of personal rights
accorded to their servants, and in terms of the legislative and
judicial powers wielded within the boundaries of their property.
As Smith put it, in an illuminating passage, 'That authority and

those jurisdictions all necessarily flowed from the state of property and manners just now described.'[36]

Such an explanation of the great authority and power held by
the proprietors of land, also helped to explain their influence as
a group and especially the fact that 'The proprietors of land
were anciently the legislators of every part of Europe'.[37] Having
come this far, Smith went on to suggest that the period in
question must have been relatively unstable in a political sense;
a problem which arises because property is here vested in a
relatively small number of proprietors, each of whom is econo-
mically and militarily self sufficient. As Smith recognized, the
internal warfare which resulted from this situation inevitably
produced a degree of civil instability which neither the institution of kingship, nor the formality of the feudal constitution,
could control. The reason, Smith suggested, was that 'the
authority of government still continued to be . . . too weak in
the head and too strong in the inferior members'.[38]

All the features we have so far considered were clearly
represented as the inevitable consquences of a particular mode of
earning subsistence, and as features which are bound to be
eliminated with the transition to a qualitatively different type
of economic organization. It is to the analysis of this process
that we now turn; a process which, in Smith's opinion, was set
in motion by the inevitable development of manufactures and
accelerated by the prevailing problems of political instability.

Even within the framework of a basically agrarian economy,
Smith recognized that certain manufactures and services would
be necessary, since, 'without the assistance of some artificers . . .
the cultivation of land cannot be carried on'.[39] Hence the need
for wheelwrights, tanners, carpenters, and masons; groups which
were not bound to particular geographical areas and which
thus naturally congregated in cities for their mutual advantage
and protection. With the gradual development of agriculture in
a quantitative sense, and the increase in population, Smith suggested that cities would naturally grow in importance. This
same development, it was argued, naturally led to the appearance of a source of royal revenue which could be used to offset
the power of the landed proprietors, thus causing a gradual
dilution of the Assemblies previously dominated by them.[40]

Given a situation of political instability generated by the wealth of the proprietors, it was thus in the interest of kings to encourage the cities, and to grant them certain privileges of self government in exchange for what Smith called a 'rent certain'. However, Smith was careful to argue that the grants given to the cities were to a certain extent a function of the weakness of the kings, pointing out that, 'The Princes who lived upon the worst terms with their Barons seem . . . to have been the most liberal in grants of this kind'.[41] Now this development was important, Smith argued, both for its short and long run effects. In the short run, the immediate consequence of the growth of cities was to enhance the wealth and power of the King at the expense of both Lords and Commons. On the other hand, he noted that, in the long run, the same phenomenon would tend to have economic, political, and sociological effects of a broadly liberalizing kind.

To begin with, Smith suggested that royal policy with respect to the cities, at least as manifested in England, France, and Germany, resulted in the voluntary creation within these states, of a 'sort of independent republics' with the rights of self government. It was then within the cities that a relatively high degree of personal liberty and security of property was first developed, creating a context where economic activity might flourish. Smith concluded: 'That industry, therefore, which aims at something more than . . . subsistence, was established in cities long before it was commonly practised by the occupiers of land in the country.'[42] The initial stimulus to manufactures was provided by personal security, but Smith also noted that their development must have been profoundly affected by the markets available. Plainly, in a situation where domestic agriculture remains in a 'rude' state, the extent of the market for manufactured products would be limited, so that the main source of stimulus must have been foreign trade. Following this line of argument, Smith noted that the growth of manufactures at this stage depended to a very large extent on the proximity of cities to the sea coast and to navigable rivers; factors which served to explain the rapid development of the Hans towns, together with Venice, Genoa, and Pisa.[43] Inter-regional and international contacts thus provided the necessary outlets for manufacturing activity; contacts which, he thought, inevitably led to the gradual refinement and development of primitive (domestic) production, not least because of the changes in taste which they helped to induce.

Now this argument enabled Smith to point out that the development of cities, such as Pisa, was to some extent independent of the development of the agricultural hinterland, meaning that they represented enclaves of prosperity based largely on foreign trade. But he also observed that the quantitative development of manufactures would inevitably provide a stimulus to domestic agriculture, citing three reasons in support of this contention. First, he suggested that the growth of cities would encourage agricultural production, since 'by affording a great and ready market for the rude produce of the country, they gave encouragement to its cultivation and further improvement'.[44] Secondly, he suggested that the acquisition of lands by the emergent merchant classes would stimulate agricultural production, since the latter class would tend to regard land as an investment rather than as a source of personal power. But thirdly, and 'by far the most important of all their effects' was, Smith felt, the gradual introduction of personal liberty and security among the occupiers of land; thus bringing to the agrarian sector the same conditions which prevailed in the cities. It is interesting to observe that Smith directly attributed this important change to the appearance of a relatively sophisticated manufacturing sector. The reasons are perhaps obvious, but they deserve some elaboration at this point, if only for the light thus shed on the more sociological aspects of the argument.

To begin with, Smith suggested that the quantitative development of manufactures would give a stimulus to agricultural production, by providing the proprietors with a source of expenditure. Thus, whereas in the initial stages of the third economic period the lords could only expend their wealth in aggrandisement or in the maintenance of dependents, the appearance of manufactures on a relatively large scale

... furnished the great proprietors with something for which they could exchange the whole surplus produce of their lands, and which they could consume themselves without sharing it either with tenants or retainers. All for ourselves, and nothing for other people, seems, in every age of the world, to have been the vile maxim of the masters of mankind.[45]

Vile or no, in such a case it is evident that the rude produce of lands represents an equivalent which can be used in exchange for manufactured goods, thus giving the proprietors a natural motive to increase their command over that equivalent; a motive whose expression had two interesting effects. First, Smith observed that a desire to increase the means of exchange, led the owners of land to dismiss their unnecessary tenants and retainers, thus reducing the population on the land 'to the number necessary for cultivating it, according to the imperfect state of cultivation and improvement in those times'.[46] Secondly, Smith suggested that the same motive led to the gradual elimination of the slavery which originally prevailed among the occupiers of land, not from a sense of duty or humanity, but from a regard to self-interest on the part of the owner. The purpose in short was to increase the produce of the land and thus command over the equivalent to be used in exchange; an object which could only be attained by admitting those who had been slaves in effect, to certain rights of property and security, since 'a person who can acquire no property, can have no other interest but to eat as much and to labour as little as possible'.[47] It was in such terms that Smith explained the gradual (historical) change in the status of the occupiers of land, which, starting from the state of villeinage, culminated in the appearance of farmers properly so called, that is, those 'who cultivated the land with their own stock, paying a rent certain'.[48] Finally, Smith suggested that the same motive which had led to the developments just noted, would lead the proprietors to maximize their (monetary) rents; a change which could only be acceptable in return for leases sufficiently long to permit the farmers to earn a suitable return on their invested capital.

Now while this argument, taken as a whole, helps to elucidate the (historical) causes of agricultural development, it is plainly important in a more purely sociological sense. To begin with, Smith is here suggesting that the presence of a source of expenditure (manufactures) leads to the development of the means of exchange (agriculture), thus causing a change in the form of leases and giving the occupiers of land a degree of personal freedom previously impossible. Furthermore, the same argument enabled Smith to point out that the appearance of a new means of using wealth (in exchange) inevitably caused a gradual reduction in the number of dependents the proprietors of land could maintain, with consequent effects on the power and authority wielded by the members of that class. As he put it, the great proprietors, given the development of manufactures, could now exchange 'the maintenance, or what is the same thing, the price of the maintenance of a thousand men for a year, and with it the whole weight and authority which it could give them'.[49] Under such circumstances it was suggested that as the power of the proprietors declined, the degree of freedom enjoyed by individuals must correspondingly increase until a situation was reached where 'a regular government was established in the country as well as in the city'.[50] But this, Smith insisted, was the result of natural (inevitable) forces, and not the reflection of some high motive or deliberate act of policy on the part of either the proprietors or the merchants. Thus, on the one hand, he argued that the proprietors who used the produce of their lands in exchange for manufactures only sought to gratify 'the most childish vanity'; while on the other, the merchants and artificers only acted on the (self-interested) principle of 'turning a penny wherever a penny was to be got'. He added: 'Neither of them had either the knowledge or foresight of that great revolution which the folly of the one, and the industry of the other, was gradually bringing about.'[51] Once again, we find an example of the typical Smithian thesis, that man is led, as if by an Invisible Hand, to promote ends which were no part of his original intention.

4

The argument we have just reviewed would seem to be important for a number of reasons. Most obviously, the analysis may be seen as a useful contribution to a theory of history which was widely held at the time, and which is remarkable for the emphasis given to economic forces. Again, it is evident that this same theory purports to explain the links which connect civilized with barbarous society, thus focusing attention on the phenomenon, and inevitability, of change. As we have already suggested, the presence of this theme in Smith's thought helps to explain the character of the *Moral Sentiments*, while the theory in its fullest form goes some way towards explaining why there is likely to be some variation in customs and standards of accepted behaviour over time. However, for our purpose, it is perhaps of more importance to observe that the analysis considered in this section serves to expose the manner in which the modern exchange economy had come, or was coming, into being, together with the nature of the social and political structure inevitably created by it.

Looking at the question in this way, Smith clearly regarded the 'great revolution' to which we have just alluded, as one which ushered in a series of changes in the economic, political, and social structure.

In the economic sphere, the significant development was the appearance of a basically two-sector economy, leading to a division in society as between those engaged in manufacture and those engaged in agriculture. In Smith's own words:

The great commerce of every civilized society is that carried on between the inhabitants of the town and those of the country. It consists in the exchange of rude for manufactured products, either immediately or by the intervention of money, or of some sort of paper which represents money.[52]

In the *political* sphere, Smith recognized that the continuing development of new sources of wealth (commerce and manufactures) meant that the power of the landed proprietors must progressively decline; changes which were most obviously reflected in the contemporary rise of the English Commons, and in those events which culminated in the Revolution Settlement of 1688.[53] The change in the balance of power was seen *directly* to reflect the development of new sources of wealth so that John Millar only provided a summary of his master's argument in remarking that under such conditions:

... the pre-rogatives of the monarch and of the ancient nobility will be undermined ... the privileges of the people will be extended in the same proportion, and ... power, the usual attendant of wealth will be in some measure diffused over all the members of the community.[54]

As far as the structure of *society* was concerned, Smith was, of course, well aware that any single community at any point in time will be made up of a series of 'different orders and societies'.[55] The analysis was not designed to question or ignore such a truth, but rather to suggest that the new economic order must involve changes in man's 'general system of behaviour', together with a degree of personal freedom hitherto impossible. The reason was found to lie in the gradual substitution of a cash for a service nexus; in the gradual substitution of dependence on *forces* (the market) for direct dependence on men (such as the proprietors). The phenomenon of *authority* is not of course eliminated by the new economic order, and Smith took due note of the fact that men are generally disposed to admire and respect the great, well born, and wealthy, in this as in the three preceding periods of society.[56] Nor did Smith suggest that the phenomenon of *dependence* is eliminated in the fourth period. Indeed he quite explicitly argued that the contrary would be the case. For example, Smith observed that in this stage the farmers *depend* on the proprietors of land for the use of that factor; the undertaker (capitalist) *depends* on his customers for a living; the labourer *depends* on both major groups for his employment. The significant point is rather that in this period, *and in no other*, these services command a price, thus eliminating the service relationships of the previous stage. The occupier *pays* for the use of land, thus giving the proprietor an income in the form of rent; the worker is *paid*, in the form of wages, for the use of his labour power, while the undertaker who acquires an income in the form of profit 'derives his subsistence from the employment not of one, but of one hundred or a thousand different customers. Though in some measure obliged to them all, he is not absolutely dependent on any one of them'.[57]

Given the advent of the exchange or 'commercial' economy, we thus find society divided into three 'great constituent orders', landlords, capitalists, and wage labour. As we have just seen, all of these groups are linked by a complex pattern of interdependencies, a pattern which is compatible with a considerable degree of personal freedom, and which reflects the existence of a distinct mode of earning subsistence. It is to the economic aspect of these relationships that we now turn; the last chapter, to use Professor Macfie's happy phrase, in 'a more comprehensive study of man in society'.[58]

SECTION 3: POLITICAL ECONOMY

I

In *The Wealth of Nations*, Smith attempted to explain the *modus operandi* of a type of economy which corresponds to the 'commercial' stage of the theory of history. The main features of the modern exchange economy are thus implicit in the argument of the previous section, but they may be usefully developed at this point as a means of stating the main components of the model.

To begin with, Smith was concerned with a basically two-sector case (agriculture and manufacture), where the creation of commodities requires the use of three distinct factors of production. Corresponding to the three factors (land, labour, capital), Smith isolated three forms of monetary return (rent, wages, profit), each of which represents the reward appropriate to the provision of three distinct types of service. Thus, for example, *wages* are paid in exchange for the use of the factor labour, thus providing the members of a distinct social group with an equivalent (money) which may be used in exchange for commodities. Similarly, *rent* is paid for the use of the factor land, since this resource is part of the private property of individuals. Finally, *profit* represents the return on capital, while it is also a form of compensation which accrues to those (capitalists) who undertake the strategic role of combining the factors of production.[1] Once again, this form of return represents a type of income which is earned by a distinct group in society; a group which falls into divisions, corresponding to the two main forms of productive activity. Thus, for example, the farmers properly so called fulfil what is now known as the entrepreneurial function, in that they cultivate (leased) land 'with their own stock', while the 'undertakers' fulfil a similar role with respect to manufacturers.

The major sectors and groups may then be described as providing the main components of Smith's model. It will be remembered that each group has distinct (economic) functions, while it will be recalled from the previous section that the existence of the exchange economy necessarily implies a certain pattern of social relations between them. However, in considering the economic *as a distinct area of human experience*, Smith's argument depends upon two elements in addition to those already mentioned. First, Smith required to make some judgement as to the activities of men, and in fact relied on what were previously defined as the 'selfish propensities'.[2] Smith was not of course suggesting that these propensities provided of themselves an adequate statement of man's psychology. He was simply arguing that within the economic sphere, mankind is motivated (broadly speaking) by a desire for gain, and indeed that this is a characteristic feature of our experience. As he put it, in a famous passage: 'It is not from the benevolence of the butcher, the brewer, or the baker, that we expect our dinner, but from their regard to their own self interest.'[3] Secondly, Smith recognized that in examining economic phenomena, he was concerned with one aspect of the activities of man in society, and that the argument must thus depend on some prior judgement as to the nature of the social bond. The formal analysis of the latter problem is of course contained in the *Moral Sentiments*, but it may be noted that only part of the argument there stated is relevant at this stage. That is to say, all that is necessary for the purposes of Smith's *economic* analysis is that the individual be restrained from hurting his fellows, both in respect of their persons *and property*.

Now given the basic hypothesis (self-interest), the main elements of the model (sectors, classes, etc.), and the condition of security (justice), Smith set out to show how an economy of the type outlined would work or function. As we shall see, the characteristic emphasis throughout his work is on the interdependence of economic phenomena; the characteristic thesis, that of 'unintended social outcomes'.

However, it is perhaps worth noting that Smith's basic themes and purposes found precedents, particularly in the works of those who were also concerned with the socio-economic analysis of the theory of history. Among the latter writers we must number Sir James Steuart[4], but the most notable precursors were a group of thinkers whom Smith met during his travels on the Continent, and who were the authors of a 'system' which he regarded as 'perhaps the nearest approximation to the truth that has yet been published upon the subject of political economy'.[5]

The Physiocrats, of whom Quesnai and Mirabeau are now the most famous, were in fact among the first thinkers to state and examine the proposition that 'in nature everything is intertwined, everything runs through circular courses which are interlaced with one another'.[6] In explaining this phenomenon, the 'economists' used a model not dissimilar to that employed by Smith, but which was first formally expounded in Quesnai's *Tableau Economique* of 1758.[7] The argument features, as Smith noted, a number of 'arithmetical formularies', but its importance derives from the fact that it shows the working of the economy during a given time period (a year), and demonstrates the interconnexions between sectors and social groups in terms of a flow of goods and money. It would be difficult indeed to overstate the importance of the analysis of the 'circular flow', which marks, as Cannan pointed out, 'an enormous advance in economic theory';[8] the first study of the whole organism.

Here as elsewhere, Smith was hardly the first in the field, although once again his contribution was one of originality and genius.

In what follows we shall be mainly concerned with Smith's handling of the common theme of 'interdependence'; a theme which is developed in two distinct ways. First, Smith considered the (economic) interdependence of individuals, and by this means successively introduced the problems of exchange value, price, and allocation. Secondly, he showed the interdependence of groups and sectors in a manner reminiscent of the Physiocrats, but in a form which permitted him to emphasize the major issues of economic growth and capital accumulation. As we shall see, the theory of distribution provides the formal link between the two parts of the argument, while in addition the key concept of the division of labour is common to both.

2

Although Smith's model has several distinct elements, the feature on which he placed most emphasis is the *division of labour*.[9] In terms of the content of the model outlined in the previous section, a division of labour is of course implied in the existence of distinct *sectors* or types of productive activity. But Smith also emphasized the fact that there was specialization by types of employment and even within each employment. To illustrate the basic point, Smith chose the celebrated example of the pin; a very 'trifling manufacture' which none the less required some eighteen distinct processes for its completion.

In Smith's hands, the argument was important for two main reasons. First, he was at some pains to point out that the division of labour (by process) helped to explain the relatively high productivity of labour in modern times; a phenomenon which he ascribed to:

a) The increase in 'dexterity' which inevitably results from making a single, relatively simple operation 'the sole employment of the labourer'.

b) The saving of time which would otherwise be lost in 'passing from one type of work to another'.

c) The associated use of machines which 'facilitate and abridge labour, and enable one man to do the work of many'.[10]

He further observed that the existence of specialization (by employment) necessarily involves a high degree of interdependence, in that each separate *manufacture* tends to rely on the output of other industries for different goods and services. It thus follows that the individual consumer who purchases a single commodity, must at the same time acquire, in effect, the separate outputs of a 'great variety of labour'. Smith added, 'If we examine ... all these things ... we shall be sensible that without the assistance and co-operation of many thousands, the very meanest person in a civilized country could not be provided [for]'.[11]

However, the aspect of this discussion which is most immediately relevant is the light which it throws on the necessity of *exchange*. As Smith observed, once the division of labour is established, our own labour can supply us with only a very

small part of our wants. He thus noted that even in the barter
economy the individual can best satisfy the whole range of his
needs by exchanging the surplus part of his own production,
receiving in return the products of others. Where the division of
labour is thoroughly established, it is then to be expected that
each individual is in a sense *dependent* on his fellows, and that
'Every man ... lives by exchanging, or becomes in some
measure a merchant'.[12]

This observation brought Smith directly to the problem of
value, and it is noteworthy that in order to simplify the analysis
he in fact used the analytical (as distinct from historical) device
of the barter economy. However, despite the attempt made to
simplify and to be 'perspicuous', these passages in the book
remain somewhat obscure, very largely because Smith uses a
single term 'exchangeable value' in handling two distinct, but
related problems.[13]

The first problem concerns the forces which determine the
rate at which one good, or units of one good, may be exchanged
for another; the second is concerned basically with the means by
which we can measure the value of the total *stock* of goods
created by an individual, and which are used in exchange for
others. We may take these issues in turn.

As regards the *rate* of exchange, Smith isolated two relevant
factors: the usefulness of the good *to be acquired*, and the 'cost'
incurred in creating the commodity *to be given up*. The first of
the relevant relationships then is obviously that which exists
between 'usefulness' and value, and the elements of Smith's
argument become apparent in his handling of the famous paradox, namely that 'the things which have the greatest value in
use (e.g. water) have frequently little or no value in exchange;
and, on the contrary, those things which have the greatest value
in exchange (e.g. diamonds) have frequently little or no value in
use'.[14]

The solution to this paradox can be stated in two stages,
where the first involves an explanation as to why two such
goods have *some* value; and the second, an explanation as to
why the two goods have *different* values.

Smith's handling of the first part of the problem is based on
his recognition that both goods are considered to be 'useful'

although noting that the 'utilities' of each are qualitatively different. For example, water represents a source of satisfaction to us (utility), precisely because it has a value *in use* (drinking, washing, etc.), while diamonds give us a measure of satisfaction, not because they are *usable* but because they are beautiful. In the former case (water) we place a value on the good because we can use it in a practical way, while in the latter case (diamonds) we place a value on the good because it appeals to our 'senses', an appeal which, as Smith observed, constitutes a ground 'of preference', 'merit', or 'source of pleasure'.[15] He concluded: 'The demand for the precious stones arises altogether from their beauty.'[16] The utilities of the two goods thus emerge as being qualitatively different, although the significant point is seen to be that *both* have *some* value precisely because they represent sources of satisfaction to the individual. It would thus appear that Smith regarded *value* as a function of utility, or 'usefulness' broadly defined.

Smith was then left with the second part of the initial problem, namely the explanation as to why the two goods have *different* values. Here again, the answer provided, while simple, is clear, embodying in effect the argument that merit (value) is a function of scarcity. As Smith put it 'the merit of an object which is in any degree either useful or beautiful, is greatly enhanced by its scarcity'.[17] Even more specifically he remarked:

Cheapness is in fact the same thing with plenty. It is only on account of the plenty of water that it is so cheap as to be got for the lifting; and on account of the scarcity of diamonds (for their real use seems not yet to have been discovered) that they are so dear.[18]

Having come thus far, Smith introduced the second major element in the problem by observing that the rate at which the individual will exchange one good for another must be affected not only by the utility of the good to be acquired, but also by the 'toil and trouble' involved in creating the good exchanged. In this connexion he clearly recognized that in acquiring the means of exchange (goods in the barter case), the individual must undergo 'the fatigues of labour'[19] and thus 'lay down' a 'portion of his ease, his liberty, his happiness'.[20]

In dealing with the rate of exchange, Smith placed most

emphasis on this side of the problem, and explicitly argued that in the case of the barter economy 'the proportion between the quantities of labour necessary for acquiring different objects, seems to be the only circumstance which can afford any rule for exchanging them for one another'.[21] Thus he suggested that if it takes twice the labour to kill a beaver as it does to kill a deer, then 'one beaver should naturally exchange for two deer'.[22] Smith left the analysis at this point, although it will be apparent from the previous argument that the rate of exchange above-mentioned can only prevail where the ratios of the relevant utilities and disutilities are the same for the respective hunters.

So far we have been mainly concerned with stating those elements which may determine the rate at which an individual is prepared to give up units of one commodity in order to pro-cure, through exchange, particular units of another. We have thus (implicitly) worked in terms of *single units* of two different goods, and suggested that Smith's argument taken as a whole indicates that the relevant utilities and disutilities must govern the choice made. This is plainly one way of looking at the problem of exchange value, but Smith seems to have treated it, not as an end in itself, but as a means of elucidating those factors which govern the value of *the whole stock of goods* which the individual creates, and which he proposes to use in exchange.

Looking at the problem *in this way*, Smith then went on to argue that:

The value of any commodity ... to the person who possesses it and who means not to use or consume it himself, but to exchange it for other commodities, is equal to the quantity of labour which it en-ables him to purchase or command. Labour therefore is the real measure of the exchangeable value of all commodities.[23]

This is at first sight a rather odd statement, but Smith's mean-ing becomes clear when he remarked that the value of a good (to the individual) must always be in proportion to 'the quantity of other men's labour, *or what is the same thing of the produce* of other men's labour which it enables him to purchase or com-mand. The exchangeable value of everything must always be precisely equal to the extent of this power'.[24] In other words,

Smith is here arguing that the *real* value of the goods which the workman has to dispose of (in effect his income) must be *measured* by the quantity of goods (expressed in terms of labour units) which he can command, and which he receives once the whole volume of (separate) exchanges has taken place. If we remain for the moment with the primitive state, we may clarify the conclusion just mentioned, and at the same time show a connexion between this and the preceding analysis. In the case of the barter economy, it will be recalled that the individual is assumed to create a single (complete) product, which then becomes his personal (disposable) property. Now if, as Smith suggested, the *rate* of exchange between goods is always equal to the ratio of the labour embodied in them, then it follows that the exchangeable value of the whole *stock* of goods must be equal to the labour required to make it. In other words, the labour embodied in the stock of goods made by the individual must be equal to the labour embodied in the goods received; i.e. that quantity of goods which the original stock enables the possessor to purchase or command. Given this, it will now be apparent that the argument thus far has two important features. First, Smith suggests that in the barter economy, the labour which the individual expends, and which is embodied in the good *he* creates, must exchange for or command an equal quantity. In short, in this state, labour embodied equals labour commanded, the essential premises being that *all* goods exchange at a given (previously defined) rate and that labour is the sole factor of production. Secondly, Smith suggests that the extent to which the individual can satisfy his needs through exchanging his produce for that of others, must be determined by the quantity of other men's output (in labour units) which he receives in exchange. Evidently, this is one way of measuring the economic welfare (command over goods), of individuals, and one which indicates the necessity of measuring welfare in *real* terms. Now it is noteworthy that Smith's statement of the first result helped him to clarify the meaning of the second, and also that he considered the former to be of restricted, and the latter of universal, validity. To begin with, it is evident that in the modern economy labour is no longer the sole factor of production, in that 'in this state of things, the whole produce of labour

does not always belong to the labourer'.[25] This means of course
that the labour commanded by virtue of our possession of a
stock of goods must always exceed the (*direct*) labour embodied
in them, by virtue of the allowance which must be made for the
contribution of capital and land. In short, the equality between
labour embodied and labour commanded appears to be relevant
to the primitive (barter) economy and to no other. However,
Smith did not consider that the recognition of this truth did any
violence to his second result; namely, that the real value of
income must be determined by the produce of other men's
labour (in labour units) which it enables the recipient to purchase or command.

As Smith observed, a clear difference between the barter and
modern economies is to be found in the fact that, while in the
former, goods are exchanged for goods, in the latter, goods are
exchanged for a sum of money, which may then be expended in
purchasing other goods.[26] Under such circumstances the individual, as Smith saw, very naturally estimates the value of his
receipts (received in return for undergoing the 'fatigues' of
labour) in terms of money, rather than in terms of the quantity
of goods he can acquire by virtue of his expenditure. However,
Smith was at some pains to insist that the real measure of welfare (i.e. our ability to satisfy our wants) was to be found in 'the
money's worth', rather than the money, where the former is
determined by the quantity of products (labour 'commanded')
which either individuals or groups can purchase. On this basis,
Smith went on to distinguish between the nominal and the real
value of income, pointing out that if the three 'original sources
of (monetary) revenue in modern times are wages, rent, and
profit, then the real value of each, must ultimately be measured
'by the quantity of labour which they can, each of them, purchase or command'.[27]

The distinction between real and money income being established, the remainder of chapter 5 is largely concerned with a
defence of the labour unit as the only stable basis on which the
real value of income may be established both at any one point in
time and over time.[28] Smith thus began a (perhaps vain) search
for an absolute measure of value: a search which was to be
continued by Ricardo and Marx.

3

It will be apparent from the previous argument that Smith regarded rent, wages, and profit, as the types of return payable to the three 'great constituent orders' of society, and as the price paid for the use of the three factors of production. The revenues which accrue to individuals and groups in society, and which permit them to *purchase* commodities, thus appear to be costs incurred by those who *create* commodities. These points were made quite explicitly by Smith when he remarked:

As the price or exchangeable value of every particular commodity taken separately, resolves itself into some one or other, or all of these three parts, so that of all commodities, which compose the whole annual produce ... taken complexly must resolve itself into the same three parts, and be parcelled out among different inhabitants of the country, either as the wages of their labour, the profits of their stock, or the rent of their land.[29]

This argument obviously raises the problem of price and its determinants, and it is to this area of analysis (following Smith) that we now turn.[30] However, before going further, it may be useful to clarify some of the features of the argument.

To begin with, Smith assumes the existence of given 'ordinary' or 'average' rates of wages, profit, and rent; rates which may be said to prevail within any given society or neighbourhood, during any given (annual) period. This assumption is of considerable importance, and for two main reasons. First, it indicates that in dealing with the problem of price, Smith was implicitly using the analytical device of a static system, and working in terms of a given (stable) stock of factors together with a given (stable) level of aggregate demand for them.[31] Secondly, the assumption of given (stable) rates of return is important in that these are rates which affect the supply price of commodities and rates over which the individual seller has no control.

With these two points forming Smith's major premises, he proceeded to examine the determinants of price, and to produce a discussion which seems to involve two distinct, but related, problems. First, Smith set out to show those forces which determine the prices of *particular* commodities, elucidating in the process the nature of *partial* equilibrium. Secondly, he would appear to have used the above analysis as a means of explaining the phenomenon of *general* equilibrium, and thus those forces which determine the manner in which a (given) stock of factors of production is allocated between different uses or employments. We may take these issues in turn.

In dealing with the first aspect of the problem, Smith implicitly examines the case of a single commodity manufactured by a number of sellers, opening the analysis by establishing an important distinction between 'natural' and 'market price'. *Natural price* is defined as that amount which is 'neither more nor less than what is sufficient to pay the rent of land, the wages of labour, and the profits of stock ... according to their natural rates'.[32] In other words, where natural price prevails, the seller is just able to cover his costs of production, including a margin for 'ordinary or average' profit. By contrast, *market price* is defined as that price which may prevail at any given point in time, being regulated 'by the proportion between the quantity which is actually brought to market, and the demand of those who are willing to pay the natural price of the commodity' (the effectual demanders').[33] Now these two 'prices' are interrelated, the essential point being that while in the short run market and natural price may diverge, in the long run they will tend to coincide. Natural price thus emerges as an *equilibrium* price, and one which will obtain when the commodity in question is in fact sold at its cost of production. The latter point may be illustrated by examining the consequences of divergences between the two prices.

If, for example, the quantity offered by the seller was less than that which the consumers were prepared to take at a particular (natural) price, the consequence would be a competition among the consumers to procure some of a relatively limited stock. Under such circumstances, Smith argued that the 'market' will rise above the 'natural' price, the extent of the divergence being determined by 'the greatness of the deficiency' and varying 'according as the acquisition of the commodity happens to be of more or less importance' to the buyer. In making the latter point, Smith took due note of the fact that where a relative shortage occurs of goods which are 'necessaries' of life, the extent of the divergence between the two prices (in effect the demand and supply prices) would be greater than that which would occur in other cases (e.g. luxuries).

Under such circumstances, the price received by the seller must exceed the natural price (cost of production), with the result that rates of return paid to the factors in this employment also rise above their 'ordinary' level. The consequence of such a divergence between the returns paid in a particular employment, and the 'natural' rates prevailing must then be an inflow of resources to this relatively profitable field, leading to an expansion in the supply of the commodity, and a return to that position where the commodity is sold at its natural price. Given a relative shortage of the commodity in the market, Smith thus concluded, 'The quantity brought hither will soon be sufficient to supply the effectual demand. All the different parts of its price will soon sink to their natural rate and the whole price to its natural price.'[34]

Smith's second case is one where the quantity brought to market exceeds that which the consumers are willing to take at a particular (natural) price. Under these circumstances, he argued, the supply offered cannot be disposed of at the natural price, so that part of the total output must be sold 'to those who are willing to pay less, and the low price which they give for it must reduce the price of the whole'.[35] In such a case, the market price must fall below the natural, where the degree of divergence will be determined by the extent of the excess supply, and vary according to the competition generated among the sellers; a competition which will itself vary 'according as it happens to be more or less important to them to get immediately rid of the commodity'.[36] Once again, Smith noted that the type of good involved would be important as regards the competition engendered by a relative excess, and observed that oversupply of a perishable commodity 'will occasion a much greater competition than in that of durable commodities'.[37] However, given some divergence between market and natural price, the consequence in this case must be that the rates of return payable to factors in this employment fall below their 'ordinary' rates, thus prompting producers to

... withdraw a part of their labour or stock from this employment. The quantity brought to market will soon be no more than sufficient

to supply the effectual demand. All the different parts of its price
will rise to their natural rate, and the whole price to its natural
price.[38]

Taking the two cases of divergence, it thus becomes apparent
that the price paid by the consumers in taking a particular
quantity of some commodity, will tend to coincide with that
price which the seller requires to cover his costs for that level of
output. In short, the 'natural price' emerges as that equilibrium
or 'central' price, 'to which the prices of all commodities are
continually gravitating'.[39]

Now it will be apparent that the conclusion just stated
depends on certain assumptions which are so far implicit. To
begin with, it is evident that the process by which natural price
is established in the event of divergence from it, depends upon
the reaction of producers to short run changes in their rates of
return. Looked at in this way, it becomes apparent that the
conclusion reached (equilibrium) must depend on Smith's use of
the hypothesis of economic rationality, as noted above. In addition, Smith also observed that the result attained (namely that
commodities in the long run are sold at their cost of production)
can only hold good where there is perfect liberty; in the absence
of monopoly powers, transport problems, secrets in manufacture, etc. The cost of production solution is, in short, only to be
expected where free (perfect) competition prevails.[40]

Having come thus far, it is now possible to consider the
second aspect of Smith's argument, and to proceed from the
discussion of partial to that of general, equilibrium.

Perhaps the main contribution of Smith's price theory lies in
the fact that it enables us to see what conditions have to be
satisfied before the economy as a whole can be said to be in a
state of 'balance'. For example, the first stage of the discussion
establishes that, in the case of any one commodity, equilibrium
will be attained where the good is sold at its natural price, and
where each of the (relevant) factors is paid for at its natural rate.
Under these circumstances, equilibrium obtains of course, precisely because there can be no tendency for resources to increase
or decrease in this *particular* type of employment. Now it is
evident that if this process, and this result, holds good for all
commodities taken separately, it must also apply to all com-

modities 'taken complexly', at least where perfect competition
prevails. That is, where the conditions which form the assumptions of the partial equilibrium case, are satisfied *over the whole
economy*, a position of equilibrium will be attained where *each*
different type of good is sold at its natural price, and where *each*
factor in each employment is paid at its natural rate. The
economy can then be said to be in a position of 'balance'[41] since
where the above conditions *are* satisfied there can be no tendency to move resources *within* or *between* employments, and
because, where the necessary conditions *are not* satisfied, they
will naturally tend to be re-established.

To illustrate the latter point, suppose we start from a position
of (general) equilibrium, and assume a change in the pattern of
consumer demand (other things remaining equal). In the case of
commodities for which demand is reduced, market price would
fall below the natural price, reflecting the fact that consumers
are now prepared to take a smaller amount of the good than
that originally offered. In other cases, where demand is increased (in the sense of an upward shift in the schedule), market
price must rise above the natural price, in the short run, indicating that the quantity offered by the seller is now relatively
scarce in relation to the current level of (effectual) demand for
it. A divergence of the market and natural prices of *commodities* must then cause the rates of return payable to factors
to fall below, and rise above their natural rates, in the employments affected. On Smith's argument, the latter situation
must, in its turn, cause a movement of resources from those
fields which are relatively poorly paid, into those which are
relatively highly paid; a process of transfer which must continue
until each factor in each of the relevant employments is paid at
the same (natural) rate. At the same time, it is evident that the
movement of resources must mean an expansion in the supply
of the commodity for which demand has risen, and a contraction in that (or those) for which demand has fallen; a process
which will continue until each of the relevant commodities is
once again sold at its natural price. The attainment of a new
balance thus involves a re-allocation of resources, and a tendency
to establish equilibrium (simultaneously) in the commodity and
factor markets, the condition being that each good is sold for its

natural price, and each factor at its natural rate. It will be observed that the departure from, and re-attainment of, a position of (general) equilibrium, depends upon the essentially self-interested actions and reactions of consumers and producers. Smith's treatment of price and allocation thus provides one of the best examples of his emphasis on 'interdependence' and one of the most dramatic examples of his thesis of the Invisible Hand.

However, while this argument would appear to express the logic of Smith's treatment, he did modify the conclusions reached in two important respects.

First, while Smith certainly conceived of general equilibrium in terms of a situation where there was no tendency for resources to move between employments, he also recognized that a position of 'balance' need not involve an equality between monetary rates of return. The point follows directly from Smith's recognition of the fact that employments differ qualitatively and that such differences may serve to explain why, even in a position of 'balance', different money rates prevail. As Smith put it, 'certain circumstances in the employments themselves . . . either really, or at least in the imaginations of men, make up for a small pecuniary gain in some, and counterbalance a great one in others'.[42] Thus, for example, he noted that money wage rates would tend to vary between different types of employment according to the difficulty of learning the trade, the constancy of employment and the degree of trust involved. Similarly, he observed that both wages and profits would vary with differences in the agreeableness of the work, and with the probability of success in particular fields. In short, he was suggesting that money rates of return would only tend to equality within employments of similar kinds, and that over the whole economy the relevant balance would be one involving *net advantages*.[43] It will be observed that this argument involves an important *modification* to the definition of (general) equilibrium previously used, and that, as Smith pointed out, the (modified) result will only hold good where there is a perfect liberty for labour and stock to move between employments.[44]

Secondly, Smith observed that in the real world the conditions necessary for the attainment of equilibrium (as previously

defined) were unlikely to be satisfied, placing most emphasis on
the problems presented by current 'regulations of police'.[45] Of
these, he singled out monopoly powers, since 'the price of
monopoly is upon every occasion the highest which can be
got',[46] and thus unlikely to be regulated by cost of production.
He was also a bitter critic of the privileges of corporations,
which effectively served to hinder the movement of capital between areas; of the Poor Laws, which had a similar effect with
respect to labour; and of the Statutes of Apprenticeship, which
artificially controlled the numbers of workmen in particular
types of employment.[47] Smith deplored all such regulations,
both because they were violations of man's 'natural liberty', and
because they 'break what may be called the natural balance of
industry', thus constraining productive activity in an 'unnatural
[less beneficial] channel'.[48]

4

Abstracting from the fact of legislative obstacles and qualita-
tive differences in employments, it will be recalled that Smith's
theory of price was built up on the assumption of given rates of
factor payment.[49] Following on from this argument, Smith's next
task was to elucidate the forces which determine the *level* of
('ordinary or average') rates of return during any given time
period, or over time, applying to the problem the simple 'demand and supply' type of analysis just considered. We may take
the relevant issues in turn, reviewing them only in such detail as
may be necessary for the present argument.

As regards *wages*,[50] Smith observed that payment for the use
of the factor labour was a feature of modern society; a payment
which is made by those classes who require the factor (undertakers, farmers) and which is necessary to compensate the
disutility of work. The process of wage determination may then
be viewed as a kind of bargain or contract:

What are the common wages of labour, depends everywhere upon
the contract usually made between ... two parties whose interests
are by no means the same. The workmen desire to get as much, the
masters to give as little as possible. The former are disposed to

combine in order to raise, the latter in order to lower the wages of labour.[51]

In Smith's judgement, the balance of advantage in determining the terms of this 'contract' must generally lie with the 'masters', the reason being that while the law permitted their 'combinations', it prevented those of the workers. However, Smith was careful to point out that the bargaining strength of the two parties would itself be affected by demand and supply relationships, irrespective of legal privileges. Thus, for example, where labour is relatively abundant, wage rates will tend to be low, partly because individuals will have to compete for such employment as is available, and partly because, while 'in the long run, the workman may be as necessary to his master as his master is to him, the necessity is not so immediate'.[52] On the other hand, where labour is relatively scarce, 'The scarcity of hands occasions a competition among masters, who bid against one another, in order to get workmen, and thus voluntarily break through the natural combination of masters not to raise wages.'[53]

Having come thus far, Smith clarified the argument by pointing out that wage rates may be relatively high or low, depending on the available supply of labour and the size of the funds (or capital stock) available for its purchase. He did not in fact set out to define some upper limit for wages, but he did suggest that the lowest limit, in the long term, must be determined by the needs of subsistence, since,

A man must live by his work, and his wages must at least be sufficient to maintain him. They must even upon some occasions be somewhat more, otherwise it would be impossible for him to bring up a family, and the race of such workmen could not last beyond the first generation.[54]

In Smith's analysis, the importance of the 'subsistence wage' lies in the fact that it constitutes the long run supply price of labour, the argument being in effect that over time labour may be produced at constant cost, leading to the conclusion that the subsistence wage could be regarded as a kind of 'natural' or equilibrium rate. Smith in fact made use of three cases to illustrate an argument which is analogous to the previous treatment of equilibrium price. To begin with, it will be apparent that in a position of long run equilibrium, the demand for, and supply of, labour must be such that a particular level of population is in receipt of a subsistence wage. Under such circumstances, we find a position of equilibrium in the sense that there can be no tendency for population to increase or diminish; a condition which will obtain so long as there is no change in the size of the wages fund.[55] This is Smith's example of the stationary state, as illustrated by the experience of China. Secondly, Smith examined a case, again starting from a position of equilibrium, where there is a fall in the demand for labour either in any one year, or continuously over a number of years. In graphical terms, the argument might be illustrated in terms of a downward shift, or a series of such shifts, in the position of the demand curve, reflecting a single, or continuing decline in the size of the funds destined for the employment of labour. Under such circumstances, the actual wage rate paid must fall below the subsistence rate, resulting in a fall in population until the quantity is such as to permit subsistence wages to be paid. This example represents Smith's 'declining' state, the cases cited being Bengal and certain East Indian colonies; areas where the decline in the wages fund had led to want, 'famine and mortality', until, 'the number of inhabitants . . . was reduced to what could easily be maintained by the revenue and stock which remained . . .'[56] Finally we have Smith's 'advancing state' where an increase, or series of (annual) increases in the size of the wages fund, causes rates in excess of the subsistence level to be paid to a given level of population. If we start as before from a position of long run equilibrium, we can think of this case as involving an upward shift in the demand curve for labour, leading to rates in excess of the subsistence level at least for as long as it takes to increase the level of population; an increase which, he said, would inevitably follow from the higher standard of living involved. However, Smith also pointed out that the feature of the 'advancing state' would be a continuous upward movement in the demand curve for labour, thus making it possible for high wage rates to be paid over a number of years, and indeed for as long as the *rate* of increase in the demand for labour exceeded the rate of increase in supply. Smith considered the case of North

America to be a good example of the trend, but also that many
European countries, including Great Britain, showed the same
tendency, albeit to a lesser degree. In the case of Britain, for
example, Smith pointed out that (real) wages had increased
during the eighteenth century, and that as a matter of fact they
were well above subsistence level at the time of writing.[57] It is
interesting to observe that Smith felt that high wages were to be
approved of both on the grounds of equity and of the improved
productivity of labour which results.[58]

Now while this argument runs in terms of an analysis of
equilibrium similar in kind to that used in dealing with the
theory of (commodity) price, it will be apparent that it examines
adjustments very much longer term in character than those so
far considered. On the other hand, the argument *is* important as
regards the static aspects of Smith's analysis in the sense that it
helps to elucidate the forces which determine the level of wages
during the course of a single time period, such as a year, and
thus the level of the 'ordinary or average' rates which Smith
took as given in handling the problem of price. Certainly, what
has been said so far serves to show that in any one time period
(such as a year), wage rates may be equal to, above, or below,
the subsistence rate; that such rates are a function of the size of
the wages fund and the level of population, and that particular
rates, once established will remain stable so long as there is no
change in any of the relevant aggregates.

As far as *profit* is concerned, it is interesting to observe that
Smith did not consider this form of return to be the reward
payable for undertaking the managerial function of 'inspection
and direction' but rather as the compensation for the trouble
taken, and the risks incurred, in combining the factors of production. As he put it:

As soon as stock has accumulated in the hands of particular persons,
some of them will naturally employ it in setting to work industrious
people, whom they will supply with materials and subsistence in
order to make a profit by the sale of their work, or by what their
labour adds to the value of the materials.[59]

Looked at in this way, the profits which accrue to individual
producers must obviously be affected by the selling price of the

commodity and costs of production (including wages). Profits are thus likely to be particularly sensitive to changes in the direction of demand, together with the 'good or bad fortune' of rivals and customers; facts make it difficult to speak of an 'ordinary or average' rate of return. However, Smith did suggest that the rate of interest would provide a reasonably accurate index of profit levels at any one time and over time, basically on the ground that the rate payable for borrowed funds would reflect the profits to be gained from their use: 'It may be laid down as a maxim, that wherever a great deal can be made by the use of money, a great deal will commonly be given for the use of it; and that wherever little can be made by it, less will commonly be given for it.'[60]

In this connexion Smith was careful to argue that the rate of interest payable would be in proportion to the *clear or neat* profit, rather than *gross* profit, that is, to the profit remaining after making allowance for the necessary risk premium required by the *entrepreneur*.[61]

As least as a broad generalization, Smith felt able to suggest that the rate of profit accruing at any one point in time (other things remaining equal, and with wage rates given) would be determined by the quantity of stock (capital) available, taken in conjunction with the volume of business to be transacted by it, or the extent of the outlets for profitable investment. It thus followed that over time the rate of profit will tend to decline, partly in consequence of the gradual increase of stock, and partly because of the increasing difficulty of finding 'a profitable method of employing any new capital'. As he put it, in another passage:

When the stocks of many rich merchants are turned into the same trade, their mutual competition tends to lower its profit; and when there is a like increase of stock in all the different trades carried on in the same society; the same competition must produce the same effect in them all.[62]

It then follows that 'the diminution of profit is the natural effect of . . . prosperity'.[63]

In the long term, Smith concluded that just as wages would sink towards subsistence levels, so profit would progressively decline until the rate of *clear* profit was just sufficient to meet the necessary interest payments, including a risk premium for the *lender*.[64] Historically, the pattern of events involves a progression from the 'advancing' to the 'stationary' state (such as China), although Smith did observe that two sets of circumstances might serve to reverse the associated trend of profits. First, he suggested that a declining state (such as Bengal) would feature a gradual reduction in capital stock and thus a tendency to increased rates of profit. Secondly, he pointed out that even in advancing states, the tendency for profits to fall might be reversed or temporarily halted, due to the acquisition of new investment outlets, or of new territories as a result of conquest. For example, in the case of Great Britain, Smith pointed out that the acquisitions made after 'the late war' must necessarily have increased the rate of profit, despite the advancing tendency of the country, since, 'so great an accession of new business to be carried on by the old stock, must necessarily have diminished the quantity employed in a great number of particular branches, in which the competition being less, the profits must have been greater'.[65]

However, the basic points which Smith was endeavouring to establish seem clear. If we look at the long term trends of the economy, the tendency is for profits (like wages) to fall. If we look at the economy at a particular point in time (say a single year), then it appears that the 'ordinary or average' rate of profit prevailing must be a function of the quantity of stock, and the 'proportion of business' to which it can be applied. However, Smith made an important qualification to the latter point when he indicated that even where the quantity of stock remains the same (say, in two different years), other things remaining equal, the rate of profit will also be related to the prevailing wage rates. Thus for example, if labour is relatively abundant in relation to a given capital stock (i.e. the wages fund), the rate of profit will be higher, and wage rates lower, than they would be where labour was relatively scarce.

Smith's handling of the third and last type of return need not detain us, and it will be sufficient, for our present purposes, to notice only the salient features of his treatment. Smith formally defined *rent* as the 'price paid for the use of land'; a price paid because land is of itself productive, part of the property of individuals, and (presumably) scarce.[66] Looking at the question in this way, Smith was careful to argue that rent constitutes a pure surplus in the sense that it accrues to the owner of land independently of any effort made by him, so that the proprietors emerge as 'the only one of the three orders whose revenue costs them neither labour nor care, but comes to them, as it were, of its own accord'.[67] Moreover, Smith suggested that rent payments are somewhat akin to a 'monopoly price' at least in the broad sense that they are generally the highest which can be got in the 'actual circumstances of the land'.[68] The reference to 'actual circumstances' is important, at least in so far as Smith recognized that rent payments would vary both with the fertility and situation of the land involved.

Smith generally took the view that land used for the production of human food would always yield a rent, and indeed computed that rent would be of the order of one third of the gross produce. Morever, he suggested that in the long term, rent payments would tend to increase, at least absolutely, due to the increased use of the available stock (of land) which the growth of population inevitably involves. As Smith put it: 'The extension of improvement and cultivation tend to raise it directly. The landlords' share of the produce necessarily increases with the increase of the produce.' He added that the real value of the landlords' receipts would also tend to increase over time, since 'all those improvements in the productive powers of labour, which tend directly to reduce the real price of manufactures, tend indirectly to raise the real rent of land'.[69]

However, two aspects of Smith's argument would appear to be of particular importance in the present context. First, the analysis serves to suggest that at any point in time, or during any given annual period, rent payments will be a function of the proportion of the fixed stock (of land) used, where the latter is in turn a function of the level of population. Secondly, Smith's argument indicates that during any given annual period, rent payments will be related, not only to the productivity of the soil, but also to the prevailing rates of wages and profit. Or, as Smith put it:

Rent, it is to be observed ... enters into the composition of the price of commodities in a different way from wages and profit. High or low wages and profit are the causes of high or low price; high or low rent is the effect of it. It is because high or low wages and profit must be paid in order to bring a particular commodity to market, that its price is high or low. But it is because its price is high or low, a great deal more, or very little more, or no more, than what is sufficient to pay those wages and profit, that it affords a high rent, or a low rent, or no rent at all.[70]

While we will have occasion to return later to Smith's theory of distribution taken as a whole, some of its features may be worth emphasizing before going further.

(1) Smith here establishes a point which we previously asserted to be true, namely that in modern society there are *three* original sources of revenue, or forms of return, which accrue to individual members of the three 'great constituent' social orders: proprietors, labour, and capitalists.

(2) Smith makes some attempt, in each case, to explain the nature of the type of return involved and to elucidate *why* it is paid or acquired. Thus, for example, he pointed out that payment in the form of wages must be made in exchange for the use of the factor labour, partly because the service relationships of the feudal period no longer apply, and partly because it is necessary to compensate the disutility of work. Similarly, he argued that profit accrued to those who combined the factors of production in creating (and selling) commodities. It will be noted that in this case the entrepreneurs must purchase producers' goods (materials, labour) before commodities can be made, meaning that at least some portion of their income must be *saved*, i.e. devoted to purposes other than the satisfaction of immediately *personal* needs (consumption).

(3) In explaining the forces which determine rates of return, the argument throughout has a static element (linking it to the theory of price) at least in so far as Smith was concerned to elucidate those forces which determine the 'ordinary or average' rates of return which prevail in any given (annual) period. It will be observed that in this case Smith treats factors of production as fixed stocks (quantities), and that he suggests a certain interdependence with respect to the rates of return prevailing in the course of a single year. As we have seen, rent payments are

affected by the prevailing rates of profit and wages, while, in addition, profits are affected by the existing wage levels.

4. The argument just reviewed also has a dynamic element, at least in the sense that Smith was partly concerned with long run trends in rates of return, treating factors as flows rather than stocks. Once again it will be recalled that these trends are inter-related and that they apparently depend on the process of capital accumulation. Thus, for example, Smith suggests that profits will decline as the size of the capital stock (wages fund) in-creases; that high rates of accumulation will generate high market wage rates, leading to an increase in the level of popu-lation, a movement back towards subsistence levels, and changes in rent payments which reflect the inevitable increase in the output of food. However, it is interesting to note that at this stage of the argument, no explanation is offered as to the *source* of the increase in capital; a lack which is supplied in the pre-dominantly macroeconomic analysis of Book 2.

5

The 'static' and 'dynamic' themes which are present in the theory of distribution are continued in the second book; the former in the attempt made to show the working of the economy *as a whole* during a particular annual period; the latter in the analysis of trends over a number of years. Specifically, the first theme is developed in the form of an analysis of the 'cir-cular flow', which shows the connexion between *aggregate* in-come, output, and expenditure, while the second is developed in the form of a theory of growth. Both of these (macroeconomic) areas of analysis may be seen to be inter-related, while in addi-tion both would appear to be connected with the previous treat-ment of price and distribution. We may take these issues in turn.

Smith's analysis of the 'circular flow' may be seen as a direct development of certain results already stated in connec-tion with the theory of price. To begin with, it will be recalled that costs of production are incurred by those who create com-modities, thus providing individuals with the means of ex-change. It therefore follows that if the price of each good (in a position of equilibrium) comprehends payments made for rent, wages, and profit, according to their natural rates, then 'it must be so for all commodities which compose the whole annual produce'. On this basis, Smith concluded that 'The whole price or exchangeable value of that annual produce must resolve itself into the same three parts, and be parcelled out among the different inhabitants . . .'[71] If, for the moment we ignore the problem of distribution (i.e. of a given level of income between rent, wages, and profit), the result which Smith is here endeavouring to establish may be stated to involve a relationship between aggregate output and aggregate income. Or, as he put it: 'The gross revenue of all the inhabitants of a great country comprehends the whole annual produce of their land and labour.'[72]

Now it will be evident that a particular level of income, created by a particular level of (aggregate) output, represents that power to purchase goods which is available to all the members of 'a great society'. Smith then went on to observe that this level of *purchasing power* would be divided into two funds, consumption and saving, adding, 'The principle which prompts us to expense (consumption), is the passion for present enjoyment. . . . But the principle which prompts us to save, is the desire of bettering our condition.'[73] In fact, Smith offered no *formal* explanation of the forces which would determine the actual distribution of (aggregate) income or purchasing power between these two uses, at any particular point in time. He did however suggest that the proprietors and labourers would tend to devote a high proportion of their income to consumption, the latter by virtue of the size of their receipts (in relation to their basic needs), and the former by virtue of the habits of 'expense' associated with that class. The problem of balancing future against present enjoyments thus appears to be mainly relevant for the entrepreneurial group: a group whose functions and objectives necessarily dispose it to frugality.

But Smith did clarify the problems here considered from the standpoint of *expenditure*. For example, he duly noted that the proportion of annual income earmarked for *consumption*, taking all groups 'complexly' would be used to purchase consumption goods both perishable and durable in character. He also noted that this type of expenditure could involve the purchase of *services*; services of a kind which do not *directly* contribute to the annual *output* of *commodities* (in physical terms) and which thus cannot be said to contribute to that level of income associated with it. Smith formally described such labour as 'unproductive', but without denying that services of this kind are useful. For example, he pointed out that the services of 'players, buffoons, opera singers, and musicians' have a certain *value* because they represent sources of satisfaction to those who pay for them. Similarly, he pointed out that the services provided by governments, and which are paid for out of *taxes*, have a value, the reason being that society could not subsist without them. However all such services are by definition unproductive:

> The sovereign ... with all the officers both of justice and war ... the whole army and navy, are unproductive labourers. They are the servants of the public, and are maintained by a part of the annual produce of the industry of other people.[74]

As regards the use of *savings*, Smith suggested that the proportion of income devoted to this purpose would provide or contribute to the 'capitals' used by the entrepreneur; 'capitals' which would be used for productive purposes, since by definition, the whole object of savings is to secure future, as distinct from present, benefits (in the form of profit). Given this point, Smith went on to suggest that 'capitals' (as presently defined) could be used in a number of ways, each one of which involves, in effect, the purchase of 'investment' goods or factors of production. Specifically, he suggested that capitals may be employed in the cultivation of lands, mines, or fisheries; in the production of all types of manufactured goods (including consumer and producer's goods), or in either the wholesale or the retail trades.[75] However, it is perhaps more relevant for our immediate purpose to observe that Smith defined *all* 'capitals' in terms of two main categories. *Fixed Capital* he defined as that portion of savings used to purchase 'useful machines' or to improve, for example, the productive powers of land, the characteristic feature being that goods are created, and profits ultimately acquired, by using and *retaining* possession of the investment goods involved. *Circulating Capital* Smith defined as that portion of savings used to purchase *investment* goods other than 'fixed' implements, such as labour power or raw materials, the characteristic feature being that goods are produced through temporarily 'parting with' the funds so used. Smith was in fact careful to argue that different trades would use different proportions of fixed and circulating capital, and that 'no fixed capital can yield any revenue but by means of a circulating capital'.[76]

In terms of the argument thus far, it will be apparent that some contribution is made to an understanding of the essential nature of the circular flow, in the sense that Smith here establishes a connexion between the levels of output, income, and expenditure. Specifically, it would appear that a particular level of output must include consumption and investment goods, that the level of income thus created may be distributed between two funds, consumption and saving, and that these funds, when employed to make purchases, may be used to take off the market the consumption and investment goods which themselves made up the level of production in question.

Up to this point, we have simply been working in terms of aggregates, i.e. in terms of total output, income, and expenditure. However, taking the results already established as given, Smith in fact offered a more elaborate version of the flow; one which enabled him to make more allowance for the existence of the three social orders (and thus the problem of the distribution of income), together with the three main forms of economic activity – manufacture, agriculture, commerce.

Suppose, for example, that we examine the performance of the economy during a particular year, from the standpoint of the beginning of the period in question. Under these circumstances it may be reasonable to assume that there will be certain stocks of goods in existence, reflecting the level of output attained in the previous period, together with the quantities of (consumption and investment) goods purchased during it; stocks which may be divided into three main parts.

First, there is that part of total stock which is reserved for immediate consumption, and which is held by *all* consumers (capitalists, labour, and proprietors). The characteristic feature of this part of the total stock is that it affords no revenue to its possessors, since it consists in 'the stock of food, clothes, household furniture, etc., . . . which has been purchased by their proper consumers, but which are not yet entirely consumed'.[77]

Secondly, there is that part of the total stock which may be described as 'fixed capital' and which will again be distributed between the various groups in society. This part of the stock, Smith suggested, is composed of the 'useful machines' purchased in preceding periods and held by the capitalists engaged in manufacture; the quantity of useful buildings and of 'improved land' in the possession of the capitalist farmers and proprietors, together with the 'acquired and useful abilities' of all the inhabitants.

Thirdly, there is that part of the total stock which may be described as 'circulating capital' and which again has several components, these being:

a) The quantity of money necessary to carry on the process of circulation. In this connexion Smith observed that:

The sole use of money is to circulate consumeable goods. . . . The quantity of money therefore, which can be annually employed in any country, must be determined by the value of the consumeable goods annually circulated within it.[78]

b) The stock of provisions and other agricultural products which are available for sale during the current period, but which are still in the hands of either the farmers or merchants.

c) The stock of raw materials and work in process, which is held by merchants, undertakers, or those capitalists engaged in the agricultural sector (including mining, etc.).

d) The stock of manufactured goods (consumption and investment) created during the previous period, but which remain in the hands of undertakers and merchants at the beginning of the present year. Finally, we may assume a particular level of (aggregate) income available for expenditure in the current period; a level of income which will of course be determined by the volume of output produced and sold during the previous period. In this connection Smith was careful to draw a distinction between the 'gross' and 'net' revenue available, the latter being determined by gross income, less the cost of maintaining the money supply and the fixed capital.[79] Perhaps the logic of the process can be best represented by artificially splitting up the activities involved. Let us suppose for example that at the beginning of the time period in question, the major capitalist groups possess the total net receipts earned from the sale of products in the previous period, and that the undertakers engaged in agriculture open by transmitting the total rent due to the proprietors of land, for the use of that factor. The income thus provided will enable the proprietors to make the necessary purchases of consumption (and investment) goods in the current period, thus contributing to reduce the stocks of such goods with which the undertakers and merchants began the period. Secondly, let us assume that the undertakers engaged in both sectors, together with the merchant groups transmit to wage labour the content of the wages fund, thus providing this socio-economic class with an income which can be used in the current period. It is worth noting in this connexion that the capitalist groups transmit a fund to wage labour which formed a part of their *savings*, providing by this means an income (wages) which is available for *consumption* purposes. Thirdly, the undertakers in agriculture and manufactures will make purchases of consumption and investment goods from each other (through the medium of retail and wholesale merchants) thus generating a series of expenditures $(C + S)$ linking the two sectors. Finally the process of circulation may be seen to be completed by the purchases made by individual undertakers within their own sectors. Once again these purchases will include consumption and investment goods, thus contributing still further to reduce the stocks of commodities which were available for sale when the period under examination began.

Given these points, we can represent the working of the system in terms of a series of flows whereby money income (accruing in the form of rent, wages, and profit) is exchanged for commodities in such a way as to involve a series of withdrawals from the 'circulating' capital of society. As Smith pointed out, the consumption goods thus withdrawn from the existing stock may be entirely used up within the current period, or used to *increase* the stock 'reserved for immediate consumption' or to replace the more durable goods (e.g. clothes) which had reached the end of their life in the course of the same period. Similarly, the undertakers as a result of their purchases, will add to their stocks of raw materials and/or their fixed capital, or replace the machines which had finally worn out in the current period. Looked at in this way, the 'circular flow' may be seen to involve a certain level of purchases which takes (C + I) goods from the market, but at the same time a continuous process of replacement by virtue of the productive activity which is currently carried on.

The argument which we have just reviewed is interesting for a number of reasons. First, it is worth noting that the basic model of the 'flow' does not feature in Smith's *Lectures* and that if physiocratic influence was at work on him, then this must be the most likely area. Secondly, it should be noted that in choosing to examine the working of the economy within a given time period such as a year, Smith gave his 'model' a broadly static character, albeit one which includes a time dimension. As we have seen, Smith set out to illustrate the patterns of interdependence which link the sectors and classes which make up the system in terms of a number of *processes* which *unfold* within the (single) time period examined, just as his theory of price was designed to illustrate the *processes* by virtue of which resources were allocated between different uses. Thirdly, it is noteworthy that in using a model based on a year as the relevant time period, Smith did not try to formulate *equilibrium* conditions at least in the sense that he did not (as Quesnai had done) try to develop a model using specified assumptions of a quantitative kind as a means of showing what must happen before the next time period could open under identical conditions to those prevailing in the period actually examined. Indeed, Smith's lack of concern, not with macro-statics, but with macro-static *equilibrium* was to some extent announced by the fact that in developing his model of the flow, he made allowance for the problem of the different *rates* at which goods are used up.

Nor in dealing with the 'flow' did Smith suggest that the level of output attained during any given period would be exactly sufficient to replace the goods used up in it. On the contrary, he argued that output levels attained in any one year would be likely to exceed previous levels; an important reminder

that Smith's predominant concern was with economic growth.
In this connexion, Smith noted that:

The annual produce of the land and labour of any nation can be
increased in its value by no other means, but by increasing either
the number of its productive labourers, or the productive powers of
those labourers who had before been employed.[80]

Smith also observed that both the above sources of increased output required an 'additional capital' devoted either to increasing
the size of the wages fund or to the purchase of 'machines and
instruments which facilitate and abridge labour';[81] an additional
capital which can only be acquired through extra (net) savings.

It may be useful at this stage to illustrate the burden of
Smith's argument in terms of a simple example. Let us suppose
that the annual period 't + 1' has opened under conditions
identical to those which obtained in the period 't'; that during
the current period the capitalist groups decide to devote a smaller
proportion of their income to consumption, and that the greater
savings thus made are used to maintain productive labour or
to purchase machines. Under these circumstances Smith's theory
of price prompts the conclusion, in the first instance, that the
output of consumption goods will contract, and that of investment goods expand, thus leaving the same level of output as
before although changing its composition. This type of change
in the direction of (aggregate) demand, (and thus in the composition of output) would obviously be quite compatible with
the maintenance of static equilibrium at least in the relatively
short run (say, during the course of a single month). However,
in the longer run (i.e. during the course of the current annual
period) Smith argued, in cases of this kind, that total output
would necessarily *increase*, by virtue of the greater productive
capacity created by the increased output of investment goods
and the employment of a greater quantity of productive (output
creating) labour. Given an alteration in the proportions in which
a particular level of (aggregate) income is devoted to the purchase of consumption and investment goods, we would then
expect a *short run* change in the *composition* of output and, in
consequence, a *long run* change in the *level* of output and income, leading to an expansion in the size of the 'circular flow'.

On this basis, Smith concluded that every increase in capital would naturally tend to enhance:

the exchangeable value of the annual produce of the land and labour of the inhabitants, the real value and revenue of all its inhabitants.[82]

It will be observed, in terms of our example, that net savings attained during the course of a single (annual) period will lead indirectly to higher output and income, where the latter become available either during the course of the period examined or in subsequent years. The argument can of course be extended from this point in that the higher levels of output and income attained in any one year make it possible to reach still higher levels of savings and investment in subsequent years, thus generating still further increases in output and income. Once started, the process of capital accumulation and thus economic growth may be seen as self-generating, indicating that Smith's 'flow' is to be regarded as a spiral, rather than a circle of given dimensions. This indeed is the burden of Smith's argument in Book 2; a fact which helps to explain three of its recurrent themes. First, Smith frequently argues that net savings will always be *possible* during each annual period; that such savings will be made, by virtue of 'frugality', and prompted by:

the desire of bettering our condition, a desire which, though generally calm and dispassionate, comes with us from the womb and never leaves us till we go into the grave.[83]

Secondly, he argues that savings once made will always be *used* either to make purchases of investment goods or to employ productive (output creating) labour:

What is annually saved is as regularly consumed as what is annually spent, and nearly in the same time too, but it is consumed by a different set of people . . .[84]

Thirdly, Smith consistently suggests that savings when used must create successively higher levels of output, since:

Parsimony, by increasing the fund which is destined for the maintenance of productive hands, tends to increase the number of those whose labour adds to the subject upon which it is bestowed. It tends therefore, to increase the exchangeable value of the annual produce of the land and labour of the country. It puts into motion an addi-

provide a plentiful revenue or subsistence for the people, or more
properly to enable them to provide such a revenue or subsistence for
themselves.[95]

But of course Smith went much further than this, and in a
number of interesting ways. To begin with he was, as we have
already noted, acutely conscious of historical time and of the
fact that institutions which had been once appropriate to particular conditions did not themselves pass away when 'the circumstances, which first gave occasion to them, and which could
alone render them reasonable, are no more'.[96] Smith thus ascribed
to the State a responsibility for *reform*; a responsibility for removing various institutional and legal impediments to the system of natural liberty, such as the laws of succession and entail,
the privileges or corporations, and the statutes of apprenticeship
– all of which adversely affected the free transfer of resources
between employments and violated the liberty of the subject. In
a rather similar way, Smith objected to positions of privilege,
such as monopoly powers,[97] regarding these as creatures of the
civil law. He also rejected the prevailing (mercantile) system of
national policy which sought to control the use of resources in
such a way as to ensure a favourable balance of payments and
to create a self-supporting politico-economic unit from the contemporary relationship between Great Britain and her (especially
American) colonies. As in the case of monopoly powers in
general, Smith objected to policies of control and restraint at
the national level on the ground that they disturbed the alloca-
tive mechanism; artificially restricted the extent of the market,
and thus limited the possibilities for economic growth. The
general position is usefully summarized in Smith's statement
that:

No regulation of commerce can increase the quantity of industry in
any society beyond what its capital can maintain. It can only divert
a part of it into a direction into which it might not otherwise have
gone: and it is by no means certain that this artificial direction is
likely to be more advantageous to the society than that into which
it would have gone of its own accord.[98]

The functions of the State are therefore something other than
minimal in that Smith here calls for the abolition of institutions

and customs which are the remnants of the past; for the abolition of positions of monopoly and privilege, and for a general reform of national policy. At the same time, however, Smith's historical perspective also taught him that the same forces which had given the House of Commons a superior degree of influence had also made it an important focus for partial interests of a mercantile kind, thus making it unlikely that the necessary reforms would ever be executed at least in their entirety. Indeed, Smith was particularly scathing with regard to the political powers exercised by economic interests and frequently insisted that legislative proposals emanating from members of the mercantile classes :

ought always to be listened to with great precaution, and ought never to be adopted till after having been long and carefully examined, not only with the most scrupulous, but with the most suspicious attention. It comes from an order of men, whose interest is never exactly the same with that of the public, who have generally an interest to deceive and even to oppress the public, and who accordingly have, upon many occasions, both deceived and oppressed it.[99]

At this level of debate, there is a bleak realism about Smith's analysis, of a kind which led him to regard complete freedom of trade as an ideal unlikely to be attained in fact, even while he felt moved to confirm that the individual's natural drive to better his condition would be capable of surmounting :

a hundred impertinent obstructions with which the folly of human laws too often encumbers its operations; though the effect of those obstructions is always more or less to encroach upon its freedom, or diminish its security.[100]

If points such as these contribute to qualify the rather 'optimistic' thesis with which Smith is generally associated, the impression is further confirmed by those passages in the *Wealth of Nations* which bear more directly on the analysis of the *Moral Sentiments*. In the former work, it will be remembered that welfare is typically defined in material terms; in terms of the level of real income, i.e. the extent to which the individual can command the produce (or labour) of others. On the other hand, in the philosophical work welfare was defined more in terms of the *quality* of life attainable, where 'quality' refers to a level of moral experience greater than that involved in the 'mercenary exchange of good offices according to an agreed valuation'. There is of course no inconsistency between these two positions, since the two major books, while analytically linked, in fact refer to different areas of human experience. But at the same time Smith made a number of points in the *Wealth of Nations* which establish an important link between the philosophical and economic aspects of his study, and which also remind us that while economic growth may bring material benefit, it could also erode those faculties and propensities by virtue of which we are capable of attaining some degree of moral existence; qualities such as reason, imagination, sympathy, and fellow feeling. As he pointed out, the development of productive forces had created great cities and 'manufactories', wherein the individual worker was 'little attended to', where he lost his 'character', and where the mechanisms of the impartial spectator might well break down. Similarly, he suggested that the division of labour, which had brought in its train great benefits in terms of output, might lead to 'mental mutilation' through narrowing the range of activities undertaken by individuals. Indeed, Smith quite explicitly pointed out that where the individual is confined to the performance of a small number of simple operations, day after day, and for a high proportion of each day, he:

... has no occasion to exert his understanding, or to exercise his invention ... He naturally loses, therefore, the habit of such exertion, and generally becomes as stupid and ignorant as it is possible for a human creature to become. The torpor of his mind renders him, not only incapable of relishing or bearing a part in any rational conversation, but of conceiving any generous, noble or tender sentiment, and consequently of forming any just judgement concerning many even of the ordinary duties of private life. Of the great and extensive interests of his country he is altogether incapable of judging; and unless very particular pains have been taken to render him otherwise, he is equally incapable of defending his country in war.

To leave the point in no doubt, he continued:

His dexterity at his own particular trade, seems in this manner to be acquired at the expence of his intellectual, social, and martial virtues. But in every improved and civilized society this is the state into which the labouring poor, that is, the great body of the people, must necessarily fall, unless government takes some pains to prevent it.[101]

On the grounds of welfare, Smith then argued that governments should take pains to offset the (inevitable) effects of economic advance, by assuming at least some responsibility for 'cultural' activities. Smith defended this type of function at some length, not only because of the benefit which would accrue to individuals and thus the society to which they belonged, but also because the ordinary man, if left in a 'mutilated and deformed' state, would become the dupe of political, religious, and economic interests. On this ground he defended the encouragement of 'public shows' which, 'without indecency', might relieve the boredom and drabness of their lives. But by far the most important and positive of his suggestions was that governments should take steps to encourage basic education; an education of that kind and quality which was already available in Scotland through the agency of the parish school.

Writing as an *economist*, Smith's tone is basically optimistic, despite occasional references to the classic eighteenth-century theme of 'growth and decay'. But writing as a *social* scientist, Smith's tone is starkly realistic, at least in so far as he recognized those problems which the development of productive forces might bring. Thus the teaching of the economist is modified; the unproductive labour so severely criticized from the standpoint of the theory of growth, finally emerges as being productive of benefit to society at large. The negative functions of government defended on the basis of the economic work, are later extended to include a cultural purpose; a purpose which argues a recognition of the fact that we cannot simply conceive of welfare in economic terms.[102] Such arguments are not simply the *obiter dicta* of a great man; but rather the reflection of Smith's mastery of a wide range of disciplines, which include, as we have seen, philosophy, politics, history and economics.

NOTES TO INTRODUCTION

1. John Rae, *Life of Adam Smith* (1895), p. 286.
2. ibid.
3. Quoted in Sir James Steuart, *Principles of Political Economy* (1767, ed. Skinner, 1966) at p. lv.
4. Essays, p. 44. Smith in fact argued that the thinker would tend to produce systems in the sense just used, because of a natural dislike of the apparently unconnected and an equally natural preference for order. He applied this 'psychological law' to even the most ordinary business of life, and speaks frequently of the fact that 'the happy contrivance of a production of art' is 'often more highly valued than the very end for which it was intended'; of our 'love of system', and of our regard to 'the beauty of order, of art, of contrivance'. On this subject see the *Moral Sentiments*, Part 4, chapter 1 'Of the Effect of Utility upon the Sentiment of Approbation'. In the intellectual sphere, this same dislike of the chaotic and preference for order also explains, for Smith, our drive towards, and interest in, the philosophical system. Intellectual effort is prompted by a sense of wonder and the discomfort felt in contemplating 'disjointed objects' or 'jarring appearances'. Philosophy, by representing the 'invisible chains which bind together' the operations of nature, allays 'the tumult of imagination', and at the same time admits us to that pleasure which comes from observing 'the resemblances which are discoverable betwixt different objects'. (*Philosophical Essays*, pp. 10 and 20 ff.) These views tell us something of Smith's own purposes as a thinker, but they were also used by him to explain the history of ideas, and especially the development of ancient astronomy, physics, logic, and metaphysics. Perhaps the most successful of these essays is the first, and its title certainly deserves quotation, being: 'The Principles which lead and direct philosophical enquiries illustrated by the History of Astronomy.' It is interesting to observe that this essay was written prior to 1758 (op. cit., p. 90).
5. The comment appears in the advertisement to the 6th edition of the *Moral Sentiments*, and in the concluding paragraphs of earlier versions of that work.
6. The range of topics just considered scarcely exhausts the subjects on which Smith might claim expert knowledge. As a lecturer in Glasgow College, from 1751–64, he delivered material on areas as diverse (to modern eyes) as rhetoric, natural theology, ethics, jurisprudence, and economics. One of Smith's pupils, John Millar, supplied an account of his professor's lectures to Dugald Stewart when the latter was writing his biographical memoir. See Stewart's *Works* (vol. 10), p. 12.

SECTION I

1. The most useful commentaries may be: Glen Morrow, *The Ethical and Economic Theories of Adam Smith*, Cornell Studies in Philosophy, No. 13; 'The Significance of the Doctrine of Sympathy in Hume and Adam Smith', *Philosophical Review*, No. 32 (1923); 'Adam Smith: Moralist and Philosopher' in *Adam Smith 1776–1926*, ed. Hollander (1928); A. L. Macfie, *The Individual in Society, Papers on Adam Smith*, (1967); Dugald Stewart, *Biographical Memoir*, section 2.

2. For commentary on the School and its members, see James McCosh, *The Scottish Philosophy* (1875).

3. Quoted in Thomas Reid's *Collected Works*, ed. Sir William Hamilton (1846), p. 13. On the subject of method, see Reid's *Essays on the Intellectual Powers of Man* (1785) essay 1, chapter 1; cf. Adam Ferguson, *Institutes of Moral Philosophy* (3rd ed. 1785), sections 1–8, together with the same author's *Principles of Moral and Political Science* (1792), Part 1, chapter 2, section 9; chapter 3, section 11. For related commentary, see Dugald Stewart's *Account of the Life and Writings of Thomas Reid*, in *Collected Works*, vol. 10; A. W. Small, *Adam Smith and Modern Sociology* (1907), pp. 28–9; G. Bryson, *Man and Society* (1945), chapters 1 and 2; H. J. Bitterman, 'Adam Smith's Empiricism and the Law of Nature', in *Journal of Political Economy*, vol. 48 (1940).

4. David Hume, *A Treatise of Human Nature* (Everyman Library), p. 5.

5. *Theory of the Moral Sentiments* (6th ed. 1790), vol. 2, pp. 196–7. In handling the first problem Smith in fact rejected the argument of Hutcheson that we distinguish between objects of approval and disapproval by virtue of our possession of a 'moral sense', where the latter is defined as a reflex sense, akin to our sense of beauty, shame or ridicule. Smith criticized this type of argument, largely on the ground that it is odd that anything akin to a *moral* sense 'should hitherto have been so little taken notice of, as not to have got a name in any language', vol. 2, p. 354. For commentary on this aspect of Hutcheson's approach, see Part 7, section 3, chapters 2 and 3 (hence cited as 7.3.2, where part, section, and chapter number are given, or as 7.2, where only part and chapter number is supplied). Francis Hutcheson was of course Professor of Moral Philosophy at Glasgow when Smith was a student, and author of *A System of Moral Philosophy* (1755). A similar critical spirit is to be found in Smith's handling of what he took to be the second major question of moral philosophy; that concerning the problem of 'wherein does virtue consist?' In dealing with this issue, Hutcheson had argued that virtue consists in benevolence; a position which Smith rejected on the ground that it gave prominence to the 'milder' virtues, at the expense of the more demanding virtue of 'self command'. Smith also criticized Hutcheson's argument because of its denial that actions based on self love could ever be regarded as virtuous. For comment, see 7.2.3.

It is perhaps worth observing in this place that Smith also rejected Hume's solution to this (second) problem; a solution which grounded our approval of an action on our perception of its utility. Smith commented:

First of all, it seems impossible that . . . we should have no other reason for praising a man than that for which we commend a chest of drawers. And, secondly, it will be found upon examination that the usefulness of any disposition of mind is seldom the first ground of our approbation, and that the sentiment of approbation always involves in it a sense of propriety quite distinct from the perception of utility. (Vol. 1, p. 476–7 and see 4.1. and 2.)

Smith's comments on other classical and contemporary philosophers may be found in Part 7 of the *Moral Sentiments*.

6. Smith quite characteristically placed a good deal of emphasis on the existence of man's selfish, or at least self-regarding propensities; a position in marked contrast to that adopted by his old teacher Francis Hutcheson. Hutcheson had in fact argued that benevolent actions alone are worthy of approval; a quality which, Smith insisted, may be expected of the Deity, but:

so imperfect a creature as man, the support of whose existence requires so many things external to him, must often act from many other motives. The condition of human nature were peculiary hard if these affections, which by the very nature of our being, ought frequently to influence our conduct, could upon no occasion appear virtuous or deserve esteem and commendation from anybody.

(Vol. 2, p. 297.)

7. Vol. 1, pp. 1–2, and see 1.1.1.
8. ibid.
9. Vol. 1, pp. 28–9.
10. Vol. 1, p. 30.
11. Vol. 1, pp. 276–7, and see 3.1.
12. Vol. 1, p. 23, and see 1.1.3.
13. ibid.
14. Vol. 1, p. 38, and see 1.1.4. and 5.
15. Vol. 1, p. 39.
16. Vol. 1, p. 292, and see 3.2.
17. ibid.
18. Vol. 1, p. 321.
19. Vol. 1, p. 205, and see 2.2.2.
20. For an analysis of this question, see especially 3.4.
21. Vol. 1, p. 389.
22. Vol. 1, p. 391.
23. Vol. 1, p. 393.
24. ibid.
25. Vol. 1, p. 395.
26. For an analysis of this question see especially 3.5
27. Vol. 1, p. 122, and see 1.3.1. and 2.
28. Vol. 1, p. 464, and see 4.1.
29. Vol. 1, p. 141, and see 1.3.2.
30. Vol. 1, p. 225, and see 2.2.3.
31. Vol. 1, p. 207.
32. Vol. 1, p. 211.

33. Vol. 1, p. 229.
34. Vol. 1, p. 223.
35. Vol. 2, p. 395, and see 7.4.
36. Vol. 1, p. 218, and see 2.2.3.
37. Vol. 1, p. 414, and see 3.5.
38. This approach is sometimes described as 'functionalist', and as involving the doctrine of 'unintended social outcomes'. On this subject, see Louis Schneider, *The Scottish Moralists on Human Nature and Society* (1967). The solitary reference to the 'Invisible Hand' appears in *The Wealth of Nations* (Modern Library ed.) at p. 423. References are much more frequent in the *Moral Sentiments*; see for example 2.1.5; 3.2. and 4.1. For comment on this concept see A. L. Macfie, op. cit., essay 6 'The Invisible Hand in *The Theory of the Moral Sentiments*'.
39. Smith, op. cit., vol. 1, p. 203, and see 2.2.1.
40. Vol. 1, p. 442, and see 3.6.
41. Vol. 1, p. 214, and see 2.2.3.
42. ibid, p. 215.
43. Examination of the two major works has led to arguments for and against the view that they are consistent with each other. The question of consistency was probably first considered by August Oncken, in 'Das Adam Smith-Problem', *Zeitschrift fuer Sozialwissenschaft* (1898). However, the consistency of the two books is defended in A. L. Macfie, op. cit., essays 4 and 6; O. H. Taylor, 'Economics and the Idea of Ius Naturale', *Quarterly Journal of Economics*, No. 44 (1930); A. W. Small, op. cit., p. 5.
44. Recognition of this feature of Smith's philosophy, called forth a very perceptive comment from Edmund Burke. In a letter to Smith, dated 10 September 1759, Burke wrote:
A theory like yours, founded on the nature of man, which is always the same, will last, when those that are founded upon his opinions, which are always changing, will and must be forgotten.
(Quoted in C. R. Fay, *The World of Adam Smith* (1960) at p. 9.)
45. Smith in fact seems to have had an interest in this type of problem which dates back to his *Edinburgh Lectures* of 1748–51. W. R. Scott drew attention to the presence of an historical treatment of jurisprudence in these lectures, and suggested that they may have had a very direct influence on work of a similar kind undertaken by Adam Ferguson, Gilbert Stuart, and William Robertson. In the latter connexion, Scott indeed quoted a statement from one of Smith's auditors, one Collander of Craigforth, to the effect that 'Dr Robertson had borrowed the first volume of his History of Charles V from them (the lectures), as every student could testify'; *Adam Smith as Student and Professor* (1937), p. 55, and see generally chapter 5.

SECTION 2

1. For a discussion of the debts owed to Smith by his contemporaries, see W. R. Scott, op. cit., pp. 55–6; 63–4; 118–19.
For a discussion of the work done by the School as a whole, see: W. C. Lehmann, *John Millar of Glasgow* (1960); R. Pascal, 'Property and

Society: The Scottish Historical School of the Eighteenth Century', *Modern Quarterly*, (March 1938); D. Forbes, 'Scientific Whiggism: Adam Smith and John Millar', *Cambridge Journal*, vol. 7 (1953–4); G. Bryson, *Man and Society* (1945); R. L. Meek, 'The Scottish Contribution to Marxist Sociology' (1954) in *Economics, Ideology and Other Essays* (1967); A. Skinner, 'Economics and History: The Scottish Enlightenment', *Scottish Journal of Political Economy*, vol. 12 (1965); 'Natural History in the Age of Adam Smith', *Political Studies*, vol. 15 (1967); A. L. Macfie, 'The Scottish Tradition in Economic Thought', *S.J.P.E.*, vol. 1 (1955); 'John Millar', *S.J.P.E.*, vol. 7 (1961).

2. The *New Science* was first published in 1725, and the definitive edition in 1744. Bergin and Fisch brought out a new edition of the work in 1948, and of Vico's *Autobiography* in 1945. For a comment on Vico see Forbes, op. cit., pp. 658–9, and C. E. Vaughan, *History of Political Philosophy* (1925), chapter 5.

3. *Works*, vol. 10, p. 34.

4. Letter to Rochefoucauld, dated November 1785, quoted Meek, p. 35*n*. The conjectural historical approach is particularly marked in Smith's *Essays* (1795) and is also a feature of both the lectures on Justice, and Rhetoric.

5. J. H. Burton, *The Life of David Hume* (1846), vol. 1, p. 269.

6. Of the classical philosophers, three in particular are worthy of note: Plato, *Laws*, Book 3; Aristotle, *Politics*, Book 1; Lucretius, *De Rerum Natura*, Book 5. For comment on the classical historians, see Smith's *Lectures on Rhetoric*, lectures 16–19, but especially lecture 19 'Of the History of Historians'.

As regards Rousseau, the main relevant works are: *Discourse on the Arts and Sciences* (1750) and the *Discourse on the Origin of Inequality* (1754). It is interesting to observe that Adam Smith reviewed Rousseau's work in the ill-fated *Edinburgh Review* for 1755–6.

7. *Oeuvres*, vol. 24, quoted in J. B. Black, *The Art of History* (1922), p. 34. Black's work also contains a very useful analysis of the 'Scottish' contribution including that of Hume. Cf. C. Becker's *Heavenly City* (1932), chap. 3.

8. Lord Kames, (Henry Home), *Sketches of the History of Man* (1774), vol. 2, p. 2. On the influence of Montesquieu, see I. Ross, 'A Consideration of Lord Kames' Historical Law Tracts', *Texas Studies in Literature and Language*, vol. 8 (1967); F. T. H. Fletcher, 'English Imitators of Montesquieu', *Revue de Litterature Comparée*, vol. 13 (1933).

9. *Esprit des Lois*, (1748) and see also the same author's *Considerations of the Causes of the Greatness of the Romans and their Decline*, ed. D. Lowenthal (1965).

10. John Millar, *Historical View of the English Government* (1786, new edition in 4 vols., 1803), vol. 2, p. 429.

11. The argument again finds precedents; especially in physiocratic writing: see, for example, Turgot's *Reflections on the Formation and Distribution of Riches* (1766); *Notes on Universal History* (1750). See also R. L. Meek, *The Economics of Physiocracy* (1962), translations, part 1 'Philo-

sophy and Sociology'. A further notable example of a writer who used the socio-economic argument is Sir James Steuart, *Principles of Political Economy* (1767), ed. Skinner (1966).

12. Smith, *The Moral Sentiments*, part 4 'Of the Effect of Utility upon the Sentiment of Approbation'; *Lectures on Justice*, part 2, division 2, sections 1–2 'Of the Natural Wants of Mankind'.

13. op. cit., p. 107.
14. The *Historical Law Tracts* (1758, 4th ed. 1792), p. 56.
15. *Collected Works*, ed. Dugald Stewart (1809), vol. 5, pp. 111 and 128.
16. The analysis mainly appears in the *Lectures on Justice*, part 1 'Of Public Jurisprudence'; *The Wealth of Nations* Books 3 and 5.
17. *The Wealth of Nations* (Modern Library ed.) p. 653.
18. ibid.
19. *Lectures on Justice*, p. 14.
20. *The Wealth of Nations*, p. 653.
21. op. cit., p. 670.
22. ibid.
23. op. cit., p. 670; *Lectures*, p. 15.
24. *The Wealth of Nations*, p. 674.
25. op. cit., p. 671.
26. op. cit., p. 672.
27. op. cit., p. 673.
28. ibid.
29. op. cit., p. 20 (125).
30. *Lectures*, p. 22 ff.
31. *Lectures*, p. 116.
32. *Wealth*, p. 361 (484).
33. op. cit., pp. 361–2 (486).
34. op. cit., p. 385; cf. *Lectures*, p. 42 (508).
35. *Wealth*, pp. 385–6 (508–9).
36. op. cit., p. 387 (511).
37. op. cit., p. 369 (493).
38. *Lectures*, p. 39; *Wealth*, p. 388 (512).
39. op. cit., p. 358 (481).
40. *Lectures*, pp. 40–45, *Wealth*, pp. 373–9 (496 ff).
41. op. cit., p. 377 (500).
42. op. cit., p. 379 (502).
43. op. cit., p. 381 (503).
44. op. cit., p. 384 (507).
45. op. cit., p. 388 (512).
46. op. cit., p. 390 (514).
47. op. cit., p. 365 (488).
48. op. cit., p. 368 (491).
49. op. cit., p. 389 (512).
50. op. cit., p. 391 (514).
51. op. cit., pp. 391–2 (515).
52. op. cit., p. 356 (479).

53. *Lectures*, pp. 40–46.

54. *Origins of the Distinction of Ranks* (1771), ed. Lehmann (1960), p. 292. Millar was always 'happy to acknowledge' the debt he owed to Smith's lectures. He provided one of the most complete statements of the thesis which we have examined, in his *Historical View of the English Government*. See especially vol. 4. The acknowledgement of Smith's example occurs in vol. 2, at p. 429.

55. *Moral Sentiments*, 6.2.2. 'Of the Order in which Societies are by Nature recommended to our Benificence'.

56. *Moral Sentiments*, part 3, section 3 'Of the Propriety of Action'.

57. *Wealth*, p. 390 (513).

58. *The Individual in Society*, p. 16, and see essay 2 'The Scottish Tradition in Economic Thought'.

SECTION 3

1. The distinctions used here, between factors and types of return, were not always made by Smith's contemporaries, and of themselves amount to a considerable clarification. Of particular importance is Smith's handling of the concept of profit. See R. L. Meek, 'Adam Smith and the Classical Concept of Profit', *Scottish Journal of Political Economy*, vol. 1, (1954).

2. It will be recalled from section 1 (above) that this description occurs in the *Moral Sentiments*, and that Smith's statement as to the objectives of self-interested action is a complex one – much more so indeed than that contained in the post-Benthamite hypothesis of economic man. On this subject see also A. L. Macfie, op. cit., essays 3 and 4.

3. *The Wealth of Nations*, p. 14 (119).

4. Sir James Steuart, *The Principles of Political Economy* (1767), ed. Skinner (1966).

5. op. cit., p. 642. For Smith's comment on the French School, see Book 4, chapter 9. On Smith's contact with the School between 1764 and 1766, see Rae, op. cit., pp. 200–220. Since the discovery of the Glasgow (Cannan) *Lectures* it has generally been held that at most the Physiocrats could have acted as a kind of catalyst to Smith's thought. On this subject, see especially Cannan's introduction to the *Lectures*, pp. xxiii–iv; xxviii–xxxi. See also I. C. Lunberg's *Turgot's Unknown Translator* for an alternative view, and for comment, Viner's *Guide*, pp. 128–38.

On the subject of influences, Smith's teacher, Francis Hutcheson, should also be mentioned. See Cannan's introduction to *The Wealth of Nations*, pp. xliv–li; the *Lectures*, pp. xxv–vi and also W. R. Scott's *Francis Hutcheson* (1900), chapter 11. The interested reader might also consult David Hume's *Economic Writings* (ed. Rotwein, 1955).

6. From Quesnai's *Dialogues*, quoted in R. L. Meek's *Economics of Physiocracy* (1962), at p. 204.

7. A *variorum* edition of this work is presented in Meek, op. cit.

8. Cannan, op. cit., p. xxix.

9. The main discussion of this topic will be found in Book 1, chapters 1–3.

10. *The Wealth of Nations*, p. 7 (112). For a useful comment on the various senses in which Smith used the term 'division of labour', see Viner's *Guide*, pp. 103–9, 'Pins (and Needles) and Nails'.

11. *The Wealth of Nations*, p. 12 (117).

12. op. cit., p. 22 (120). Smith in fact regarded the division of labour as both the cause and consequence of exchange. In a famous passage, which also provides an example of the thesis of 'unintended outcomes, he remarked (below p. 117) that the institution is not the effect of 'human wisdom', but rather the consequence of man's 'propensity to truck, barter, and exchange one thing for another'.

13. The main discussion of value theory, appears in Book 1, chapters 5 and 6.

14. op. cit., p. 28 (131). For a discussion of Smith's treatment of the paradox of value, see Schumpeter's *History of Economic Analysis*, Part 2, chapter 6, section 3 'Digression on Value'. Schumpeter's view which is widely accepted, is that Smith quite failed to solve the problem; a view which, perhaps, does less than justice to his treatment of the subject.

15. *Lectures* (ed. Cannan), Division 2, section 1 'Of the Natural Wants of Mankind'. On this subject, see also the *Moral Sentiments*, especially Part 4, chapter 1, 'Of the Beauty which the Appearance of Utility bestows upon all the Productions of Art and of the Extensive Influence of this Species of Beauty'.

16. *The Wealth of Nations*, p. 172 (277).

17. ibid., cf. *Lectures*, p. 159.

18. op. cit., p. 157.

19. *The Wealth of Nations*, p. 30 (133).

20. *The Wealth of Nations*, p. 33 (136).

21. op. cit., p. 47 (150).

22. ibid. Smith did however observe that some allowance would have to be made for differences in the quality or type of labour involved, e.g. with respect to the degrees of hardship and ingenuity involved. This qualification was of considerable importance in the modern state, where as Smith observed, the disutility involved in labour would vary with the type of employment. The argument is developed in Book 1, chapter 10, part 1.

23. op. cit., p. 30 (133).

24. op. cit., p. 31 (134). Italics supplied.

25. op. cit., p. 49 (152). For an elaboration of this argument, see Book 1, chapter 6.

26. On this subject, see Book 1, chapter 4 'Of the Origin and Use of Money'.

27. op. cit., p. 50 (153).

28. While the remainder of the chapter is perhaps most easily understood after the rest of the work has been read, the elements of the argument may be briefly elaborated at this point. If we seek to *compare* levels of real income at different points in time, it is obviously necessary to

employ a stable unit of measurement or value coefficient. In Smith's opinion, the labour unit alone was stable, the reason being that the disutility of labour may be said to be constant over time (136); an argument which serves to remind us that Smith's labour unit is expressed in terms of disutility and not (directly) man hours. The choice of unit may be further clarified by considering the problems of the wage unit, where the latter is defined as the return payable per labour unit, or the return required to induce the individual to undergo the disutility involved (to 'forego his ease and happiness'). Looked at in this way, Smith regarded a wage unit expressed in money terms as adequate over short periods, but not over long – the reason being that money was liable to changes in its value, either through debasement of the standard, or through the effects of discoveries such as the American mines. Over long periods, he regarded a wage unit expressed in terms of wage goods (corn) as adequate, but not over short – the reason being that in the short run (a number of years) the real wage of the labourer was likely to vary with the rate of economic growth. In the longer run, the relevant unit (corn) was however considered to be adequate, because here wages were held to tend towards subsistence levels. Smith did not then deny the usefulness of the money or corn unit, but he did insist, because labour was always stable in *its* value (in terms of the disutility incurred), that the labour unit was the only universal and invariable standard on which comparisons could be based. It will be observed that the argument thus far seems to imply that the disutility of work is the same for all individuals in all employments. However, Smith did observe (note 22 above) that employments differ qualitatively, being more or less agreeable or disagreeable, etc. Given this point, it then becomes necessary to express the disutility involved in one hour of 'hard' labour, in terms of a number of units of common labour power. On Smith's argument, the relevant proportions would be adequately expressed by the money wage differentials established by the 'higgling and bargaining' of the market. The interested reader should take chapters 5 and 11 in conjunction, and consult M. Blaug's *Economic Theory in Retrospect* (1962), pp. 48–52.

29. op. cit., p. 52 (155).

30. The main discussion is to be found in Book 1, chapters 6 and 7. It is perhaps worth noting that in these chapters Smith is generally held to have gone on to state a 'cost of production' theory of value, after having restricted the labour theory to the 'primitive' state. In a sense, this is of course perfectly true, although it may be observed that the discussion of rates of exchange is not unconnected with the treatment of price theory, at least in the broad sense that the link established between value and utility is connected with the problem of demand, while the view that labour requires a reward to compensate the disutility of work is associated with the problem of supply price.

31. The assumption is stated at the beginning of chapter 7, although the discussion of the theory of distribution appears in chapters 8–11.

32. op. cit., p. 55 (158).

33. op. cit., p. 56 (158).

34. op. cit., p. 58 (160). This, and subsequent stages of the argument can

be illustrated graphically. If we plot price per unit on one axis, and
quantities of the commodity on the other, we may use a downward slop-
ing demand curve, and a long run supply curve in the form of a horizontal

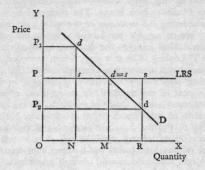

straight line. The latter procedure is justified at least in so far as Smith
implicitly assumes that natural price remains constant irrespective of output. Given these points, Smith's equilibrium position is represented by
that point at which the DD curve intersects the (long run) SS curve; this
being the position where the price paid (the demand price) for the quantity
OM is the same as the natural (supply) price of that quantity. If for example, the quantity offered was less than OM, (say ON), the market price
would be OP_1 and the supply price OP, indicating that profits in excess of the 'ordinary' would accrue, causing an expansion of supply back
towards the equilibrium level of OM. In the contrary case, if the quantity
offered was greater than the equilibrium amount (OR rather than OM),
the market price would fall below the natural price (OP_2 as compared to
OP) thus generating losses and causing a contraction in supply back to OM.
    Diagram 2 represents a simple extension of the argument, which Smith
himself made. Starting from a position of equilibrium as defined, suppose an upward shift in the DD curve. If we assume that in the very short

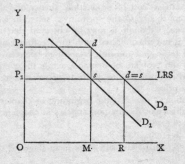

run (Marshallian market period) supply is inelastic, then the initial consequence of the shift is that price rises from OP 1 to OP 2, indicating a divergence of market and natural price. In the long run, the consequence is that resources flow into this employment, causing supply of the good to increase, until a position is reached where market price falls to equality with the natural price, a greater quantity of the good being produced. It is important to note that under the conditions assumed, the position of the DD curve determines the amount of the good produced, and that *price* is determined by cost of production.

35. op. cit., p. 57 (159).
36. ibid.
37. ibid.
38. ibid (160).
39. op. cit., p. 58 (160).
40. Smith enumerates these assumptions at pp. 60–62 (163–5).
41. *Lectures* (ed. Cannan), p. 180.
42. *The Wealth of Nations*, p. 99 (202). The analysis of this problem occurs in chapter 10, part 1. See note 28 above for another respect in which the analysis is relevant.
43. op. cit., p. 99 (202).
44. The other necessary assumptions are: 'First, the employments must be well known and long established in the neighbourhood; secondly, they must be in their ordinary, or what may be called their natural state; and thirdly, they must be the sole or principal occupations of those who occupy them.' op. cit., p. 114 *et seq.*; (217).
It is worth noting that the argument concerning 'net advantages' provides a clear link with the analysis of man's psychology contained in the *Moral Sentiments*. This is very obvious in Smith's discussion of the agreeable or disagreeable nature of employments, and of the effect which this must have on pecuniary rates of return. He noted for example, the impact of fashion, and of what is considered by men in general to be honourable or disgraceful, the point being that where an occupation is generally approved of, this fact alone constitutes an important part of the reward. Where on the contrary it is considered disgraceful to make a parade of certain abilities, this fact means that a higher rate of monetary reward is required; required, that is, to induce men to suffer the penalty of disapproval. See, for example, p. 107 (209).
45. Where 'police' means (Government) policy.
46. op. cit., p. 61 (164).
47. On this subject, see chapter 10, part 2, and the closing passages of chapter 7.
48. *Lectures* (ed. Cannan), p. 246 and cf. pp. 180–82. As early as the 1750s, Smith had already stated his celebrated doctrine that 'it is by far the best policy to leave things to their natural course'. See also, Dugald Stewart, op. cit., p. 68, where Smith's views on natural liberty are dated from 1755.
49. Above, p. 52.
50. This subject is chiefly handled in Book 1, chapter 8.

51. op. cit., p. 66 (169).

52. ibid.

53. op. cit., p. 68 (171).

54. ibid (170).

55. The argument may be illustrated diagrammatically, where we have population (working) on the X axis and the (real) wage rate on the Y axis. With a given demand curve (DD 1) and a given long-run supply curve, equilibrium is attained where the level of population OM is in receipt of the subsistence wage, W_1. If population was greater than the amount OM, the wage payable would be W_2, indicating that wage payments would be below the subsistence level, and causing a contraction in supply back to the quantity OM, where a subsistence wage can be paid to a smaller population. Similarly, if the level of population was less than OM, the wage payable would be W_3, indicating that wages are in excess of the subsistence level (or supply price). Under these circumstances, and with a 'generative faculty' of constant force, more children can survive, leading to a long-run expansion to that level (OM) where no further increase is possible. As Smith pointed out, 'It is in this manner that the demand for men, like that for any other commodity, necessarily regulates the production of men'. The argument may be extended to take account of shifts in the demand curve for labour, exactly in the same manner as for changes in the demand for particular commodities. See note 34, above.

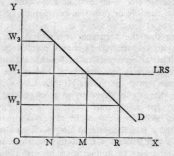

56. op. cit., p. 73 (175).

57. op. cit., pp. 74 f (176 ff.).

58. 'It is but equity besides, that they who feed, cloath and lodge the whole body of the people, should have such a share of the produce of their own labour as to be themselves tolerably well fed, cloathed, and lodged,' (181). For Smith's views on the causes of the increase in productivity which high wages involve, see pp. 81 and 86 (184, 190).

59. op. cit., pp. 48–9 (151). This subject is mainly considered in Book 1, chapter 9.

60. op. cit., p. 88 (191).

61. op. cit., pp. 96 ff. (198).

62. op. cit., p. 87 (190).

63. op. cit., p. 91 (194).

64. op. cit., p. 97 (199). The theory of interest, is considered in Book 2, chapter 4.

65. op. cit., pp. 93–4 (196).

66. This subject is considered in Book 1, chapter 11.

67. op. cit., p. 249 (357).

68. op. cit., p. 144 (247).

69. op. cit., pp. 247–8 (356).

70. op. cit., pp. 145–6 (249).

71. op. cit., p. 270, and see above, section 3 of this part (382).

72. op. cit., p. 271 (382).

73. op. cit., p. 324 (441).

74. op. cit., p. 315. On this subject, see chapter 3 (430).

75. These subjects are considered in chapter 5.

76. On these topics, see especially, chapter 1 of Book 2.

77. op. cit., p. 264 (375).

78. op. cit., p. 323. On the relationship between the quantity of money and the 'value of consumeable goods', see especially chapter 2, (439).

79. op. cit., p. 271 (382).

80. op. cit., p. 326 (443).

81. ibid, (443).

82. op. cit., p. 321 (437).

83. op. cit., p. 324 (441).

84. op. cit., p. 321 (438).

85. ibid. (437).

86. On this subject, see chapter 5 of Book 2. In Smith's opinion, agriculture would set in motion the greatest quantity of industry, for an equal quantity of 'capital' used; followed by manufactures and commerce (domestic and foreign). It is interesting to observe that while Smith rejected the physiocratic view that agriculture alone was productive, he still accepted the argument that of all types of productive activity, agriculture was the *most* productive

87. op. cit., p. 329 (446). It is to be observed that this argument is directly linked to the psychology of the *Moral Sentiments*, where Smith explains the drive to better one's condition (fortune) in terms of the desire to become an object of approval to one's fellows. On this subject, see above section 1, pp. 23 ff. and the *Moral Sentiments*, part 1, section 3, chapter 2 'Of Ambition and the Distinction of Ranks'. Smith also argued that the personal qualities necessary for the acquisition of fortune were objects of approval to mankind thus stimulating individuals to acquire them. The end (fortune) is thus seen by Smith to be quite as 'natural' as the means (prudence and frugality for example) since both represent activities or qualities with which the 'spectator' is likely to sympathize. In this connection Smith made two points. First, he suggested that the man of enterprise is always approved of, while ambition too 'is always admired in the world' – provided that this passion is kept 'within the bounds of prudence and justice'. On this subject, see part 3, chapter 6. Secondly, Smith argued that the willingness of individuals to forego present enjoyments, and thus

to accumulate stock through frugality, was also an admired quality since it involved the virtue of self-command. He added:

> Hence arises that eminent esteem with which all men naturally regard a steady perseverance in the practice of frugality, industry and application, though directed to no other purpose than the acquisition of fortune.

See for example, part 4, chapter 2 'Of the Beaunty and Influence of Utility Upon Men'. Very similar points are made in part 7, section 2, chapter 3, where Smith suggests:

> The habits of economy, industry, discretion, attention and application of thought, are generally supposed to be cultivated from self-interested motives, and at the same time are apprehended to be very praiseworthy qualities which deserve the esteem and approbation of everybody.

88. *Adam Smith, 1776–1926* (Chicago, 1928), p. 116, 118. See also Jacob Hollander's comments in the same volume, at pp. 15–19.

89. Dugald Stewart, loc. cit., p. 278. Similar comments appear at pp. 69–70.

90. On this general subject, see especially Jacob Viner's essay 'Adam Smith and Laisser-Faire' in *Adam Smith, 1776–1926*; and A. S. Skinner, 'Adam Smith and the Role of the State' (Glasgow University Press, 1973).

91. *op. cit.*, p. 651.

92. *op. cit.*, p. 681. For comment see Lionel Robbins's *Theory of Economic Policy* (1953), especially Lectures 1 and 2.

93. *op. cit.*, p. 678. For comment see Nathan Rosenberg, 'Some Institutional Aspects of the *Wealth of Nations*' in the *Journal of Political Economy*, vol. 68 (1960).

94. Smith was particularly scathing on the subject of the universities, and pointed out that large public endowments paid irrespective of effort encourage sloth, especially in those cases where the government of the college is in the hands of those who happen to be subject to it. Here the teachers 'are likely to make a common cause, to be very indulgent to one another, and every man to consent that his neighbour may neglect his duty, provided he himself is allowed to neglect his own'. (718). Smith also objected to a system which bound the student to one college, and to the lack of choice of teacher – all of which contributed to explain poor teaching and unwillingness to innovate. As he pointed out in another connexion: several of those learned societies have chosen to remain ... the sanctuaries in which exploded doctrines and obsolete prejudices found sanctuary and protection'. (727). The Scottish universities were exempted from this general condemnation, not because they had better men, but because the conditions of corruption if not wholly absent, were less marked than they were in contemporary Oxford.

95. *op. cit.*, p. 397.

96. *op. cit.*, p. 362 (485).

97. Smith did however defend temporary monopolies, for example of the kind granted to a group of merchants who had undertaken a 'dangerous and expensive experiment, of which the public is afterwards to reap the benefit'. In the same way, he considered it appropriate to give certain

exclusive rights for a limited period, e.g. to the inventors of new machines or the authors of new books. *op. cit.*, p. 712.

98. *op. cit.*, p. 421. The argument that regulation would upset the 'natural balance of industry' dates back to Smith's Glasgow lectures.

99. *op. cit.*, p. 250. *cf.* George Stigler, 'Adam Smith's Travels on the Ship of State' in *History of Political Economy*, vol. 3 (1971).

100. *op. cit.*, p. 508.

101. *op. cit.*, pp. 734-5, and see also pp. 735-40. Similar points appear in the *Lectures* (ed. Cannan), pp. 255-8. On this subject, see E. G. West, 'Adam Smith's two views on the Division of Labour', *Economica*, February, 1964 and N. Rosenberg, 'Adam Smith on the Division of Labour: Two Views or One', *Economica*, May, 1965. It is interesting to note that Smith's views on the social effects of the division of labour were widely stated. See for example, John Millar's *Historical View* (1803 ed.), vol. 4, chapter 4; Adam Ferguson, *History of Civil Society* (1767), Part 4, sections 1 and 2. Ferguson in particular was most eloquent on the subject, and was in fact quoted with approval by Marx in his *Poverty of Philosophy* (Lawrence & Wishart) at p. 110, the relevant passage being:

It may even be doubted, whether the measure of national capacity increases with the advancement of arts. Many mechanical arts indeed, require no capacity; they succeed best under a total suppression of sentiment and reason; and ignorance is the mother of industry as well as of superstition. Reflection and fancy are subject to err; but a habit of moving the hand or the foot, is independent of either. Manufactures, accordingly, prosper most, where the mind is least consulted, and where the workshop may, without any great effort of imagination, be considered as an engine, the parts of which are men.

(Ferguson, *op. cit.*, pp. 182-3; ed. Forbes (1966).)

For recent comment on this subject see E. G. West, 'The Political Economy of Alienation' *Oxford Economic Papers*, vol. 21 (1969); and R. Hamowy, 'Adam Smith, Adam Ferguson, and the Division of Labour', *Economica*, August, 1968.

102. *cf.* J. M. A. Gee, 'Adam Smith's Social Welfare Function', *Scottish Journal of Political Economy*, vol. 15 (1968).

Facsimile title page of the first edition
of *The Wealth of Nations*.

AN

INQUIRY

INTO THE

Nature and Caufes

OF THE

WEALTH OF NATIONS.

By ADAM SMITH, LL. D. and F. R. S.

Formerly Profeffor of Moral Philofophy in the Univerfity of GLASGOW.

IN TWO VOLUMES.

VOL. I.

LONDON:

PRINTED FOR W. STRAHAN; AND T. CADELL, IN THE STRAND.

MDCCLXXVI.

CONTENTS

Omissions:

The reader interested in Smith's discussion of principles might usefully
omit (initially) the following passages:

Book 1, chapter 5, pp. 141–50. From the last paragraph on p. 141 to
the end of the chapter.

Chapter 10, pp. 222–47. Part 2 of this chapter.

Chapter 11, pp. 255–65. From the second paragraph on p. 255 to the
end of Part 1 of this chapter.

Chapter 11, pp. 282–350; 359–67. The Digression on Silver.

Book 2, chapter 2, pp. 394–429. From the second paragraph on p. 394
to the end of the chapter.

Book 3, chapters 1–4, pp. 479–520.

INTRODUCTION AND PLAN OF THE WORK

THE annual labour of every nation is the fund which originally supplies it with all the necessaries and conveniences of life
which it annually consumes, and which consists always either in
the immediate produce of that labour, or in what is purchased
with that produce from other nations.

According therefore as this produce, or what is purchased
with it, bears a greater or smaller proportion to the number of
those who are to consume it, the nation will be better or worse
supplied with all the necessaries and conveniences for which it
has occasion.

But this proportion must in every nation be regulated by two
different circumstances; first, by the skill, dexterity, and judgement with which its labour is generally applied; and, secondly,
by the proportion between the number of those who are employed in useful labour, and that of those who are not so employed. Whatever be the soil, climate, or extent of territory of
any particular nation, the abundance or scantiness of its annual
supply must, in that particular situation, depend upon those two
circumstances.

The abundance or scantiness of this supply, too, seems to
depend more upon the former of those two circumstances than
upon the latter. Among the savage nations of hunters and
fishers, every individual who is able to work, is more or less
employed in useful labour, and endeavours to provide, as well
as he can, the necessaries and conveniences of life, for himself, or
such of his family or tribe as are either too old, or too young, or
too infirm to go a hunting and fishing. Such nations, however,
are so miserably poor that, from mere want, they are frequently
reduced, or, at least, think themselves reduced, to the necessity
sometimes of directly destroying, and sometimes of abandoning
their infants, their old people, and those afflicted with lingering

diseases, to perish with hunger, or to be devoured by wild beasts. Among civilized and thriving nations, on the contrary, though a great number of people do not labour at all, many of whom consume the produce of ten times, frequently of a hundred times more labour than the greater part of those who work; yet the produce of the whole labour of the society is so great that all are often abundantly supplied, and a workman, even of the lowest and poorest order, if he is frugal and industrious, may enjoy a greater share of the necessaries and conveniences of life than it is possible for any savage to acquire.

The causes of this improvement, in the productive powers of labour, and the order, according to which its produce is naturally distributed among the different ranks and conditions of men in the society, make the subject of the First Book of this Inquiry.

Whatever be the actual state of the skill, dexterity, and judgement with which labour is applied in any nation, the abundance or scantiness of its annual supply must depend, during the continuance of that state, upon the proportion between the number of those who are annually employed in useful labour, and that of those who are not so employed. The number of useful and productive labourers, it will hereafter appear, is everywhere in proportion to the quantity of capital stock which is employed in setting them to work, and to the particular way in which it is so employed. The Second Book, therefore, treats of the nature of capital stock, of the manner in which it is gradually accumulated, and of the different quantities of labour which it puts into motion, according to the different ways in which it is employed.

Nations tolerably well advanced as to skill, dexterity, and judgement, in the application of labour, have followed very different plans in the general conduct or direction of it; and those plans have not all been equally favourable to the greatness of its produce. The policy of some nations has given extraordinary encouragement to the industry of the country; that of others to the industry of towns. Scarce any nation has dealt equally and impartially with every sort of industry. Since the downfall of the Roman empire, the policy of Europe has been more favourable to arts, manufactures, and commerce, the industry of towns, than to agriculture, the industry of the country. The circumstances which seem to have introduced and established this policy are explained in the Third Book.

Though those different plans were, perhaps, first introduced by the private interests and prejudices of particular orders of men, without any regard to, or foresight of, their consequences upon the general welfare of the society; yet they have given occasion to very different theories of political economy; of which some magnify the importance of that industry which is carried on in towns, others of that which is carried on in the country. Those theories have had a considerable influence, not only upon the opinions of men of learning, but upon the public conduct of princes and sovereign states. I have endeavoured, in the Fourth Book, to explain, as fully and distinctly as I can, those different theories, and the principal effects which they have produced in different ages and nations.

To explain in what has consisted the revenue of the great body of the people, or what has been the nature of those funds which, in different ages and nations, have supplied their annual consumption, is the object of these Four first Books. The Fifth and last Book treats of the revenue of the sovereign, or commonwealth. In this book I have endeavoured to show, first, what are the necessary expenses of the sovereign, or commonwealth; which of those expenses ought to be defrayed by the general contribution of the whole society; and which of them by that of some particular party only, or of some particular members of it; secondly, what are the different methods in which the whole society may be made to contribute towards defraying the expenses incumbent on the whole society, and what are the principal advantages and inconveniences of each of those methods: and, thirdly and lastly, what are the reasons and causes which have induced almost all modern governments to mortgage some part of this revenue, or to contract debts, and what have been the effects of those debts upon the real wealth, the annual produce of the land and labour of the society.

BOOK ONE

*Of the Causes of Improvement in the
Productive Powers of Labour, and of the Order
According to Which its Produce Is Naturally
Distributed Among the Different Ranks
of the People*

CHAPTER I

OF THE DIVISION OF LABOUR

THE greatest improvement in the productive powers of labour, and the greater part of the skill, dexterity, and judgement with which it is anywhere directed, or applied, seem to have been the effects of the division of labour.

The effects of the division of labour, in the general business of society, will be more easily understood by considering in what manner it operates in some particular manufactures. It is commonly supposed to be carried furthest in some very trifling ones; not perhaps that it really is carried further in them than in others of more importance: but in those trifling manufactures which are destined to supply the small wants of but a small number of people, the whole number of workmen must necessarily be small; and those employed in every different branch of the work can often be collected into the same workhouse, and placed at once under the view of the spectator. In those great manufactures, on the contrary, which are destined to supply the great wants of the great body of the people, every different branch of the work employs so great a number of workmen that it is impossible to collect them all into the same workhouse. We can seldom see more, at one time, than those employed in one single branch. Though in such manufactures, therefore, the work may really be divided into a much greater number of parts than in those of a more trifling nature, the division is not near so obvious, and has accordingly been much less observed.

To take an example, therefore, from a very trifling manufacture; but one in which the division of labour has been very often taken notice of, the trade of the pin-maker; a workman not educated to this business (which the division of labour has rendered a distinct trade), nor acquainted with the use of the machinery employed in it (to the invention of which the same division of labour has probably given occasion), could scarce, perhaps, with his utmost industry, make one pin in a day, and certainly could not make twenty. But in the way in which this business is now carried on, not only the whole work is a peculiar trade, but it is divided into a number of branches, of which the greater part are likewise peculiar trades. One man draws out the wire, another straights it, a third cuts it, a fourth points it, a fifth grinds it at the top for receiving the head; to make the head requires three distinct operations; to put it on is a peculiar business, to whiten the pins is another; it is even a trade by itself to put them into the paper; and the important business of making a pin is, in this manner, divided into about eighteen distinct operations, which, in some manufactories, are all performed by distinct hands, though in others the same man will sometimes perform two or three of them. I have seen a small manufactory of this kind where ten men only were employed, and where some of them consequently performed two or three distinct operations. But though they were very poor, and therefore but indifferently accommodated with the necessary machinery, they could, when they exerted themselves, make among them about twelve pounds of pins in a day. There are in a pound upwards of four thousand pins of a middling size. Those ten persons, therefore, could make among them upwards of forty-eight thousand pins in a day. Each person, therefore, making a tenth part of forty-eight thousand pins, might be considered as making four thousand eight hundred pins in a day. But if they had all wrought separately and independently, and without any of them having been educated to this peculiar business, they could certainly not each of them have made twenty, perhaps not one pin in a day; that is, certainly, not the two hundred and fortieth, perhaps not the four thousand eight hundredth part of what they are at present capable of performing, in consequence of a proper division and combination of their different operations.

In every other art and manufacture, the effects of the division of labour are similar to what they are in this very trifling one; though, in many of them, the labour can neither be so much subdivided, nor reduced to so great a simplicity of operation. The division of labour, however, so far as it can be introduced, occasions, in every art, a proportionable increase of the productive powers of labour. The separation of different trades and employments from one another seems to have taken place in consequence of this advantage. This separation, too, is generally carried furthest in those countries which enjoy the highest degree of industry and improvement; what is the work of one man in a rude state of society being generally that of several in an improved one. In every improved society, the farmer is generally nothing but a farmer; the manufacturer, nothing but a manufacturer. The labour, too, which is necessary to produce any one complete manufacture is almost always divided among a great number of hands. How many different trades are employed in each branch of the linen and woollen manufactures, from the growers of the flax and the wool, to the bleachers and smoothers of the linen, or to the dyers and dressers of the cloth! The nature of agriculture, indeed, does not admit of so many subdivisions of labour, nor of so complete a separation of one business from another, as manufactures. It is impossible to separate so entirely the business of the grazier from that of the corn-farmer as the trade of the carpenter is commonly separated from that of the smith. The spinner is almost always a distinct person from the weaver; but the ploughman, the harrower, the sower of the seed, and the reaper of the corn, are often the same. The occasions for those different sorts of labour returning with the different seasons of the year, it is impossible that one man should be constantly employed in any one of them. This impossibility of making so complete and entire a separation of all the different branches of labour employed in agriculture is perhaps the reason why the improvement of the productive powers of labour in this art does not always keep pace with their improvement in manufactures. The most opulent nations, indeed, generally excel all their neighbours in agriculture as well as in manufactures; but they are commonly more distinguished by their superiority in the latter than in the former. Their lands are in general better cultivated, and having more labour and expense bestowed upon them, produce more in proportion to the extent and natural fertility of the ground. But this superiority of produce is seldom much more than in proportion to the superiority of labour and expense. In agriculture, the labour of the rich country is not always much more productive than that of the poor; or, at least, it is never so much more productive as it commonly is in manufactures. The corn of the rich country, therefore, will not always, in the same degree of goodness, come cheaper to market than that of the poor. The corn of Poland, in the same degree of goodness, is as cheap as that of France, notwithstanding the superior opulence and improvement of the latter country. The corn of France is, in the corn provinces, fully as good, and in most years nearly about the same price with the corn of England, though, in opulence and improvement, France is perhaps inferior to England. The corn-lands of England, however, are better cultivated than those of France, and the corn-lands of France are said to be much better cultivated than those of Poland. But though the poor country, notwithstanding the inferiority of its cultivation, can, in some measure, rival the rich in the cheapness and goodness of its corn, it can pretend to no such competition in its manufactures; at least if those manufactures suit the soil, climate, and situation of the rich country. The silks of France are better and cheaper than those of England, because the silk manufacture, at least under the present high duties upon the importation of raw silk, does not so well suit the climate of England as that of France. But the hardware and the coarse woollens of England are beyond all comparison superior to those of France, and much cheaper too in the same degree of goodness. In Poland there are said to be scarce any manufactures of any kind, a few of those coarser household manufactures excepted, without which no country can well subsist.

This great increase of the quantity of work which, in consequence of the division of labour, the same number of people are capable of performing, is owing to three different circumstances; first, to the increase of dexterity in every particular workman; secondly, to the saving of the time which is commonly lost in passing from one species of work to another; and lastly, to the invention of a great number of machines which facilitate and abridge labour, and enable one man to do the work of many.

First, the improvement of the dexterity of the workman necessarily increases the quantity of the work he can perform; and the division of labour, by reducing every man's business to some one simple operation, and by making this operation the sole employment of his life, necessarily increases very much the dexterity of the workman. A common smith, who, though accustomed to handle the hammer, has never been used to make nails, if upon some particular occasion he is obliged to attempt it, will scarce, I am assured, be able to make above two or three hundred nails in a day, and those too very bad ones. A smith who has been accustomed to make nails, but whose sole or principal business has not been that of a nailer, can seldom with his utmost diligence make more than eight hundred or a thousand nails in a day. I have seen several boys under twenty years of age who had never exercised any other trade but that of making nails, and who, when they exerted themselves, could make, each of them, upwards of two thousand three hundred nails in a day. The making of a nail, however, is by no means one of the simplest operations. The same person blows the bellows, stirs or mends the fire as there is occasion, heats the iron, and forges every part of the nail: in forging the head too he is obliged to change his tools. The different operations into which the making of a pin, or of a metal button, is subdivided, are all of them much more simple, and the dexterity of the person, of whose life it has been the sole business to perform them, is usually much greater. The rapidity with which some of the operations of those manufactures are performed, exceeds what the human hand could, by those who had never seen them, be supposed capable of acquiring.

Secondly, the advantage which is gained by saving the time commonly lost in passing from one sort of work to another is much greater than we should at first view be apt to imagine it. It is impossible to pass very quickly from one kind of work to another that is carried on in a different place and with quite different tools. A country weaver, who cultivates a small farm, must lose a good deal of time in passing from his loom to the field, and from the field to his loom. When the two trades can be carried on in the same workhouse, the loss of time is no doubt much less. It is even in this case, however, very considerable. A man commonly saunters a little in turning his hand from one sort of employment to another. When he first begins the new work he is seldom very keen and hearty; his mind, as they say, does not go to it, and for some time he rather trifles than applies to good purpose. The habit of sauntering and of

indolent careless application, which is naturally, or rather necessarily acquired by every country workman who is obliged to
change his work and his tools every half hour, and to apply his
hand in twenty different ways almost every day of his life,
renders him almost always slothful and lazy, and incapable of
any vigorous application even on the most pressing occasions.
Independent, therefore, of his deficiency in point of dexterity,
this cause alone must always reduce considerably the quantity
of work which he is capable of performing.

Thirdly, and lastly, everybody must be sensible how much
labour is facilitated and abridged by the application of proper
machinery. It is unnecessary to give any example. I shall only
observe, therefore, that the invention of all those machines by
which labour is so much facilitated and abridged seems to have
been originally owing to the division of labour. Men are much
more likely to discover easier and readier methods of attaining
any object when the whole attention of their minds is directed
towards that single object than when it is dissipated among a
great variety of things. But in consequence of the division of
labour, the whole of every man's attention comes naturally to be
directed towards some one very simple object. It is naturally to
be expected, therefore, that some one or other of those who are
employed in each particular branch of labour should soon find
out easier and readier methods of performing their own particular work, wherever the nature of it admits of such improvement. A great part of the machines made use of in those manufactures in which labour is most subdivided, were originally the
inventions of common workmen, who, being each of them employed in some very simple operation, naturally turned their
thoughts towards finding out easier and readier methods of performing it. Whoever has been much accustomed to visit such
manufactures must frequently have been shown very pretty
machines, which were the inventions of such workmen in order
to facilitate and quicken their own particular part of the work.
In the first fire-engines, a boy was constantly employed to open
and shut alternately the communication between the boiler and
the cylinder, according as the piston either ascended or de-
scended. One of those boys, who loved to play with his companions, observed that, by tying a string from the handle of the

valve which opened this communication to another part of the machine, the valve would open and shut without his assistance, and leave him at liberty to divert himself with his play-fellows. One of the greatest improvements that has been made upon this machine, since it was first invented, was in this manner the discovery of a boy who wanted to save his own labour.

All the improvements in machinery, however, have by no means been the inventions of those who had occasion to use the machines. Many improvements have been made by the ingenuity of the makers of the machines, when to make them became the business of a peculiar trade; and some by that of those who are called philosophers or men of speculation, whose trade it is not to do anything, but to observe everything; and who, upon that account, are often capable of combining together the powers of the most distant and dissimilar objects. In the progress of society, philosophy or speculation becomes, like every other employment, the principal or sole trade and occupation of a particular class of citizens. Like every other employment too, it is subdivided into a great number of different branches, each of which affords occupation to a peculiar tribe or class of philosophers; and this subdivision of employment in philosophy, as well as in every other business, improves dexterity, and saves time. Each individual becomes more expert in his own peculiar branch, more work is done upon the whole, and the quantity of science is considerably increased by it.

It is the great multiplication of the productions of all the different arts, in consequence of the division of labour, which occasions, in a well-governed society, that universal opulence which extends itself to the lowest ranks of the people. Every workman has a great quantity of his own work to dispose of beyond what he himself has occasion for; and every other workman being exactly in the same situation, he is enabled to exchange a great quantity of his own goods for a great quantity, or, what comes to the same thing, for the price of a great quantity of theirs. He supplies them abundantly with what they have occasion for, and they accommodate him as amply with what he has occasion for, and a general plenty diffuses itself through all the different ranks of the society.

Observe the accommodation of the most common artificer or

day-labourer in a civilized and thriving country, and you will perceive that the number of people of whose industry a part, though but a small part, has been employed in procuring him this accommodation, exceeds all computation. The woollen coat, for example, which covers the day-labourer, as coarse and rough as it may appear, is the produce of the joint labour of a great multitude of workmen. The shepherd, the sorter of the wool, the wool-comber or carder, the dyer, the scribbler, the spinner, the weaver, the fuller, the dresser, with many others, must all join their different arts in order to complete even this homely production. How many merchants and carriers, besides, must have been employed in transporting the materials from some of those workmen to others who often live in a very distant part of the country! How many merchants and carriers, besides, must how many ship-builders, sailors, sail-makers, rope-makers, must have been employed in order to bring together the different drugs made use of by the dyer, which often come from the remotest corners of the world! What a variety of labour, too, is necessary in order to produce the tools of the meanest of those workmen! To say nothing of such complicated machines as the ship of the sailor, the mill of the fuller, or even the loom of the weaver, let us consider only what a variety of labour is requisite in order to form that very simple machine, the shears with which the shepherd clips the wool. The miner, the builder of the furnace for smelting the ore, the seller of the timber, the burner of the charcoal to be made use of in the smelting-house, the brick-maker, the brick-layer, the workmen who attend the furnace, the mill-wright, the forger, the smith, must all of them join their different arts in order to produce them. Were we to examine, in the same manner, all the different parts of his dress and household furniture, the coarse linen shirt which he wears next his skin, the shoes which cover his feet, the bed which he lies on, and all the different parts which compose it, the kitchen-grate at which he prepares his victuals, the coals which he makes use of for that purpose, dug from the bowels of the earth, and brought to him perhaps by a long sea and a long land carriage, all the other utensils of his kitchen, all the furniture of his table, the knives and forks, the earthen or pewter plates upon which he serves up and divides his victuals, the different hands employed in preparing his bread and his beer, the glass window which lets in the heat and the light, and keeps out the wind and the rain, with all the knowledge and art requisite for preparing that beautiful and happy invention, without which these northern parts of the world could scarce have afforded a very comfortable habitation, together with the tools of all the different workmen employed in producing those different conveniences; if we examine, I say, all these things, and consider what a variety of labour is employed about each of them, we shall be sensible that, without the assistance and co-operation of many thousands, the very meanest person in a civilized country could not be provided, even according to what we very falsely imagine the easy and simple manner in which he is commonly accommodated. Compared, indeed, with the more extravagant luxury of the great, his accommodation must no doubt appear extremely simple and easy; and yet it may be true, perhaps, that the accommodation of a European prince does not always so much exceed that of an industrious and frugal peasant as the accommodation of the latter exceeds that of many an African king, the absolute master of the lives and liberties of ten thousand naked savages.

CHAPTER II

OF THE PRINCIPLE WHICH GIVES OCCASION TO THE DIVISION OF LABOUR

THIS division of labour, from which so many advantages are derived, is not originally the effect of any human wisdom, which foresees and intends that general opulence to which it gives occasion. It is the necessary, though very slow and gradual consequence of a certain propensity in human nature which has in view no such extensive utility; the propensity to truck, barter, and exchange one thing for another.

Whether this propensity be one of those original principles in human nature of which no further account can be given; or whether, as seems more probable, it be the necessary consequences of the faculties of reason and speech, it belongs not to our present subject to inquire. It is common to all men, and to be found in no other race of animals, which seem to know neither this nor any other species of contracts. Two greyhounds, in running down the same hare, have sometimes the appearance of acting in some sort of concert. Each turns her towards his companion, or endeavours to intercept her when his companion turns her towards himself. This, however, is not the effect of any contract, but of the accidental concurrence of their passions in the same object at that particular time. Nobody ever saw a dog make a fair and deliberate exchange of one bone for another with another dog. Nobody ever saw one animal by its gestures and natural cries signify to another, this is mine, that yours; I am willing to give this for that. When an animal wants to obtain something either of a man or of another animal, it has no other means of persuasion but to gain the favour of those whose service it requires. A puppy fawns upon its dam, and a spaniel endeavours by a thousand attractions to engage the attention of its master who is at dinner, when it wants to be fed by him. Man sometimes uses the same arts with his brethren, and when he has no other means of engaging them to act according to his inclinations, endeavours by every servile and fawning attention to obtain their good will. He has not time, however, to do this upon every occasion. In civilized society he stands at all times in need of the co-operation and assistance of great multitudes, while his whole life is scarce sufficient to gain the friendship of a few persons. In almost every other race of animals each individual, when it is grown up to maturity, is entirely independent, and in its natural state has occasion for the assistance of no other living creature. But man has almost constant occasion for the help of his brethren, and it is in vain for him to expect it from their benevolence only. He will be more likely to prevail if he can interest their self-love in his favour, and show them that it is for their own advantage to do for him what he requires of them. Whoever offers to another a bargain of any kind, proposes to do this. Give me that which I want, and you shall have this which you want, is the meaning of every such offer; and it is in this manner that we obtain from one another the far greater part of those good offices which we stand in need of. It is not from the benevolence of the butcher, the brewer, or the baker that we expect our dinner, but from their regard to their own interest. We address ourselves, not to their humanity but to their self-love, and never talk to them of our own necessities but of their advantages. Nobody but a beggar chooses to depend chiefly upon the benevolence of his fellow-citizens. Even a beggar does not depend upon it entirely. The charity of well-disposed people, indeed, supplies him with the whole fund of his subsistence. But though this principle ultimately provides him with all the necessaries of life which he has occasion for, it neither does nor can provide him with them as he has occasion for them. The greater part of his occasional wants are supplied in the same manner as those of other people, by treaty, by barter, and by purchase. With the money which one man gives him he purchases food. The old clothes which another bestows upon him he exchanges for other old clothes which suit him better, or for lodging, or for food, or for money, with which he can buy either food, clothes, or lodging, as he has occasion.

As it is by treaty, by barter, and by purchase that we obtain from one another the greater part of those mutual good offices which we stand in need of, so it is this same trucking disposition which originally gives occasion to the division of labour. In a tribe of hunters or shepherds a particular person makes bows and arrows, for example, with more readiness and dexterity than any other. He frequently exchanges them for cattle or for venison with his companions; and he finds at last that he can in this manner get more cattle and venison than if he himself went to the field to catch them. From a regard to his own interest, therefore, the making of bows and arrows grows to be his chief business, and he becomes a sort of armourer. Another excels in making the frames and covers of their little huts or movable houses. He is accustomed to be of use in this way to his neighbours, who reward him in the same manner with cattle and with venison, till at last he finds it his interest to dedicate himself entirely to this employment, and to become a sort of house-carpenter. In the same manner a third becomes a smith or a brazier, a fourth a tanner or dresser of hides or skins, the principal part of the clothing of savages. And thus the certainty of being able to exchange all that surplus part of the produce of his own labour, which is over and above his own consumption, for such parts of the produce of other men's labour as he may have occasion for, encourages every man to apply himself to a particular occupation, and to cultivate and bring to perfection whatever talent or genius he may possess for that particular species of business.

The difference of natural talents in different men is, in reality, much less than we are aware of; and the very different genius which appears to distinguish men of different professions, when grown up to maturity, is not upon many occasions so much the cause as the effect of the division of labour. The difference between the most dissimilar characters, between a philosopher and a common street porter, for example, seems to arise not so much from nature as from habit, custom, and education. When they came into the world, and for the first six or eight years of their existence, they were perhaps very much alike, and neither their parents nor play-fellows could perceive any remarkable difference. About that age, or soon after, they come to be employed in very different occupations. The difference of talents comes then to be taken notice of, and widens by degrees, till at last the vanity of the philosopher is willing to acknowledge scarce any resemblance. But without the disposition to truck, barter, and exchange, every man must have procured to himself every necessary and conveniency of life which he wanted. All must have had the same duties to perform, and the same work to do, and there could have been no such difference of employment as could alone give occasion to any great difference of talents.

As it is this disposition which forms that difference of talents, so remarkable among men of different professions, so it is this same disposition which renders that difference useful. Many tribes of animals acknowledged to be all of the same species derive from nature a much more remarkable distinction of genius, than what, antecedent to custom and education, appears to take place among men. By nature a philosopher is not in genius and disposition half so different from a street porter, as a mastiff is from a greyhound, or a greyhound from a spaniel, or this last from a shepherd's dog. Those different tribes of animals, however, though all of the same species, are of scarce any use to one another. The strength of the mastiff is not in the least supported either by the swiftness of the greyhound, or by the sagacity of the spaniel, or by the docility of the shepherd's dog. The effects of those different geniuses and talents, for want of the power or disposition to barter and exchange, cannot be brought into a common stock, and do not in the least contribute to the better accommodation and conveniency of the species. Each animal is still obliged to support and defend itself, separately and independently, and derives no sort of advantage from that variety of talents with which nature has distinguished its fellows. Among men, on the contrary, the most dissimilar geniuses are of use to one another; the different produces of their respective talents, by the general disposition to truck, barter, and exchange, being brought, as it were, into a common stock, where every man may purchase whatever part of the produce of the other men's talents he has occasion for.

CHAPTER III

THAT THE DIVISION OF LABOUR IS LIMITED BY THE EXTENT OF THE MARKET

As it is the power of exchanging that gives occasion to the division of labour, so the extent of this division must always be limited by the extent of that power, or, in other words, by the extent of the market. When the market is very small, no person can have any encouragement to dedicate himself entirely to one employment, for want of the power to exchange all that surplus part of the produce of his own labour, which is over and above his own consumption, for such parts of the produce of other men's labour as he has occasion for.

There are some sorts of industry, even of the lowest kind, which can be carried on nowhere but in a great town. A porter, for example, can find employment and subsistence in no other place. A village is by much too narrow a sphere for him; even an ordinary market town is scarce large enough to afford him constant occupation. In the lone houses and very small villages which are scattered about in so desert a country as the Highlands of Scotland, every farmer must be butcher, baker, and brewer for his own family. In such situations we can scarce expect to find even a smith, a carpenter, or a mason, within less than twenty miles of another of the same trade. The scattered families that live at eight or ten miles distance from the nearest of them must learn to perform themselves a great number of little pieces of work, for which, in more populous countries, they would call in the assistance of those workmen. Country workmen are almost everywhere obliged to apply themselves to all the different branches of industry that have so much affinity to one another as to be employed about the same sort of materials. A country carpenter deals in every sort of work that is made of wood : a country smith in every sort of work that is made of iron. The former is not only a carpenter, but a joiner, a cabinet-maker, and even a carver in wood, as well as a wheelwright, a plough-wright, a cart and waggon maker. The employments of the latter are still more various. It is impossible there should be such a trade as even that of a nailer in the remote and inland parts of the Highlands of Scotland. Such a workman at the rate of a thousand nails a day, and three hundred working days in the year, will make three hundred thousand nails in the year. But in such a situation it would be impossible to dispose of one thousand, that is, of one day's work in the year.

As by means of water-carriage a more extensive market is opened to every sort of industry than what land-carriage alone can afford it, so it is upon the sea-coast, and along the banks of navigable rivers, that industry of every kind naturally begins to subdivide and improve itself, and it is frequently not till a long time after that those improvements extend themselves to the inland parts of the country. A broad-wheeled waggon, attended by two men, and drawn by eight horses, in about six weeks' time carries and brings back between London and Edinburgh near four ton weight of goods. In about the same time a ship navigated by six or eight men, and sailing between the ports of London and Leith, frequently carries and brings back two hundred ton weight of goods. Six or eight men, therefore, by the help of water-carriage, can carry and bring back in the same time the same quantity of goods between London and Edinburgh, as fifty broad-wheeled waggons, attended by a hundred men, and drawn by four hundred horses. Upon two hundred tons of goods, therefore, carried by the cheapest land-carriage from London to Edinburgh, there must be charged the maintenance of a hundred men for three weeks, and both the maintenance, and, what is nearly equal to the maintenance, the wear and tear of four hundred horses as well as of fifty great waggons. Whereas, upon the same quantity of goods carried by water, there is to be charged only the maintenance of six or eight men, and the wear and tear of a ship of two hundred tons burden, together with the value of the superior risk, or the difference of the insurance between land and water-carriage. Were there no other communication between those two places, therefore, but by land-carriage, as no goods could be transported from the one to the other, except such whose price was very considerable in proportion to their weight, they could carry on but a small part of that commerce which at present subsists between them, and consequently could give but a small part of that encouragement which they at present mutually afford to each other's industry. There could be little or no commerce of any kind between the distant parts of the world. What goods could bear the expense of land-carriage between London and Calcutta? Or if there were any so precious as to be able to support this expense, with what safety could they be transported through the territories of so many barbarous nations? Those two cities, however, at present carry on a very considerable commerce with each other, and by mutually affording a market, give a good deal of encouragement to each other's industry.

Since such, therefore, are the advantages of water-carriage, it is natural that the first improvements of art and industry should be made where this conveniency opens the whole world for a market to the produce of every sort of labour, and that they should always be much later in extending themselves into the inland parts of the country. The inland parts of the country can for a long time have no other market for the greater part of their goods, but the country which lies round about them, and separates them from the sea-coast, and the great navigable rivers. The extent of their market, therefore, must for a long time be in proportion to the riches and populousness of that country, and consequently their improvement must always be posterior to the improvement of that country. In our North American colonies the plantations have constantly followed either the sea-coast or the banks of the navigable rivers, and have scarce anywhere extended themselves to any considerable distance from both.

The nations that, according to the best authenticated history, appear to have been first civilized, were those that dwelt round the coast of the Mediterranean Sea. That sea, by far the greatest inlet that is known in the world, having no tides, nor consequently any waves except such as are caused by the wind only, was, by the smoothness of its surface, as well as by the multitude of its islands, and the proximity of its neighbouring shores, extremely favourable to the infant navigation of the world; when, from their ignorance of the compass, men were afraid to quit the view of the coast, and from the imperfection of the art of shipbuilding, to abandon themselves to the boisterous waves of the ocean. To pass beyond the pillars of Hercules, that is, to sail out of the Straits of Gibraltar, was, in the ancient world, long considered as a most wonderful and dangerous exploit of navigation. It was late before even the Phoenicians and Carthaginians, the most skilful navigators and ship-builders of those old times, attempted it, and they were for a long time the only nations that did attempt it.

Of all the countries on the coast of the Mediterranean Sea, Egypt seems to have been the first in which either agriculture or manufactures were cultivated and improved to any considerable degree. Upper Egypt extends itself nowhere above a few miles from the Nile, and in Lower Egypt that great river breaks itself into many different canals, which, with the assistance of a little art, seem to have afforded a communication by water-carriage, not only between all the great towns, but between all the considerable villages, and even to many farm-houses in the country; nearly in the same manner as the Rhine and the Maese do in Holland at present. The extent and easiness of this inland navigation was probably one of the principal causes of the early improvement in Egypt.

The improvements in agriculture and manufactures seem likewise to have been of very great antiquity in the provinces of Bengal, in the East Indies, and in some of the eastern provinces of China; though the great extent of this antiquity is not authenticated by any histories of whose authority we, in this part of the world, are well assured. In Bengal the Ganges and several other great rivers form a great number of navigable canals in the same manner as the Nile does in Egypt. In the Eastern provinces of China, too, several great rivers form, by their different branches, a multitude of canals, and by communicating with one another afford an inland navigation much more extensive than that either of the Nile or the Ganges, or perhaps than both of them put together. It is remarkable that neither the ancient Egyptians, nor the Indians, nor the Chinese, encouraged foreign commerce, but seem all to have derived their great opulence from this inland navigation.

All the inland parts of Africa, and all that part of Asia which lies any considerable way north of the Euxine and Caspian seas, the ancient Scythia, the modern Tartary and Siberia, seem in all ages of the world to have been in the same barbarous and uncivilized state in which we find them at present. The Sea of Tartary is the frozen ocean which admits of no navigation, and though some of the greatest rivers in the world run through that country, they are at too great a distance from one another to carry commerce and communication through the greater part of it. There are in Africa none of those great inlets, such as the Baltic and Adriatic seas in Europe, the Mediterranean and Euxine seas in both Europe and Asia, and the gulfs of Arabia, Persia, India, Bengal, and Siam, in Asia, to carry maritime commerce into the interior parts of that great continent: and the great rivers of Africa are at too great a distance from one another to give occasion to any considerable inland navigation. The commerce besides which any nation can carry on by means of a river which does not break itself into any great number of branches or canals, and which runs into another territory before it reaches the sea, can never be very considerable; because it is always in the power of the nations who possess that other territory to obstruct the communication between the upper country and the sea. The navigation of the Danube is of very little use to the different states of Bavaria, Austria, and Hungary, in comparison of what it would be if any of them possessed the whole of its course till it falls into the Black Sea.

CHAPTER IV

OF THE ORIGIN AND USE OF MONEY

WHEN the division of labour has been once thoroughly established, it is but a very small part of a man's wants which the produce of his own labour can supply. He supplies the far greater part of them by exchanging that surplus part of the produce of his own labour, which is over and above his own consumption, for such parts of the produce of other men's labour as he has occasion for. Every man thus lives by exchanging, or becomes in some measure a merchant, and the society itself grows to be what is properly a commercial society.

But when the division of labour first began to take place, this power of exchanging must frequently have been very much clogged and embarrassed in its operations. One man, we shall suppose, has more of a certain commodity than he himself has occasion for, while another has less. The former consequently would be glad to dispose of, and the latter to purchase, a part of this superfluity. But if this latter should chance to have nothing that the former stands in need of, no exchange can be made between them. The butcher has more meat in his shop than he himself can consume, and the brewer and the baker would each of them be willing to purchase a part of it. But they have nothing to offer in exchange, except the different productions of their respective trades, and the butcher is already provided with all the bread and beer which he has immediate occasion for. No exchange can, in this case, be made between them. He cannot be their merchant, nor they his customers; and they are all of them thus mutually less serviceable to one another. In order to avoid the inconveniency of such situations, every prudent man in every period of society, after the first establishment of the division of labour, must naturally have endeavoured to manage

his affairs in such a manner as to have at all times by him,
besides the peculiar produce of his own industry, a certain
quantity of some one commodity or other, such as he imagined
few people would be likely to refuse in exchange for the produce of their industry.

Many different commodities, it is probable, were successively
both thought of and employed for this purpose. In the rude ages
of society, cattle are said to have been the common instrument
of commerce; and, though they must have been a most inconvenient one, yet in old times we find things were frequently
valued according to the number of cattle which had been given
in exchange for them. The armour of Diomede, says Homer,
cost only nine oxen; but that of Glaucus cost an hundred oxen.
Salt is said to be the common instrument of commerce and
exchanges in Abyssinia; a species of shells in some parts of the
coast of India; dried cod at Newfoundland; tobacco in Virginia;
sugar in some of our West India colonies; hides or dressed
leather in some other countries; and there is at this day a village
in Scotland where it is not uncommon, I am told, for a workman
to carry nails instead of money to the baker's shop or the alehouse.

In all countries, however, men seem at last to have been
determined by irresistible reasons to give the preference, for this
employment, to metals above every other commodity. Metals
can not only be kept with as little loss as any other commodity,
scarce anything being less perishable than they are, but they can
likewise, without any loss, be divided into any number of parts,
as by fusion those parts can easily be reunited again; a quality
which no other equally durable commodities possess, and which
more than any other quality renders them fit to be the instruments of commerce and circulation. The man who wanted to
buy salt, for example, and had nothing but cattle to give in
exchange for it, must have been obliged to buy salt to the value
of a whole ox, or a whole sheep at a time. He could seldom buy
less than this, because what he was to give for it could seldom
be divided without loss; and if he had a mind to buy more, he
must, for the same reasons, have been obliged to buy double or
triple the quantity, the value, to wit, of two or three oxen, or of
two or three sheep. If, on the contrary, instead of sheep or oxen,

he had metals to give in exchange for it, he could easily proportion the quantity of the metal to the precise quantity of the commodity which he had immediate occasion for.

Different metals have been made use of by different nations for this purpose. Iron was the common instrument of commerce among the ancient Spartans; copper among the ancient Romans; and gold and silver among all rich and commercial nations.

Those metals seem originally to have been made use of for this purpose in rude bars, without any stamp or coinage. Thus we are told by Pliny,[1] upon the authority of Timaeus, an ancient historian, that till the time of Servius Tullius, the Romans had no coined money, but made use of unstamped bars of copper, to purchase whatever they had occasion for. These rude bars, therefore, performed at this time the function of money.

The use of metals in this rude state was attended with two very considerable inconveniences; first, with the trouble of weighing; and, secondly, with that of assaying them. In the precious metals, where a small difference in the quantity makes a great difference in the value, even the business of weighing, with proper exactness, requires at least very accurate weights and scales. The weighing of gold in particular is an operation of some nicety. In the coarser metals, indeed, where a small error would be of little consequence, less accuracy would, no doubt, be necessary. Yet we should find it excessively troublesome, if every time a poor man had occasion either to buy or sell a farthing's worth of goods, he was obliged to weigh the farthing. The operation of assaying is still more difficult, still more tedious, and, unless a part of the metal is fairly melted in the crucible, with proper dissolvents, any conclusion that can be drawn from it, is extremely uncertain. Before the institution of coined money, however, unless they went through this tedious and difficult operation, people must always have been liable to the grossest frauds and impositions, and instead of a pound weight of pure silver, or pure copper, might receive in exchange for their goods an adulterated composition of the coarsest and cheapest materials, which had, however, in their outward

1. Plir. Hist. Nat. lib. 33, cap. 3.

appearance, been made to resemble those metals. To prevent such abuses, to facilitate exchanges, and thereby to encourage all sorts of industry and commerce, it has been found necessary, in all countries that have made any considerable advances towards improvement, to affix a public stamp upon certain quantities of such particular metals as were in those countries commonly made use of to purchase goods. Hence the origin of coined money, and those public offices called mints; institutions exactly of the same nature with those of the aulnagers and stamp-masters of woollen and linen cloth. All of them are equally meant to ascertain, by means of a public stamp, the quantity and uniform goodness of those different commodities when brought to market.

The first public stamps of this kind that were affixed to the current metals, seem in many cases to have been intended to ascertain, what it was both most difficult and most important to ascertain, the goodness or fineness of the metal, and to have resembled the sterling mark which is at present affixed to plate and bars of silver, or the Spanish mark which is sometimes affixed to ingots of gold, and which being struck only upon one side of the piece, and not covering the whole surface, ascertains the fineness, but not the weight of the metal. Abraham weighs to Ephron the four hundred shekels of silver which he had agreed to pay for the field of Machpelah. They are said, how-ever, to be the current money of the merchant, and yet are received by weight and not by tale, in the same manner as ingots of gold and bars of silver are at present. The revenues of the ancient Saxon kings of England are said to have been paid, not in money but in kind, that is, in victuals and provisions of all sorts. William the Conqueror introduced the custom of pay-ing them in money. This money, however, was, for a long time, received at the exchequer, by weight and not by tale.

The inconveniency and difficulty of weighing those metals with exactness gave occasion to the institution of coins, of which the stamp, covering entirely both sides of the piece and some-times the edges too, was supposed to ascertain not only the fineness, but the weight of the metal. Such coins, therefore, were received by tale as at present, without the trouble of weighing.

The denominations of those coins seem originally to have

expressed the weight or quantity of metal contained in them. In the time of Servius Tullius, who first coined money at Rome, the Roman As or Pondo contained a Roman pound of good copper. It was divided in the same manner as our Troyes pound, into twelve ounces, each of which contained a real ounce of good copper. The English pound sterling, in the time of Edward I, contained a pound, Tower weight, of silver, of a known fineness. The Tower pound seems to have been something more than the Roman pound, and something less than the Troyes pound. This last was not introduced into the mint of England till the 18th of Henry VIII. The French livre contained in the time of Charlemagne a pound, Troyes weight, of silver of a known fineness. The fair of Troyes in Champaign was at that time frequented by all the nations of Europe, and the weights and measures of so famous a market were generally known and esteemed. The Scots money pound contained, from the time of Alexander the First to that of Robert Bruce, a pound of silver of the same weight and fineness with the English pound sterling. English, French, and Scots pennies, too, contained all of them originally a real pennyweight of silver, the twentieth part of an ounce and the two-hundred-and-fortieth part of a pound. The shilling too seems originally to have been the denomination of a weight. *When wheat is at twelve shillings the quarter,* says an ancient statute of Henry III, *then wastel bread of a farthing shall weigh eleven shillings and four pence.* The proportion, however, between the shilling and either the penny on the one hand, or the pound on the other, seems not to have been so constant and uniform as that between the penny and the pound. During the first race of the kings of France, the French sou or shilling appears upon different occasions to have contained five, twelve, twenty, and forty pennies. Among the ancient Saxons a shilling appears at one time to have contained only five pennies, and it is not improbable that it may have been as variable among them as among their neighbours, the ancient Franks. From the time of Charlemagne among the French, and from that of William the Conqueror among the English, the proportion between the pound, the shilling, and the penny, seems to have been uniformly the same as at present, though the value of each has been very different. For in every country of the world,

I believe, the avarice and injustice of princes and sovereign states, abusing the confidence of their subjects, have by degrees diminished the real quantity of metal, which had been originally contained in their coins. The Roman As, in the latter ages of the Republic, was reduced to the twenty-fourth part of its original value, and, instead of weighing a pound, came to weigh only half an ounce. The English pound and penny contain at present about a third only; the Scots pound and penny about a thirty-sixth; and the French pound and penny about a sixty-sixth part of their original value. By means of those operations the princes and sovereign states which performed them were enabled, in appearance, to pay their debts and to fulfil their engagements with a smaller quantity of silver than would otherwise have been requisite. It was indeed in appearance only; for their creditors were really defrauded of a part of what was due to them. All other debtors in the state were allowed the same privilege, and might pay with the same nominal sum of the new and debased coin whatever they had borrowed in the old. Such operations, therefore, have always proved favourable to the debtor, and ruinous to the creditor, and have sometimes produced a greater and more universal revolution in the fortunes of private persons, than could have been occasioned by a very great public calamity.

It is in this manner that money has become in all civilized nations the universal instrument of commerce, by the intervention of which goods of all kinds are bought and sold, or exchanged for one another.

What are the rules which men naturally observe in exchanging them either for money or for one another, I shall now proceed to examine. These rules determine what may be called the relative or exchangeable value of goods.

The word VALUE, it is to be observel, has two different meanings, and sometimes expresses the utility of some particular object, and sometimes the power of purchasing other goods which the possession of that object conveys. The one may be called 'value in use'; the other, 'value in exchange'. The things which have the greatest value in use have frequently little or no value in exchange; and, on the contrary, those which have the greatest value in exchange have frequently little or no value in use. Nothing is more useful than water: but it will purchase scarce anything; scarce anything can be had in exchange for it. A diamond, on the contrary, has scarce any value in use; but a very great quantity of other goods may frequently be had in exchange for it.

In order to investigate the principles which regulate the exchangeable value of commodities, I shall endeavour to show,

First, what is the real measure of this exchangeable value; or, wherein consists the real price of all commodities.

Secondly, what are the different parts of which this real price is composed or made up.

And, lastly, what are the different circumstances which sometimes raise some or all of these different parts of price above, and sometimes sink them below their natural or ordinary rate; or, what are the causes which sometimes hinder the market price, that is, the actual price of commodities, from coinciding exactly with what may be called their natural price.

I shall endeavour to explain, as fully and distinctly as I can, those three subjects in the three following chapters, for which I must very earnestly entreat both the patience and attention of the reader: his patience in order to examine a detail which may perhaps in some places appear unnecessarily tedious; and his attention in order to understand what may, perhaps, after the fullest explication which I am capable of giving of it, appear still in some degree obscure. I am always willing to run some hazard of being tedious in order to be sure that I am perspicuous; and after taking the utmost pains that I can to be perspicuous, some obscurity may still appear to remain upon a subject in its own nature extremely abstracted.

CHAPTER V

OF THE REAL AND NOMINAL PRICE OF COMMODITIES, OR THEIR PRICE IN LABOUR, AND THEIR PRICE IN MONEY

EVERY man is rich or poor according to the degree in which he can afford to enjoy the necessaries, conveniences, and amusements of human life. But after the division of labour has once thoroughly taken place, it is but a very small part of these with which a man's own labour can supply him. The far greater part of them he must derive from the labour of other people, and he must be rich or poor according to the quantity of that labour which he can command, or which he can afford to purchase. The value of any commodity, therefore, to the person who possesses it, and who means not to use or consume it himself, but to exchange it for other commodities, is equal to the quantity of labour which it enables him to purchase or command. Labour, therefore, is the real measure of the exchangeable value of all commodities.

The real price of everything, what everything really costs to the man who wants to acquire it, is the toil and trouble of acquiring it. What everything is really worth to the man who has acquired it, and who wants to dispose of it or exchange it for something else, is the toil and trouble which it can save to himself, and which it can impose upon other people. What is bought with money or with goods is purchased by labour as much as what we acquire by the toil of our own body. That money or those goods indeed save us this toil. They contain the value of a certain quantity of labour which we exchange for what is supposed at the time to contain the value of an equal quantity. Labour was the first price, the original purchase-money that was paid for all things. It was not by gold or by silver, but by labour, that all the wealth of the world was originally purchased; and its value, to those who possess it, and who want to exchange it for some new productions, is precisely equal to the quantity of labour which it can enable them to purchase or command.

Wealth, as Mr Hobbes says, is power. But the person who either acquires, or succeeds to a great fortune, does not necessarily acquire or succeed to any political power, either civil or military. His fortune may, perhaps, afford him the means of acquiring both, but the mere possession of that fortune does not necessarily convey to him either. The power which that possession immediately and directly conveys to him, is the power of purchasing; a certain command over all the labour, or over all the produce of labour, which is then in the market. His fortune is greater or less, precisely in proportion to the extent of this power; or to the quantity either of other men's labour, or, what is the same thing, of the produce of other men's labour, which it enables him to purchase or command. The exchangeable value of everything must always be precisely equal to the extent of this power which it conveys to its owner.

But though labour be the real measure of the exchangeable value of all commodities, it is not that by which their value is commonly estimated. It is often difficult to ascertain the proportion between two different quantities of labour. The time spent in two different sorts of work will not always alone determine this proportion. The different degrees of hardship endured, and of ingenuity exercised, must likewise be taken into account. There may be more labour in an hour's hard work than in two hours' easy business; or in an hour's application to a trade which it cost ten years' labour to learn, than in a month's industry at an ordinary and obvious employment. But it is not easy to find any accurate measure either of hardship or ingenuity. In exchanging, indeed, the different productions of different sorts of labour for one another, some allowance is commonly made for both. It is adjusted, however, not by any accurate measure, but by the higgling and bargaining of the market, according to that sort of rough equality which, though not exact, is sufficient for carrying on the business of common life.

Every commodity, besides, is more frequently exchanged for, and thereby compared with, other commodities than with labour. It is more natural, therefore, to estimate its exchangeable value by the quantity of some other commodity than by that of the labour which it can purchase. The greater part of people, too, understand better what is meant by a quantity of a particular commodity than by a quantity of labour. The one is a plain and palpable object; the other an abstract notion, which, though it can be made sufficiently intelligible, is not altogether so natural and obvious.

But when barter ceases, and money has become the common instrument of commerce, every particular commodity is more frequently exchanged for money than for any other commodity. The butcher seldom carries his beef or his mutton to the baker, or the brewer, in order to exchange them for bread or for beer; but he carries them to the market, where he exchanges them for money, and afterwards exchanges that money for bread and for beer. The quantity of money which he gets for them regulates, too, the quantity of bread and beer which he can afterwards purchase. It is more natural and obvious to him, therefore, to estimate their value by the quantity of money, the commodity for which he immediately exchanges them, than by that of bread and beer, the commodities for which he can exchange them only by the intervention of another commodity; and rather to say that his butcher's meat is worth threepence or fourpence a pound, than that it is worth three or four pounds of bread, or three or four quarts of small beer. Hence it comes to pass that the exchangeable value of every commodity is more frequently estimated by the quantity of money, than by the quantity either of labour or of any other commodity which can be had in exchange for it.

Gold and silver, however, like every other commodity, vary in their value, are sometimes cheaper and sometimes dearer, sometimes of easier and sometimes of more difficult purchase. The quantity of labour which any particular quantity of them can purchase or command, or the quantity of other goods which it will exchange for, depends always upon the fertility or barrenness of the mines which happen to be known about the time when such exchanges are made. The discovery of the abundant mines of America reduced, in the sixteenth century, the value of gold and silver in Europe to about a third of what it had been before. As it cost less labour to bring those metals from the mine to the market, so when they were brought thither they could purchase or command less labour; and this revolution in their value, though perhaps the greatest, is by no means the only one of which history gives some account. But as a measure of quantity, such as the natural foot, fathom, or handful, which is continually varying in its own quantity, can never be an accurate measure of the quantity of other things; so a commodity which is itself continually varying in its own value, can never be an accurate measure of the value of other commodities. Equal quantities of labour, at all times and places, may be said to be of equal value to the labourer. In his ordinary state of health, strength, and spirits; in the ordinary degree of his skill and dexterity, he must always lay down the same portion of his ease, his liberty, and his happiness. The price which he pays must always be the same, whatever may be the quantity of goods which he receives in return for it. Of these, indeed, it may sometimes purchase a greater and sometimes a smaller quantity; but it is their value which varies, not that of the labour which purchases them. At all times and places that is dear which it is difficult to come at, or which it costs much labour to acquire; and that cheap which is to be had easily, or with very little labour. Labour alone, therefore, never varying in its own value, is alone the ultimate and real standard by which the value of all commodities can at all times and places be estimated and compared. It is their real price; money is their nominal price only.

But though equal quantities of labour are always of equal value to the labourer, yet to the person who employs him they appear sometimes to be of greater and sometimes of smaller value. He purchases them sometimes with a greater and sometimes with a smaller quantity of goods, and to him the price of labour seems to vary like that of all other things. It appears to him dear in the one case, and cheap in the other. In reality, however, it is the goods which are cheap in the one case, and dear in the other.

In this popular sense, therefore, labour, like commodities, may be said to have a real and a nominal price. Its real price may be said to consist in the quantity of the necessaries and conveniences of life which are given for it; its nominal price, in the quantity of money. The labourer is rich or poor, is well or ill rewarded, in proportion to the real, not to the nominal price of his labour.

The distinction between the real and the nominal price of

commodities and labour is not a matter of mere speculation, but may sometimes be of considerable use in practice. The same real price is always of the same value; but on account of the variations in the value of gold and silver, the same nominal price is sometimes of very different values. When a landed estate, therefore, is sold with a reservation of a perpetual rent, if it is intended that this rent should always be of the same value, it is of importance to the family in whose favour it is reserved that it should not consist in a particular sum of money. Its value would in this case be liable to variations of two different kinds; first, to those which arise from the different quantities of gold and silver which are contained at different times in coin of the same denomination; and, secondly, to those which arise from the different values of equal quantities of gold and silver at different times.

Princes and sovereign states have frequently fancied that they had a temporary interest to diminish the quantity of pure metal contained in their coins; but they seldom have fancied that they had any to augment it. The quantity of metal contained in the coins, I believe of all nations, has, accordingly, been almost continually diminishing, and hardly ever augmenting. Such variations, therefore, tend almost always to diminish the value of a money rent.

The discovery of the mines of America diminished the value of gold and silver in Europe. This diminution, it is commonly supposed, though I apprehend without any certain proof, is still going on gradually, and is likely to continue to do so for a long time. Upon this supposition, therefore, such variations are more likely to diminish than to augment the value of a money rent, even though it should be stipulated to be paid, not in such a quantity of coined money of such a denomination (in so many pounds sterling, for example), but in so many ounces either of pure silver, or of silver of a certain standard.

The rents which have been reserved in corn have preserved their value much better than those which have been reserved in money, even where the denomination of the coin has not been altered. By the 18th of Elizabeth it was enacted, That a third of the rent of all college leases should be reserved in corn, to be paid, either in kind, or according to the current prices at the nearest public market. The money arising from this corn rent, though originally but a third of the whole, is in the present times, according to Doctor Blackstone, commonly near double of what arises from the other two-thirds. The old money rents of colleges must, according to this account, have sunk almost to a fourth part of their ancient value; or are worth little more than a fourth part of the corn which they were formerly worth. But since the reign of Philip and Mary the denomination of the English coin has undergone little or no alteration, and the same number of pounds, shillings, and pence have contained very nearly the same quantity of pure silver. This degradation, therefore, in the value of the money rents of colleges, has arisen altogether from the degradation in the value of silver.

When the degradation in the value of silver is combined with the diminution of the quantity of it contained in the coin of the same denomination, the loss is frequently still greater. In Scotland, where the denomination of the coin has undergone much greater alterations than it ever did in England, and in France, where it has undergone still greater than it ever did in Scotland, some ancient rents, originally of considerable value, have in this manner been reduced almost to nothing.

Equal quantities of labour will at distant times be purchased more nearly with equal quantities of corn, the subsistence of the labourer, than with equal quantities of gold and silver, or perhaps of any other commodity. Equal quantities of corn, therefore, will, at distant times, be more nearly of the same real value, or enable the possessor to purchase or command more nearly the same quantity of the labour of other people. They will do this, I say, more nearly than equal quantities of almost any other commodity; for even equal quantities of corn will not do it exactly. The subsistence of the labourer, or the real price of labour, as I shall endeavour to show hereafter, is very different upon different occasions; more liberal in a society advancing to opulence than in one that is standing still; and in one that is standing still than in one that is going backwards. Every other commodity, however, will at any particular time purchase a greater or smaller quantity of labour in proportion to the quantity of subsistence which it can purchase at that time. A rent therefore reserved in corn is liable only to the variations in the

THE PRICE OF COMMODITIES

quantity of labour which a certain quantity of corn can purchase. But a rent reserved in any other commodity is liable not only to the variations in the quantity of labour which any particular quantity of corn can purchase, but to the variations in the quantity of corn which can be purchased by any particular quantity of that commodity.

Though the real value of a corn rent, it is to be observed, however, varies much less from century to century than that of a money rent, it varies much more from year to year. The money price of labour, as I shall endeavour to show hereafter, does not fluctuate from year to year with the money price of corn, but seems to be everywhere accommodated, not to the temporary or occasional, but to the average or ordinary price of that necessary of life. The average or ordinary price of corn again is regulated, as I shall likewise endeavour to show hereafter, by the value of silver, by the richness or barrenness of the mines which supply the market with that metal, or by the quantity of labour which must be employed, and consequently of corn which must be consumed, in order to bring any particular quantity of silver from the mine to the market. But the value of silver, though it sometimes varies greatly from century to century, seldom varies much from year to year, but frequently continues the same, or very nearly the same, for half a century or a century together. The ordinary or average money price of corn, therefore, may, during so long a period, continue the same or very nearly the same too, and along with it the money price of labour, provided, at least, the society continues, in other respects, in the same or nearly in the same condition. In the meantime the temporary and occasional price of corn may frequently be double, one year, of what it had been the year before, or fluctuate, for example, from five and twenty to fifty shillings the quarter. But when corn is at the latter price, not only the nominal, but the real value of a corn rent will be double of what it is when at the former, or will command double the quantity either of labour or of the greater part of other commodities; the money price of labour, and along with it that of most other things, continuing the same during all these fluctuations.

Labour, therefore, it appears evidently, is the only universal, as well as the only accurate measure of value, or the only standard by which we can compare the values of different commodities at all times, and at all places. We cannot estimate, it is allowed, the real value of different commodities from century to century by the quantities of silver which were given for them. We cannot estimate it from year to year by the quantities of corn. By the quantities of labour we can, with the greatest accuracy, estimate it both from century to century and from year to year. From century to century, corn is a better measure than silver, because, from century to century, equal quantities of corn will command the same quantity of labour more nearly than equal quantities of silver. From year to year, on the contrary, silver is a better measure than corn, because equal quantities of it will more nearly command the same quantity of labour.

But though in establishing perpetual rents, or even in letting very long leases, it may be of use to distinguish between real and nominal price; it is of none in buying and selling, the more common and ordinary transactions of human life.

At the same time and place the real and the nominal price of all commodities are exactly in proportion to one another. The more or less money you get for any commodity, in the London market for example, the more or less labour it will at that time and place enable you to purchase or command. At the same time and place, therefore, money is the exact measure of the real exchangeable value of all commodities. It is so, however, at the same time and place only.

Though at distant places, there is no regular proportion between the real and the money price of commodities, yet the merchant who carries goods from the one to the other has nothing to consider but their money price, or the difference between the quantity of silver for which he buys them, and that for which he is likely to sell them. Half an ounce of silver at Canton in China may command a greater quantity both of labour and of the necessaries and conveniences of life than an ounce at London. A commodity, therefore, which sells for half an ounce of silver at Canton may there be really dearer, of more real importance to the man who possesses it there, than a commodity which sells for an ounce at London is to the man who possesses it at London. If a London merchant, however, can buy at Canton for half an ounce of silver, a commodity which he can afterwards sell at London for an ounce, he gains a hundred per cent by the bargain, just as much as if an ounce of silver was at London exactly of the same value as at Canton. It is of no importance to him that half an ounce of silver at Canton would have given him the command of more labour and of a greater quantity of the necessaries and conveniences of life than an ounce can do at London. An ounce at London will always give him the command of double the quantity of all these which half an ounce would have done there, and this is precisely what he wants.

As it is the nominal or money price of goods, therefore, which finally determines the prudence or imprudence of all purchases and sales, and thereby regulates almost the whole business of common life in which price is concerned, we cannot wonder that it should have been so much more attended to than the real price.

In such a work as this, however, it may sometimes be of use to compare the different real values of a particular commodity at different times and places, or the different degrees of power over the labour of other people which it may, upon different occasions, have given to those who possessed it. We must in this case compare, not so much the different quantities of silver for which it was commonly sold, as the different quantities of labour which those different quantities of silver could have purchased. But the current prices of labour at distant times and places can scarce ever be known with any degree of exactness. Those of corn, though they have in few places been regularly recorded, are in general better known and have been more frequently taken notice of by historians and other writers. We must generally, therefore, content ourselves with them, not as being always exactly in the same proportion as the current prices of labour, but as being the nearest approximation which can commonly be had to that proportion. I shall hereafter have occasion to make several comparisons of this kind.

In the progress of industry, commercial nations have found it convenient to coin several different metals into money; gold for larger payments, silver for purchases of moderate value, and copper, or some other coarse metal, for those of still smaller consideration. They have always, however, considered one of those metals as more peculiarly the measure of value than any of the other two; and this preference seems generally to have been given to the metal which they happened first to make use of as the instrument of commerce. Having once begun to use it as their standard, which they must have done when they had no other money, they have generally continued to do so even when the necessity was not the same.

The Romans are said to have had nothing but copper money till within five years before the first Punic war,[1] when they first began to coin silver. Copper, therefore, appears to have continued always the measure of value in that republic. At Rome all accounts appear to have been kept, and the value of all estates to have been computed either in *Asses* or in *Sestertii*. The *As* was always the denomination of a copper coin. The word *Sestertius* signifies two *Asses* and a half. Though the *Sestertius,* therefore, was originally a silver coin, its value was estimated in copper. At Rome, one who owed a great deal of money was said to have a great deal of other people's copper.

The northern nations who established themselves upon the ruins of the Roman empire, seem to have had silver money from the first beginning of their settlements, and not to have known either gold or copper coins for several ages thereafter. There were silver coins in England in the time of the Saxons; but there was little gold coined till the time of Edward III nor any copper till that of James I of Great Britain. In England, therefore, and for the same reason, I believe, in all other modern nations of Europe, all accounts are kept, and the value of all goods and of all estates is generally computed in silver : and when we mean to express the amount of a person's fortune, we seldom mention the number of guineas, but the number of pounds sterling which we suppose would be given for it.

Originally, in all countries, I believe, a legal tender of payment could be made only in the coin of that metal, which was peculiarly considered as the standard or measure of value. In England, gold was not considered as a legal tender for a long time after it was coined into money. The proportion between

1. Pliny, lib. xxxiii. c. 3.

the values of gold and silver money was not fixed by any public
law or proclamation; but was left to be settled by the market. If
a debtor offered payment in gold, the creditor might either re-
ject such payment altogether, or accept of it at such a valuation
of the gold as he and his debtor could agree upon. Copper is not
at present a legal tender except in the change of the smaller
silver coins. In this state of things the distinction between the
metal which was the standard, and that which was not the
standard, was something more than a nominal distinction.

In process of time, and as people became gradually more
familiar with the use of the different metals in coin, and consequently better acquainted with the proportion between their
respective values, it has in most countries, I believe, been found
convenient to ascertain this proportion, and to declare by a
public law that a guinea, for example, of such a weight and
fineness, should exchange for one-and-twenty shillings, or be a
legal tender for a debt of that amount. In this state of things,
and during the continuance of any one regulated proportion of
this kind, the distinction between the metal which is the standard, and that which is not the standard, becomes little more
than a nominal distinction.

In consequence of any change, however, in this regulated
proportion, this distinction becomes, or at least seems to become, something more than nominal again. If the regulated
value of a guinea, for example, was either reduced to twenty, or
raised to two-and-twenty shillings, all accounts being kept and
almost all obligations for debt being expressed in silver money,
the greater part of payments could in either case be made with
the same quantity of silver money as before; but would require
very different quantities of gold money; a greater in the one
case, and a smaller in the other. Silver would appear to be more
invariable in its value than gold. Silver would appear to
measure the value of gold, and gold would not appear to
measure the value of silver. The value of gold would seem to
depend upon the quantity of silver which it would exchange
for; and the value of silver would not seem to depend upon the
quantity of gold which it would exchange for. This difference,
however, would be altogether owing to the custom of keeping
accounts, and of expressing the amount of all great and small

sums rather in silver than in gold money. One of Mr Drummond's notes for five-and-twenty or fifty guineas would, after an alteration of this kind, be still payable with five-and-twenty or fifty guineas in the same manner as before. It would, after such an alteration, be payable with the same quantity of gold as before, but with very different quantities of silver. In the payment of such a note, gold would appear to be more invariable in its value than silver. Gold would appear to measure the value of silver, and silver would not appear to measure the value of gold. If the custom of keeping accounts, and of expressing promissory notes and other obligations for money in this manner, should ever become general, gold, and not silver, would be considered as the metal which was peculiarly the standard or measure of value.

In reality, during the continuance of any one regulated proportion between the respective values of the different metals in coin, the value of the most precious metal regulates the value of the whole coin. Twelve copper pence contain half a pound, avoirdupois, of copper, of not the best quality, which, before it is coined, is seldom worth sevenpence in silver. But as by the regulation twelve such pence are ordered in exchange for a shilling, they are in the market considered as worth a shilling, and a shilling can at any time be had for them. Even before the late reformation of the gold coin of Great Britain, the gold, that part of it at least which circulated in London and its neighbourhood, was in general less degraded below its standard weight than the greater part of the silver. One-and-twenty worn and defaced shillings, however, were considered as equivalent to a guinea, which perhaps, indeed, was worn and defaced too, but seldom so much so. The late regulations have brought the gold coin as near perhaps to its standard weight as it is possible to bring the current coin of any nation; and the order, to receive no gold at the public offices but by weight, is likely to preserve it so, as long as that order is enforced. The silver coin still continues in the same worn and degraded state as before the reformation of the gold coin. In the market, however, one-and-twenty shillings of this degraded silver coin are still considered as worth a guinea of this excellent gold coin.

The reformation of the gold coin has evidently raised the value of the silver coin which can be exchanged for it.

In the English mint a pound weight of gold is coined into forty-four guineas and a half, which, at one-and-twenty shillings the guinea, is equal to forty-six pounds fourteen shillings and sixpence. An ounce of such gold coin, therefore, is worth £3 17s. 10½d. in silver. In England no duty or seignorage is paid upon the coinage, and he who carries a pound weight or an ounce weight of standard gold bullion to the mint, gets back a pound weight or an ounce weight of gold in coin, without any deduction. Three pounds seventeen shillings and tenpence half-penny an ounce, therefore, is said to be the mint price of gold in England, or the quantity of gold coin which the mint gives in return for standard gold bullion.

Before the reformation of the gold coin, the price of standard gold bullion in the market had for many years been upwards of £3 18s. sometimes £3 19s. and very frequently £4 an ounce; that sum, it is probable, in the worn and degraded gold coin, seldom containing more than an ounce of standard gold. Since the reformation of the gold coin, the market price of standard gold bullion seldom exceeds £3 17s. 7d. an ounce. Before the reformation of the gold coin, the market price was always more or less above the mint price. Since that reformation, the market price has been constantly below the mint price. But that market price is the same whether it is paid in gold or in silver coin. The late reformation of the gold coin, therefore, has raised not only the value of the gold coin, but likewise that of the silver coin in proportion to gold bullion, and probably, too, in proportion to all other commodities; though the price of the greater part of other commodities being influenced by so many other causes, the rise in the value either of gold or silver coin in proportion to them may not be so distinct and sensible.

In the English mint a pound weight of standard silver bullion is coined into sixty-two shillings, containing, in the same man-ner, a pound weight of standard silver. Five shillings and two-pence an ounce, therefore, is said to be the mint price of silver in England, or the quantity of silver coin which the mint gives in return for standard silver bullion. Before the reformation of the gold coin, the market price of standard silver bullion was, upon different occasions, five shillings and fourpence, five shil-lings and fivepence, five shillings and sixpence, five shillings and sevenpence, and very often five shillings and eightpence an ounce. Five shillings and sevenpence, however, seems to have been the most common price. Since the reformation of the gold coin, the market price of standard silver bullion has fallen occasionally to five shillings and threepence, five shillings and fourpence, and five shillings and fivepence an ounce, which last price it has scarce ever exceeded. Though the market price of silver bullion has fallen considerably since the reformation of the gold coin, it has not fallen so low as the mint price.

In the proportion between the different metals in the English coin, as copper is rated very much above its real value, so silver is rated somewhat below it. In the market of Europe, in the French coin and in the Dutch coin, an ounce of fine gold exchanges for about fourteen ounces of fine silver. In the English coin, it exchanges for about fifteen ounces, that is, for more silver than it is worth according to the common estimation of Europe. But as the price of copper in bars is not, even in England, raised by the high price of copper in English coin, so the price of silver in bullion is not sunk by the low rate of silver in English coin. Silver in bullion still preserves its proper proportion to gold; for the same reason that copper in bars preserves its proper proportion to silver.

Upon the reformation of the silver coin in the reign of William III the price of silver bullion still continued to be somewhat above the mint price. Mr Locke imputed this high price to the permission of exporting silver bullion, and to the prohibition of exporting silver coin. This permission of exporting, he said, rendered the demand for silver bullion greater than the demand for silver coin. But the number of people who want silver coin for the common uses of buying and selling at home, is surely much greater than that of those who want silver bullion either for the use of exportation or for any other use. There subsists at present a like permission of exporting gold bullion, and a like prohibition of exporting gold coin; and yet the price of gold bullion has fallen below the mint price. But in the English coin silver was then, in the same manner as now, under-rated in proportion to gold, and the gold coin (which at that time too was not supposed to require any reformation) regulated then, as well as now, the real value of the whole coin.

As the reformation of the silver coin did not then reduce the price of silver bullion to the mint price, it is not very probable that a like reformation will do so now.

Were the silver coin brought back as near to its standard weight as the gold, a guinea, it is probable, would, according to the present proportion, exchange for more silver in coin than it would purchase in bullion. The silver coin containing its full standard weight, there would in this case be a profit in melting it down, in order, first, to sell the bullion for gold coin, and afterwards to exchange this gold coin for silver coin to be melted down in the same manner. Some alteration in the present proportion seems to be the only method of preventing this inconveniency.

The inconveniency perhaps would be less if silver was rated in the coin as much above its proper proportion to gold as it is at present rated below it; provided it was at the same time enacted that silver should not be a legal tender for more than the change of a guinea, in the same manner as copper is not a legal tender for more than the change of a shilling. No creditor could in this case be cheated in consequence of the high valuation of silver in coin; as no creditor can at present be cheated in consequence of the high valuation of copper. The bankers only would suffer by this regulation. When a run comes upon them they sometimes endeavour to gain time by paying in sixpences, and they would be precluded by this regulation from this discreditable method of evading immediate payment. They would be obliged in consequence to keep at all times in their coffers a greater quantity of cash than at present; and though this might no doubt be a considerable inconveniency to them, it would at the same time be a considerable security to their creditors.

Three pounds seventeen shillings and tenpence halfpenny (the mint price of gold) certainly does not contain, even in our present excellent gold coin, more than an ounce of standard gold, and it may be thought, therefore, should not purchase more standard bullion. But gold in coin is more convenient than gold in bullion, and though, in England, the coinage is free, yet the gold which is carried in bullion to the mint can seldom be returned in coin to the owner till after a delay of several weeks. In the present hurry of the mint, it could not be returned till after a delay of several months. This delay is equivalent to a small duty, and renders gold in coin somewhat more valuable than an equal quantity of gold in bullion. If in the English coin silver was rated according to its proper proportion to gold, the price of silver bullion would probably fall below the mint price even without any reformation of the silver coin; the value even of the present worn and defaced silver coin being regulated by the value of the excellent gold coin for which it can be changed.

A small seignorage or duty upon the coinage of both gold and silver would probably increase still more the superiority of those metals in coin above an equal quantity of either of them in bullion. The coinage would in this case increase the value of the metal coined in proportion to the extent of this small duty; for the same reason that the fashion increases the value of plate in proportion to the price of that fashion. The superiority of coin above bullion would prevent the melting down of the coin, and would discourage its exportation. If upon any public exigency it should become necessary to export the coin, the greater part of it would soon return again of its own accord. Abroad it could sell only for its weight in bullion. At home it would buy more than that weight. There would be a profit, therefore, in bringing it home again. In France a seignorage of about eight per cent is imposed upon the coinage, and the French coin, when exported, is said to return home again of its own accord.

The occasional fluctuations in the market price of gold and silver bullion arise from the same causes as the like fluctuations in that of all other commodities. The frequent loss of those metals from various accidents by sea and by land, the continual waste of them in gilding and plating, in lace and embroidery, in the wear and tear of coin, and in that of plate; require, in all countries which possess no mines of their own, a continual importation, in order to repair this loss and this waste. The merchant importers, like all other merchants, we may believe, endeavour, as well as they can, to suit their occasional importations to what, they judge, is likely to be the immediate demand. With all their attention, however, they sometimes over-do the business, and sometimes under-do it. When they import more bullion than is wanted, rather than incur the risk and trouble of exporting it again, they are sometimes willing to sell a part of it

for something less than the ordinary or average price. When, on
the other hand, they import less than is wanted, they get something more than this price. But when, under all those occasional
fluctuations, the market price either of gold or silver bullion
continues for several years together steadily and constantly,
either more or less above, or more or less below the mint price,
we may be assured that this steady and constant, either superiority or inferiority of price, is the effect of something in the state of
the coin, which, at that time, renders a certain quantity of coin
either of more value or of less value than the precise quantity of
bullion which it ought to contain. The constancy and steadiness
of the effect supposes a proportionable constancy and steadiness
in the cause.

The money of any particular country is, at any particular time
and place, more or less an accurate measure of value according
as the current coin is more or less exactly agreeable to its standard, or contains more or less exactly the precise quantity of
pure gold or pure silver which it ought to contain. If in England, for example, forty-four guineas and a half contained
exactly a pound weight of standard gold, or eleven ounces of
fine gold and one ounce of alloy, the gold coin of England
would be as accurate a measure of the actual value of goods at
any particular time and place as the nature of the thing would
admit. But if, by rubbing and wearing, forty-four guineas and a
half generally contain less than a pound weight of standard
gold; the diminution, however, being greater in some pieces
than in others; the measure of value comes to be liable to the
same sort of uncertainty to which all other weights and
measures are commonly exposed. As it rarely happens that these
are exactly agreeable to their standard, the merchant adjusts the
price of his goods, as well as he can, not to what those weights
and measures ought to be, but to what, upon an average, he
finds by experience they actually are. In consequence of a like
disorder in the coin, the price of goods comes, in the same
manner, to be adjusted, not to the quantity of pure gold or
silver which the coin ought to contain, but to that which, upon
an average, it is found by experience, it actually does contain.

By the money-price of goods, it is to be observed, I understand always the quantity of pure gold or silver for which they

are sold, without any regard to the denomination of the coin. Six shillings and eightpence, for example, in the time of Edward I, I consider as the same money-price with a pound sterling in the present times; because it contained, as nearly as we can judge, the same quantity of pure silver.

CHAPTER VI

OF THE COMPONENT PARTS OF THE PRICE OF COMMODITIES

IN that early and rude state of society which precedes both the accumulation of stock and the appropriation of land, the proportion between the quantities of labour necessary for acquiring different objects seems to be the only circumstance which can afford any rule for exchanging them for one another. If among a nation of hunters, for example, it usually costs twice the labour to kill a beaver which it does to kill a deer, one beaver should naturally exchange for or be worth two deer. It is natural that what is usually the produce of two days' or two hours' labour, should be worth double of what is usually the produce of one day's or one hour's labour.

If the one species of labour should be more severe than the other, some allowance will naturally be made for this superior hardship; and the produce of one hour's labour in the one way may frequently exchange for that of two hours' labour in the other.

Or if the one species of labour requires an uncommon degree of dexterity and ingenuity, the esteem which men have for such talents will naturally give a value to their produce, superior to what would be due to the time employed about it. Such talents can seldom be acquired but in consequence of long application, and the superior value of their produce may frequently be no more than a reasonable compensation for the time and labour which must be spent in acquiring them. In the advanced state of society, allowances of this kind, for superior hardship and superior skill, are commonly made in the wages of labour; and something of the same kind must probably have taken place in its earliest and rudest period.

In this state of things, the whole produce of labour belongs to the labourer; and the quantity of labour commonly employed in acquiring or producing any commodity is the only circumstance which can regulate the quantity of labour which it ought commonly to purchase, command, or exchange for.

As soon as stock has accumulated in the hands of particular persons, some of them will naturally employ it in setting to work industrious people, whom they will supply with materials and subsistence, in order to make a profit by the sale of their work, or by what their labour adds to the value of the materials. In exchanging the complete manufacture either for money, for labour, or for other goods, over and above what may be sufficient to pay the price of the materials, and the wages of the workmen, something must be given for the profits of the undertaker of the work who hazards his stock in this adventure. The value which the workmen add to the materials, therefore, resolves itself in this case into two parts, of which the one pays their wages, the other the profits of their employer upon the whole stock of materials and wages which he advanced. He could have no interest to employ them, unless he expected from the sale of their work something more than what was sufficient to replace his stock to him; and he could have no interest to employ a great stock rather than a small one, unless his profits were to bear some proportion to the extent of his stock.

The profits of stock, it may perhaps be thought, are only a different name for the wages of a particular sort of labour, the labour of inspection and direction. They are, however, altogether different, are regulated by quite different principles, and bear no proportion to the quantity, the hardship, or the ingenuity of this supposed labour of inspection and direction. They are regulated altogether by the value of the stock employed, and are greater or smaller in proportion to the extent of this stock. Let us suppose, for example, that in some particular place, where the common annual profits of manufacturing stock are ten per cent, there are two different manufactures, in each of which twenty workmen are employed at the rate of fifteen pounds a year each, or at the expense of three hundred a year in each manufactory. Let us suppose, too, that the coarse materials annually wrought up in the one cost only seven hundred pounds, while the finer materials in the other cost seven thousand. The capital annually employed in the one will in this case amount only to one thousand pounds; whereas that employed in the other will amount to seven thousand three hundred pounds. At the rate of ten per cent, therefore, the undertaker of the one will expect a yearly profit of about one hundred pounds only; while that of the other will expect about seven hundred and thirty pounds. But though their profits are so very different, their labour of inspection and direction may be either altogether or very nearly the same. In many great works almost the whole labour of this kind is committed to some principal clerk. His wages properly express the value of this labour of inspection and direction. Though in settling them some regard is had commonly, not only to his labour and skill, but to the trust which is reposed in him, yet they never bear any regular proportion to the capital of which he oversees the management; and the owner of this capital, though he is thus discharged of almost all labour, still expects that his profits should bear a regular proportion to his capital. In the price of commodities, therefore, the profits of stock constitute a component part altogether different from the wages of labour, and regulated by quite different principles.

In this state of things, the whole produce of labour does not always belong to the labourer. He must in most cases share it with the owner of the stock which employs him. Neither is the quantity of labour commonly employed in acquiring or producing any commodity, the only circumstance which can regulate the quantity which it ought commonly to purchase, command, or exchange for. An additional quantity, it is evident, must be due for the profits of the stock which advanced the wages and furnished the materials of that labour.

As soon as the land of any country has all become private property, the landlords, like all other men, love to reap where they never sowed, and demand a rent even for its natural produce. The wood of the forest, the grass of the field, and all the natural fruits of the earth, which, when land was in common, cost the labourer only the trouble of gathering them, come, even to him, to have an additional price fixed upon them. He must then pay for the licence to gather them; and he must give up to the landlord a portion of what his labour either collects or produces. This portion, or, what comes to the same thing, the price of this portion, constitutes the rent of land, and in the price of the greater part of commodities makes a third component part.

The real value of all the different component parts of price, it must be observed, is measured by the quantity of labour which they can, each of them, purchase or command. Labour measures the value not only of that part of price which resolves itself into labour, but of that which resolves itself into rent, and of that which resolves itself into profit.

In every society the price of every commodity finally resolves itself into some one or other, or all of those three parts; and in every improved society, all the three enter more or less, as component parts, into the price of the far greater part of commodities.

In the price of corn, for example, one part pays the rent of the landlord, another pays the wages or maintenance of the labourers and labouring cattle employed in producing it, and the third pays the profit of the farmer. These three parts seem either immediately or ultimately to make up the whole price of corn. A fourth part, it may perhaps be thought, is necessary for replacing the stock of the farmer, or for compensating the wear and tear of his labouring cattle, and other instruments of husbandry. But it must be considered that the price of any instrument of husbandry, such as a labouring horse, is itself made up of the same three parts; the rent of the land upon which he is reared, the labour of tending and rearing him, and the profits of the farmer who advances both the rent of this land, and the wages of this labour. Though the price of the corn, therefore, may pay the price as well as the maintenance of the horse, the whole price still resolves itself either immediately or ultimately into the same three parts of rent, labour, and profit.

In the price of flour or meal, we must add to the price of the corn, the profits of the miller, and the wages of his servants; in the price of bread, the profits of the baker, and the wages of his servants; and in the price of both, the labour of transporting the corn from the house of the farmer to that of the miller, and from that of the miller to that of the baker, together with the profits of those who advance the wages of that labour.

The price of flax resolves itself into the same three parts as that of corn. In the price of linen we must add to this price the wages of the flax-dresser, of the spinner, of the weaver, of the bleacher, etc., together with the profits of their respective employers.

As any particular commodity comes to be more manufactured, that part of the price which resolves itself into wages and profit comes to be greater in proportion to that which resolves itself into rent. In the progress of the manufacture, not only the number of profits increase, but every subsequent profit is greater than the foregoing; because the capital from which it is derived must always be greater. The capital which employs the weavers, for example, must be greater than that which employs the spinners; because it not only replaces that capital with its profits, but pays, besides, the wages of the weavers; and the profits must always bear some proportion to the capital.

In the most improved societies, however, there are always a few commodities of which the price resolves itself into two parts only, the wages of labour, and the profits of stock; and a still smaller number, in which it consists altogether in the wages of labour. In the price of sea-fish, for example, one part pays the labour of the fishermen, and the other the profits of the capital employed in the fishery. Rent very seldom makes any part of it, though it does sometimes, as I shall show hereafter. It is otherwise, at least through the greater part of Europe, in river fisheries. A salmon fishery pays a rent, and rent, though it cannot well be called the rent of land, makes a part of the price of a salmon as well as wages and profit. In some parts of Scotland a few poor people make a trade of gathering, along the sea-shore, those little variegated stones commonly known by the name of Scotch Pebbles. The price which is paid to them by the stone cutter is altogether the wages of their labour; neither rent nor profit make any part of it.

But the whole price of any commodity must still finally resolve itself into some one or other, or all of those three parts; as whatever part of it remains after paying the rent of the land,

and the price of the whole labour employed in raising, manufacturing, and bringing it to market, must necessarily be profit to somebody.

As the price or exchangeable value of every particular commodity, taken separately, resolves itself into some one or other or all of those three parts; so that of all the commodities which compose the whole annual produce of the labour of every country, taken complexly, must resolve itself into the same three parts, and be parcelled out among different inhabitants of the country, either as the wages of their labour, the profits of their stock, or the rent of their land. The whole of what is annually either collected or produced by the labour of every society, or what comes to the same thing, the whole price of it, is in this manner originally distributed among some of its different members. Wages, profit, and rent, are the three original sources of all revenue as well as of all exchangeable value. All other revenue is ultimately derived from some one or other of these.

Whoever derives his revenue from a fund which is his own, must draw it either from his labour, from his stock, or from his land. The revenue derived from labour is called wages. That derived from stock, by the person who manages or employs it, is called profit. That derived from it by the person who does not employ it himself, but lends it to another, is called the interest or the use of money. It is the compensation which the borrower pays to the lender, for the profit which he has an opportunity of making by the use of the money. Part of that profit naturally belongs to the borrower, who runs the risk and takes the trouble of employing it; and part to the lender, who affords him the opportunity of making this profit. The interest of money is always a derivative revenue, which, if it is not paid from the profit which is made by the use of the money, must be paid from some other source of revenue, unless perhaps the borrower is a spendthrift, who contracts a second debt in order to pay the interest of the first. The revenue which proceeds altogether from land, is called rent, and belongs to the landlord. The revenue of the farmer is derived partly from his labour, and partly from his stock. To him, land is only the instrument which enables him to earn the wages of this labour, and to make the profits of this stock. All taxes, and all the revenue which is founded upon them, all salaries, pensions, and annuities of every kind, are ultimately derived from some one or other of those three original sources of revenue, and are paid either immediately or mediately from the wages of labour, the profits of stock, or the rent of land.

When those three different sorts of revenue belong to different persons, they are readily distinguished; but when they belong to the same they are sometimes confounded with one another, at least in common language.

A gentleman who farms a part of his own estate, after paying the expense of cultivation, should gain both the rent of the landlord and the profit of the farmer. He is apt to denominate, however, his whole gain, profit, and thus confounds rent with profit, at least in common language. The greater part of our North American and West Indian planters are in this situation. They farm, the greater part of them, their own estates, and accordingly we seldom hear of the rent of a plantation, but frequently of its profit.

Common farmers seldom employ any overseer to direct the general operations of the farm. They generally, too, work a good deal with their own hands, as ploughmen, harrowers, etc. What remains of the crop after paying the rent, therefore, should not only replace to them their stock employed in cultivation, together with its ordinary profits, but pay them the wages which are due to them, both as labourers and overseers. Whatever remains, however, after paying the rent and keeping up the stock, is called profit. But wages evidently make a part of it. The farmer, by saving these wages, must necessarily gain them. Wages, therefore, are in this case confounded with profit.

An independent manufacturer, who has stock enough both to purchase materials, and to maintain himself till he can carry his work to market, should gain both the wages of a journeyman who works under a master, and the profit which that master makes by the sale of the journeyman's work. His whole gains, however, are commonly called profit, and wages are, in this case too, confounded with profit.

A gardener who cultivates his own garden with his own hands, unites in his own person the three different characters of landlord, farmer, and labourer. His produce, therefore, should pay him the rent of the first, the profit of the second, and the wages of the third. The whole, however, is commonly considered as the earnings of his labour. Both rent and profit are, in this case, confounded with wages.

As in a civilized country there are but few commodities of which the exchangeable value arises from labour only, rent and profit contributing largely to that of the far greater part of them, so the annual produce of its labour will always be sufficient to purchase or command a much greater quantity of labour than what was employed in raising, preparing, and bringing that produce to market. If the society were annually to employ all the labour which it can annually purchase, as the quantity of labour would increase greatly every year, so the produce of every succeeding year would be of vastly greater value than that of the foregoing. But there is no country in which the whole annual produce is employed in maintaining the industrious. The idle everywhere consume a great part of it; and according to the different proportions in which it is annually divided between those two different orders of people, its ordinary or average value must either annually increase, or diminish, or continue the same from one year to another.

CHAPTER VII

OF THE NATURAL AND MARKET PRICE OF COMMODITIES

THERE is in every society or neighbourhood an ordinary or average rate both of wages and profit in every different employment of labour and stock. This rate is naturally regulated, as I shall show hereafter, partly by the general circumstances of the society, their riches or poverty, their advancing, stationary, or declining condition; and partly by the particular nature of each employment.

There is likewise in every society or neighbourhood an ordinary or average rate of rent, which is regulated too, as I shall show hereafter, partly by the general circumstances of the society or neighbourhood in which the land is situated, and partly by the natural or improved fertility of the land.

These ordinary or average rates may be called the natural rates of wages, profit, and rent, at the time and place in which they commonly prevail.

When the price of any commodity is neither more nor less than what is sufficient to pay the rent of the land, the wages of the labour, and the profits of the stock employed in raising, preparing, and bringing it to market, according to their natural rates, the commodity is then sold for what may be called its natural price.

The commodity is then sold precisely for what it is worth, or for what it really costs the person who brings it to market; for though in common language what is called the prime cost of any commodity does not comprehend the profit of the person who is to sell it again, yet if he sell it at a price which does not allow him the ordinary rate of profit in his neighbourhood, he is evidently a loser by the trade; since by employing his stock in some other way he might have made that profit. His profit, besides, is his revenue, the proper fund of his subsistence. As, while he is preparing and bringing the goods to market, he advances to his workmen their wages, or their subsistence; so he advances to himself, in the same manner, his own subsistence, which is generally suitable to the profit which he may reasonably expect from the sale of his goods. Unless they yield him this profit, therefore, they do not repay him what they may very properly be said to have really cost him.

Though the price, therefore, which leaves him this profit is not always the lowest at which a dealer may sometimes sell his goods, it is the lowest at which he is likely to sell them for any considerable time; at least where there is perfect liberty, or where he may change his trade as often as he pleases.

The actual price at which any commodity is commonly sold is called its market price. It may either be above, or below, or exactly the same with its natural price.

The market price of every particular commodity is regulated by the proportion between the quantity which is actually brought to market, and the demand of those who are willing to pay the natural price of the commodity, or the whole value of

the rent, labour, and profit, which must be paid in order to
bring it thither. Such people may be called the effectual demanders, and their demand the effectual demand; since it may
be sufficient to effectuate the bringing of the commodity to
market. It is different from the absolute demand. A very poor
man may be said in some sense to have a demand for a coach
and six; he might like to have it; but his demand is not an
effectual demand, as the commodity can never be brought to
market in order to satisfy it.

When the quantity of any commodity which is brought to
market falls short of the effectual demand, all those who are
willing to pay the whole value of the rent, wages, and profit,
which must be paid in order to bring it thither, cannot be supplied with the quantity which they want. Rather than want it
altogether, some of them will be willing to give more. A competition will immediately begin among them, and the market
price will rise more or less above the natural price, according as
either the greatness of the deficiency, or the wealth and wanton
luxury of the competitors, happen to animate more or less the
eagerness of the competition. Among competitors of equal
wealth and luxury the same deficiency will generally occasion a
more or less eager competition, according as the acquisition of
the commodity happens to be of more or less importance to
them. Hence the exorbitant price of the necessaries of life during the blockade of a town or in a famine.

When the quantity brought to market exceeds the effectual
demand, it cannot be all sold to those who are willing to pay the
whole value of the rent, wages, and profit, which must be paid
in order to bring it thither. Some part must be sold to those
who are willing to pay less, and the low price which they give
for it must reduce the price of the whole. The market price will
sink more or less below the natural price, according as the
greatness of the excess increases more or less the competition of
the sellers, or according as it happens to be more or less important to them to get immediately rid of the commodity. The
same excess in the importation of perishable, will occasion a
much greater competition than in that of durable commodities; in
the importation of oranges, for example, than in that of old iron.

When the quantity brought to market is just sufficient to

supply the effectual demand, and no more, the market price naturally comes to be either exactly, or as nearly as can be judged of, the same with the natural price. The whole quantity upon hand can be disposed of for this price, and cannot be disposed of for more. The competition of the different dealers obliges them all to accept of this price, but does not oblige them to accept of less.

The quantity of every commodity brought to market naturally suits itself to the effectual demand. It is the interest of all those who employ their land, labour, or stock, in bringing any commodity to market, that the quantity never should exceed the effectual demand; and it is the interest of all other people that it never should fall short of that demand.

If at any time it exceeds the effectual demand, some of the component parts of its price must be paid below their natural rate. If it is rent, the interest of the landlords will immediately prompt them to withdraw a part of their land; and if it is wages or profit, the interest of the labourers in the one case, and of their employers in the other, will prompt them to withdraw a part of their labour or stock from this employment. The quantity brought to market will soon be no more than sufficient to supply the effectual demand. All the different parts of its price will rise to their natural rate, and the whole price to its natural price.

If, on the contrary, the quantity brought to market should at any time fall short of the effectual demand, some of the component parts of its price must rise above their natural rate. If it is rent, the interest of all other landlords will naturally prompt them to prepare more land for the raising of this commodity; if it is wages or profit, the interest of all other labourers and dealers will soon prompt them to employ more labour and stock in preparing and bringing it to market. The quantity brought thither will soon be sufficient to supply the effectual demand. All the different parts of its price will soon sink to their natural rate, and the whole price to its natural price.

The natural price, therefore, is, as it were, the central price, to which the prices of all commodities are continually gravitating. Different accidents may sometimes keep them suspended a good deal above it, and sometimes force them down even somewhat below it. But whatever may be the obstacles which hinder them from settling in this centre of repose and continuance, they are ✓ constantly tending towards it.

The whole quantity of industry annually employed in order to bring any commodity to market naturally suits itself in this manner to the effectual demand. It naturally aims at bringing always that precise quantity thither which may be sufficient to supply, and no more than supply, that demand.

But in some employments the same quantity of industry will in different years produce very different quantities of commodities; while in others it will produce always the same, or very nearly the same. The same number of labourers in husbandry will, in different years, produce very different quantities of corn, wine, oil, hops, etc. But the same number of spinners and weavers will every year produce the same or very nearly the same quantity of linen and woollen cloth. It is only the average produce of the one species of industry which can be suited in any respect to the effectual demand; and as its actual produce is frequently much greater and frequently much less than its average produce, the quantity of the commodities brought to market will sometimes exceed a good deal, and sometimes fall short a good deal, of the effectual demand. Even though that demand therefore should continue always the same, their market price will be liable to great fluctuations, will sometimes fall a good deal below, and sometimes rise a good deal above their natural price. In the other species of industry, the produce of equal quantities of labour being always the same, or very nearly the same, it can be more exactly suited to the effectual demand. While that demand continues the same, therefore, the market price of the commodities is likely to do so too, and to be either altogether, or as nearly as can be judged of, the same with the natural price. That the price of linen and woollen cloth is liable neither to such frequent nor to such great variations as the price of corn, every man's experience will inform him. The price of the one species of commodities varies only with the variations in the demand: that of the other varies, not only with the variations in the demand, but with the much greater and more frequent variations in the quantity of what is brought to market in order to supply that demand.

The occasional and temporary fluctuations in the market price of any commodity fall chiefly upon those parts of its price which resolve themselves into wages and profit. That part which resolves itself into rent is less affected by them. A rent certain in money is not in the least affected by them either in its rate or in its value. A rent which consists either in a certain proportion or in a certain quantity of the rude produce, is no doubt affected in its yearly value by all the occasional and temporary fluctuations in the market price of that rude produce; but it is seldom affected by them in its yearly rate. In settling the terms of the lease, the landlord and farmer endeavour, according to their best judgement, to adjust that rate, not to the temporary and occasional, but to the average and ordinary price of the produce.

Such fluctuations affect both the value and the rate either of wages or of profit, according as the market happens to be either over-stocked or under-stocked with commodities or with labour; with work done, or with work to be done. A public mourning raises the price of black cloth (with which the market is almost always under-stocked upon such occasions), and augments the profits of the merchants who possess any considerable quantity of it. It has no effect upon the wages of the weavers. The market is under-stocked with commodities, not with labour; with work done, not with the work to be done. It raises the wages of journeymen tailors. The market is here under-stocked with labour. There is an effectual demand for more labour, for more work to be done than can be had. It sinks the price of coloured silks and cloths, and thereby reduces the profits of the merchants who have any considerable quantity of them upon hand. It sinks, too, the wages of the workmen employed in preparing such commodities, for which all demand is stopped for six months, perhaps for a twelvemonth. The market is here over-stocked both with commodities and with labour.

But though the market price of every particular commodity is in this manner continually gravitating, if one may say so, towards the natural price, yet sometimes particular accidents, sometimes natural causes, and sometimes particular regulations of police, may, in many commodities, keep up the market price, for a long time together, a good deal above the natural price.

When by an increase in the effectual demand, the market

price of some particular commodity happens to rise a good deal above the natural price, those who employ their stocks in supplying that market are generally careful to conceal this change. If it was commonly known, their great profit would tempt so many new rivals to employ their stocks in the same way that, the effectual demand being fully supplied, the market price would soon be reduced to the natural price, and perhaps for some time even below it. If the market is at a great distance from the residence of those who supply it, they may sometimes be able to keep the secret for several years together, and may so long enjoy their extraordinary profits without any new rivals. Secrets of this kind, however, it must be aknowledged, can seldom be long kept; and the extraordinary profit can last very little longer than they are kept. when market price rises above natural competition

Secrets in manufactures are capable of being longer kept than secrets in trade. A dyer who has found the means of producing a particular colour with materials which cost only half the price of those commonly made use of, may, with good management, enjoy the advantage of his discovery as long as he lives, and even leave it as a legacy to his posterity. His extraordinary gains arise from the high price which is paid for his private labour. They properly consist in the high wages of that labour. But as they are repeated upon every part of his stock, and as their whole amount bears, upon that account, a regular proportion to it, they are commonly considered as extraordinary profits of stock.

Such enhancements of the market price are evidently the effects of particular accidents, of which, however, the operation may sometimes last for many years together.

Some natural productions require such a singularity of soil and situation that all the land in a great country, which is fit for producing them, may not be sufficient to supply the effectual demand. The whole quantity brought to market, therefore, may be disposed of to those who are willing to give more than what is sufficient to pay the rent of the land which produced them, together with the wages of the labour, and the profits of the stock which were employed in preparing and bringing them to market, according to their natural rates. Such commodities may continue for whole centuries together to be sold at this high price; and that part of it which resolves itself into the rent of land is in this case the part which is generally paid above its natural rate. The rent of the land which affords such singular and esteemed productions, like the rent of some vineyards in France of a peculiarly happy soil and situation, bears no regular proportion to the rent of other equally fertile and equally well-cultivated land in its neighbourhood. The wages of the labour and the profits of the stock employed in bringing such commodities to market, on the contrary, are seldom out of their natural proportion to those of the other employments of labour and stock in their neighbourhood.

Such enhancements of the market price are evidently the effect of natural causes which may hinder the effectual demand from ever being fully supplied, and which may continue, therefore, to operate for ever.

A monopoly granted either to an individual or to a trading company has the same effect as a secret in trade or manufactures. The monopolists, by keeping the market constantly under-stocked, by never fully supplying the effectual demand, sell their commodities much above the natural price, and raise their emoluments, whether they consist in wages or profit, greatly above their natural rate.

The price of monopoly is upon every occasion the highest which can be got. The natural price, or the price of free competition, on the contrary, is the lowest which can be taken, not upon every occasion, indeed, but for any considerable time together. The one is upon every occasion the highest which can be squeezed out of the buyers, or which, it is supposed, they will consent to give: the other is the lowest which the sellers can commonly afford to take, and at the same time continue their business.

The exclusive privileges of corporations, statutes of apprenticeship, and all those laws which restrain, in particular employments, the competition to a smaller number than might otherwise go into them, have the same tendency, though in a less degree. They are a sort of enlarged monopolies, and may frequently, for ages together, and in whole classes of employments, keep up the market price of particular commodities above the natural price, and maintain both the wages of the labour and the profits of the stock employed about them some-what above their natural rate.

Such enhancements of the market price may last as long as the regulations of police which give occasion to them.

The market price of any particular commodity, though it may continue long above, can seldom continue long below its natural price. Whatever part of it was paid below the natural rate, the persons whose interest it affected would immediately feel the loss, and would immediately withdraw either so much land, or so much labour, or so much stock, from being employed about it, that the quantity brought to market would soon be no more than sufficient to supply the effectual demand. Its market price, therefore, would soon rise to the natural price. This at least would be the case where there was perfect liberty.

The same statutes of apprenticeship and other corporation laws, indeed, which, when a manufacture is in prosperity, enable the workman to raise his wages a good deal above their natural rate, sometimes oblige him, when it decays, to let them down a good deal below it. As in the one case they exclude many people from his employment, so in the other they exclude him from many employments. The effect of such regulations, however, is not near so durable in sinking the workman's wages below, as in raising them above their natural rate. Their opera-tion in the one way may endure for many centuries, but in the other it can last no longer than the lives of some of the work-men who were bred to the business in the time of its prosperity. When they are gone, the number of those who are afterwards educated to the trade will naturally suit itself to the effectual demand. The police must be as violent as that of Indostan or ancient Egypt (where every man was bound by a principle of religion to follow the occupation of his father, and was sup-posed to commit the most horrid sacrilege if he changed it for another), which can in any particular employment, and for several generations together, sink either the wages of labour or the profits of stock below their natural rate.

This is all that I think necessary to be observed at present concerning the deviations, whether occasional or permanent, of the market price of commodities from the natural price.

The natural price itself varies with the natural rate of each of its component parts, of wages, profit, and rent; and in every society this rate varies according to their circumstances, according to their riches or poverty, their advancing, stationary, or declining condition. I shall, in the four following chapters, endeavour to explain, as fully and distinctly as I can, the causes of those different variations.

First, I shall endeavour to explain what are the circumstances which naturally determine the rate of wages, and in what manner those circumstances are affected by the riches or poverty, by the advancing, stationary, or declining state of the society.

Secondly, I shall endeavour to show what are the circumstances which naturally determine the rate of profit, and in what manner, too, those circumstances are affected by the like variations in the state of the society.

Though pecuniary wages and profit are very different in the different employments of labour and stock; yet a certain proportion seems commonly to take place between both the pecuniary wages in all the different employments of labour, and the pecuniary profits in all the different employments of stock. This proportion, it will appear hereafter, depends partly upon the nature of the different employments, and partly upon the different laws and policy of the society in which they are carried on. But though in many respects dependent upon the laws and policy, this proportion seems to be little affected by the riches or poverty of that society; by its advancing, stationary, or declining condition; but to remain the same or very nearly the same in all those different states. I shall, in the third place, endeavour to explain all the different circumstances which regulate this proportion.

In the fourth and last place, I shall endeavour to show what are the circumstances which regulate the rent of land, and which either raise or lower the real price of all the different substances which it produces.

CHAPTER VIII

OF THE WAGES OF LABOUR

THE produce of labour constitutes the natural recompense or wages of labour.

In that original state of things, which precedes both the appropriation of land and the accumulation of stock, the whole produce of labour belongs to the labourer. He has neither landlord nor master to share with him.

Had this state continued, the wages of labour would have augmented with all those improvements in its productive powers to which the division of labour gives occasion. All things would gradually have become cheaper. They would have been produced by a smaller quantity of labour; and as the commodities produced by equal quantities of labour would naturally in this state of things be exchanged for one another, they would have been purchased likewise with the produce of a smaller quantity.

But though all things would have become cheaper in reality, in appearance many things might have become dearer than before, or have been exchanged for a greater quantity of other goods. Let us suppose, for example, that in the greater part of employments the productive powers of labour had been improved to tenfold, or that a day's labour could produce ten times the quantity of work which it had done originally; but that in a particular employment they had been improved only to double, or that a day's labour could produce only twice the quantity of work which it had done before. In exchanging the produce of a day's labour in the greater part of employments for that of a day's labour in this particular one, ten times the original quantity of work in them would purchase only twice the original quantity in it. Any particular quantity in it, therefore, a pound weight, for example, would appear to be five times dearer than before. In reality, however, it would be twice as cheap. Though it required five times the quantity of other goods to purchase it, it would require only half the quantity of labour either to purchase or to produce it. The acquisition, therefore, would be twice as easy as before.

But this original state of things, in which the labourer enjoyed the whole produce of his own labour, could not last beyond the first introduction of the appropriation of land and the accumulation of stock. It was at an end, therefore, long before the most considerable improvements were made in the productive powers of labour, and it would be to no purpose to trace further what might have been its effect upon the recompense or wages of labour.

As soon as land becomes private property, the landlord demands a share of almost all the produce which the labourer can either raise, or collect from it. His rent makes the first deduction from the produce of the labour which is employed upon land.

It seldom happens that the person who tills the ground has wherewithal to maintain himself till he reaps the harvest. His maintenance is generally advanced to him from the stock of a master, the farmer who employs him, and who would have no interest to employ him, unless he was to share in the produce of his labour, or unless his stock was to be replaced to him with a profit. This profit makes a second deduction from the produce of the labour which is employed upon land.

The produce of almost all other labour is liable to the like deduction of profit. In all arts and manufactures the greater part of the workmen stand in need of a master to advance them the materials of their work, and their wages and maintenance till it be completed. He shares in the produce of their labour, or in the value which it adds to the materials upon which it is bestowed; and in this share consists his profit.

It sometimes happens, indeed, that a single independent workman has stock sufficient both to purchase the materials of his work, and to maintain himself till it be completed. He is both master and workman, and enjoys the whole produce of his own labour, or the whole value which it adds to the materials upon which it is bestowed. It includes what are usually two distinct revenues, belonging to two distinct persons, the profits of stock, and the wages of labour.

Such cases, however, are not very frequent, and in every part of Europe, twenty workmen serve under a master for one that is independent; and the wages of labour are everywhere under-

stood to be, what they usually are, when the labourer is one
person, and the owner of the stock which employs him another.

What are the common wages of labour, depends everywhere
upon the contract usually made between those two parties,
whose interests are by no means the same. The workmen desire
to get as much, the masters to give as little as possible. The
former are disposed to combine in order to raise, the latter in
order to lower the wages of labour.

It is not, however, difficult to foresee which of the two parties
must, upon all ordinary occasions, have the advantage in the
dispute, and force the other into a compliance with their terms.
The masters, being fewer in number, can combine much more
easily; and the law, besides, authorises, or at least does not prohibit their combinations, while it prohibits those of the workmen. We have no acts of parliament against combining to lower
the price of work; but many against combining to raise it. In all
such disputes the masters can hold out much longer. A landlord, a farmer, a master manufacturer, or merchant, though they
did not employ a single workman, could generally live a year or
two upon the stocks which they have already acquired. Many
workmen could not subsist a week, few could subsist a month,
and scarce any a year without employment. In the long-run the
workman may be as necessary to his master as his master is to
him; but the necessity is not so immediate.

We rarely hear, it has been said, of the combinations of
masters, though frequently of those of workmen. But whoever
imagines, upon this account, that masters rarely combine, is as
ignorant of the world as of the subject. Masters are always and
everywhere in a sort of tacit, but constant and uniform combination, not to raise the wages of labour above their actual rate.
To violate this combination is everywhere a most unpopular
action, and a sort of reproach to a master among his neighbours
and equals. We seldom, indeed, hear of this combination, because it is the usual, and one may say, the natural state of
things, which nobody ever hears of. Masters, too, sometimes
enter into particular combinations to sink the wages of labour
even below this rate. These are always conducted with the
utmost silence and secrecy, till the moment of execution, and
when the workmen yield, as they sometimes do, without resis-

tance, though severely felt by them, they are never heard of by other people. Such combinations, however, are frequently resisted by a contrary defensive combination of the workmen; who sometimes too, without any provocation of this kind, combine of their own accord to raise the price of their labour. Their usual pretences are, sometimes the high price of provisions; sometimes the great profit which their masters make by their work. But whether their combinations be offensive or defensive, they are always abundantly heard of. In order to bring the point to a speedy decision, they have always recourse to the loudest clamour, and sometimes to the most shocking violence and outrage. They are desperate, and act with the folly and extravagance of desperate men, who must either starve, or frighten their masters into an immediate compliance with their demands. The masters upon these occasions are just as clamorous upon the other side, and never cease to call aloud for the assistance of the civil magistrate, and the rigorous execution of those laws which have been enacted with so much severity against the combinations of servants, labourers, and journeymen. The workmen, accordingly, very seldom derive any advantage from the violence of those tumultuous combinations, which, partly from the interposition of the civil magistrate, partly from the superior steadiness of the masters, partly from the necessity which the greater part of the workmen are under of submitting for the sake of present subsistence, generally end in nothing, but the punishment or ruin of the ringleaders.

But though in disputes with their workmen, masters must generally have the advantage, there is, however, a certain rate below which it seems impossible to reduce, for any considerable time, the ordinary wages, even of the lowest species of labour.

A man must always live by his work, and his wages must at least be sufficient to maintain him. They must even upon most occasions be somewhat more; otherwise it would be impossible for him to bring up a family, and the race of such workmen could not last beyond the first generation. Mr Cantillon seems, upon this account, to suppose that the lowest species of common labourers must everywhere earn at least double their own maintenance, in order that one with another they may be enabled to bring up two children; the labour of the wife, on account of her necessary attendance on the children, being supposed no more than sufficient to provide for herself. But one-half the children born, it is computed, die before the age of manhood. The poorest labourers, therefore, according to this account, must, one with another, attempt to rear at least four children, in order that two may have an equal chance of living to that age. But the necessary maintenance of four children, it is supposed, may be nearly equal to that of one man. The labour of an able-bodied slave, the same author adds, is computed to be worth double his maintenance; and that of the meanest labourer, he thinks, cannot be worth less than that of an able-bodied slave. Thus far at least seems certain, that, in order to bring up a family, the labour of the husband and wife together must, even in the lowest species of common labour, be able to earn something more than what is precisely necessary for their own maintenance; but in what proportion, whether in that above mentioned, or in any other, I shall not take upon me to determine.

There are certain circumstances, however, which sometimes give the labourers an advantage, and enable them to raise their wages considerably above this rate; evidently the lowest which is consistent with common humanity.

When in any country the demand for those who live by wages, labourers, journeymen, servants of every kind, is continually increasing; when every year furnishes employment for a greater number than had been employed the year before, the workmen have no occasion to combine in order to raise their wages. The scarcity of hands occasions a competition among masters, who bid against one another, in order to get workmen, and thus voluntarily break through the natural combination of masters not to raise wages.

The demand for those who live by wages, it is evident, cannot increase but in proportion to the increase of the funds which are destined for the payment of wages. These funds are of two kinds; first, the revenue which is over and above what is necessary for the maintenance; and, secondly, the stock which is over and above what is necessary for the employment of their masters.

When the landlord, annuitant, or monied man, has a greater

revenue than what he judges sufficient to maintain his own family, he employs either the whole or a part of the surplus in maintaining one or more menial servants. Increase this surplus, and he will naturally increase the number of those servants.

When an independent workman, such as a weaver or shoe-maker, has got more stock than what is sufficient to purchase the materials of his own work, and to maintain himself till he can dispose of it, he naturally employs one or more journeymen with the surplus, in order to make a profit by their work. Increase this surplus, and he will naturally increase the number of his journeymen.

The demand for those who live by wages, therefore, necessarily increases with the increase of the revenue and stock of every country, and cannot possibly increase without it. The increase of revenue and stock is the increase of national wealth. The demand for those who live by wages, therefore, naturally increases with the increase of national wealth, and cannot possibly increase without it.

It is not the actual greatness of national wealth, but its continual increase, which occasions a rise in the wages of labour. It is not, accordingly, in the richest countries, but in the most thriving, or in those which are growing rich the fastest, that the wages of labour are highest. England is certainly, in the present times, a much richer country than any part of North America. The wages of labour, however, are much higher in North America than in any part of England. In the province of New York, common labourers earn[1] three shillings and six-pence currency, equal to two shillings sterling, a day; ship carpenters, ten shillings and sixpence currency, with a pint of rum worth sixpence sterling, equal in all to six shillings and sixpence sterling; house carpenters and bricklayers, eight shil-lings currency, equal to four shillings and sixpence sterling; journeymen tailors, five shillings currency, equal to about two shillings and tenpence sterling. These prices are all above the London price; and wages are said to be as high in the other colonies as in New York. The price of provisions is everywhere in North America much lower than in England. A dearth has

1. This was written in 1773, before the commencement of the late dis-turbances.

never been known there. In the worst seasons they have always had a sufficiency for themselves, though less for exportation. If the money price of labour, therefore, be higher than it is anywhere in the mother country, its real price, the real command of the necessaries and conveniences of life which it conveys to the labourer must be higher in a still greater proportion.

But though North America is not yet so rich as England, it is much more thriving, and advancing with much greater rapidity to the further acquisition of riches. The most decisive mark of the prosperity of any country is the increase of the number of its inhabitants. In Great Britain, and most other European countries, they are not supposed to double in less than five hundred years. In the British colonies in North America, it has been found that they double in twenty or five-and-twenty years. Nor in the present times is this increase principally owing to the continual importation of new inhabitants, but to the great multiplication of the species. Those who live to old age, it is said, frequently see there from fifty to a hundred, and sometimes many more, descendants from their own body. Labour is there so well rewarded that a numerous family of children, instead of being a burden, is a source of opulence and prosperity to the parents. The labour of each child, before it can leave their house, is computed to be worth a hundred pounds clear gain to them. A young widow with four or five young children, who, among the middling or inferior ranks of people in Europe, would have so little chance for a second husband, is there frequently courted as a sort of fortune. The value of the children is the greatest of all encouragements to marriage. We cannot, therefore, wonder that the people in North America should generally marry very young. Notwithstanding the great increase occasioned by such early marriages, there is a continual complaint of the scarcity of hands in North America. The demand for labourers, the funds destined for maintaining them, increase, it seems, still faster than they can find labourers to employ.

Though the wealth of a country should be very great, yet if it has been long stationary, we must not expect to find the wages of labour very high in it. The funds destined for the payment of wages, the revenue and stock of its inhabitants, may be of the greatest extent; but if they have continued for several centuries of the same, or very nearly of the same extent, the number of labourers employed every year could easily supply, and even more than supply, the number wanted the following year. There could seldom be any scarcity of hands, nor could the masters be obliged to bid against one another in order to get them. The hands, on the contrary, would, in this case, naturally multiply beyond their employment. There would be a constant scarcity of employment, and the labourers would be obliged to bid against one another in order to get it. If in such a country the wages of labour had ever been more than sufficient to maintain the labourer, and to enable him to bring up a family, the competition of the labourers, and the interest of the masters would soon reduce them to this lowest rate which is consistent with common humanity. China has been long one of the richest, that is, one of the most fertile, best cultivated, most industrious, and most populous countries in the world. It seems, however, to have been long stationary. Marco Polo, who visited it more than five hundred years ago, describes its cultivation, industry, and populousness, almost in the same terms in which they are described by travellers in the present times. It had perhaps, even long before his time, acquired that full complement of riches which the nature of its laws and institutions permits it to acquire. The accounts of all travellers, inconsistent in many other respects, agree in the low wages of labour, and in the difficulty which a labourer finds in bringing up a family in China. If by digging the ground a whole day he can get what will purchase a small quantity of rice in the evening, he is contented. The condition of artificers is, if possible, still worse. Instead of waiting indolently in their workhouses, for the calls of their customers, as in Europe, they are continually running about the streets with the tools of their respective trades, offering their service, and as it were begging employment. The poverty of the lower ranks of people in China far surpasses that of the most beggarly nations in Europe. In the neighbourhood of Canton many hundred, it is commonly said, many thousand families have no habitation on the land, but live constantly in little fishing boats upon the rivers and canals. The subsistence which they find there is so scanty that they are eager to fish up the nastiest garbage thrown overboard from any European ship.

Any carrion, the carcase of a dead dog or cat, for example, though half putrid and stinking, is as welcome to them as the most wholesome food to the people of other countries. Marriage is encouraged in China, not by the profitableness of children, but by the liberty of destroying them. In all great towns several are every night exposed in the street, or drowned like puppies in the water. The performance of this horrid office is even said to be the avowed business by which some people earn their subsistence.

China, however, though it may perhaps stand still, does not seem to go backwards. Its towns are nowhere deserted by their inhabitants. The lands which had once been cultivated are nowhere neglected. The same or very nearly the same annual labour must therefore continue to be performed, and the funds destined for maintaining it must not, consequently, be sensibly diminished. The lowest class of labourers, therefore, notwithstanding their scanty subsistence, must some way or another make shift to continue their race so far as to keep up their usual numbers.

But it would be otherwise in a country where the funds destined for the maintenance of labour were sensibly decaying. Every year the demand for servants and labourers would, in all the different classes of employments, be less than it had been the year before. Many who had been bred in the superior classes, not being able to find employment in their own business, would be glad to seek it in the lowest. The lowest class being not only over-stocked with its own workmen, but with the overflowings of all the other classes, the competition for employment would be so great in it, as to reduce the wages of labour to the most miserable and scanty subsistence of the labourer. Many would not be able to find employment even upon these hard terms, but would either starve, or be driven to seek a subsistence either by begging, or by the perpetration perhaps of the greatest enormities. Want, famine, and mortality would immediately prevail in that class, and from thence extend themselves to all the superior classes, till the number of inhabitants in the country was reduced to what could easily be maintained by the revenue and stock which remained in it, and which had escaped either the tyranny or calamity which had destroyed the rest. This per-

haps is nearly the present state of Bengal, and of some other of
the English settlements in the East Indies. In a fertile country
which had before been much depopulated, where subsistence,
consequently, should not be very difficult, and where, notwithstanding three or four hundred thousand people die of hunger
in one year, we may be assured that the funds destined for the
maintenance of the labouring poor are fast decaying. The
difference between the genius of the British constitution which
protects and governs North America, and that of the mercantile company which oppresses and domineers in the East
Indies, cannot perhaps be better illustrated than by the different
state of those countries.

The liberal reward of labour, therefore, as it is the necessary
effect, so it is the natural symptom of increasing national
wealth. The scanty maintenance of the labouring poor, on the
other hand, is the natural symptom that things are at a stand,
and their starving condition that they are going fast backwards.

In Great Britain the wages of labour seem, in the present
times, to be evidently more than what is precisely necessary to
enable the labourer to bring up a family. In order to satisfy
ourselves upon this point it will not be necessary to enter into
any tedious or doubtful calculation of what may be the lowest
sum upon which it is possible to do this. There are many plain
symptoms that the wages of labour are nowhere in this country
regulated by this lowest rate which is consistent with common
humanity.

First, in almost every part of Great Britain there is a distinction, even in the lowest species of labour, between summer and
winter wages. Summer wages are always highest. But on
account of the extraordinary expense of fuel, the maintenance of
a family is most expensive in winter. Wages, therefore, being
highest when this expense is lowest, it seems evident that they
are not regulated by what is necessary for this expense; but by
the quantity and supposed value of the work. A labourer, it
may be said indeed, ought to save part of his summer wages in
order to defray his winter expense; and that through the whole
year they do not exceed what is necessary to maintain his family
through the whole year. A slave, however, or one absolutely
dependent on us for immediate subsistence, would not be

treated in this manner. His daily subsistence would be proportioned to his daily necessities.

Secondly, the wages of labour do not in Great Britain fluctuate with the price of provisions. These vary everywhere from
year to year, frequently from month to month. But in many
places the money price of labour remains uniformly the same
sometimes for half a century together. If in these places, therefore, the labouring poor can maintain their families in dear
years, they must be at their ease in times of moderate plenty,
and in affluence in those of extraordinary cheapness. The high
price of provisions during these ten years past has not in many
parts of the kingdom been accompanied with any sensible rise
in the money price of labour. It has, indeed, in some, owing
probably more to the increase of the demand for labour than to
that of the price of provisions.

Thirdly, as the price of provisions varies more from year to
year than the wages of labour, so, on the other hand, the wages
of labour vary more from place to place than the price of provisions. The prices of bread and butcher's meat are generally the
same or very nearly the same through the greater part of the
united kingdom. These and most other things which are sold by
retail, the way in which the labouring poor buy all things, are
generally fully as cheap or cheaper in great towns than in the
remoter parts of the country, for reasons which I shall have
occasion to explain hereafter. But the wages of labour in a great
town and its neighbourhood are frequently a fourth or a fifth
part, twenty or five-and-twenty per cent higher than at a few
miles distance. Eighteenpence a day may be reckoned the
common price of labour in London and its neighbourhood. At a
few miles distance it falls to fourteen and fifteen pence. Tenpence may be reckoned its price in Edinburgh and its neighbourhood. At a few miles distant it falls to eightpence, the usual
price of common labour through the greater part of the low
country of Scotland, where it varies a good deal less than in
England. Such a difference of prices, which it seems is not
always sufficient to transport a man from one parish to another,
would necessarily occasion so great a transportation of the most
bulky commodities, not only from one parish to another, but
from one end of the kingdom, almost from one end of the

world to the other, as would soon reduce them more nearly to a level. After all that has been said of the levity and inconstancy of human nature, it appears evidently from experience that a man is of all sorts of luggage the most difficult to be transported. If the labouring poor, therefore, can maintain their families in those parts of the kingdom where the price of labour is lowest, they must be in affluence where it is highest.

Fourthly, the variations in the price of labour not only do not correspond either in place or time with those in the price of provisions, but they are frequently quite opposite.

Grain, the food of the common people, is dearer in Scotland than in England, whence Scotland receives almost every year very large supplies. But English corn must be sold dearer in Scotland, the country to which it is brought, than in England, the country from which it comes; and in proportion to its quality it cannot be sold dearer in Scotland than the Scotch corn that comes to the same market in competition with it. The quality of grain depends chiefly upon the quantity of flour or meal which it yields at the mill, and in this respect English grain is so much superior to the Scotch that, though often dearer in appearance, or in proportion to the measure of its bulk, it is generally cheaper in reality, or in proportion to its quality, or even to the measure of its weight. The price of labour, on the contrary, is dearer in England than in Scotland. If the labouring poor, therefore, can maintain their families in the one part of the united kingdom, they must be in affluence in the other. Oatmeal indeed supplies the common people in Scotland with the greatest and the best part of their food, which is in general much inferior to that of their neighbours of the same rank in England. This difference, however, in the mode of their subsistence is not the cause, but the effect of the difference in their wages; though, by a strange misapprehension, I have frequently heard it represented as the cause. It is not because one man keeps a coach while his neighbour walks a-foot that the one is rich and the other poor; but because the one is rich he keeps a coach, and because the other is poor he walks a-foot.

During the course of the last century, taking one year with another, grain was dearer in both parts of the united kingdom than during that of the present. This is a matter of fact which cannot now admit of any reasonable doubt; and the proof of it is, if possible, still more decisive with regard to Scotland than with regard to England. It is in Scotland supported by the evidence of the public fiars, annual valuations made upon oath, according to the actual state of the markets, of all the different sorts of grain in every different county of Scotland. If such direct proof could require any collateral evidence to confirm it, I would observe that this has likewise been the case in France, and probably in most other parts of Europe. With regard to France there is the clearest proof. But though it is certain that in both parts of the united kingdom grain was somewhat dearer in the last century than in the present, it is equally certain that labour was much cheaper. If the labouring poor, therefore, could bring up their families then, they must be much more at their ease now. In the last century, the most usual day-wages of common labour through the greater part of Scotland were sixpence in summer and fivepence in winter. Three shillings a week, the same price very nearly, still continues to be paid in some parts of the Highlands and Western Islands. Through the greater part of the low country the most usual wages of common labour are now eightpence a day, tenpence, sometimes a shilling about Edinburgh, in the counties which border upon England, probably on account of that neighbourhood, and in a few other places where there has lately been a considerable rise in the demand for labour, about Glasgow, Carron, Ayrshire, etc. In England the improvements of agriculture, manufactures, and commerce began much earlier than in Scotland. The demand for labour, and consequently its price, must necessarily have increased with those improvements. In the last century, accordingly, as well as in the present, the wages of labour were higher in England than in Scotland. They have risen, too, considerably since that time, though, on account of the greater variety of wages paid there in different places, it is more difficult to ascertain how much. In 1614, the pay of a foot soldier was the same as in the present times, eightpence a day. When it was first established it would naturally be regulated by the usual wages of common labourers, the rank of people from which foot soldiers are commonly drawn. Lord Chief Justice Hales, who wrote in the time of Charles II, computes the necessary expense of a labourer's family, consisting of six persons, the father and mother, two children able to do something, and two not able, at ten shillings a week, or twenty-six pounds a year. If they cannot earn this by their labour, they must make it up, he supposes, either by begging or stealing. He appears to have inquired very carefully into this subject.[1] In 1688, Mr Gregory King, whose skill in political arithmetic is so much extolled by Doctor Davenant, computed the ordinary income of labourers and out-servants to be fifteen pounds a year to a family, which he supposed to consist, one with another, of three and a half persons. His calculation, therefore, though different in appearance, corresponds very nearly at bottom with that of Judge Hales. Both suppose the weekly expense of such families to be about twenty pence a head. Both the pecuniary income and expense of such families have increased considerably since that time through the greater part of the kingdom; in some places more, and in some less; though perhaps scarce anywhere so much as some exaggerated accounts of the present wages of labour have lately represented them to the public. The price of labour, it must be observed, cannot be ascertained very accurately anywhere, different prices being often paid at the same place and for the same sort of labour, not only according to the different abilities of the workmen, but according to the easiness or hardness of the masters. Where wages are not regulated by law, all that we can pretend to determine is what are the most usual; and experience seems to show that law can never regulate them properly, though it has often pretended to do so.

The real recompense of labour, the real quantity of the necessaries and conveniences of life which it can procure to the labourer, has, during the course of the present century, increased perhaps in a still greater proportion than its money price. Not only grain has become somewhat cheaper, but many other things from which the industrious poor derive an agreeable and wholesome variety of food have become a great deal cheaper. Potatoes, for example, do not at present, through the greater part of the kingdom, cost half the price which they used to do thirty or forty years ago. The same thing may be said of

1. See his scheme for the maintenance of the Poor, in Burn's *History of the Poor-laws*.

turnips, carrots, cabbages; things which were formerly never raised but by the spade, but which are now commonly raised by the plough. All sorts of garden stuff, too, has become cheaper. The greater part of the apples and even of the onions consumed in Great Britain were in the last century imported from Flanders. The great improvements in the coarser manufactures of both linen and woollen cloth furnish the labourers with cheaper and better clothing; and those in the manufactures of the coarser metals, with cheaper and better instruments of trade, as well as with many agreeable and convenient pieces of household furniture. Soap, salt, candles, leather, and fermented liquors have, indeed, become a good deal dearer; chiefly from the taxes which have been laid upon them. The quantity of these, however, which the labouring poor are under any necessity of consuming, is so very small, that the increase in their price does not compensate the diminution in that of so many other things. The common complaint that luxury extends itself even to the lowest ranks of the people, and that the labouring poor will not now be contented with the same food, clothing, and lodging which satisfied them in former times, may convince us that it is not the money price of labour only, but its real recompense, which has augmented.

Is this improvement in the circumstances of the lower ranks of the people to be regarded as an advantage or as an inconveniency to the society? The answer seems at first sight abundantly plain. Servants, labourers, and workmen of different kinds, make up the far greater part of every great political society. But what improves the circumstances of the greater part can never be regarded as an inconveniency to the whole. No society can surely be flourishing and happy, of which the far greater part of the members are poor and miserable. It is but equity, besides, that they who food, clothe, and lodge the whole body of the people, should have such a share of the produce of their own labour as to be themselves tolerably well fed, clothed, and lodged.

Poverty, though it no doubt discourages, does not always prevent marriage. It seems even to be favourable to generation. A half-starved Highland woman frequently bears more than twenty children, while a pampered fine lady is often incapable of bearing any, and is generally exhausted by two or three. Barrenness, so frequent among women of fashion, is very rare among those of inferior station. Luxury in the fair sex, while it inflames perhaps the passion for enjoyment, seems always to weaken, and frequently to destroy altogether, the powers of generation.

But poverty, though it does not prevent the generation, is extremely unfavourable to the rearing of children. The tender plant is produced, but in so cold a soil and so severe a climate, soon withers and dies. It is not uncommon, I have been frequently told, in the Highlands of Scotland for a mother who has borne twenty children not to have two alive. Several officers of great experience have assured me, that so far from recruiting their regiment, they have never been able to supply it with drums and fifes from all the soldiers' children that were born in it. A greater number of fine children, however, is seldom seen anywhere than about a barrack of soldiers. Very few of them, it seems, arrive at the age of thirteen or fourteen. In some places one half the children born die before they are four years of age; in many places before they are seven; and in almost all places before they are nine or ten. This great mortality, however, will everywhere be found chiefly among the children of the common people, who cannot afford to tend them with the same care as those of better station. Though their marriages are generally more fruitful than those of people of fashion, a smaller proportion of their children arrive at maturity. In foundling hospitals, and among the children brought up by parish charities, the mortality is still greater than among those of the common people.

Every species of animals naturally multiplies in proportion to the means of their subsistence, and no species can ever multiply beyond it. But in civilized society it is only among the inferior ranks of people that the scantiness of subsistence can set limits to the further multiplication of the human species; and it can do so in no other way than by destroying a great part of the children which their fruitful marriages produce.

The liberal reward of labour, by enabling them to provide better for their children, and consequently to bring up a greater number, naturally tends to widen and extend those limits. It deserves to be remarked, too, that it necessarily does this as nearly as possible in the proportion which the demand for labour requires. If this demand is continually increasing, the reward of labour must necessarily encourage in such a manner the marriage and multiplication of labourers, as may enable them to supply that continually increasing demand by a continually increasing population. If the reward should at any time be less than what was requisite for this purpose, the deficiency of hands would soon raise it; and if it should at any time be more, their excessive multiplication would soon lower it to this necessary rate. The market would be so much under-stocked with labour in the one case, and so much over-stocked in the other, as would soon force back its price to that proper rate which the circumstances of the society required. It is in this manner that the demand for men, like that for any other commodity, necessarily regulates the production of men; quickens it when it goes on too slowly, and stops it when it advances too fast. It is this demand which regulates and determines the state of propagation in all the different countries of the world, in North America, in Europe, and in China; which renders it rapidly progressive in the first, slow and gradual in the second, and altogether stationary in the last.

The wear and tear of a slave, it has been said, is at the expense of his master; but that of a free servant is at his own expense. The wear and tear of the latter, however, is, in reality, as much at the expense of his master as that of the former. The wages paid to journeymen and servants of every kind must be such as may enable them, one with another, to continue the race of journeymen and servants, according as the increasing, diminishing, or stationary demand of the society may happen to require. But though the wear and tear of a free servant be equally at the expense of his master, it generally costs him much less than that of a slave. The fund destined for replacing or repairing, if I may say so, the wear and tear of the slave, is commonly managed by a negligent master or careless overseer. That destined for performing the same office with regard to the free man, is managed by the free man himself. The disorders which generally prevail in the economy of the rich, naturally introduce themselves into the management of the former: the strict frugality and parsimonious attention of the poor as naturally establish themselves in that of the latter. Under such different management, the same purpose must require very different degrees of expense to execute it. It appears, accordingly, from the experience of all ages and nations, I believe, that the work done by freemen comes cheaper in the end than that performed by slaves. It is found to do so even at Boston, New York, and Philadelphia, where the wages of common labour are so very high.

The liberal reward of labour, therefore, as it is the effect of increasing wealth, so it is the cause of increasing population. To complain of it is to lament over the necessary effect and cause of the greatest public prosperity.

It deserves to be remarked, perhaps, that it is in the progressive state, while the society is advancing to the further acquisition, rather than when it has acquired its full complement of riches, that the condition of the labouring poor, of the great body of the people, seems to be the happiest and the most comfortable. It is hard in the stationary, and miserable in the declining state. The progressive state is in reality the cheerful and the hearty state to all the different orders of the society. The stationary is dull; the declining, melancholy.

The liberal reward of labour, as it encourages the propagation, so it increases the industry of the common people. The wages of labour are the encouragement of industry, which, like every other human quality, improves in proportion to the encouragement it receives. A plentiful subsistence increases the bodily strength of the labourer, and the comfortable hope of bettering his condition, and of ending his days perhaps in ease and plenty, animates him to exert that strength to the utmost. Where wages are high, accordingly, we shall always find the workmen more active, diligent, and expeditious than where they are low : in England, for example, than in Scotland; in the neighbourhood of great towns than in remote country places. Some workmen, indeed, when they can earn in four days what will maintain them through the week, will be idle the other three. This, however, is by no means the case with the greater part. Workmen, on the contrary, when they are liberally paid by the piece, are very apt to over-work themselves, and to ruin their health and constitution in a few years. A carpenter in London, and in some other places, is not supposed to last in his utmost vigour above eight years. Something of the same kind happens in many other trades, in which the workmen are paid by the piece, as they generally are in manufactures, and even in country labour, wherever wages are higher than ordinary. Almost every class of artificers is subject to some peculiar infirmity occasioned by excessive application to their peculiar species of work. Ramuzzini, an eminent Italian physician, has written a particular book concerning such diseases. We do not reckon our soldiers the most industrious set of people among us. Yet when soldiers have been employed in some particular sorts of work, and liberally paid by the piece, their officers have frequently been obliged to stipulate with the undertaker, that they should not be allowed to earn above a certain sum every day, according to the rate at which they were paid. Till this stipulation was made, mutual emulation and the desire of greater gain frequently prompted them to over-work themselves, and to hurt their health by excessive labour. Excessive application during four days of the week is frequently the real cause of the idleness of the other three, so much and so loudly complained of. Great labour, either of mind or body, continued for several days together, is in most men naturally followed by a great desire of relaxation, which, if not restrained by force or by some strong necessity, is almost irresistible. It is the call of nature, which requires to be relieved by some indulgence, sometimes of ease only, but sometimes, too, of dissipation and diversion. If it is not complied with, the consequences are often dangerous, and sometimes fatal, and such as almost always, sooner or later, bring on the peculiar infirmity of the trade. If masters would always listen to the dictates of reason and humanity, they have frequently occasion rather to moderate than to animate the application of many of their workmen. It will be found, I believe, in every sort of trade, that the man who works so moderately as to be able to work constantly not only preserves his health the longest, but, in the course of the year, executes the greatest quantity of work.

In cheap years, it is pretended, workmen are generally more idle, and in dear ones more industrious than ordinary. A plentiful subsistence, therefore, it has been concluded, relaxes, and a scanty one quickens their industry. That a little more plenty than ordinary may render some workmen idle, cannot well be doubted; but that it should have this effect upon the greater part, or that men in general should work better when they are ill fed than when they are well fed, when they are disheartened than when they are in good spirits, when they are frequently sick than when they are generally in good health, seems not very probable. Years of dearth, it is to be observed, are generally among the common people years of sickness and mortality, which cannot fail to diminish the produce of their industry.

In years of plenty, servants frequently leave their masters, and trust their subsistence to what they can make by their own industry. But the same cheapness of provisions, by increasing the fund which is destined for the maintenance of servants, encourages masters, farmers especially, to employ a greater number. Farmers upon such occasions expect more profit from their corn by maintaining a few more labouring servants than by selling it at a low price in the market. The demand for servants increases, while the number of those who offer to supply that demand diminishes. The price of labour, therefore, frequently rises in cheap years.

In years of scarcity, the difficulty and uncertainty of subsistence make all such people eager to return to service. But the high price of provisions, by diminishing the funds destined for the maintenance of servants, disposes masters rather to diminish than to increase the number of those they have. In dear years, too, poor independent workmen frequently consume the little stocks with which they had used to supply themselves with the materials of their work, and are obliged to become journeymen for subsistence. More people want employment than can easily get it; many are willing to take it upon lower terms than ordinary, and the wages of both servants and journeymen frequently sink in dear years.

Masters of all sorts, therefore, frequently make better bargains with their servants in dear than in cheap years, and find them more humble and dependent in the former than in the latter. They naturally, therefore, commend the former as more favourable to industry. Landlords and farmers, besides, two of the largest classes of masters, have another reason for being pleased with dear years. The rents of the one and the profits of the other depend very much upon the price of provisions. Nothing can be more absurd, however, than to imagine that men in general should work less when they work for themselves, than when they work for other people. A poor independent workman will generally be more industrious than even a journeyman who works by the piece. The one enjoys the whole produce of his own industry; the other shares it with his master. The one, in his separate independent state, is less liable to the temptations of bad company, which in large manufactories so frequently ruin the morals of the other. The superiority of the independent workman over those servants who are hired by the month or by the year, and whose wages and maintenance are the same whether they do much or do little, is likely to be still greater. Cheap years tend to increase the proportion of independent workmen to journeymen and servants of all kinds, and dear years to diminish it.

A French author of great knowledge and ingenuity, Mr Messance, receiver of the tailles in the election of St Etienne, endeavours to show that the poor do more work in cheap than in dear years, by comparing the quantity and value of the goods made upon those different occasions in three different manufactures; one of coarse woollens carried on at Elbeuf; one of linen, and another of silk, both which extend through the whole generality of Rouen. It appears from his account, which is copied from the registers of the public offices, that the quantity and value of the goods made in all those three manufactures has generally been greater in cheap than in dear years; and that it has always been greatest in the cheapest, and least in the dearest years. All the three seem to be stationary manufactures, or which, though their produce may vary somewhat from year to year, are upon the whole neither going backwards nor forwards.

The manufacture of linen in Scotland, and that of coarse woollens in the West Riding of Yorkshire, are growing manufactures, of which the produce is generally, though with some variations, increasing both in quantity and value. Upon examining, however, the accounts which have been published of their

annual produce, I have not been able to observe that its variations have had any sensible connection with the dearness or
cheapness of the seasons. In 1740, a year of great scarcity, both
manufactures, indeed, appear to have declined very considerably. But in 1756, another year of great scarcity, the Scotch
manufacture made more than ordinary advances. The Yorkshire manufacture, indeed, declined, and its produce did not
rise to what it had been in 1755 till 1766, after the repeal of the
American Stamp Act. In that and the following year it greatly
exceeded what it had ever been before, and it has continued to
advance ever since.

The produce of all great manufactures for distant sale must
necessarily depend, not so much upon the dearness or cheapness
of the seasons in the countries where they are carried on as upon
the circumstances which affect the demand in the countries
where they are consumed; upon peace or war, upon the prosperity or declension of other rival manufacturers, and upon the
good or bad humour of their principal customers. A great part
of the extraordinary work, besides, which is probably done in
cheap years, never enters the public registers of manufactures.
The men servants who leave their masters become independent
labourers. The women return to their parents, and commonly
spin in order to make clothes for themselves and their families.
Even the independent workmen do not always work for public
sale, but are employed by some of their neighbours in manufactures for family use. The produce of their labour, therefore,
frequently makes no figure in those public registers of which
the records are sometimes published with so much parade, and
from which our merchants and manufacturers would often
vainly pretend to announce the prosperity or declension of the
great empires.

Though the variations in the price of labour not only do not
always correspond with those in the price of provisions, but are
frequently quite opposite, we must not, upon this account,
imagine that the price of provisions has no influence upon that
of labour. The money price of labour is necessarily regulated by
two circumstances; the demand for labour, and the price of the
necessaries and conveniences of life. The demand for labour,
according as it happens to be increasing, stationary, or declin-

ing, or to require an increasing, stationary, or declining population, determines the quantity of the necessaries and conveniences of life which must be given to the labourer; and the money price of labour is determined by what is requisite for purchasing this quantity. Though the money price of labour, therefore, is sometimes high where the price of provisions is low, it would be still higher, the demand continuing the same, if the price of provisions was high.

It is because the demand for labour increases in years of sudden and extraordinary plenty, and diminishes in those of sudden and extraordinary scarcity, that the money price of labour sometimes rises in the one and sinks in the other.

In a year of sudden and extraordinary plenty, there are funds in the hands of many of the employers of industry sufficient to maintain and employ a greater number of industrious people than had been employed the year before; and this extraordinary number cannot always be had. Those masters, therefore, who want more workmen bid against one another, in order to get them, which sometimes raises both the real and the money price of their labour.

The contrary of this happens in a year of sudden and extraordinary scarcity. The funds destined for employing industry are less than they had been the year before. A considerable number of people are thrown out of employment, who bid against one another, in order to get it, which sometimes lowers both the real and the money price of labour. In 1740, a year of extraordinary scarcity, many people were willing to work for bare subsistence. In the succeeding years of plenty, it was more difficult to get labourers and servants.

The scarcity of a dear year, by diminishing the demand for labour, tends to lower its price, as the high price of provisions tends to raise it. The plenty of a cheap year, on the contrary, by increasing the demand, tends to raise the price of labour, as the cheapness of provisions tends to lower it. In the ordinary variations of the price of provisions those two opposite causes seem to counterbalance one another, which is probably in part the reason why the wages of labour are everywhere so much more steady and permanent than the price of provisions.

The increase in the wages of labour necessarily increases the price of many commodities, by increasing that part of it which resolves itself into wages, and so far tends to diminish their consumption both at home and abroad. The same cause, however, which raises the wages of labour, the increase of stock, tends to increase its productive powers, and to make a smaller quantity of labour produce a greater quantity of work. The owner of the stock which employs a great number of labourers, necessarily endeavours, for his own advantage, to make such a proper division and distribution of employment that they may be enabled to produce the greatest quantity of work possible. For the same reason, he endeavours to supply them with the best machinery which either he or they can think of. What takes place among the labourers in a particular workhouse takes place, for the same reason, among those of great society. The greater their number, the more they naturally divide themselves into different classes and subdivisions of employment. More heads are occupied in inventing the most proper machinery for executing the work of each, and it is, therefore, more likely to be invented. There are many commodities, therefore, which, in consequence of these improvements, come to be produced by so much less labour than before that the increase of its price is more than compensated by the diminution of its quantity.

CHAPTER IX

OF THE PROFITS OF STOCK

THE rise and fall in the profits of stock depend upon the same causes with the rise and fall in the wages of labour, the increasing or declining state of the wealth of the society; but those causes affect the one and the other very differently.

The increase of stock, which raises wages, tends to lower profit. When the stocks of many rich merchants are turned into the same trade their mutual competition naturally tends to lower its profit; and when there is a like increase of stock in all the different trades carried on in the same society, the same competition must produce the same effect in them all.

THE PROFITS OF STOCK

It is not easy, it has already been observed, to ascertain what are the average wages of labour even in a particular place, and at a particular time. We can, even in this case, seldom determine more than what are the most usual wages. But even this can seldom be done with regard to the profits of stock. Profit is so very fluctuating that the person who carries on a particular trade cannot always tell you himself what is the average of his annual profit. It is affected not only by every variation of price in the commodities which he deals in, but by the good or bad fortune both of his rivals and of his customers, and by a thousand other accidents to which goods when carried either by sea or by land, or even when stored in a warehouse, are liable. It varies, therefore, not only from year to year, but from day to day, and almost from hour to hour. To ascertain what is the average profit of all the different trades carried on in a great kingdom must be much more difficult; and to judge of what it may have been formerly, or in remote periods of time, with any degree of precision, must be altogether impossible.

But though it may be impossible to determine, with any degree of precision, what are or were the average profits of stock, either in the present or in ancient times, some notion may be formed of them from the interest of money. It may be laid down as a maxim, that wherever a great deal can be made by the use of money, a great deal will commonly be given for the use of it; and that wherever little can be made by it, less will commonly be given for it. According, therefore, as the usual market rate of interest varies in any country, we may be assured that the ordinary profits of stock must vary with it, must sink as it sinks, and rise as it rises. The progress of interest, therefore, may lead us to form some notion of the progress of profit.

By the 37th of Henry VIII all interest above ten per cent was declared unlawful. More, it seems, had sometimes been taken before that. In the reign of Edward VI religious zeal prohibited all interest. This prohibition, however, like all others of the same kind, is said to have produced no effect, and probably rather increased than diminished the evil of usury. The statute of Henry VIII was revived by the 13th of Elizabeth, cap. 8, and ten per cent continued to be the legal rate of interest till the 21st of James I, when it was restricted to eight per cent. It was reduced to six per cent soon after the restoration, and by the 12th of Queen Anne to five per cent. All these different statutory regulations seem to have been made with great propriety. They seem to have followed and not to have gone before the market rate of interest, or the rate at which people of good credit usually borrowed. Since the time of Queen Anne, five per cent seems to have been rather above than below the market rate. Before the late war, the government borrowed at three per cent; and people of good credit in the capital, and in many other parts of the kingdom, at three and a half, four, and four and a half per cent.

Since the time of Henry VIII the wealth and revenue of the country have been continually advancing, and, in the course of their progress, their pace seems rather to have been gradually accelerated than retarded. They seem not only to have been going on, but to have been going on faster and faster. The wages of labour have been continually increasing during the same period, and in the greater part of the different branches of trade and manufactures the profits of stock have been diminishing.

It generally requires a greater stock to carry on any sort of trade in a great town than in a country village. The great stocks employed in every branch of trade, and the number of rich competitors, generally reduce the rate of profit in the former below what it is in the latter. But the wages of labour are generally higher in a great town than in a country village. In a thriving town the people who have great stocks to employ frequently cannot get the number of workmen they want, and therefore bid against one another in order to get as many as they can, which raises the wages of labour, and lowers the profits of stock. In the remote parts of the country there is frequently not stock sufficient to employ all the people, who therefore bid against one another in order to get employment, which lowers the wages of labour and raises the profits of stock.

In Scotland, though the legal rate of interest is the same as in England, the market rate is rather higher. People of the best credit there seldom borrow under five per cent. Even private bankers in Edinburgh give four per cent upon their promissory notes, of which payment either in whole or in part may be demanded at pleasure. Private bankers in London give no interest for the money which is deposited with them. There are few trades which cannot be carried on with a smaller stock in Scotland than in England. The common rate of profit, therefore, must be somewhat greater. The wages of labour, it has already been observed, are lower in Scotland than in England. The country, too, is not only much poorer, but the steps by which it advances to a better condition, for it is evidently advancing, seem to be more slower and more tardy.

The legal rate of interest in France has not, during the course of the present century, been always regulated by the market rate.[1] In 1720 interest was reduced from the twentieth to the fiftieth penny, or from five to two per cent. In 1724 it was raised to the thirtieth penny, or to $3\frac{1}{2}$ per cent. In 1725 it was again raised to the twentieth penny, or to five per cent. In 1766, during the administration of Mr Laverdy, it was reduced to the twenty-fifth penny, or to four per cent. The Abbe Terray raised it afterwards to the old rate of five per cent. The supposed purpose of many of those violent reductions of interest was to prepare the way for reducing that of the public debts; a purpose which has sometimes been executed. France is perhaps in the present times not so rich a country as England; and though the legal rate of interest has in France frequently been lower than in England, the market rate has generally been higher; for there, as in other countries, they have several very safe and easy methods of evading the law. The profits of trade, I have been assured by British merchants who had traded in both countries, are higher in France than in England; and it is no doubt upon this account that many British subjects choose rather to employ their capitals in a country where trade is in disgrace, than in one where it is highly respected. The wages of labour are lower in France than in England. When you go from Scotland to England, the difference which you may remark between the dress and countenance of the common people in the one country and in the other sufficiently indicates the difference in their condition. The contrast is still greater when you return from France. France, though no doubt a richer country than Scotland, seems not to be going forward so fast. It is a common and even a

1. See Denisart. *Article Taux des Interets*, tom. iii. p. 18.

popular opinion in the country that it is going backwards; an opinion which, I apprehend, is ill founded even with regard to France, but which nobody can possibly entertain with regard to Scotland, who sees the country now, and who saw it twenty or thirty years ago.

The province of Holland, on the other hand, in proportion to the extent of its territory and the number of its people, is a richer country than England. The government there borrows at two per cent. and private people of good credit at three. The wages of labour are said to be higher in Holland than in England, and the Dutch, it is well known, trade upon lower profits than any people in Europe. The trade of Holland, it has been pretended by some people, is decaying, and it may perhaps be true that some particular branches of it are so. But these symptoms seem to indicate sufficiently that there is no general decay. When profit diminishes, merchants are very apt to complain that trade decays; though the diminution of profit is the natural effect of its prosperity, or of a greater stock being employed in it than before. During the late war the Dutch gained the whole carrying trade of France, of which they still retain a very large share. The great property which they possess both in the French and English funds, about forty millions, it is said, in the latter (in which I suspect, however, there is a considerable exaggeration); the great sums which they lend to private people in countries where the rate of interest is higher than in their own, are circumstances which no doubt demonstrate the redundancy of their stock, or that it has increased beyond what they can employ with tolerable profit in the proper business of their own country: but they do not demonstrate that that business has decreased. As the capital of a private man, though acquired by a particular trade, may increase beyond what he can employ in it, and yet that trade continue to increase too; so may likewise the capital of a great nation.

In our North American and West Indian colonies, not only the wages of labour, but the interest of money, and consequently the profits of stock, are higher than in England. In the different colonies both the legal and the market rate of interest run from six to eight per cent. High wages of labour and high profits of stock, however, are things, perhaps, which scarce ever go together, except in the peculiar circumstances of new colonies. A new colony must always for some time be more under-stocked in proportion to the extent of its territory, and more under-peopled in proportion to the extent of its stock, than the greater part of other countries. They have more land than they have stock to cultivate. What they have, therefore, is applied to the cultivation only of what is most fertile and most favourably situated, the land near the sea shore, and along the banks of navigable rivers. Such land, too, is frequently purchased at a price below the value even of its natural produce. Stock employed in the purchase and improvement of such lands must yield a very large profit, and consequently afford to pay a very large interest. Its rapid accumulation in so profitable an employment enables the planter to increase the number of his hands faster than he can find them in a new settlement. Those whom he can find, therefore, are very liberally rewarded. As the colony increases, the profits of stock gradually diminish. When the most fertile and best situated lands have been all occupied, less profit can be made by the cultivation of what is inferior both in soil and situation, and less interest can be afforded for the stock which is so employed. In the greater part of our colonies, accordingly, both the legal and the market rate of interest have been considerably reduced during the course of the present century. As riches, improvement, and population have increased, interest has declined. The wages of labour do not sink with the profits of stock. The demand for labour increases with the increase of stock whatever be its profits; and after these are diminished, stock may not only continue to increase, but to increase much faster than before. It is with industrious nations who are advancing in the acquisition of riches as with industrious individuals. A great stock, though with small profits, generally increases faster than a small stock with great profits. Money, says the proverb, makes money. When you have got a little, it is often easy to get more. The great difficulty is to get that little. The connexion between the increase of stock and that of industry, or of the demand for useful labour, has partly been explained already, but will be explained more fully hereafter in treating of the accumulation of stock.

The acquisition of new territory, or of new branches of trade, may sometimes raise the profits of stock, and with them the interest of money, even in a country which is fast advancing in the acquisition of riches. The stock of the country not being sufficient for the whole accession of business, which such acquisitions present to the different people among whom it is divided, is applied to those particular branches only which afford the greatest profit. Part of what had before been employed in other trades is necessarily withdrawn from them, and turned into some of the new and more profitable ones. In all those old trades, therefore, the competition comes to be less than before. The market comes to be less fully supplied with many different sorts of goods. Their price necessarily rises more or less, and yields a greater profit to those who deal in them, who can, therefore, afford to borrow at a higher interest. For some time after the conclusion of the late war, not only private people of the best credit, but some of the greatest companies in London, commonly borrowed at five per cent, who before that had not been used to pay more than four, and four and a half per cent. The great accession both of territory and trade, by our acquisitions in North America and the West Indies, will sufficiently account for this, without supposing any diminution in the capital stock of the society. So great an accession of new business to be carried on by the old stock must necessarily have diminished the quantity employed in a great number of particular branches, in which the competition being less, the profits must have been greater. I shall hereafter have occasion to mention the reasons which dispose me to believe that the capital stock of Great Britain was not diminished even by the enormous expense of the late war.

The diminution of the capital stock of the society, or of the funds destined for the maintenance of industry, however, as it lowers the wages of labour, so it raises the profits of stock, and consequently the interest of money. By the wages of labour being lowered, the owners of what stock remains in the society can bring their goods at less expense to market than before, and less stock being employed in supplying the market than before, they can sell them dearer. Their goods cost them less, and they get more for them. Their profits, therefore, being augmented at both ends, can well afford a large interest. The great fortunes so suddenly and so easily acquired in Bengal and the other British settlements in the East Indies may satisfy us that, as the wages of labour are very low, so the profits of stock are very high in those ruined countries. The interest of money is proportionably so. In Bengal, money is frequently lent to the farmers at forty, fifty, and sixty per cent and the succeeding crop is mortgaged for the payment. As the profits which can afford such an interest must eat up almost the whole rent of the landlord, so such enormous usury must in its turn eat up the greater part of those profits. Before the fall of the Roman republic, a usury of the same kind seems to have been common in the provinces, under the ruinous administration of their proconsuls. The virtuous Brutus lent money in Cyprus at eight-and-forty per cent as we learn from the letters of Cicero.

In a country which had acquired that full complement of riches which the nature of its soil and climate, and its situation with respect to other countries, allowed it to acquire; which could, therefore, advance no further, and which was not going backwards, both the wages of labour and the profits of stock would probably be very low. In a country fully peopled in proportion to what either its territory could maintain or its stock employ, the competition for employment would necessarily be so great as to reduce the wages of labour to what was barely sufficient to keep up the number of labourers, and, the country being already fully peopled, that number could never be augmented. In a country fully stocked in proportion to all the business it had to transact, as great a quantity of stock would be employed in every particular branch as the nature and extent of the trade would admit. The competition, therefore, would everywhere be as great, and consequently the ordinary profit as low as possible.

But perhaps no country has ever yet arrived at this degree of opulence. China seems to have been long stationary, and had probably long ago acquired that full complement of riches which is consistent with the nature of its laws and institutions. But this complement may be much inferior to what, with other laws and insitutions, the nature of its soil, climate, and situation might admit of. A country which neglects or despises foreign commerce, and which admits the vessels of foreign nations into one or two of its ports only, cannot transact the same quantity of business which it might do with different laws and institutions. In a country too, where, though the rich or the owners of large capitals enjoy a good deal of security, the poor or the owners of small capitals enjoy scarce any, but are liable, under the pretence of justice, to be pillaged and plundered at any time by the inferior mandarines, the quantity of stock employed in all the different branches of business transacted within it can never be equal to what the nature and extent of that business might admit. In every different branch, the oppression of the poor must establish the monopoly of the rich, who, by engrossing the whole trade to themselves, will be able to make very large profits. Twelve per cent accordingly is said to be the common interest of money in China, and the ordinary profits of stock must be sufficient to afford this large interest.

A defect in the law may sometimes raise the rate of interest considerably above what the condition of the country, as to wealth or poverty, would require. When the law does not enforce the performance of contracts, it puts all borrowers nearly upon the same footing with bankrupts or people of doubtful credit in better regulated countries. The uncertainty of recovering the money makes the lender exact the same usurious interest which is usually required from bankrupts. Among the barbarous nations who over-ran the western provinces of the Roman empire, the performance of contracts was left for many ages to the faith of the contracting parties. The courts of justice of their kings seldom intermeddled in it. The high rate of interest which took place in those ancient times may perhaps be partly accounted for from this cause.

When the law prohibits interest altogether, it does not prevent it. Many people must borrow, and nobody will lend without such a consideration for the use of their money as is suitable not only to what can be made by the use of it, but to the difficulty and danger of evading the law. The high rate of interest among all Mahometan nations is accounted for by Mr Montesquieu, not from their poverty, but partly from this, and partly from the difficulty of recovering the money.

The lowest ordinary rate of profit must always be something more than what is sufficient to compensate the occasional losses to which every employment of stock is exposed. It is this surplus only which is neat or clear profit. What is called gross profit comprehends frequently, not only this surplus, but what is retained for compensating such extraordinary losses. The interest which the borrower can afford to pay is in proportion to the clear profit only.

The lowest ordinary rate of interest must, in the same manner, be something more than sufficient to compensate the occasional losses to which lending, even with tolerable prudence, is exposed. Were it not more, charity or friendship could be the only motives for lending.

In a country which had acquired its full complement of riches, where in every particular branch of business there was the greatest quantity of stock that could be employed in it, as the ordinary rate of clear profit would be very small, so the usual market rate of interest which could be afforded out of it would be so low as to render it impossible for any but the very wealthiest people to live upon the interest of their money. All people of small or middling fortunes would be obliged to superintend themselves the employment of their own stocks. It would be necessary that almost every man should be a man of business, or engage in some sort of trade. The province of Holland seems to be approaching near to this state. It is there unfashionable not to be a man of business. Necessity makes it usual for almost every man to be so, and custom everywhere regulates fashion. As it is ridiculous not to dress, so is it, in some measure, not to be employed, like other people. As a man of a civil profession seems awkward in a camp or a garrison, and is even in some danger of being despised there, so does an idle man among men of business.

The highest ordinary rate of profit may be such as, in the price of the greater part of commodities, eats up the whole of what should go to the rent of the land, and leaves only what is sufficient to pay the labour of preparing and bringing them to market, according to the lowest rate at which labour can anywhere be paid, the bare subsistence of the labourer. The workman must always have been fed in some way or other while he was about the work; but the landlord may not always have been paid. The profits of the trade which the servants of the East

India Company carry on in Bengal may not perhaps be very far from this rate.

The proportion which the usual market rate of interest ought to bear to the ordinary rate of clear profit, necessarily varies as profit rises or falls. Double interest is in Great Britain reckoned what the merchants call a good, moderate, reasonable profit; terms which I apprehend mean no more than a common and usual profit. In a country where the ordinary rate of clear profit is eight or ten per cent, it may be reasonable that one half of it should go to interest, wherever business is carried on with borrowed money. The stock is at the risk of the borrower, who, as it were, insures it to the lender; and four or five per cent may, in the greater part of trades, be both a sufficient profit upon the risk of this insurance, and a sufficient recompense for the trouble of employing the stock. But the proportion between interest and clear profit might not be the same in countries where the ordinary rate of profit was either a good deal lower, or a good deal higher. If it were a good deal lower, one half of it perhaps could not be afforded for interest; and more might be afforded if it were a good deal higher.

In countries which are fast advancing to riches, the low rate of profit may, in the price of many commodities, compensate the high wages of labour, and enable those countries to sell as cheap as their less thriving neighbours, among whom the wages of labour may be lower.

In reality high profits tend much more to raise the price of work than high wages. If in the linen manufacture, for example, the wages of the different working people, the flax-dressers, the spinners, the weavers, etc., should, all of them, be advanced twopence a day; it would be necessary to heighten the price of a piece of linen only by a number of twopences equal to the number of people that had been employed about it, multiplied by the number of days during which they had been so employed. That part of the price of the commodity which resolved itself into wages would, through all the different stages of the manufacture, rise only in arithmetical proportion to this rise of wages. But if the profits of all the different employers of those working people should be raised five per cent, that part of the price of the commodity which resolved itself into profit would, through all the different stages of the manufacture, rise in geometrical proportion to this rise of profit. The employer of the flax-dressers would in selling his flax require an additional five per cent upon the whole value of the materials and wages which he advanced to his workmen. The employer of the spinners would require an additional five per cent both upon the advanced price of the flax and upon the wages of the spinners. And the employer of the weavers would require a like five per cent both upon the advanced price of the linen yarn and upon the wages of the weavers. In raising the price of commodities the rise of wages operates in the same manner as simple interest does in the accumulation of debt. The rise of profit operates like compound interest. Our merchants and master-manufacturers complain much of the bad effects of high wages in raising the price, and thereby lessening the sale of their goods both at home and abroad. They say nothing concerning the bad effects of high profits. They are silent with regard to the pernicious effects of their own gains. They complain only of those of other people.

CHAPTER X

OF WAGES AND PROFIT IN THE DIFFERENT EMPLOYMENTS OF LABOUR AND STOCK

THE whole of the advantages and disadvantages of the different employments of labour and stock must, in the same neighbourhood, be either perfectly equal or continually tending to equality. If in the same neighbourhood, there was any employment evidently either more or less advantageous than the rest, so many people would crowd into it in the one case, and so many would desert it in the other, that its advantages would soon return to the level of other employments. This at least would be the case in a society where things were left to follow their natural course, where there was perfect liberty, and where every man was perfectly free both to choose what occupation he thought proper, and to change it as often as he thought proper.

Every man's interest would prompt him to seek the advantageous, and to shun the disadvantageous employment.

Pecuniary wages and profit, indeed, are everywhere in Europe extremely different according to the different employments of labour and stock. But this difference arises partly from certain circumstances in the employments themselves, which, either really, or at least in the imaginations of men, make up for a small pecuniary gain in some, and counterbalance a great one in others; and partly from the policy of Europe, which nowhere leaves things at perfect liberty.

The particular consideration of those circumstances and of that policy will divide this chapter into two parts.

PART I

Inequalities arising from the Nature of the Employments themselves

The five following are the principal circumstances which, so far as I have been able to observe, make up for a small pecuniary gain in some employments, and counterbalance a great one in others : first, the agreeableness or disagreeableness of the employments themselves; secondly, the easiness and cheapness, or the difficulty and expense of learning them; thirdly, the constancy or inconstancy of employment in them; fourthly, the small or great trust which must be reposed in those who exercise them; and fifthly, the probability or improbability of success in them.

First, the wages of labour vary with the ease or hardship, the cleanliness or dirtiness, the honourableness or dishonourableness of the employment. Thus in most places, take the year round, a journeyman tailor earns less than a journeyman weaver. His work is much easier. A journeyman weaver earns less than a journeyman smith. His work is not always easier, but it is much cleanlier. A journeyman blacksmith, though an artificer, seldom earns so much in twelve hours as a collier, who is only a labourer, does in eight. His work is not quite so dirty, is less dangerous, and is carried on in daylight, and above ground. Honour makes a great part of the reward of all honourable professions. In point of pecuniary gain, all things considered, they are generally under-recompensed, as I shall endeavour to show by and by. Disgrace has the contrary effect. The trade of a butcher is a brutal and an odious business; but it is in most places more profitable than the greater part of common trades. The most detestable of all employments, that of public executioner, is, in proportion to the quantity of work done, better paid than any common trade whatever.

Hunting and fishing, the most important employments of mankind in the rude state of society, became in its advanced state their most agreeable amusements, and they pursue for pleasure what they once followed from necessity. In the advanced state of society, therefore, they are all very poor people who follow as a trade what other people pursue as a pastime. Fishermen have been so since the time of Theocritus.[1] A poacher is everywhere a very poor man in Great Britain. In countries where the rigour of the law suffers no poachers, the licensed hunter is not in a much better condition. The natural taste for those employments makes more people follow them than can live comfortably by them, and the produce of their labour, in proportion to its quantity, comes always too cheap to market to afford anything but the most scanty subsistence to the labourers.

Disagreeableness and disgrace affect the profits of stock in the same manner as the wages of labour. The keeper of an inn or tavern, who is never master of his own house, and who is exposed to the brutality of every drunkard, exercises neither a very agreeable nor a very creditable business. But there is scarce any common trade in which a small stock yields so great a profit.

Secondly, the wages of labour vary with the easiness and cheapness, or the difficulty and expense of learning the business.

When any expensive machine is erected, the extraordinary work to be performed by it before it is worn out, it must be expected, will replace the capital laid out upon it, with at least the ordinary profits. A man educated at the expense of much labour and time to any of those employments which require extraordinary dexterity and skill, may be compared to one of those expensive machines. The work which he learns to perform, it must be expected, over and above the usual wages of

1. See Idyllium xxi.

common labour, will replace to him the whole expense of his
education, with at least the ordinary profits of an equally
valuable capital. It must do this, too, in a reasonable time,
regard being had to the very uncertain duration of human life,
in the same manner as to the more certain duration of the
machine.

The difference between the wages of skilled labour and those
of common labour is founded upon this principle.

The policy of Europe considers the labour of all mechanics,
artificers, and manufacturers, as skilled labour; and that of all
country labourers as common labour. It seems to suppose that of
the former to be of a more nice and delicate nature than that of
the latter. It is so perhaps in some cases; but in the greater part
is it quite otherwise, as I shall endeavour to show by and by.
The laws and customs of Europe, therefore, in order to qualify
any person for exercising the one species of labour, impose the
necessity of an apprenticeship, though with different degrees of
rigour in different places. They leave the other free and open to
everybody. During the continuance of the apprenticeship, the
whole labour of the apprentice belongs to his master. In the
meantime he must, in many cases, be maintained by his parents
or relations, and in almost all cases must be clothed by them.
Some money, too, is commonly given to the master for teaching
him his trade. They who cannot give money give time, or become bound for more than the usual number of five years; a consideration which, though it is not always advantageous to the
master, on account of the usual idleness of apprentices, is always
disadvantageous to the apprentice. In country labour, on the
contrary, the labourer, while he is employed about the easier,
learns the more difficult parts of his business, and his own
labour maintains him through all the different stages of his
employment. It is reasonable, therefore, that in Europe the
wages of mechanics, artificers, and manufacturers, should be
somewhat higher than those of common labourers. They are so
accordingly, and their superior gains make them in most places
be considered as a superior rank of people. This superiority,
however, is generally very small; the daily or weekly earnings of
journeymen in the more common sorts of manufactures, such as
those of plain linen and woollen cloth, computed at an average,

are, in most places, very little more than the day wages of common labourers. Their employment, indeed, is more steady and uniform, and the superiority of their earnings, taking the whole year together, may be somewhat greater. It seems evidently, however, to be no greater than what is sufficient to compensate the superior expense of their education.

Education in the ingenious arts and in the liberal professions is still more tedious and expensive. The pecuniary recompense, therefore, of painters and sculptors, of lawyers and physicians, ought to be much more liberal; and it is so accordingly.

The profits of stock seem to be very little affected by the easiness or difficulty of learning the trade in which it is employed. All the different ways in which stock is commonly employed in great towns seem, in reality, to be almost equally easy and equally difficult to learn. One branch either of foreign or domestic trade cannot well be a much more intricate business than another.

Thirdly, the wages of labour in different occupations vary with the constancy or inconstancy of employment.

Employment is much more constant in some trades than in others. In the greater part of manufactures, a journeyman may be pretty sure of employment almost every day in the year that he is able to work. A mason or bricklayer, on the contrary, can work neither in hard frost nor in foul weather, and his employment at all times depends upon the occasional calls of his customers. He is liable, in consequence, to be frequently without any. What he earns, therefore, while he is employed, must not only maintain him while he is idle, but make him some compensation for those anxious and desponding moments which the thought of so precarious a situation must sometimes occasion. Where the computed earnings of the greater part of manufacturers, accordingly, are nearly upon a level with the day wages of common labourers, those of masons and bricklayers are generally from one half more to double those wages. Where common labourers earn four and five shillings a week, masons and bricklayers frequently earn seven and eight; where the former earn six, the latter often earn nine and ten; and where the former earn nine and ten, as in London, the latter commonly earn fifteen and eighteen. No species of skilled labour, however, seems more easy to learn than that of masons and bricklayers. Chairmen in London, during the summer season, are said sometimes to be employed as bricklayers. The high wages of those workmen, therefore, are not so much the recompense of their skill, as the compensation for the inconstancy of their employment.

A house carpenter seems to exercise rather a nicer and more ingenious trade than a mason. In most places, however, for it is not universally so, his day-wages are somewhat lower. His employment, though it depends much, does not depend so entirely upon the occasional calls of his customers; and it is not liable to be interrupted by the weather.

When the trades which generally afford constant employment happen in a particular place not to do so, the wages of the workmen always rise a good deal above their ordinary proportion to those of common labour. In London almost all journeymen artificers are liable to be called upon and dismissed by their masters from day to day, and from week to week, in the same manner as day-labourers in other places. The lowest order of artificers, journeymen tailors, accordingly, earn there half a crown a-day, though eighteenpence may be reckoned the wages of common labour. In small towns and country villages, the wages of journeymen tailors frequently scarce equal those of common labour; but in London they are often many weeks without employment, particularly during the summer.

When the inconstancy of employment is combined with the hardship, disagreeableness and dirtiness of the work, it sometimes raises the wages of the most common labour above those of the most skilful artificers. A collier working by the piece is supposed, at Newcastle, to earn commonly about double, and in many parts of Scotland about three times the wages of common labour. His high wages arise altogether from the hardship, disagreeableness, and dirtiness of his work. His employment may, upon most occasions, be as constant as he pleases. The coalheavers in London exercise a trade which in hardship, dirtiness, and disagreeableness, almost equals that of colliers; and from the unavoidable irregularity in the arrivals of coal-ships, the employment of the greater part of them is necessarily very inconstant. If colliers, therefore, commonly earn double and triple

the wages of common labour, it ought not to seem unreasonable
that coal-heavers should sometimes earn four and five times
those wages. In the inquiry made into their condition a few
years ago, it was found that at the rate at which they were then
paid, they could earn from six to ten shillings a day. Six shillings are about four times the wages of common labour in London, and in every particular trade the lowest common earnings
may always be considered as those of the far greater number.
How extravagant soever those earnings may appear, if they
were more than sufficient to compensate all the disagreeable
circumstances of the business, there would soon be so great a
number of competitors as, in a trade which has no exclusive
privilege, would quickly reduce them to a lower rate.

The constancy or inconstancy of employment cannot affect
the ordinary profits of stock in any particular trade. Whether
the stock is or is not constantly employed depends, not upon the
trade, but the trader.

Fourthly, the wages of labour vary accordingly to the small or
great trust which must be reposed in the workmen.

The wages of goldsmiths and jewellers are everywhere
superior to those of many other workmen, not only of equal,
but of much superior ingenuity, on account of the precious
materials with which they are intrusted.

We trust our health to the physician; our fortune and sometimes our life and reputation to the lawyer and attorney. Such
confidence could not safely be reposed in people of a very mean
or low condition. Their reward must be such, therefore, as may
give them that rank in the society which so important a trust
requires. The long time and the great expense which must be
laid out in their education, when combined with this circumstance, necessarily enhance still further the price of their labour.

When a person employs only his own stock in trade, there is
no trust; and the credit which he may get from other people
depends, not upon the nature of his trade, but upon their
opinion of his fortune, probity, and prudence. The different
rates of profit, therefore, in the different branches of trade, cannot arise from the different degrees of trust reposed in the
traders.

Fifthly, the wages of labour in different employments vary

according to the probability or improbability of success in them.

The probability that any particular person shall ever be qualified for the employment to which he is educated is very different in different occupations. In the greater part of mechanic trades, success is almost certain; but very uncertain in the liberal professions. Put your son apprentice to a shoemaker, there is little doubt of his learning to make a pair of shoes; but send him to study the law, it is at least twenty to one if ever he makes such proficiency as will enable him to live by the business. In a perfectly fair lottery, those who draw the prizes ought to gain all that is lost by those who draw the blanks. In a profession where twenty fail for one that succeeds, that one ought to gain all that should have been gained by the unsuccessful twenty. The counsellor at law who, perhaps, at near forty years of age, begins to make something by his profession, ought to receive the retribution, not only of his own so tedious and expensive eduction, but that of more than twenty others who are never likely to make anything by it. How extravagant soever the fees of counsellors at law may sometimes appear, their real retribution is never equal to this. Compute in any particular place what is likely to be annually gained, and what is likely to be annually spent, by all the different workmen in any common trade, such as that of shoemakers or weavers, and you will find that the former sum will generally exceed the latter. But make the same computation with regard to all the counsellors and students of law, in all the different inns of court, and you will find that their annual gains bear but a very small proportion to their annual expense, even though you rate the former as high, and the latter as low, as can well be done. The lottery of the law, therefore, is very far from being a perfectly fair lottery; and that, as well as many other liberal and honourable professions, are, in point of pecuniary gain, evidently under-recompensed.

Those professions keep their level, however, with other occupations, and, notwithstanding these discouragements, all the most generous and liberal spirits are eager to crowd into them. Two different causes contribute to recommend them. First, the desire of the reputation which attends upon superior excellence in any of them; and, secondly, the natural confidence which every man has more or less, not only in his own abilities, but in his own good fortune.

To excel in any profession, in which but few arrive at mediocrity, is the most decisive mark of what is called genius or superior talents. The public admiration which attends upon such distinguished abilities makes always a part of their reward; a greater or smaller in proportion as it is higher or lower in degree. It makes a considerable part of that reward in the profession of physic; a still greater perhaps in that of law; in poetry and philosophy it makes almost the whole.

There are some very agreeable and beautiful talents of which the possession commands a certain sort of admiration; but of which the exercise for the sake of gain is considered, whether from reason or prejudice, as a sort of public prostitution. The pecuniary recompense, therefore, of those who exercise them in this manner must be sufficient, not only to pay for the time, labour, and expense of acquiring the talents, but for the discredit which attends the employment of them as the means of subsistence. The exorbitant rewards of players, opera-singers, opera-dancers, etc., are founded upon those two principles; the rarity and beauty of the talents, and the discredit of employing them in this manner. It seems absurd at first sight that we should despise their persons and yet reward their talents with the most profuse liberality. While we do the one, however, we must of necessity do the other. Should the public opinion or prejudice ever alter with regard to such occupations, their pecuniary recompense would quickly diminish. More people would apply to them, and the competition would quickly reduce the price of labour. Such talents, though far from being common, are by no means so rare as is imagined. Many people possess them in great perfection, who disdain to make this use of them; and many more are capable of acquiring them if anything could be made honourably by them.

The overweening conceit which the greater part of men have of their abilities is an ancient evil remarked by the philosophers and moralists of all ages. Their absurd presumption in their own good fortune has been less taken notice of. It is, however, if possible, still more universal. There is no man living who, when in tolerable health and spirits, has not some share of it. The chance of gain is by every man more or less over-valued, and the chance of loss is by most men under-valued, and by scarce any man, who is in tolerable health and spirits, valued more than it is worth.

That the chance of gain is naturally over-valued, we may learn from the universal success of lotteries. The world neither ever saw, nor ever will see, a perfectly fair lottery; or one in which the whole gain compensated the whole loss; because the undertaker could make nothing by it. In the state lotteries the tickets are really not worth the price which is paid by the original subscribers, and yet commonly sell in the market for twenty, thirty, and sometimes forty per cent advance. The vain hope of gaining some of the great prizes is the sole cause of this demand. The soberest people scarce look upon it as a folly to pay a small sum for the chance of gaining ten or twenty thousand pounds; though they know that even that small sum is perhaps twenty or thirty per cent more than the chance is worth. In a lottery in which no prize exceeded twenty pounds, though in other respects it approached much nearer to a perfectly fair one than the common state lotteries, there would not be the same demand for tickets. In order to have a better chance for some of the great prizes, some people purchase several tickets, and others, small share in a still greater number. There is not, however, a more certain proposition in mathematics than that the more tickets you adventure upon, the more likely you are to be a loser. Adventure upon all the tickets in the lottery, and you lose for certain; and the greater the number of your tickets the nearer you approach to this certainty.

That the chance of loss is frequently under-valued, and scarce ever valued more than it is worth, we may learn from the very moderate profit of insurers. In order to make insurance, either from fire or sea-risk, a trade at all, the common premium must be sufficient to compensate the common losses, to pay the expense of management, and so afford such a profit as might have been drawn from an equal capital employed in any common trade. The person who pays no more than this evidently pays no more than the real value of the risk, or the lowest price at which he can reasonably expect to insure it. But though many people have made a little money by insurance, very few have made a great fortune; and from this consideration alone, it seems evident enough that the ordinary balance of profit and loss is not more advantageous in this than in other common trades by which so many people make fortunes. Moderate, however, as the premium of insurance commonly is, many people despise the risk too much to care to pay it. Taking the whole kingdom at an average, nineteen houses in twenty, or rather perhaps ninety-nine in a hundred, are not insured from fire. Sea risk is more alarming to the greater part of people, and the proportion of ships insured to those not insured is much greater. Many sail, however, at all seasons, and even in time of war, without any insurance. This may sometimes perhaps be done without any imprudence. When a great company, or even a great merchant, has twenty or thirty ships at sea, they may, as it were, insure one another. The premium saved upon them all may more than compensate such losses as they are likely to meet with in the common course of chances. The neglect of insurance upon shipping, however, in the same manner as upon houses, is, in most cases, the effect of no such nice calculation, but of mere thoughtless rashness and presumptuous contempt of the risk.

The contempt of risk and the presumptuous hope of success are in no period of life more active than at the age at which young people choose their professions. How little the fear of misfortune is then capable of balancing the hope of good luck appears still more evidently in the readiness of the common people to enlist as soldiers, or to go to sea, than in the eagerness of those of better fashion to enter into what are called the liberal professions.

What a common soldier may lose is obvious enough. Without regarding the danger, however, young volunteers never enlist so readily as at the beginning of a new war; and though they have scarce any chance of preferment, they figure to themselves, in their youthful fancies, a thousand occasions of acquiring honour and distinction which never occur. These romantic hopes make the whole price of their blood. Their pay is less than that of common labourers, and in actual service their fatigues are much greater.

The lottery of the sea is not altogether so disadvantageous as that of the army. The son of a creditable labourer or artificer may frequently go to sea with his father's consent; but if he enlists as a soldier, it is always without it. Other people see some chance of his making something by the one trade: nobody but himself sees any of his making anything by the other. The great admiral is less the object of public admiration than the great general, and the highest success in the sea service promises a less brilliant fortune and reputation than equal success in the land. The same difference runs through all the inferior degrees of preferment in both. By the rules of precedency a captain in the navy ranks with a colonel in the army; but he does not rank with him in the common estimation. As the great prizes in the lottery are less, the smaller ones must be more numerous. Common sailors, therefore, more frequently get some fortune and preferment than common soldiers; and the hope of those prizes is what principally recommends the trade. Though their skill and dexterity are much superior to that of almost any artificers, and though their whole life is one continual scene of hardship and danger, yet for all this dexterity and skill, for all those hardships and dangers, while they remain in the condition of common sailors, they receive scarce any other recompense but the pleasure of exercising the one and of surmounting the other. Their wages are not greater than those of common labourers at the port which regulates the rate of seamen's wages. As they are continually going from port to port, the monthly pay of those who sail from all the different ports of Great Britain is more nearly upon a level than that of any other workmen in those different places; and the rate of the port to and from which the greatest number sail, that is the port of London, regulates that of all the rest. At London the wages of the greater part of the different classes of workmen are about double those of the same classes at Edinburgh. But the sailors who sail from the port of London seldom earn above three or four shillings a month more than those who sail from the port of Leith, and the difference is frequently not so great. In time of peace, and in the merchant service, the London price is from a guinea to about seven-and-twenty shillings the calendar month. A common labourer in London, at the rate of nine or ten shillings a week, may earn in the calendar month from forty to five-

and-forty shillings. The sailor, indeed, over and above his pay, is supplied with provisions. Their value, however, may not perhaps always exceed the difference between his pay and that of the common labourer; and though it sometimes should, the excess will not be clear gain to the sailor, because he cannot share it with his wife and family, whom he must maintain out of his wages at home.

The dangers and hairbreadth escapes of a life of adventures, instead of disheartening young people, seem frequently to recommend a trade to them. A tender mother, among the inferior ranks of people, is often afraid to send her son to school at a seaport town, lest the sight of the ships and the conversation and adventures of the sailors should entice him to go to sea. The distant prospect of hazards, from which we can hope to extricate ourselves by courage and address, is not disagreeable to us, and does not raise the wages of labour in any employment. It is otherwise with those in which courage and address can be of no avail. In trades which are known to be very unwholesome, the wages of labour are always remarkably high. Unwholesomeness is a species of disagreeableness, and its effects upon the wages of labour are to be ranked under that general head.

In all the different employments of stock, the ordinary rate of profit varies more or less with the certainty or uncertainty of the returns. These are in general less uncertain in the inland than in the foreign trade, and in some branches of foreign trade than in others; in the trade to North America, for example, than in that to Jamaica. The ordinary rate of profit always rises more or less with the risk. It does not, however, seem to rise in proportion to it, or so as to compensate it completely. Bankruptcies are most frequent in the most hazardous trades. The most hazardous of all trades, that of a smuggler, though when the adventure succeeds it is likewise the most profitable, is the infallible road to bankruptcy. The presumptuous hope of success seems to act here as upon all other occasions, and to entice so many adventurers into those hazardous trades, that their competition reduces their profit below what is sufficient to compensate the risk. To compensate it completely, the common returns ought, over and above the ordinary profits of stock, not only to make up for all occasional losses, but to afford a surplus profit to the adventurers of the same nature with the profit of insurers. But if the common returns were sufficient for all this, bankruptcies would not be more frequent in these than in other trades.

Of the five circumstances, therefore, which vary the wages of labour, two only affect the profits of stock; the agreeableness or disagreeableness of the business, and the risk or security with which it is attended. In point of agreeableness or disagreeableness, there is little or no difference in the far greater part of the different employments of stock; but a great deal in those of labour; and the ordinary profit of stock, though it rises with the risk, does not always seem to rise in proportion to it. It should follow from all this, that, in the same society or neighbourhood, the average and ordinary rates of profit in the different employments of stock should be more nearly upon a level than the pecuniary wages of the different sorts of labour. They are so accordingly. The difference between the earnings of a common labourer and those of a well employed lawyer or physician, is evidently much greater than that between the ordinary profits in any two different branches of trade. The apparent difference, besides, in the profits of different trades, is generally a deception arising from our not always distinguishing what ought to be considered as wages, from what ought to be considered as profit.

Apothecaries' profit is become a bye-word, denoting something uncommonly extravagant. This great apparent profit, however, is frequently no more than the reasonable wages of labour. The skill of an apothecary is a much nicer and more delicate matter than that of any artificer whatever; and the trust which is reposed in him is of much greater importance. He is the physician of the poor in all cases, and of the rich when the distress or danger is not very great. His reward, therefore, ought to be suitable to his skill and his trust, and it arises generally from the price at which he sells his drugs. But the whole drugs which the best employed apothecary, in a large market town, will sell in a year, may not perhaps cost him above thirty or forty pounds. Though he should sell them, therefore, for three or four hundred, or at a thousand per cent profit, this may frequently be no more than the reasonable wages of his labour charged, in the only way in which he can charge them, upon the price of his drugs. The greater part of the apparent profit is real wages disguised in the garb of profit.

In a small seaport town, a little grocer will make forty or fifty per cent upon a stock of a single hundred pounds, while a considerable wholesale merchant in the same place will scarce make eight or ten per cent upon a stock of ten thousand. The trade of the grocer may be necessary for the conveniency of the inhabitants, and the narrowness of the market may not admit the employment of a larger capital in the business. The man, however, must not only live by his trade, but live by it suitably to the qualifications which it requires. Besides possessing a little capital, he must be able to read, write, and account, and must be a tolerable judge too of, perhaps, fifty or sixty different sorts of goods, their prices, qualities, and the markets where they are to be had cheapest. He must have all the knowledge, in short, that is necessary for a great merchant, which nothing hinders him from becoming but the want of sufficient capital. Thirty or forty pounds a year cannot be considered as too great a recompense for the labour of a person so accomplished. Deduct this from the seemingly great profits of his capital, and little more will remain, perhaps, than the ordinary profits of stock. The greater part of the apparent profit is, in this case too, real wages.

The difference between the apparent profit of the retail and that of the wholesale trade, is much less in the capital than in small towns and country villages. Where ten thousand pounds can be employed in the grocery trade, the wages of the grocer's labour make but a very trifling addition to the real profits of so great a stock. The apparent profits of the wealthy retailer, therefore, are there more nearly upon a level with those of the wholesale merchant. It is upon this account that goods sold by retail are generally as cheap and frequently much cheaper in the capital than in small towns and country villages. Grocery goods, for example, are generally much cheaper; bread and butcher's meat frequently as cheap. It costs no more to bring grocery goods to the great town than to the country village; but it costs a great deal more to bring corn and cattle, as the greater part of them must be brought from a much greater distance. The prime cost of grocery goods, therefore, being the same in both places, they are cheapest where the least profit is charged upon them.

The prime cost of bread and butcher's meat is greater in the great town than in the country village; and though the profit is less, therefore, they are not always cheaper there, but often equally cheap. In such articles as bread and butcher's meat, the same cause, which diminishes apparent profit, increases prime cost. The extent of the market, by giving employment to greater stocks, diminishes apparent profit; but by requiring supplies from a greater distance, it increases prime cost. This diminution of the one and increase of the other seem, in most cases, nearly to counter-balance one another, which is probably the reason that, though the prices of corn and cattle are commonly very different in different parts of the kingdom, those of bread and butcher's meat are generally very nearly the same through the greater part of it.

Though the profits of stock both in the wholesale and retail trade are generally less in the capital than in small towns and country villages, yet great fortunes are frequently acquired from small beginnings in the former, and scarce ever in the latter. In small towns and country villages, on account of the narrowness of the market, trade cannot always be extended as stock extends. In such places, therefore, though the rate of a particular person's profits may be very high, the sum or amount of them can never be very great, nor consequently that of his annual accumulation. In great towns, on the contrary, trade can be extended as stock increases, and the credit of a frugal and thriving man increases much faster than his stock. His trade is extended in proportion to the amount of both, and the sum or amount of his profits is in proportion to the extent of his trade, and his annual accumulation in proportion to the amount of his profits. It seldom happens, however, that great fortunes are made even in great towns by any one regular, established, and well-known branch of business, but in consequence of a long life of industry, frugality, and attention. Sudden fortunes, indeed, are sometimes made in such places by what is called the trade of speculation. The speculative merchant exercises no one regular, established, or well-known branch of business. He is a corn merchant this year, and a wine merchant the next, and a sugar, tobacco or tea merchant the year after. He enters into every trade when he foresees that it is likely to be more than commonly profitable, and he quits it when he foresees that its profits are likely to return to the level of other trades. His profits and losses, therefore, can bear no regular proportion to those of any one established and well-known branch of business. A bold adventurer may sometimes acquire a considerable fortune by two or three successful speculations; but is just as likely to lose one by two or three unsuccessful ones. This trade can be carried on nowhere but in great towns. It is only in places of the most extensive commerce and correspondence that the intelligence requisite for it can be had.

The five circumstances above mentioned, though they occasion considerable inequalities in the wages of labour and profits of stock, occasion none in the whole of the advantages and disadvantages, real or imaginary, of the different employments of either. The nature of those circumstances is such that they make up for a small pecuniary gain in some, and counterbalance a great one in others.

In order, however, that this equality may take place in the whole of their advantages or disadvantages, three things are requisite even where there is the most perfect freedom. First, the employments must be well known and long established in the neighbourhood; secondly, they must be in their ordinary, or what may be called their natural state; and, thirdly, they must be the sole or principal employments of whose who occupy them.

First, this equality can take place only in those employments which are well known, and have been long established in the neighbourhood.

Where all other circumstances are equal, wages are generally higher in new than in old trades. When a projector attempts to establish a new manufacture, he must at first entice his workmen from other employments by higher wages than they can either earn in their own trades, or than the nature of his work would otherwise require, and a considerable time must pass away before he can venture to reduce them to the common level. Manufactures for which the demand arises altogether from fashion and fancy are continually changing, and seldom last long enough to be considered as old established manufactures. Those, on the contrary, for which the demand arises chiefly from use or necessity, are less liable to change, and the same form or fabric may continue in demand for whole centuries together. The wages of labour, therefore, are likely to be higher in manufactures of the former than in those of the latter kind. Birmingham deals chiefly in manufactures of the former kind; Sheffield in those of the latter; and the wages of labour in those two different places are said to be suitable to this difference in the nature of their manufactures.

The establishment of any new manufacture, of any new branch of commerce, or of any new practice in agriculture, is always a speculation, from which the projector promises himself extraordinary profits. These profits sometimes are very great, and sometimes, more frequently, perhaps, they are quite otherwise; but in general they bear no regular proportion to those of other old trades in the neighbourhood. If the project succeeds, they are commonly at first very high. When the trade or practice becomes thoroughly established and well known, the competition reduces them to the level of other trades.

Secondly, this equality in the whole of the advantages and disadvantages of the different employments of labour and stock, can take place only in the ordinary, or what may be called the natural state of those employments.

The demand for almost every different species of labour is sometimes greater and sometimes less than usual. In the one case the advantages of the employment rise above, in the other they fall below the common level. The demand for country labour is greater at hay-time and harvest than during the greater part of the year; and wages rise with the demand. In time of war, when forty or fifty thousand sailors are forced from the merchant service into that of the king, the demand for sailors to merchant ships necessarily rises with their scarcity, and their wages upon such occasions rise from a guinea and seven-and-twenty shillings, to forty shillings and three pounds a month. In a decaying manufacture, on the contrary, many workmen, rather than quit their old trade, are contented with smaller wages than would otherwise be suitable to the nature of their employment.

The profits of stock vary with the price of the commodities in which it is employed. As the price of any commodity rises above the ordinary or average rate, the profits of at least some part of the stock that is employed in bringing it to market, rise above their proper level, and as it falls they sink below it. All commodities are more or less liable to variations of price, but some are much more so than others. In all commodities which are produced by human industry, the quantity of industry annually employed is necessarily regulated by the annual demand, in such a manner that the average annual produce may, as nearly as possible, be equal to the average annual consumption. In some employments, it has already been observed, the same quantity of industry will always produce the same, or very nearly the same quantity of commodities. In the linen or woollen manufactures, for example, the same number of hands will annually work up very nearly the same quantity of linen and woollen cloth. The variations in the market price of such commodities, therefore, can arise only from some accidental variations in the demand. A public mourning raises the price of black cloth. But as the demand for most sorts of plain linen and woollen cloth is pretty uniform, so is likewise the price. But there are other employments in which the same quantity of industry will not always produce the same quantity of commodities. The same quantity of industry, for example, will, in different years, produce very different quantities of corn, wine, hops, sugar, tobacco, etc. The price of such commodities, therefore, varies not only with the variations of demand, but with the much greater and more frequent variations of quantity, and is consequently extremely fluctuating. But the profit of some of the dealers must necessarily fluctuate with the price of the commodities. The operations of the speculative merchant are principally employed about such commodities. He endeavours to buy them up when he foresees that their price is likely to rise, and to sell them when it is likely to fall.

Thirdly, this equality in the whole of the advantages and disadvantages of the different employments of labour and stock can take place only in such as are the sole or principal employments of those who occupy them.

When a person derives his subsistence from one employment, which does not occupy the greater part of his time, in the intervals of his leisure he is often willing to work at another for less wages than would otherwise suit the nature of the employment.

There still subsists in many parts of Scotland a set of people called Cotters or Cottagers, though they were more frequent some years ago than they are now. They are a sort of out-servants of the landlords and farmers. The usual reward which they receive from their masters is a house, a small garden for pot-herbs, as much grass as will feed a cow, and, perhaps, an acre or two of bad arable land. When their master has occasion for their labour, he gives them, besides, two pecks of oatmeal a week, worth about sixteenpence sterling. During a great part of the year he has little or no occasion for their labour, and the cultivation of their own little possession is not sufficient to occupy the time which is left at their own disposal. When such occupiers were more numerous than they are at present, they are said to have been willing to give their spare time for a very small recompense to anybody, and to have wrought for less wages than other labourers. In ancient times they seem to have been common all over Europe. In countries ill cultivated and worse inhabited, the greater part of landlords and farmers could not otherwise provide themselves with the extraordinary number of hands which country labour requires at certain seasons. The daily or weekly recompense which such labourers occasionally received from their masters was evidently not the whole price of their labour. Their small tenement made a considerable part of it. This daily or weekly recompense, however, seems to have been considered as the whole of it, by many writers who have collected the prices of labour and provisions in ancient times, and who have taken pleasure in representing both as wonderfully low.

The produce of such labour comes frequently cheaper to market than would otherwise be suitable to its nature. Stockings in many parts of Scotland are knit much cheaper than they can anywhere be wrought upon the loom. They are the work of servants and labourers, who derive the principal part of their subsistence from some other employment. More than a thousand pair of Shetland stockings are annually imported into Leith, of which the price is from fivepence to sevenpence a pair. At Lerwick, the small capital of the Shetland Islands, tenpence a day, I have been assured, is a common price of common labour. In the same islands they knit worsted stockings to the value of a guinea a pair and upwards.

The spinning of linen yarn is carried on in Scotland nearly in the same way as the knitting of stockings, by servants who are chiefly hired for other purposes. They earn but a very scanty subsistence, who endeavour to get their whole livelihood by either of those trades. In most parts of Scotland she is a good spinner who can earn twentypence a week.

In opulent countries the market is generally so extensive that any one trade is sufficient to employ the whole labour and stock of those who occupy it. Instances of people's living by one employment, and at the same time deriving some little advantage from another, occur chiefly in poor countries. The following instance, however, of something of the same kind is to be found in the capital of a very rich one. There is no city in Europe, I believe, in which house-rent is dearer than in London, and yet I know no capital in which a furnished apartment can be hired so cheap. Lodging is not only much cheaper in London than in Paris; it is much cheaper than in Edinburgh of the same degree of goodness; and what may seem extraordinary, the dearness of house-rent is the cause of the cheapness of lodging. The dearness of house-rent in London arises, not only from those causes which render it dear in all great capitals, the dearness of labour, the dearness of all the materials of building, which must generally be brought from a great distance, and above all the dearness of ground-rent, every landlord acting the part of a monopolist, and frequently exacting a higher rent for a single acre of bad land in a town than can be had for a hundred of the best in the country; but it arises in part from the peculiar manners and customs of the people, which oblige every master of a family to hire a whole house from top to bottom. A dwelling-house in England means everything that is contained under the same roof. In France, Scotland, and many other parts of Europe, it frequently means no more than a single storey. A tradesman in London is obliged to hire a whole house in that part of the town where his customers live. His shop is upon the ground-floor, and he and his family sleep in the garret; and he endeavours to pay a part of his house-rent by letting the two middle stories to lodgers. He expects to maintain his family by his trade, and not by his lodgers. Whereas, at Paris and

Edinburgh, the people who let lodgings have commonly no other means of subsistence; and the price of the lodging must pay, not only the rent of the house, but the whole expense of the family.

PART II

Inequalities occasioned by the Policy of Europe

Such are the inequalities in the whole of the advantages and disadvantages of the different employments of labour and stock, which the defect of any of the three requisites above mentioned must occasion, even where there is the most perfect liberty. But the policy of Europe, by not leaving things at perfect liberty, occasions other inequalities of much greater importance.

It does this chiefly in the three following ways. First, by restraining the competition in some employments to a smaller number than would otherwise be disposed to enter into them; secondly, by increasing it in others beyond what it naturally would be; and, thirdly, by obstructing the free circulation of labour and stock, both from employment to employment and from place to place.

First, the policy of Europe occasions a very important inequality in the whole of the advantages and disadvantages of the different employments of labour and stock, by restraining the competition in some employments to a smaller number than might otherwise be disposed to enter into them.

The exclusive privileges of corporations are the principal means it makes use of for this purpose.

The exclusive privilege of an incorporated trade necessarily restrains the competition, in the town where it is established, to those who are free of the trade. To have served an apprenticeship in the town, under a master properly qualified, is commonly the necessary requisite for obtaining this freedom. The bye-laws of the corporation regulate sometimes the number of apprentices which any master is allowed to have, and almost always the number of years which each apprentice is obliged to serve. The intention of both regulations is to restrain the competition to a much smaller number than might otherwise be disposed to enter into the trade. The limitation of the number of apprentices restrains it directly. A long term of apprenticeship restrains it more indirectly, but as effectually, by increasing the expense of education.

In Sheffield no master cutler can have more than one apprentice at a time, by a bye-law of the corporation. In Norfolk and Norwich no master weaver can have more than two apprentices, under pain of forfeiting five pounds a month to the king. No master hatter can have more than two apprentices anywhere in England, or in the English plantations, under pain of forfeiting five pounds a month, half to the king and half to him who shall sue in any court of record. Both these regulations, though they have been confirmed by a public law of the kingdom, are evidently dictated by the same corporation spirit which enacted the bye-law of Sheffield. The silk weavers in London had scarce been incorporated a year when they enacted a bye-law restraining any master from having more than two apprentices at a time. It required a particular act of parliament to rescind this bye-law.

Seven years seem anciently to have been, all over Europe, the usual term established for the duration of apprenticeships in the greater part of incorporated trades. All such incorporations were anciently called universities, which indeed is the proper Latin name for any incorporation whatever. The university of smiths, the university of tailors, etc., are expressions which we commonly meet with in the old charters of ancient towns. When those particular incorporations which are now peculiarly called universities were first established, the term of years which it was necessary to study, in order to obtain the degree of master of arts, appears evidently to have been copied from the terms of apprenticeship in common trades, of which the incorporations were much more ancient. As to have wrought seven years under a master properly qualified was necessary in order to entitle any person to become a master, and to have himself apprenticed in a common trade; so to have studied seven years under a master properly qualified was necessary to entitle him to become a master, teacher, or doctor (words anciently synonymous) in the liberal arts, and to have scholars or apprentices (words likewise originally synonymous) to study under him.

By the 5th of Elizabeth, commonly called the Statute of

Apprenticeship, it was enacted, that no person should for the future exercise any trade, craft, or mystery at that time exercised in England, unless he had previously served to it an apprenticeship of seven years at least; and what before had been the byelaw of many particular corporations became in England the general and public law of all trades carried on in market towns. For though the words of the statute are very general, and seem plainly to include the whole kingdom, by interpretation its operation has been limited to market towns, it having been held that in country villages a person may exercise several different trades, though he has not served a seven years' apprenticeship to each, they being necessary for the conveniency of the inhabitants, and the number of people frequently not being sufficient to supply each with a particular set of hands.

By a strict interpretation of the words, too, the operation of this statute has been limited to those trades which were established in England before the 5th of Elizabeth, and has never been extended to such as have been introduced since that time. This limitation has given occasion to several distinctions which, considered as rules of police, appear as foolish as can well be imagined. It has been adjudged, for example, that a coachmaker can neither himself make nor employ journeymen to make his coach-wheels, but must buy them of a master wheelwright; this latter trade having been exercised in England before the 5th of Elizabeth. But a wheelwright, though he has never served an apprenticeship to a coachmaker, may either himself make or employ journeymen to make coaches; the trade of a coachmaker not being within the statute, because not exercised in England at the time when it was made. The manufactures of Manchester, Birmingham, and Wolverhampton, are many of them, upon this account, not within the statute, not having been exercised in England before the 5th of Elizabeth.

In France, the duration of apprenticeships is different in different towns and in different trades. In Paris, five years is the term required in a great number; but before any person can be qualified to exercise the trade as a master, he must, in many of them, serve five years more as a journeyman. During this latter term he is called the companion of his master, and the term itself is called his companionship.

In Scotland there is no general law which regulates universally the duration of apprenticeships. The term is different in different corporations. Where it is long, a part of it may generally be redeemed by paying a small fine. In most towns, too, a very small fine is sufficient to purchase the freedom of any corporation. The weavers of linen and hempen cloth, the principal manufactures of the country, as well as all other artificers subservient to them, wheel-makers, reel-makers, etc., may exercise their trades in any town corporate without paying any fine. In all towns corporate all persons are free to sell butcher's meat upon any lawful day of the week. Three years is in Scotland a common term of apprenticeship, even in some very nice trades; and in general I know of no country in Europe in which corporation laws are so little oppressive.

The property which every man has in his own labour, as it is the original foundation of all other property, so it is the most sacred and inviolable. The patrimony of a poor man lies in the strength and dexterity of his hands; and to hinder him from employing this strength and dexterity in what manner he thinks proper without injury to his neighbour is a plain violation of this most sacred property. It is a manifest encroachment upon the just liberty both of the workman and of those who might be disposed to employ him. As it hinders the one from working at what he thinks proper, so it hinders the others from employing whom they think proper. To judge whether he is fit to be employed may surely be trusted to the discretion of the employers whose interest it so much concerns. The affected anxiety of the law-giver lest they should employ an improper person is evidently as impertinent as it is oppressive.

The institution of long apprenticeships can give no security that insufficient workmanship shall not frequently be exposed to public sale. When this is done it is generally the effect of fraud, and not of inability; and the longest apprenticeship can give no security against fraud. Quite different regulations are necessary to prevent this abuse. The sterling mark upon plate, and the stamps upon linen and woollen cloth, give the purchaser much greater security than any statute of apprenticeship. He generally looks at these, but never thinks it worth while to inquire whether the workman had served a seven years' apprenticeship.

The institution of long apprenticeships has no tendency to form young people to industry. A journeyman who works by the piece is likely to be industrious, because he derives a benefit from every exertion of his industry. An apprentice is likely to be idle, and almost always is so, because he has no immediate interest to be otherwise. In the inferior employments, the sweets of labour consist altogether in the recompense of labour. They who are soonest in a condition to enjoy the sweets of it are likely soonest to conceive a relish for it, and to acquire the early habit of industry. A young man naturally conceives an aversion to labour when for a long time he receives no benefit from it. The boys who are put out apprentices from public charities are generally bound for more than the usual number of years, and they generally turn out very idle and worthless.

Apprenticeships were altogether unknown to the ancients. The reciprocal duties of master and apprentice make a considerable article in every modern code. The Roman law is perfectly silent with regard to them. I know no Greek or Latin word (I might venture, I believe, to assert that there is none) which expresses the idea we now annex to the word Apprentice, a servant bound to work at a particular trade for the benefit of a master, during a term of years, upon condition that the master shall teach him that trade.

Long apprenticeships are altogether unnecessary. The arts, which are much superior to common trades, such as those of making clocks and watches, contain no such mystery as to require a long course of instruction. The first invention of such beautiful machines, indeed, and even that of some of the instruments employed in making them, must, no doubt, have been the work of deep thought and long time, and may justly be considered as among the happiest efforts of human ingenuity. But when both have been fairly invented and are well understood, to explain to any young man, in the completest manner, how to apply the instruments and how to construct the machines, cannot well require more than the lessons of a few weeks; perhaps those of a few days might be sufficient. In the common mechanic trades, those of a few days might certainly be sufficient. The dexterity of hand, indeed, even in common trades, cannot be acquired without much practice and experi-

ence. But a young man would practice with much more diligence and attention, if from the beginning he wrought as a
journeyman, being paid in proportion to the little work which
he could execute, and paying in his turn for the materials which
he might sometimes spoil through awkwardness and inexperi-
ence. His education would generally in this way be more effectual, and always less tedious and expensive. The master, indeed,
would be a loser. He would lose all the wages of the apprentice,
which he now saves, for seven years together. In the end,
perhaps, the apprentice himself would be a loser. In a trade so
easily learnt he would have more competitors, and his wages,
when he came to be a complete workman, would be much less
than at present. The same increase in competition would reduce
the profits of the masters as well as the wages of the workmen.
The trades, the crafts, the mysteries, would all be losers. But the
public would be a gainer, the work of all artificers coming in
this way much cheaper to market.

It is to prevent this reduction of price, and consequently of
wages and profit, by restraining that free competition which
would most certainly occasion it, that all corporations, and the
greater part of corporation laws, have been established. In order
to erect a corporation, no other authority in ancient times was
requisite in many parts of Europe, but that of the town corporate in which it was established. In England, indeed, a
charter from the king was likewise necessary. But this preroga-
tive of the crown seems to have been reserved rather for extort-
ing money from the subject than for the defence of the common
liberty against such oppressive monopolies. Upon paying a fine
to the king, the charter seems generally to have been readily
granted; and when any particular class of artificers or traders
thought proper to act as a corporation without a charter, such
adulterine guilds, as they were called, were not always dis-
franchised upon that account, but obliged to fine annually to
the king for permission to exercise their usurped privileges.[1]
The immediate inspection of all corporations, and of the bye-
laws which they might think proper to enact for their own
government, belonged to the town corporate in which they were
established; and whatever discipline was exercised over them

1. See *Madox Firma Burgi*, p. 26, etc.

proceeded commonly, not from the king, but from that greater incorporation of which those subordinate ones were only parts or members.

The government of towns corporate was altogether in the hands of traders and artificers, and it was the manifest interest of every particular class of them to prevent the market from being overstocked, as they commonly express it, with their own particular species of industry, which is in reality to keep it always under-stocked. Each class was eager to establish regulations proper for this purpose, and, provided it was allowed to do so, was willing to consent that every other class should do the same. In consequence of such regulations, indeed, each class was obliged to buy the goods they had occasion for from every other within the town, somewhat dearer than they otherwise might have done. But in recompense, they were enabled to sell their own just as much dearer; so that so far it was as broad as long, as they say; and in the dealings of the different classes within the town with one another, none of them were losers by these regulations. But in their dealings with the country they were all great gainers; and in these latter dealings consists the whole trade which supports and enriches every town.

Every town draws its whole subsistence, and all the materials of its industry, from the country. It pays for these chiefly in two ways: first, by sending back to the country a part of those materials wrought up and manufactured; in which case their price is augmented by the wages of the workmen, and the profits of their masters or immediate employers; secondly, by sending to it a part both of the rude and manufactured produce, either of other countries, or of distant parts of the same country, imported into the town; in which case, too, the original price of those goods is augmented by the wages of the carriers or sailors, and by the profits of the merchants who employ them. In what is gained upon the first of those two branches of commerce consists the advantage which the town makes by its manufactures; in what is gained upon the second, the advantage of its inland and foreign trade. The wages of the workmen, and the profits of their different employers, make up the whole of what is gained upon both. Whatever regulations, therefore, tend to increase those wages and profits beyond what they otherwise would be, tend to enable the town to purchase, with a smaller quantity of its labour, the produce of a greater quantity of the labour of the country. They give the traders and artificers in the town an advantage over the landlords, farmers, and labourers in the country, and break down that natural equality which would otherwise take place in the commerce which is carried on between them. The whole annual produce of the labour of the society is annually divided between those two different sets of people. By means of those regulations a greater share of it is given to the inhabitants of the town than would otherwise fall to them; and a less to those of the country.

The price which the town really pays for the provisions and materials annually imported into it is the quantity of manufactures and other goods annually exported from it. The dearer the latter are sold, the cheaper the former are bought. The industry of the town becomes more, and that of the country less advantageous.

That the industry which is carried on in towns is, everywhere in Europe, more advantageous than that which is carried on in the country, without entering into any very nice computations, we may satisfy ourselves by one very simple and obvious observation. In every country of Europe we find, at least, a hundred people who have acquired great fortunes from small beginnings by trade and manufactures, the industry which properly belongs to towns, for one who has done so by that which properly belongs to the country, the raising of rude produce by the improvement and cultivation of land. Industry, therefore, must be better rewarded, the wages of labour and the profits of stock must evidently be greater in the one situation than in the other. But stock and labour naturally seek the most advantageous employment. They naturally, therefore, resort as much as they can to the town, and desert the country.

The inhabitants of a town, being collected into one place, can easily combine together. The most insignificant trades carried on in towns have accordingly, in some place or other, been incorporated, and even where they have never been incorporated, yet the corporation spirit, the jealousy of strangers, the aversion to take apprentices, or to communicate the secret of their trade, generally prevail in them, and often teach them, by

voluntary associations and agreements, to prevent that free
competition which they cannot prohibit by bye-laws. The trades
which employ but a small number of hands run most easily into
such combinations. Half a dozen wool-combers, perhaps, are
necessary to keep a thousand spinners and weavers at work. By
combining not to take apprentices they can not only engross the
employment, but reduce the whole manufacture into a sort of
slavery to themselves, and raise the price of their labour much
above what is due to the nature of their work.

The inhabitants of the country, dispersed in distant places,
cannot easily combine together. They have not only never been
incorporated, but the corporation spirit never has prevailed
among them. No apprenticeship has ever been thought necessary to qualify for husbandry, the great trade of the country.
After what are called the fine arts, and the liberal professions,
however, there is perhaps no trade which requires so great a
variety of knowledge and experience. The innumerable volumes
which have been written upon it in all languages may satisfy us
that, among the wisest and most learned nations, it has never
been regarded as a matter very easily understood. And from all
those volumes we shall in vain attempt to collect that knowledge of its various and complicated operations, which is commonly possessed even by the common farmer; how contemptu-
ously soever the very contemptible authors of some of them may
sometimes affect to speak of them. There is scarce any common
mechanic trade, on the contrary, of which all the operations
may not be as completely and distinctly explained in a pamphlet
of a very few pages, as it is possible for words illustrated by
figures to explain them. In the history of the arts, now publish-
ing by the French academy of sciences, several of them are
actually explained in this manner. The direction of operations,
besides, which must be varied with every change of the weather,
as well as with many other accidents, requires much more judgement and discretion than that of those which are always the
same or very nearly the same.

Not only the art of the farmer, the general direction of the
operations of husbandry, but many inferior branches of country
labour require much more skill and experience than the greater
part of mechanic trades. The man who works upon brass and

iron, works with instruments and upon materials of which the
temper is always the same, or very nearly the same. But the man
who ploughs the ground with a team of horses or oxen, works
with instruments of which the health, strength, and temper, are
very different upon different occasions. The condition of the
materials which he works upon, too, is as variable as that of the
instruments which he works with, and both require to be
managed with much judgement and discretion. The common
ploughman, though generally regarded as the pattern of
stupidity and ignorance, is seldom defective in this judgement
and discretion. He is less accustomed, indeed, to social intercourse than the mechanic who lives in a town. His voice and
language are more uncouth and more difficult to be understood
by those who are not used to them. His understanding, however, being accustomed to consider a greater variety of objects,
is generally much superior to that of the other, whose whole
attention from morning till night is commonly occupied in performing one or two very simple operations. How much the lower
ranks of people in the country are really superior to those of the
town is well known to every man whom either business or
curiosity has led to converse much with both. In China and
Indostan accordingly both the rank and the wages of country
labourers are said to be superior to those of the greater part of
artificers and manufacturers. They would probably be so everywhere, if corporation laws and the corporation spirit did not
prevent it.

The superiority which the industry of the towns has everywhere in Europe over that of the country is not altogether
owing to corporations and corporation laws. It is supported by
many other regulations. The high duties upon foreign manufactures and upon all goods imported by alien merchants, all
tend to the same purpose. Corporation laws enable the inhabitants of towns to raise their prices, without fearing to be under-
sold by the free competition of their own countrymen. Those
other regulations secure them equally against that of foreigners.
The enhancement of price occasioned by both is everywhere
finally paid by the landlords, farmers, and labourers of the
country, who have seldom opposed the establishment of such
monopolies. They have commonly neither inclination nor fitness

to enter into combinations; and the clamour and sophistry of merchants and manufacturers easily persuade them that the private interest of a part, and of a subordinate part of the society, is the general interest of the whole.

In Great Britain the superiority of the industry of the towns over that of the country seems to have been greater formerly than in the present times. The wages of country labour approach nearer to those of manufacturing labour, and the profits of stock employed in agriculture to those of trading and manufacturing stock, than they are said to have done in the last century, or in the beginning of the present. This change may be regarded as the necessary, though very late consequence of the extraordinary encouragement given to the industry of the towns. The stock accumulated in them comes in time to be so great that it can no longer be employed with the ancient profit in that species of industry which is peculiar to them. That industry has its limits like every other; and the increase of stock, by increasing the competition, necessarily reduces the profit. The lowering of profit in the town forces out stock to the country, where, by creating a new demand for country labour, it necessarily raises its wages. It then spreads itself, if I may say so, over the face of the land, and by being employed in agriculture is in part restored to the country, at the expense of which, in a great measure, it had originally been accumulated in the town. That everywhere in Europe the greatest improvements of the country have been owing to such overflowings of the stock originally accumulated in the towns, I shall endeavour to show hereafter; and at the same time to demonstrate that, though some countries have by this course attained to a considerable degree of opulence, it is in itself necessarily slow, uncertain, liable to be disturbed and interrupted by innumerable accidents, and in every respect contrary to the order of nature and of reason. The interests, prejudices, laws and customs, which have given occasion to it, I shall endeavour to explain as fully and distinctly as I can in the third and fourth books of this inquiry.

People of the same trade seldom meet together, even for merriment and diversion, but the conversation ends in a conspiracy against the public, or in some contrivance to raise prices.

It is impossible indeed to prevent such meetings, by any law which either could be executed, or would be consistent with liberty and justice. But though the law cannot hinder people of the same trade from sometimes assembling together, it ought to do nothing to facilitate such assemblies, much less to render them necessary.

A regulation which obliges all those of the same trade in a particular town to enter their names and places of abode in a public register, facilitates such assemblies. It connects individuals who might never otherwise be known to one another, and gives every man of the trade a direction where to find every other man of it.

A regulation which enables those of the same trade to tax themselves in order to provide for their poor, their sick, their widows and orphans, by giving them a common interest to manage, renders such assemblies necessary.

An incorporation not only renders them necessary, but makes the act of the majority binding upon the whole. In a free trade an effectual combination cannot be established but by the unanimous consent of every single trader, and it cannot last longer than every single trader continues of the same mind. The majority of a corporation can enact a bye-law with proper penalties, which will limit the competition more effectually and more durably than any voluntary combination whatever.

The pretence that corporations are necessary for the better government of the trade is without any foundation. The real and effectual discipline which is exercised over a workman is not that of his corporation, but that of his customers. It is the fear of losing their employment which restrains his frauds and corrects his negligence. An exclusive corporation necessarily weakens the force of this discipline. A particular set of workmen must then be employed, let them behave well or ill. It is upon this account that in many large incorporated towns no tolerable workmen are to be found, even in some of the most necessary trades. If you would have your work tolerably executed, it must be done in the suburbs, where the workmen, having no exclusive privilege, have nothing but their character to depend upon, and you must then smuggle it into the town as well as you can.

It is in this manner that the policy of Europe, by restraining the competition in some employments to a smaller number than would otherwise be disposed to enter into them, occasions a very important inequality in the whole of the advantages and disadvantages of the different employments of labour and stock.

Secondly, the policy of Europe, by increasing the competition in some employments beyond what it naturally would be, occasions another inequality of an opposite kind in the whole of the advantages and disadvantages of the different employments of labour and stock.

It has been considered as of so much importance that a proper number of young people should be educated for certain professions, that sometimes the public and sometimes the piety of private founders have established many pensions, scholarships, exhibitions, bursaries, etc., for this purpose, which draw many more people into those trades than could otherwise pretend to follow them. In all Christian countries, I believe, the education of the greater part of churchmen is paid for in this manner. Very few of them are educated altogether at their own expense. The long, tedious, and expensive education, therefore, of those who are, will not always procure them a suitable reward, the church being crowded with people who, in order to get employment, are willing to accept of a much smaller recompense than what such an education would otherwise have entitled them to; and in this manner the competition of the poor takes away the reward of the rich. It would be indecent, no doubt, to compare either a curate or a chaplain with a journeyman in any common trade. The pay of a curate or chaplain, however, may very properly be considered as of the same nature with the wages of a journeyman. They are, all three, paid for their work according to the contract which they may happen to make with their respective superiors. Till after the middle of the fourteenth century, five merks, containing about as much silver as ten pounds of our present money, was in England the usual pay of a curate or a stipendiary parish priest, as we find it regulated by the decrees of several different national councils. At the same period fourpence a day, containing the same quantity of silver as a shilling of our present money, was declared to be the pay of a master mason, and threepence a day, equal to ninepence of our present money, that of a journeyman mason.[1] The wages of both these labourers, therefore, supposing them to have been constantly employed, were much superior to those of the curate. The wages of the master mason, supposing him to have been without employment one third of the year, would have fully equalled them. By the 12th of Queen Anne, c. 12, it is declared, 'That whereas for want of sufficient maintenance and encouragement to curates, the cures have in several places been meanly supplied, the bishop is, therefore, empowered to appoint by writing under his hand and seal a sufficient certain stipend or allowance, not exceeding fifty and not less then twenty pounds a year.' Forty pounds a year is reckoned at present very good pay for a curate, and notwithstanding this act of parliament there are many curacies under twenty pounds a year. There are journeymen shoemakers in London who earn forty pounds a year, and there is scarce an industrious workman of any kind in that metropolis who does not earn more than twenty. This last sum indeed does not exceed what is frequently earned by common labourers in many country parishes. Whenever the law has attempted to regulate the wages of workmen, it has always been rather to lower them than to raise them. But the law has upon many occasions attempted to raise the wages of curates, and for the dignity of the church, to oblige the rectors of parishes to give them more than the wretched maintenance which they themselves might be willing to accept of. And in both cases the law seems to have been equally ineffectual, and has never either been able to raise the wages of curates, or to sink those of labourers to the degree that was intended; because it has never been able to hinder either the one from being willing to accept of less than the legal allowance, on account of the indigence of their situation and the multitude of their competitors; or the other from receiving more, on account of the contrary competition of those who expected to derive either profit or pleasure from employing them.

The great benefices and other ecclesiastical dignities support the honour of the church, notwithstanding the mean circumstances of some of its inferior members. The respect paid to the profession, too, makes some compensation even to them for the

1. See the Statute of Labourers, 25 Ed. III.

meanness of their pecuniary recompense. In England, and in all Roman Catholic countries, the lottery of the church is in reality much more advantageous than is necessary. The example of the churches of Scotland, of Geneva, and of several other protestant churches, may satisfy us that in so creditable a profession, in which education is so easily procured, the hopes of much more moderate benefices will draw a sufficient number of learned, decent, and respectable men into holy orders.

In professions in which there are no benefices, such as law and physic, if an equal proportion of people were educated at the public expense, the competition would soon be so great as to sink very much their pecuniary reward. It might then not be worth any man's while to educate his son to either of those professions at his own expense. They would be entirely abandoned to such as had been educated by those public charities, whose numbers and necessities would oblige them in general to content themselves with a very miserable recompense, to the entire degradation of the now respectable professions of law and physic.

That unprosperous race of men commonly called men of letters are pretty much in the situation which lawyers and physicians probably would be in upon the foregoing supposition. In every part of Europe the greater part of them have been educated for the church, but have been hindered by different reasons from entering into holy orders. They have generally, therefore, been educated at the public expense, and their numbers are everywhere so great as commonly to reduce the price of their labour to a very paltry recompense.

Before the invention of the art of printing, the only employment by which a man of letters could make anything by his talents was that of a public or private teacher, or by communicating to other people the curious and useful knowledge which he had acquired himself: and this is still surely a more honourable, a more useful, and in general even a more profitable employment than that other of writing for a bookseller, to which the art of printing has given occasion. The time and study, the genius, knowledge, and application requisite to qualify an eminent teacher of the sciences, are at least equal to what is necessary for the greatest practitioners in law and physic. But the usual reward of the eminent teacher bears no proportion to that of the lawyer or physician; because the trade of the one is crowded with indigent people who have been brought up to it at the public expense; whereas those of the other two are encumbered with very few who have not been educated at their own. The usual recompense, however, of public and private teachers, small as it may appear, would undoubtedly be less than it is, if the competition of those yet more indigent men of letters who write for bread was not taken out of the market. Before the invention of the art of printing, a scholar and a beggar seem to have been terms very nearly synonymous. The different governors of the universities before that time appear to have often granted licences to their scholars to beg.

In ancient times, before any charities of this kind had been established for the education of indigent people to the learned professions, the rewards of eminent teachers appear to have been much more considerable. Isocrates, in what is called his discourse against the sophists, reproaches the teachers of his own times with inconsistency. 'They make the most magnificent promises to their scholars, says he, and undertake to teach them to be wise, to be happy, and to be just, and in return for so important a service they stipulate the paltry reward of four or five minae. They who teach wisdom, continues he, ought certainly to be wise themselves; but if any man were to sell such a bargain for such a price, he would be convicted of the most evident folly.' He certainly does not mean here to exaggerate the reward, and we may be assured that it was not less than he represents it. Four minae were equal to thirteen pounds six shillings and eightpence: five minae to sixteen pounds thirteen shillings and fourpence. Something not less than the largest of those two sums, therefore, must at that time have been usually paid to the most eminent teachers at Athens. Isocrates himself demanded ten minae, or thirty-three pounds six shillings and eightpence, from each scholar. When he taught at Athens, he is said to have had an hundred scholars. I understand this to be the number whom he taught at one time, or who attended what he would call one course of lectures, a number which will not appear extraordinary from so great a city to so famous a teacher, who taught, too, what was at that time the most fashionable of all

sciences, rhetoric. He must have made, therefore, by each course
of lectures, a thousand minae, or £3333 6s. 8d. A thousand
minae, accordingly, is said by Plutarch in another place, to
have been his Didactron, or usual price of teaching. Many other
eminent teachers in those times appear to have acquired great
fortunes. Gorgias made a present to the temple of Delphi of his
own statue in solid gold. We must not, I presume, suppose that
it was as large as the life. His way of living, as well as that of
Hippias and Protagoras, two other eminent teachers of those
times, is represented by Plato as splendid even to ostentation.
Plato himself is said to have lived with a good deal of magnificence. Aristotle, after having been tutor to Alexander, and
most munificently rewarded, as it is universally agreed, both by
him and his father Philip, thought it worth while, notwithstanding, to return to Athens, in order to resume the teaching
of his school. Teachers of the sciences were probably in those
times less common than they came to be in an age or two afterwards, when the competition had probably somewhat reduced
both the price of their labour and the admiration for their
persons. The most eminent of them, however, appear always to
have enjoyed a degree of consideration much superior to any of
the like profession in the present times. The Athenians sent
Carneades the academic, and Diogenes the stoic, upon a solemn
embassy to Rome; and though their city had then declined from
its former grandeur, it was still an independent and considerable republic. Carneades, too, was a Babylonian by birth, and as
there never was a people more jealous of admitting foreigners to
public offices than the Athenians, their consideration for him
must have been very great.

This inequality is upon the whole, perhaps, rather advantageous than hurtful to the public. It may somewhat degrade the
profession of a public teacher; but the cheapness of literary
education is surely an advantage which greatly overbalances this
trifling inconvenience. The public, too, might derive still greater
benefit from it, if the constitution of those schools and colleges,
in which education is carried on, was more reasonable than it is
at present through the greater part of Europe.

Thirdly, the policy of Europe, by obstructing the free circulation of labour and stock both from employment to employment,

and from place to place, occasions in some cases a very inconvenient inequality in the whole of the advantages and disadvantages of their different employments.

The statute of apprenticeship obstructs the free circulation of labour from one employment to another, even in the same place. The exclusive privileges of corporations obstruct it from one place to another, even in the same employment.

It frequently happens that while high wages are given to the workmen in one manufacture, those in another are obliged to content themselves with bare subsistence. The one is in an advancing state, and has, therefore, a continual demand for new hands : the other is in a declining state, and the superabundance of hands is continually increasing. Those two manufactures may sometimes be in the same town, and sometimes in the same neighbourhood, without being able to lend the least assistance to one another. The statute of apprenticeship may oppose it in the one case, and both that and an exclusive corporation in the other. In many different manufactures, however, the operations are so much alike, that the workmen could easily change trades with one another, if those absurd laws did not hinder them. The arts of weaving plain linen and plain silk, for example, are almost entirely the same. That of weaving plain woollen is somewhat different; but the difference is so insignificant that either a linen or a silk weaver might become a tolerable workman in a very few days. If any of those three capital manufactures, therefore, were decaying, the workmen might find a resource in one of the other two which was in a more prosperous condition; and their wages would neither rise too high in the thriving, nor sink too low in the decaying manufacture. The linen manufacture indeed is, in England, by a particular statute, open to everybody; but as it is not much cultivated through the greater part of the country, it can afford no general resource to the workmen of other decaying manufactures, who, wherever the statute of apprenticeship takes place, have no other choice but either to come upon the parish, or to work as common labourers, for which, by their habits, they are much worse qualified than for any sort of manufacture that bears any resemblance to their own. They generally, therefore, choose to come upon the parish.

Whatever obstructs the free circulation of labour from one employment to another obstructs that of stock likewise; the quantity of stock which can be employed in any branch of business depending very much upon that of the labour which can be employed in it. Corporation laws, however, give less obstruction to the free circulation of stock from one place to another than to that of labour. It is everywhere much easier for a wealthy merchant to obtain the privilege of trading in a town corporate, than for a poor artificer to obtain that of working in it.

The obstruction which corporation laws give to the free circulation of labour is common, I believe, to every part of Europe. That which is given to it by the poor laws is, so far as I know, peculiar to England. It consists in the difficulty which a poor man finds in obtaining a settlement, or even in being allowed to exercise his industry in any parish but that to which he belongs. It is the labour of artificers and manufacturers only of which the free circulation is obstructed by corporation laws. The difficulty of obtaining settlements obstructs even that of common labour. It may be worth while to give some account of the rise, progress, and present state of this disorder, the greatest perhaps of any in the police of England.

When by the destruction of monasteries the poor had been deprived of the charity of those religious houses, after some other ineffectual attempts for their relief, it was enacted by the 43rd of Elizabeth, c. 2, that every parish should be bound to provide for its own poor; and that overseers of the poor should be annually appointed, who, with the churchwardens, should raise by a parish rate competent sums for this purpose.

By this statute the necessity of providing for their own poor was indispensably imposed upon every parish. Who were to be considered as the poor of each parish became, therefore, a question of some importance. This question, after some variation, was at last determined by the 13th and 14th of Charles II when it was enacted, that forty days' undisturbed residence should gain any person a settlement in any parish; but that within that time it should be lawful for two justices of the peace, upon complaint made by the churchwardens or overseers of the poor, to remove any new inhabitant to the parish where he was last legally settled; unless he either rented a tenement of ten pounds a year, or could give such security for the discharge of the parish where he was then living, as those justices should judge sufficient.

Some frauds, it is said, were committed in consequence of this statute; parish officers sometimes bribing their own poor to go clandestinely to another parish, and by keeping themselves concealed for forty days to gain a settlement there, to the discharge of that to which they properly belonged. It was enacted, therefore, by the 1st of James II that the forty days' undisturbed residence of any person necessary to gain a settlement should be accounted only from the time of his delivering notice in writing, of the place of his abode and the number of his family, to one of the churchwardens or overseers of the parish where he came to dwell.

But parish officers, it seems, were not always more honest with regard to their own, than they had been with regard to other parishes, and sometimes connived at such intrusions, receiving the notice, and taking no proper steps in consequence of it. As every person in a parish, therefore, was supposed to have an interest to prevent as much as possible their being burdened by such intruders, it was further enacted by the 3rd of William III that the forty days' residence should be accounted only from the publication of such notice in writing on Sunday in the church, immediately after divine service.

'After all,' says Doctor Burn, 'this kind of settlement, by continuing forty days after publication of notice in writing, is very seldom obtained; and the design of the acts is not so much for gaining of settlements, as for the avoiding of them, by persons coming into a parish clandestinely: for the giving of notice is only putting a force upon the parish to remove. But if a person's situation is such, that it is doubtful whether he is actually removable or not, he shall by giving of notice compel the parish either to allow him a settlement uncontested, by suffering him to continue forty days; or, by removing him, to try the right.'

This statute, therefore, rendered it almost impracticable for a poor man to gain a new settlement in the old way, by forty days' inhabitancy. But that it might not appear to preclude altogether the common people of one parish from ever establishing themselves with security in another, it appointed four other

ways by which a settlement might be gained without any notice
delivered or published. The first was, by being taxed to parish
rates and paying them; the second, by being elected into an
annual parish office, and serving in it a year; the third, by
serving an apprenticeship in the parish; the fourth, by being
hired into service there for a year, and continuing in the same
service during the whole of it.

Nobody can gain a settlement by either of the two first ways,
but by the public deed of the whole parish, who are too well
aware of the consequences to adopt any new-comer who has
nothing but his labour to support him, either by taxing him to
parish rates, or by electing him into a parish office.

No married man can well gain any settlement in either of the
last two ways. An apprentice is scarce ever married; and it is
expressly enacted that no married servant shall gain any settlement for being hired for a year. The principal effect of introducing settlement by service has been to put out in a great measure
the old fashion of hiring for a year, which before had been so
customary in England, that even at this day, if no particular
term is agreed upon, the law intends that every servant is hired
for a year. But masters are not always willing to give their
servants a settlement by hiring them in this manner; and servants are not always willing to be so hired, because, as every last
settlement discharges all the foregoing, they might thereby lose
their original settlement in the places of their nativity, the habitation of their parents and relations.

No independent workman, it is evident, whether labourer or
artificer, is likely to gain any new settlement either by apprenticeship or by service. When such a person, therefore, carried
his industry to a new parish, he was liable to be removed, how
healthy and industrious soever, at the caprice of any church-
warden or overseer, unless he either rented a tenement of ten
pounds a year, a thing impossible for one who has nothing but
his labour to live by; or could give such security for the discharge of the parish as two justices of the peace should judge
sufficient. What security they shall require, indeed, is left altogether to their discretion; but they cannot well require less than
thirty pounds, it having been enacted that the purchase even of
a freehold estate of less than thirty pounds' value shall not gain

any person a settlement, as not being sufficient for the discharge of the parish. But this is a security which scarce any man who lives by labour can give; and much greater security is frequently demanded.

In order to restore in some measure that free circulation of labour which those different statutes had almost entirely taken away, the invention of certificates was fallen upon. By the 8th and 9th of William III it was enacted, that if any person should bring a certificate from the parish where he was last legally settled, subscribed by the churchwardens and overseers of the poor, and allowed by two justices of the peace, that every other parish should be obliged to receive him; that he should not be removable merely upon account of his being likely to become chargeable, but only upon his becoming actually chargeable, and that then the parish which granted the certificate should be obliged to pay the expense both of his maintenance and of his removal. And in order to give the most perfect security to the parish where such certificated man should come to reside, it was further enacted by the same statute, that he should gain no settlement there by any means whatever, except either by renting a tenement of ten pounds a year, or by serving upon his own account in an annual parish office for one whole year; and consequently neither by notice, nor by service, nor by apprenticeship, nor by paying parish rates. By the 12th of Queen Anne too, stat. 1. c. 18, it was further enacted, that neither the servants nor apprentices of such certificated man should gain any settlement in the parish where he resided under such certificate.

Hiw far this invention has restored that free circulation of labour which the preceding statutes had almost entirely taken away, we may learn from the following very judicious observation of Doctor Burn. 'It is obvious,' says he, 'that there are divers good reasons for requiring certificates with persons coming to settle in any place; namely, that persons residing under them can gain no settlement, neither by apprenticeship, nor by service, nor by giving notice, nor by paying parish rates; that they can settle neither apprentices nor servants; that if they become chargeable, it is certainly known whither to remove them, and the parish shall be paid for the removal, and for their maintenance in the meantime; and that if they fall sick, and cannot

be removed, the parish which gave the certificate must maintain
them: none of all which can be without a certificate. Which
reasons will hold proportionably for parishes not granting certificates in ordinary cases; for it is far more than an equal chance,
but that they will have the certificated persons again, and in a
worse condition.' The moral of this observation seems to be, that
certificates ought always to be required by the parish where any
poor man comes to reside, and that they ought very seldom to
be granted by that which he proposes to leave. 'There is somewhat of hardship in this matter of certificates,' says the same
very intelligent author in his *History of the Poor Laws*, 'by
putting it in the power of a parish officer to imprison a man as
it were for life; however inconvenient it may be for him to
continue at that place where he has had the misfortune to
acquire what is called a settlement, or whatever advantage he
may propose to himself by living elsewhere.'

Though a certificate carries along with it no testimonial of
good behaviour, and certifies nothing but that the person belongs to the parish to which he really does belong, it is altogether discretionary in the parish officers either to grant or to
refuse it. A mandamus was once moved for, says Doctor Burn,
to compel the churchwardens and overseers to sign a certificate;
but the court of King's Bench rejected the motion as a very
strange attempt.

The very unequal price of labour which we frequently find in
England in places at no great distance from one another is
probably owing to the obstruction which the law of settlements
gives to a poor man who would carry his industry from one
parish to another without a certificate. A single man, indeed,
who is healthy and industrious, may sometimes reside by suffer-
ance without one; but a man with a wife and family who
should attempt to do so would in most parishes be sure of being
removed, and if the single man should afterwards marry, he
would generally be removed likewise. The scarcity of hands in
one parish, therefore, cannot always be relieved by their superabundance in another, as it is constantly in Scotland, and, I
believe, in all other countries where there is no difficulty of
settlement. In such countries, though wages may sometimes rise
a little in the neighbourhood of a great town, or wherever else

there is an extraordinary demand for labour, and sink gradually
as the distance from such places increases, till they fall back to
the common rate of the country; yet we never meet with those
sudden and unaccountable differences in the wages of neighbouring places which we sometimes find in England, where it is
often more difficult for a poor man to pass the artificial boundary of a parish than an arm of the sea or a ridge of high
mountains, natural boundaries which sometimes separate very
distinctly different rates of wages in other countries.

To remove a man who has committed no misdemeanour from
the parish where he chooses to reside is an evident violation of
natural liberty and justice. The common people of England,
however, so jealous of their liberty, but like the common people
of most other countries never rightly understanding wherein it
consists, have now for more than a century together suffered
themselves to be exposed to this oppression without a remedy.
Though men of reflection, too, have sometimes complained of
the law of settlements as a public grievance; yet it has never
been the object of any general popular clamour, such as that
against general warrants, an abusive practice undoubtedly, but
such a one as was not likely to occasion any general oppression.
There is scarce a poor man in England of forty years of age, I
will venture to say, who has not in some part of his life felt
himself most cruelly oppressed by this ill-contrived law of
settlements.

I shall conclude this long chaper with observing that, though
anciently it was usual to rate wages, first by general laws extending over the whole kingdom, and afterwards by particular
orders of the justices of peace in every particular county, both
these practices have now gone entirely into disuse. 'By the experience of above four hundred years,' says Doctor Burn, 'it
seems time to lay aside all endeavours to bring under strict
regulations, what in its own nature seems incapable of minute
limitation; for if all persons in the same kind of work were to
receive equal wages, there would be no emulation, and no room
left for industry or ingenuity.'

Particular acts of parliament, however, still attempt sometimes to regulate wages in particular trades and in particular
places. Thus the 8th of George III prohibits under heavy penal-

ties all master tailors in London, and five miles round it, from giving, and their workmen from accepting, more than two shillings and sevenpence halfpenny a day, except in the case of a general mourning. Whenever the legislature attempts to regulate the differences between masters and their workmen, its counsellors are always the masters. When the regulation, therefore, is in favour of the workmen, it is always just and equitable; but it is sometimes otherwise when in favour of the masters. Thus the law which obliges the masters in several different trades to pay their workmen in money and not in goods is quite just and equitable. It imposes no real hardship upon the masters. It only obliges them to pay that value in money, which they pretended to pay, but did not always really pay, in goods. This law is in favour of the workmen; but the 8th of George III is in favour of the masters. When masters combine together in order to reduce the wages of their workmen, they commonly enter into a private bond or agreement not to give more than a certain wage under a certain penalty. Were the workmen to enter into a contrary combination of the same kind, not to accept of a certain wage under a certain penalty, the law would punish them very severely; and if it dealt impartially, it would treat the masters in the same manner. But the 8th of George III enforces by law that very regulation which masters sometimes attempt to establish by such combinations. The complaint of the workmen, that it puts the ablest and most industrious upon the same footing with an ordinary workman, seems perfectly well founded.

In ancient times, too, it was usual to attempt to regulate the profits of merchants and other dealers, by rating the price both of provisions and other goods. The assize of bread is, so far as I know, the only remnant of this ancient usage. Where there is an exclusive corporation, it may perhaps be proper to regulate the price of the first necessary of life. But where there is none, the competition will regulate it much better than any assize. The method of fixing the assize of bread established by the 31st of George II could not be put in practice in Scotland, on account of a defect in the law; its execution depending upon the office of clerk of the market, which does not exist there. This defect was not remedied till the 3rd of George III. The want of an assize occasioned no sensible inconveniency, and the establishment of one, in the few places where it has yet taken place, has produced no sensible advantage. In the greater part of the towns of Scotland, however, there is an incorporation of bakers who claim exclusive privileges, though they are not very strictly guarded.

The proportion between the different rates both of wages and profit in the different employments of labour and stock, seems not to be much affected, as has already been observed, by the riches or poverty, the advancing, stationary, or declining state of the society. Such revolutions in the public welfare, though they affect the general rates both of wages and profit, must in the end affect them equally in all different employments. The proportion between them, therefore, must remain the same, and cannot well be altered, at least for any considerable time, by any such revolutions.

CHAPTER XI

OF THE RENT OF LAND

RENT, considered as the price paid for the use of land, is naturally the highest which the tenant can afford to pay in the actual circumstances of the land. In adjusting the terms of the lease, the landlord endeavours to leave him no greater share of the produce than what is sufficient to keep up the stock from which he furnishes the seed, pays the labour, and purchases and maintains the cattle and other instruments of husbandry, together with the ordinary profits of farming stock in the neighbourhood. This is evidently the smallest share with which the tenant can content himself without being a loser, and the landlord seldom means to leave him any more. Whatever part of the produce, or, what is the same thing, whatever part of its price is over and above this share, he naturally endeavours to reserve to himself as the rent of his land, which is evidently the highest the tenant can afford to pay in the actual circumstances of the land. Sometimes, indeed, the liberality, more frequently the ignorance, of the landlord, makes him accept of somewhat less than this portion; and sometimes too, though more rarely, the ignorance of the tenant makes him undertake to pay somewhat more, or to content himself with somewhat less than the ordinary profits of farming stock in the neighbourhood. This portion, however, may still be considered as the natural rent of land, or the rent for which it is naturally meant that land should for the most part be let.

The rent of land, it may be thought, is frequently no more than a reasonable profit or interest for the stock laid out by the landlord upon its improvement. This, no doubt, may be partly the case upon some occasions; for it can scarce ever be more than partly the case. The landlord demands a rent even for unimproved land, and the supposed interest or profit upon the expense of improvement is generally an addition to this original rent. Those improvements, besides, are not always made by the stock of the landlord, but sometimes by that of the tenant. When the lease comes to be renewed, however, the landlord commonly demands the same augmentation of rent as if they had been all made by his own.

He sometimes demands rent for what is altogether incapable of human improvement. Kelp is a species of sea-weed, which, when burnt, yields an alkaline salt, useful for making glass, soap, and for several other purposes. It grows in several parts of Great Britain, particularly in Scotland, upon such rocks only as lie within the high water mark, which are twice every day covered with the sea, and of which the produce, therefore, was never augmented by human industry. The landlord, however, whose estate is bounded by a kelp shore of this kind, demands a rent for it as much as for his corn fields.

The sea in the neighbourhood of the islands of Shetland is more than commonly abundant in fish, which make a great part of the subsistence of their inhabitants. But in order to profit by the produce of the water, they must have a habitation upon the neighbouring land. The rent of the landlord is in proportion, not to what the farmer can make by the land, but to what he can make both by the land and by the water. It is partly paid in sea-fish; and one of the very few instances in which rent makes a part of the price of that commodity is to be found in that country.

The rent of land, therefore, considered as the price paid for the use of the land, is naturally a monopoly price. It is not at all proportioned to what the landlord may have laid out upon the improvement of the land, or to what he can afford to take; but to what the farmer can afford to give.

Such parts only of the produce of land can commonly be brought to market of which the ordinary price is sufficient to replace the stock which must be employed in bringing them thither, together with its ordinary profits. If the ordinary price is more than this, the surplus part of it will naturally go to the rent of the land. If it is not more, though the commodity may be brought to market, it can afford no rent to the landlord. Whether the price is or is not more depends upon the demand.

There are some parts of the produce of land for which the demand must always be such as to afford a greater price than what is sufficient to bring them to market; and there are others for which it either may or may not be such as to afford this greater price. The former must always afford a rent to the landlord. The latter sometimes may, and sometimes may not, according to different circumstances.

Rent, it is to be observed, therefore, enters into the composition of the price of commodities in a different way from wages and profit. High or low wages and profit are the causes of high or low price; high or low rent is the effect of it. It is because high or low wages and profit must be paid, in order to bring a particular commodity to market, that its price is high or low. But it is because its price is high or low; a great deal more, or very little more, or no more, than what is sufficient to pay those wages and profit, that it affords a high rent, or a low rent, or no rent at all.

The particular consideration, first, of those parts of the produce of land which always afford some rent; secondly, of those which sometimes may and sometimes may not afford rent; and, thirdly, of the variations which, in the different periods of improvement, naturally take place in the relative value of those two different sorts of rude produce, when compared both with one another and with manufactured commodities, will divide this chapter into three parts.

PART I

Of the Produce of Land which always affords Rent

As men, like all other animals, naturally multiply in proportion to the means of their subsistence, food is always, more or less, in demand. It can always purchase or command a greater or smaller quantity of labour, and somebody can always be found who is willing to do something in order to obtain it. The quantity of labour, indeed, which it can purchase is not always equal to what it could maintain, if managed in the most economical manner, on account of the high wages which are sometimes given to labour. But it can always purchase such a quantity of labour as it can maintain, according to the rate at which that sort of labour is commonly maintained in the neighbourhood.

But land, in almost any situation, produces a greater quantity of food than what is sufficient to maintain all the labour necessary for bringing it to market, in the most liberal way in which that labour is ever maintained. The surplus, too, is always more than sufficient to replace the stock which employed that labour, together with its profits. Something, therefore, always remains for a rent to the landlord.

The most desert moors in Norway and Scotland produce some sort of pasture for cattle, of which the milk and the increase are always more than sufficient, not only to maintain all the labour necessary for tending them, and to pay the ordinary profit to the farmer or owner of the herd or flock; but to afford some small rent to the landlord. The rent increases in proportion to the goodness of the pasture. The same extent of ground not only maintains a greater number of cattle, but as they are brought within a smaller compass, less labour becomes requisite to tend them, and to collect their produce. The landlord gains both ways, by the increase of the produce and by the diminution of the labour which must be maintained out of it.

The rent of land not only varies with its fertility, whatever be its produce, but with its situation, whatever be its fertility. Land in the neighbourhood of a town gives a greater rent than land equally fertile in a distant part of the country. Though it may cost no more labour to cultivate the one than the other, it must always cost more to bring the produce of the distant land to market. A greater quantity of labour, therefore, must be maintained out of it; and the surplus, from which are drawn both the profit of the farmer and the rent of the landlord, must be diminished. But in remote parts of the country the rate of profits, as has already been shown, is generally higher than in the neighbourhood of a large town. A smaller proportion of this diminished surplus, therefore, must belong to the landlord.

Good roads, canals, and navigable rivers, by diminishing the expense of carriage, put the remote parts of the country more nearly upon a level with those in the neighbourhood of the town. They are upon that account the greatest of all improvements. They encourage the cultivation of the remote, which must always be the most extensive circle of the country. They are advantageous to the town, by breaking down the monopoly of the country in its neighbourhood. They are advantageous even to that part of the country. Though they introduce some rival commodities into the old market, they open many new markets to its produce. Monopoly, besides, is a great enemy to good management, which can never be universally established but in consequence of that free and universal competition which forces everybody to have recourse to it for the sake of self-defence. It is not more than fifty years ago that some of the counties in the neighbourhood of London petitioned the parliament against the extension of the turnpike roads into the remoter counties. Those remoter counties, they pretended, from the cheapness of labour, would be able to sell their grass and corn cheaper in the London market than themselves, and would thereby reduce their rents, and ruin their cultivation. Their rents, however, have risen, and their cultivation has been improved since that time.

A cornfield of moderate fertility produces a much greater quantity of food for man than the best pasture of equal extent. Though its cultivation requires much more labour, yet the surplus which remains after replacing the seed and maintaining all that labour, is likewise much greater. If a pound of butcher's meat, therefore, was never supposed to be worth more than a pound of bread, this greater surplus would everywhere be of greater value, and constitute a greater fund both for the profit of the farmer and the rent of the landlord. It seems to have done so universally in the rude beginnings of agriculture.

But the relative values of those two different species of food, bread and butcher's meat, are very different in the different periods of agriculture. In its rude beginnings, the unimproved wilds, which then occupy the far greater part of the country, are all abandoned to cattle. There is more butcher's meat than bread, and bread, therefore, is the food for which there is the greatest competition, and which consequently brings the greatest price. At Buenos Ayres, we are told by Ulloa, four reals, one-and-twenty pence halfpenny sterling, was, forty or fifty years ago, the ordinary price of an ox, chosen from a herd of two or three hundred. He says nothing of the price of bread, probably because he found nothing remarkable about it. An ox there, he says, costs little more than the labour of catching him. But corn can nowhere be raised without a great deal of labour, and in a country which lies upon the river Plate, at that time the direct road from Europe to the silver mines of Potosi, the money price of labour could not be very cheap. It is otherwise when cultivation is extended over the greater part of the country. There is then more bread than butcher's meat. The competition changes its direction, and the price of butcher's meat becomes greater than the price of bread.

By the extension besides of cultivation, the unimproved wilds become insufficient to supply the demand for butcher's meat. A great part of the cultivated lands must be employed in rearing and fattening cattle, of which the price, therefore, must be sufficient to pay, not only the labour necessary for tending them, but the rent which the landlord and the profit which the farmer could have drawn from such land employed in tillage. The cattle bred upon the most uncultivated moors, when brought to the same market, are, in proportion to their weight or goodness, sold at the same price as those which are reared upon the most improved land. The proprietors of those moors profit by it, and raise the rent of their land in proportion to the price of their cattle. It is not more than a century ago that in many parts of the highlands of Scotland, butcher's meat was as cheap or cheaper than even bread made of oatmeal. The union opened the market of England to the highland cattle.

Their ordinary price is at present about three times greater than at the beginning of the century, and rents of many highland estates have been tripled and quadrupled in the same time. In almost every part of Great Britain a pound of the best butcher's meat is, in the present times, generally worth more than two pounds of the best white bread; and in plentiful years it is sometimes worth three or four pounds.

It is thus that in the progress of improvement the rent and profit of unimproved pasture come to be regulated in some measure by the rent and profit of what is improved, and these again by the rent and profit of corn. Corn is an annual crop. Butcher's meat, a crop which requires four or five years to grow. As an acre of land, therefore, will produce a much smaller quantity of the one species of food than of the other, the inferiority of the quantity must be compensated by the superiority of the price. If it was more than compensated, more corn land would be turned into pasture; and if it was not compensated, part of what was in pasture would be brought back into corn.

This equality, however, between the rent and profit of grass and those of corn; of the land of which the immediate produce is food for cattle, and of that of which the immediate produce is food for men; must be understood to take place only through the greater part of the improved lands of a great country. In some particular local situations it is quite otherwise, and the rent and profit of grass are much superior to what can be made by corn.

Thus in the neighbourhood of a great town the demand for milk and for forage to horses frequently contribute, together with the high price of butcher's meat, to raise the value of grass above what may be called its natural proportion to that of corn. This local advantage, it is evident, cannot be communicated to the lands at a distance.

Particular circumstances have sometimes rendered some countries so populous that the whole territory, like the lands in the neighbourhood of a great town, has not been sufficient to produce both the grass and the corn necessary for the subsistence of their inhabitants. Their lands therefore, have been principally employed in the production of grass, the more bulky commodity, and which cannot be so easily brought from a great distance; and corn, the food of the great body of the people, has been chiefly imported from foreign countries. Holland is at present in this situation, and a considerable part of ancient Italy seems to have been so during the prosperity of the Romans. To feed well, old Cato said, as we are told by Cicero, was the first and most profitable thing in the management of a private estate; to feed tolerably well, the second; and to feed ill, the third. To plough, he ranked only in the fourth place of profit and advantage. Tillage, indeed, in that part of ancient Italy which lay in the neighbourhood of Rome, must have been very much discouraged by the distributions of corn which were frequently made to the people, either gratuitously, or at a very low price. This corn was brought from the conquered provinces, of which several, instead of taxes, were obliged to furnish a tenth part of their produce at a stated price, about sixpence a peck, to the republic. The low price at which this corn was distributed to the people must necessarily have sunk the price of what could be brought to the Roman market from Latium, or the ancient territory of Rome, and must have discouraged its cultivation in that country.

In an open country too, of which the principal produce is corn, a well-enclosed piece of grass will frequently rent higher than any corn field in its neighbourhood. It is convenient for the maintenance of the cattle employed in the cultivation of the corn, and its high rent is, in this case, not so properly paid from the value of its own produce as from that of the corn lands which are cultivated by means of it. It is likely to fall, if ever the neighbouring lands are completely enclosed. The present high rent of enclosed land in Scotland seems owing to the scarcity of enclosure, and will probably last no longer than that scarcity. The advantage of enclosure is greater for pasture than for corn. It saves the labour of guarding the cattle, which feed better, too, when they are not liable to be disturbed by their keeper or his dog.

But where there is no local advantage of this kind, the rent and profit of corn, or whatever else is the common vegetable food of the people, must naturally regulate, upon the land which is fit for producing it, the rent and profit of pasture.

The use of the artificial grasses, of turnips, carrots, cabbages, and the other expedients which have been fallen upon to make an equal quantity of land feed a greater number of cattle than when in natural grass, should somewhat reduce, it might be expected, the superiority which, in an improved country, the price of butcher's meat naturally has over that of bread. It seems accordingly to have done so; and there is some reason for believing that, at least in the London market, the price of butcher's meat in proportion to the price of bread is a good deal lower in the present times than it was in the beginning of the last century.

In the appendix of the *Life of Prince Henry*, Doctor Birch has given us an account of the prices of butcher's meat as commonly paid by that prince. It is there said that the four quarters of an ox weighing six hundred pounds usually cost him nine pounds ten shillings, or thereabouts; that is, thirty-one shillings and eightpence per hundred pounds weight. Prince Henry died on the 6th November 1612, in the nineteenth year of his age.

In March 1764, there was a parliamentary inquiry into the causes of the high price of provisions at that time. It was then, among other proof to the same purpose, given in evidence by a Virginia merchant, that in March 1763, he had victualled his ships for twenty-four or twenty-five shillings the hundredweight of beef, which he considered as the ordinary price; whereas, in that dear year, he had paid twenty-seven shillings for the same weight and sort. This high price in 1764 is, however, four shillings and eightpence cheaper than the ordinary price paid by Prince Henry; and it is the best beef only, it must be observed, which is fit to be salted for those distant voyages.

The price paid by Prince Henry amounts to $3\frac{4}{5}d.$ per pound weight of the whole carcase, coarse and choice pieces taken together; and at that rate the choice pieces could not have been sold by retail for less than $4\frac{1}{2}d.$ or $5d.$ the pound.

In the parliamentary inquiry in 1764, the witnesses stated the price of the choice pieces of the best beef to be to the consumer $4d.$ and $4\frac{1}{4}d.$ the pound; and the coarse pieces in general to be from seven farthings to $2\frac{1}{2}d.$ and $2\frac{3}{4}d.$; and this they said was in general one halfpenny dearer than the same sort of pieces had usually been sold in the month of March. But even this high price is still a good deal cheaper than what we can well suppose the ordinary retail price to have been in the time of Prince Henry.

During the twelve first years of the last century, the average price of the best wheat at the Windsor market was £1 18s. 3⅟₆d. the quarter of nine Winchester bushels.

But in the twelve years preceding 1764, including that year, the average price of the same measure of the best wheat at the same market was £2 1s. 9½d.

In the twelve first years of the last century, therefore, wheat appears to have been a good deal cheaper, and butcher's meat a good deal dearer, than in the twelve years preceding 1764, including that year.

In all great countries the greater part of the cultivated lands are employed in producing either food for men or food for cattle. The rent and profit of these regulate the rent and profit of all other cultivated land. If any particular produce afforded less, the land would soon be turned into corn or pasture; and if any afforded more, some part of the lands in corn or pasture would soon be turned to that produce.

Those productions, indeed, which require either a greater original expense of improvement, or a greater annual expense of cultivation, in order to fit the land for them, appear commonly to afford, the one a greater rent, the other a greater profit than corn or pasture. This superiority, however, will seldom be found to amount to more than a reasonable interest or compensation for this superior expense.

In a hop garden, a fruit garden, a kitchen garden, both the rent of the landlord, and the profit of the farmer, are generally greater than in a corn or grass field. But to bring the ground into this condition requires more expense. Hence a greater rent becomes due to the landlord. It requires, too, a more attentive and skilful management. Hence a greater profit becomes due to the farmer. The crop too, at least in the hop and fruit garden, is more precarious. Its price, therefore, besides compensating all occasional losses, must afford something like the profit of insurance. The circumstances of gardeners, generally mean, and always moderate, may satisfy us that their great ingenuity is not commonly over-recompensed. Their delightful art is practised by so many rich people for amusement, that little advantage is to be made by those who practise it for profit; because the persons who should naturally be their best customers supply themselves with all their most precious productions.

The advantage which the landlord derives from such improvements seems at no time to have been greater than what was sufficient to compensate the original expense of making them. In the ancient husbandry, after the vineyard, a well-watered kitchen garden seems to have been the part of the farm which was supposed to yield the most valuable produce. But Democritus, who wrote upon husbandry about two thousand years ago, and who was regarded by the ancients as one of the fathers of the art, thought they did not act wisely who enclosed a kitchen garden. The profit, he said, would not compensate the expense of a stone wall; and bricks (he meant, I suppose, bricks baked in the sun) mouldered with the rain, and the winter storm, and required continual repairs. Columella, who reports this judgement of Democritus, does not controvert it, but proposes a very frugal method of enclosing with a hedge of brambles and briars, which, he says, he had found by experience to be both a lasting and an impenetrable fence; but which, it seems, was not commonly known in the time of Democritus. Palladius adopts the opinion of Columella, which had before been recommended by Varro. In the judgement of those ancient improvers, the produce of a kitchen garden had, it seems, been little more than sufficient to pay the extraordinary culture and the expense of watering; for in countries so near the sun, it was thought proper, in those times as in the present, to have the command of a stream of water which could be conducted to every bed in the garden. Through the greater part of Europe a kitchen garden is not at present supposed to deserve a better enclosure than that recommended by Columella. In Great Britain, and some other northern countries, the finer fruits cannot be brought to perfection but by the assistance of a wall. Their price, therefore, in such countries must be sufficient to pay the expense of building and maintaining what they cannot be had without. The fruit-wall frequently surrounds the kitchen garden, which thus enjoys the benefit of an enclosure which its own produce could seldom pay for.

That the vineyard, when properly planted and brought to perfection, was the most valuable part of the farm, seems to have been an undoubted maxim in the ancient agriculture, as it is in the modern through all the wine countries. But whether it was advantageous to plant a new vineyard was a matter of dispute among the ancient Italian husbandmen, as we learn from Columella. He decides, like a true lover of all curious cultivation, in favour of the vineyard, and endeavours to show, by a comparison of the profit and expense, that it was a most advantageous improvement. Such comparisons, however, between the profit and expense of new projects are commonly very fallacious, and in nothing more so than in agriculture. Had the gain actually made by such plantations been commonly as great as he imagined it might have been, there could have been no dispute about it. The same point is frequently at this day a matter of controversy in the wine countries. Their writers on agriculture, indeed, the lovers and promoters of high cultivation, seem generally disposed to decide with Columella in favour of the vineyard. In France the anxiety of the proprietors of the old vineyards to prevent the planting of any new ones, seems to favour their opinion, and to indicate a consciousness in those who must have the experience that this species of cultivation is at present in that country more profitable than any other. It seems at the same time, however, to indicate another opinion, that this superior profit can last no longer than the laws which at present restrain the free cultivation of the vine. In 1731, they obtained an order of council prohibiting both the planting of new vineyards and the renewal of those old ones, of which the cultivation had been interrupted for two years, without a particular permission from the king, to be granted only in consequence of an information from the intendant of the province, certifying that he had examined the land, and that it was incapable of any other culture. The pretence of this order was the scarcity of corn and pasture, and the superabundance of wine. But had this superabundance been real, it would, without any order of council, have effectually prevented the plantation of new vineyards, by reducing the profits of this species of cultivation below their natural proportion to those of corn and pasture. With regard to the supposed scarcity of corn, occasioned by the multiplication of vineyards, corn is nowhere in France more carefully cultivated than in the wine provinces, where the land is fit for producing it; as in Burgundy, Guienne, and the Upper Languedoc. The numerous hands employed in the one species of cultivation necessarily encourage the other, by affording a ready market for its produce. To diminish the number of those who are capable of paying for it is surely a most unpromising expedient for encouraging the cultivation of corn. It is like the policy which would promote agriculture by discouraging manufactures.

The rent and profit of those productions, therefore, which require either a greater original expense of improvement in order to fit the land for them, or a greater annual expense of cultivation, though often much superior to those of corn and pasture, yet when they do no more than compensate such extraordinary expense, are in reality regulated by the rent and profit of those common crops.

It sometimes happens, indeed, that the quantity of land, which can be fitted for some particular produce, is too small to supply the effectual demand. The whole produce can be disposed of to those who are willing to give somewhat more than what is sufficient to pay the whole rent, wages, and profit necessary for raising and bringing it to market, according to their natural rates, or according to the rates at which they are paid in the greater part of other cultivated land. The surplus part of the price which remains after defraying the whole expense of improvement and cultivation may commonly, in this case, and in this case only, bear no regular proportion to the like surplus in corn or pasture, but may exceed it in almost any degree; and the greater part of this excess naturally goes to the rent of the landlord.

The usual and natural proportion, for example, between the rent and profit of wine and those of corn and pasture must be understood to take place only with regard to those vineyards which produce nothing but good common wine, such as can be raised almost anywhere, upon any light, gravelly, or sandy soil, and which has nothing to recommend it but its strength and wholesomeness. It is with such vineyards only that the common land of the country can be brought into competition; for with those of a peculiar quality it is evident that it cannot.

The vine is more affected by the difference of soils than any other fruit tree. From some it derives a flavour which no culture or management can equal, it is supposed, upon any other. This flavour, real or imaginary, is sometimes peculiar to the produce of a few vineyards; sometimes it extends through the greater part of a small district, and sometimes through a considerable part of a large province. The whole quantity of such wines that is brought to market falls short of the effectual demand, or the demand of those who would be willing to pay the whole rent, profit, and wages, necessary for preparing and bringing them thither, according to the ordinary rate, or according to the rate at which they are paid in common vineyards. The whole quantity, therefore, can be disposed of to those who are willing to pay more, which necessarily raises the price above that of common wine. The difference is greater or less according as the fashionableness and scarcity of the wine render the competition of the buyers more or less eager. Whatever it be, the greater part of it goes to the rent of the landlord. For though such vineyards are in general more carefully cultivated than most others, the high price of the wine seems to be not so much the effect as the cause of this careful cultivation. In so valuable a produce the loss occasioned by negligence is so great as to force even the most careless to attention. A small part of this high price, therefore, is sufficient to pay the wages of the extraordinary labour bestowed upon their cultivation, and the profits of the extraordinary stock which puts that labour into motion.

The sugar colonies possessed by the European nations in the West Indies may be compared to those precious vineyards. Their whole produce falls short of the effectual demand of Europe, and can be disposed of to those who are willing to give more than what is sufficient to pay the whole rent, profit, and wages necessary for preparing and bringing it to market, according to the rate at which they are commonly paid by any other produce. In Cochin-china the finest white sugar commonly sells for three piasters the quintal, about thirteen shillings and sixpence of our money, as we are told by Mr Poivre,[1]

1. *Voyages d'un Philosophe.*

a very careful observer of the agriculture of that country. What is there called the quintal weighs from a hundred and fifty to two hundred Paris pounds, or a hundred and seventy-five Paris pounds at a medium, which reduces the price of the hundred-weight English to about eight shillings sterling, not a fourth part of what is commonly paid for the brown or muskavada sugars imported from our colonies, and not a sixth part of what is paid for the finest white sugar. The greater part of the cultivated lands in Cochin-china are employed in producing corn and rice, the food of the great body of the people. The respective prices of corn, rice, and sugar, are there probably in the natural proportion, or in that which naturally takes place in the different crops of the geater part of cultivated land, and which recompenses the landlord and farmer, as nearly as can be computed, according to what is usually the original expense of improvement and the annual expense of cultivation. But in our sugar colonies the price of sugar bears no such proportion to that of the produce of a rice or corn field either in Europe or in America. It is commonly said that a sugar planter expects that the rum and the molasses should defray the whole expense of his cultivation, and that his sugar should be all clear profit. If this be true, for I pretend not to affirm it, it is as if a corn farmer expected to defray the expense of his cultivation with the chaff and the straw, and that the grain should be all clear profit. We see frequently societies of merchants in London and other trading towns purchase waste lands in our sugar colonies, which they expect to improve and cultivate with profit by means of factors and agents, notwithstanding the great distance and the uncertain returns from the defective administration of justice in those countries. Nobody will attempt to improve and cultivate in the same manner the most fertile lands of Scotland, Ireland, or the corn provinces of North America, though from the more exact administration of justice in these countries more regular returns might be expected.

In Virginia and Maryland the cultivation of tobacco is preferred, as more profitable, to that of corn. Tobacco might be cultivated with advantage through the greater part of Europe; but in almost every part of Europe it has become a principal subject of taxation, and to collect a tax from every different

farm in the country where this plant might happen to be cultivated would be more difficult, it has been supposed, than to
levy one upon its importation at the custom-house. The cultivation of tobacco has upon this account been most absurdly prohibited through the greater part of Europe, which necessarily
gives a sort of monopoly to the countries where it is allowed;
and as Virginia and Maryland produce the greatest quantity of
it, they share largely, though with some competitors, in the
advantage of this monopoly. The cultivation of tobacco, however, seems not to be so advantageous as that of sugar. I have
never even heard of any tobacco plantation that was improved
and cultivated by the capital of merchants who resided in Great
Britain, and our tobacco colonies send us home no such wealthy
planters as we see frequently arrive from our sugar islands.
Though from the preference given in those colonies to the
cultivation of tobacco above that of corn, it would appear that
the effectual demand of Europe for tobacco is not completely
supplied, it probably is more nearly so than that for sugar; and
though the present price of tobacco is probably more than
sufficient to pay the whole rent, wages, and profit necessary for
preparing and bringing it to market, according to the rate at
which they are commonly paid in corn land, it must not be so
much more as the present price of sugar. Our tobacco planters,
accordingly, have shown the same fear of the superabundance of
tobacco which the proprietors of the old vineyards in France
have of the superabundance of wine. By act of assembly they
have restrained its cultivation to six thousand plants, supposed
to yield a thousand weight of tobacco, for every Negro between
sixteen and sixty years of age. Such a Negro, over and above this
quantity of tobacco, can manage, they reckon, four acres of
Indian corn. To prevent the market from being overstocked,
too, they have sometimes, in plentiful years, we are told by Dr
Douglas[1] (I suspect he has been ill informed), burnt a certain
quantity of tobacco for every Negro, in the same manner as the
Dutch are said to do of spices. If such violent methods are
necessary to keep up the present price of tobacco, the superior
advantage of its culture over that of corn, if it still has any, will
not probably be of long continuance.

1. Douglas's *Summary*, vol. ii. pp. 372, 373.

It is in this manner that the rent of the cultivated land, of which the produce is human food, regulates the rent of the greater part of other cultivated land. No particular produce can long afford less; because the land would immediately be turned to another use. And if any particular produce commonly affords more, it is because the quantity of land which can be fitted for it is too small to supply the effectual demand.

In Europe, corn is the principal produce of land which serves immediately for human food. Except in particular situations, therefore, the rent of corn land regulates in Europe that of all other cultivated land. Britain need envy neither the vineyards of France nor the olive plantations of Italy. Except in particular situations, the value of these is regulated by that of corn, in which the fertility of Britain is not much inferior to that of either of those two countries.

If in any country the common and favourite vegetable food of the people should be drawn from a plant of which the most common land, with the same or nearly the same culture, produced a much greater quantity than the most fertile does of corn, the rent of the landlord, or the surplus quantity of food which would remain to him, after paying the labour and replacing the stock of the farmer, together with its ordinary profits, would necessarily be much greater. Whatever was the rate at which labour was commonly maintained in that country, this greater surplus could always maintain a greater quantity of it, and consequently enable the landlord to purchase or command a greater quantity of it. The real value of his rent, his real power and authority, his command of the necessaries and conveniences of life with which the labour of other people could supply him, would necessarily be much greater.

A rice field produces a much greater quantity of food than the most fertile corn field. Two crops in the year from thirty to sixty bushels each, are said to be the ordinary produce of an acre. Though its cultivation, therefore, requires more labour, a much greater surplus remains after maintaining all that labour. In those rice countries, therefore, where rice is the common and favourite vegetable food of the people, and where the cultivators are chiefly maintained with it, a greater share of this greater surplus should belong to the landlord than in corn countries. In

Carolina, where the planters, as in other British colonies, are generally both farmers and landlords, and where rent consequently is confounded with profit, the cultivation of rice is found to be more profitable than that of corn, though their fields produce only one crop in the year, and though, from the prevalence of the customs of Europe, rice is not there the common and favourite vegetable food of the people.

A good rice field is a bog at all seasons, and at one season a bog covered with water. It is unfit either for corn, or pasture, or vineyard, or, indeed, for any other vegetable produce that is very useful to men; and the lands which are fit for those purposes are not fit for rice. Even in the rice countries, therefore, the rent of rice lands cannot regulate the rent of the other cultivated land, which can never be turned to that produce.

The food produced by a field of potatoes is not inferior in quantity to that produced by a field of rice, and much superior to what is produced by a field of wheat. Twelve thousand weight of potatoes from an acre of land is not a greater produce than two thousand weight of wheat. The food or solid nourishment, indeed, which can be drawn from each of those two plants, is not altogether in proportion to their weight, on account of the watery nature of potatoes. Allowing, however, half the weight of this root to go to water, a very large allowance, such an acre of potatoes will still produce six thousand weight of solid nourishment, three times the quantity produced by the acre of wheat. An acre of potatoes is cultivated with less expense than an acre of wheat; the fallow, which generally precedes the sowing of wheat, more than compensating the hoeing and other extraordinary culture which is always given to potatoes. Should this root ever become in any part of Europe, like rice in some rice countries, the common and favourite vegetable food of the people, so as to occupy the same proportion of the lands in tillage which wheat and other sorts of grain for human food do at present, the same quantity of cultivated land would maintain a much greater number of people, and the labourers being generally fed with potatoes, a greater surplus would remain after replacing all the stock and maintaining all the labour employed in cultivation. A greater share of this surplus, too, would belong to the landlord. Population would increase, and rents would rise much beyond what they are at present.

The land which is fit for potatoes is fit for almost every other useful vegetable. If they occupied the same proportion of cultivated land which corn does at present, they would regulate, in the same manner, the rent of the greater part of other cultivated land.

In some parts of Lancashire it is pretended, I have been told, that bread of oatmeal is a heartier food for labouring people than wheaten bread, and I have frequently heard the same doctrine held in Scotland. I am, however, somewhat doubtful of the truth of it. The common people in Scotland, who are fed with oatmeal, are in general neither so strong, nor so handsome as the same rank of people in England who are fed with wheaten bread. They neither work so well, nor look so well; and as there is not the same difference between the people of fashion in the two countries, experience would seem to show that the food of the common people in Scotland is not so suitable to the human constitution as that of their neighbours of the same rank in England. But it seems to be otherwise with potatoes. The chairmen, porters, and coalheavers in London, and those unfortunate women who live by prostitution, the strongest men and the most beautiful women perhaps in the British dominions, are said to be the greater part of them from the lowest rank of people in Ireland, who are generally fed with this root. No food can afford a more decisive proof of its nourishing quality, or of its being peculiarly suitable to the health of the human constitution.

It is difficult to preserve potatoes through the year, and impossible to store them like corn, for two or three years together. The fear of not being able to sell them before they rot discourages their cultivation, and is, perhaps, the chief obstacle to their ever becoming in any great country, like bread, the principal vegetable food of all the different ranks of the people.

Of the Produce of Land which sometimes does, and sometimes does not, afford Rent

Human food seems to be the only produce of land which always and necessarily affords some rent to the landlord. Other sorts of produce sometimes may and sometimes may not, according to different circumstances.

After food, clothing and lodging are the two great wants of mankind.

Land in its original rude state can afford the materials of clothing and lodging to a much greater number of people than it can feed. In its improved state it can sometimes feed a greater number of people than it can supply with those materials; at least in the way in which they require them, and are willing to pay for them. In the one state, therefore, there is always a superabundance of those materials, which are frequently, upon that account, of little or no value. In the other there is often a scarcity, which necessarily augments their value. In the one state a great part of them is thrown away as useless, and the price of what is used is considered as equal only to the labour and expense of fitting it for use, and can, therefore, afford no rent to the landlord. In the other they are all made use of, and there is frequently a demand for more than can be had. Somebody is always willing to give more for every part of them than what is sufficient to pay the expense of bringing them to market. Their price, therefore, can always afford some rent to the landlord.

The skins of the larger animals were the original materials of clothing. Among nations of hunters and shepherds, therefore, whose food consists chiefly in the flesh of those animals, every man, by providing himself with food, provides himself with the materials of more clothing than he can wear. If there was no foreign commerce, the greater part of them would be thrown away as things of no value. This was probably the case among the hunting nations of North America before their country was discovered by the Europeans, with whom they now exchange their surplus peltry for blankets, fire-arms, and brandy, which gives it some value. In the present commercial state of the known world, the most barbarous nations, I believe, among whom land property is established, have some foreign commerce of this kind, and find among their wealthier neighbours such a demand for all the materials of clothing which their land produces, and which can neither be wrought up nor consumed at home, as raises their price above what it costs to send them to those wealthier neighbours. It affords, therefore, some rent to the landlord. When the greater part of the highland cattle were consumed on their own hills, the exportation of their hides made the most considerable article of the commerce of that country, and what they were exchanged for afforded some addition to the rent of the highland estates. The wool of England, which in old times could neither be consumed nor wrought up at home, found a market in the then wealthier and more industrious country of Flanders, and its price afforded something to the rent of the land which produced it. In countries not better cultivated than England was then, or than the highlands of Scotland are now, and which had no foreign commerce, the materials of clothing would evidently be so superabundant that a great part of them would be thrown away as useless, and no part could afford any rent to the landlord.

The materials of lodging cannot always be transported to so great a distance as those of clothing, and do not so readily become an object of foreign commerce. When they are superabundant in the country which produces them, it frequently happens, even in the present commercial state of the world, that they are of no value to the landlord. A good stone quarry in the neighbourhood of London would afford a considerable rent. In many parts of Scotland and Wales it affords none. Barren timber for building is of great value in a populous and well-cultivated country, and the land which produces it affords a considerable rent. But in many parts of North America the landlord would be much obliged to anybody who would carry away the greater part of his large trees. In some parts of the highlands of Scotland the bark is the only part of the wood which, for want of roads and water-carriage, can be sent to market. The timber is left to rot upon the ground. When the materials of lodging are so superabundant, the part made use of is worth only the labour and expense of fitting it for that use. It affords no rent to the landlord, who generally grants the use of it to whoever takes the trouble of asking it. The demand of wealthier nations, however, sometimes enables him to get a rent for it. The paving of the streets of London has enabled the owners of some barren rocks on the coast of Scotland to draw a rent from what never afforded any before. The woods of Norway and of the coasts of the Baltic find a market in many parts of Great Britain which they could not find at home, and thereby afford some rent to their proprietors.

Countries are populous not in proportion to the number of people whom their produce can clothe and lodge, but in proportion to that of those whom it can feed. When food is provided, it is easy to find the necessary clothing and lodging. But though these are at hand, it may often be difficult to find food. In some parts even of the British dominions what is called a house may be built by one day's labour of one man. The simplest species of clothing, the skins of animals, require somewhat more labour to dress and prepare them for use. They do not, however, require a great deal. Among savage and barbarous nations, a hundredth or little more than a hundredth part of the labour of the whole year will be sufficient to provide them with such clothing and lodging as satisfy the greater part of the people. All the other ninety-nine parts are frequently no more than enough to provide them with food.

But when by the improvement and cultivation of land the labour of one family can provide food for two, the labour of half the society becomes sufficient to provide food for the whole. The other half, therefore, or at least the greater part of them, can be employed in providing other things, or in satisfying the other wants and fancies of mankind. Clothing and lodging, household furniture, and what is called Equipage, are the principal objects of the greater part of those wants and fancies. The rich man consumes no more food than his poor neighbour. In quality it may be very different, and to select and prepare it may require more labour and art; but in quantity it is very nearly the same. But compare the spacious palace and great wardrobe of the one with the hovel and the few rags of the other, and you will be sensible that the difference between their clothing, lodging, and household furniture is almost as great in quantity as it is in quality. The desire of food is limited in every man by the narrow capacity of the human stomach; but the desire of the conveniences and ornaments of building, dress, equipage, and household furniture, seems to have no limit or certain boundary. Those, therefore, who have the command of more food than they themselves can consume, are always willing to exchange the surplus, or, what is the same thing, the price of it, for gratifications of this other kind. What is over and above satisfying the limited desire is given for the amusement of those desires which cannot be satisfied, but seem to be altogether endless. The poor, in order to obtain food, exert themselves to gratify those fancies of the rich, and to obtain it more certainly they vie with one another in the cheapness and perfection of their work. The number of workmen increases with the increasing quantity of food, or with the growing improvement and cultivation of the lands; and as the nature of their business admits of the utmost subdivisions of labour, the quantity of materials which they can work up increases in a much greater proportion than their numbers. Hence arises a demand for every sort of material which human invention can employ, either usefully or ornamentally, in building, dress, equipage, or household furniture; for the fossils and minerals contained in the bowels of the earth; the precious metals, and the precious stones.

Food is in this manner not only the original source of rent, but every other part of the produce of land which afterwards affords rent derives that part of its value from the improvement of the powers of labour in producing food by means of the improvement and cultivation of land.

Those other parts of the produce of land, however, which afterwards afford rent, do not afford it always. Even in improved and cultivated countries, the demand for them is not always such as to afford a greater price than what is sufficient to pay the labour, and replace, together with its ordinary profits, the stock which must be employed in bringing them to market. Whether it is or is not such depends upon different circumstances.

Whether a coal-mine, for example, can afford any rent depends partly upon its fertility, and partly upon its situation.

A mine of any kind may be said to be either fertile or barren, according as the quantity of mineral which can be brought from it by a certain quantity of labour is greater or less than what can be brought by an equal quantity from the greater part of other mines of the same kind.

Some coal-mines advantageously situated cannot be wrought on account of their barrenness. The produce does not pay the expense. They can afford neither profit nor rent.

There are some of which the produce is barely sufficient to pay the labour, and replace, together with its ordinary profits, the stock employed in working them. They afford some profit to the undertaker of the work, but no rent to the landlord. They can be wrought advantageously by nobody but the landlord, who, being himself undertaker of the work, gets the ordinary profit of the capital which he employs in it. Many coal-mines in Scotland are wrought in this manner, and can be wrought in no other. The landlord will allow nobody else to work them without paying some rent, and nobody can afford to pay any.

Other coal-mines in the same country, sufficiently fertile, cannot be wrought on account of their situation. A quantity of mineral sufficient to defray the expense of working could be brought from the mine by the ordinary, or even less than the ordinary, quantity of labour; but in an inland country, thinly inhabited, and without either good roads or water-carriage, this quantity could not be sold.

Coals are a less agreeable fuel than wood: they are said, too, to be less wholesome. The expense of coals, therefore, at the place where they are consumed, must generally be somewhat less than that of wood.

The price of wood again varies with the state of agriculture, nearly in the same manner, and exactly for the same reason, as the price of cattle. In its rude beginnings the greater part of every country is covered with wood, which is then a mere encumbrance of no value to the landlord, who would gladly give it to anybody for the cutting. As agriculture advances, the woods are partly cleared by the progress of tillage, and partly go to decay in consequence of the increased number of cattle. These, though they do not increase in the same proportion as corn, which is altogether the acquisition of human industry, yet multiply under the care and protection of men, who store up in the season of plenty what may maintain them in that of scarcity, who through the whole year furnish them with a greater quantity of food than uncultivated nature provides for them, and who by destroying and extirpating their enemies, secure them in the free enjoyment of all that she provides. Numerous herds of cattle, when allowed to wander through the woods, though they do not destroy the old trees, hinder any young ones from coming up, so that in the course of a century or two the whole forest goes to ruin. The scarcity of wood then raises its price. It affords a good rent, and the landlord sometimes finds that he can scarce employ his best lands more advantageously than in growing barren timber, of which the greatness of the profit often compensates the lateness of the returns. This seems in the present times to be nearly the state of things in several parts of Great Britain, where the profit of planting is found to be equal to that of either corn or pasture. The advantage which the landlord derives from planting can nowhere exceed, at least for any considerable time, the rent which these could afford him; and in an inland country which is highly cultivated, it will frequently not fall much short of this rent. Upon the sea-coast of a well-improved country, indeed, if coals can conveniently be had for fuel, it may sometimes be cheaper to bring barren timber for building from less cultivated foreign countries than to raise it at home. In the new town of Edinburgh, built within these few years, there is not, perhaps, a single stick of Scotch timber.

Whatever may be the price of wood, if that of coals is such that the expense of a coal fire is nearly equal to that of a wood one, we may be assured that at that place, and in these circumstances, the price of coals is as high as it can be. It seems to be so in some of the inland parts of England, particularly in Oxfordshire, where it is usual, even in the fires of the common people, to mix coals and wood together, and where the difference in the expense of those two sorts of fuel cannot, therefore, be very great.

Coals, in the coal countries, are everywhere much below this highest price. If they were not, they could not bear the expense of a distant carriage, either by land or by water. A small quantity only could be sold, and the coal masters and coal proprietors find it more for their interest to sell a great quantity at a price somewhat above the lowest, than a small quantity at the highest. The most fertile coal-mine, too, regulates the price of coals at all the other mines in its neighbourhood. Both the proprietor and the undertaker of the work find, the one that he can get a greater rent, the other than he can get a greater profit, by somewhat underselling all their neighbours. Their neighbours are soon obliged to sell at the same price, though they cannot so well afford it, and though it always diminishes, and sometimes takes away altogether both their rent and their profit. Some works are abandoned altogether; others can afford no rent, and can be wrought only by the proprietor.

The lowest price at which coals can be sold for any considerable time is, like that of all other commodities, the price which is barely sufficient to replace, together with its ordinary profits, the stock which must be employed in bringing them to market. At a coal-mine for which the landlord can get no rent, but which he must either work himself or let it alone altogether, the price of coals must generally be nearly about this price.

Rent, even where coals afford one, has generally a smaller share in their price than in that of most other parts of the rude produce of land. The rent of an estate above ground commonly amounts to what is supposed to be a third of the gross produce; and it is generally a rent certain and independent of the occasional variations in the crop. In coal-mines a fifth of the gross produce is a very great rent; a tenth the common rent, and it is seldom a rent certain, but depends upon the occasional variations in the produce. These are so great that, in a country where thirty years' purchase is considered as a moderate price for the property of a landed estate, ten years' purchase is regarded as a good price for that of a coal-mine.

The value of a coal-mine to the proprietor frequently depends as much upon its situation as upon its fertility. That of a metallic mine depends more upon its fertility, and less upon its situation. The coarse, and still more the precious metals, when separated from the ore, are so valuable that they can generally bear the expense of a very long land, and of the most distant sea carriage. Their market is not confined to the countries in the neighbourhood of the mine, but extends to the whole world. The copper of Japan makes an article of commerce in Europe; the iron of Spain in that of Chili and Peru. The silver of Peru finds its way, not only to Europe, but from Europe to China.

The price of coals in Westmoreland or Shropshire can have little effect on their price at Newcastle; and their price in the Lionnois can have none at all. The productions of such distant coal-mines can never be brought into competition with one another. But the productions of the most distant metallic mines frequently may, and in fact commonly are. The price, therefore, of the coarse, and still more that of the precious metals, at the most fertile mines in the world, must necessarily more or less affect their price at every other in it. The price of copper in Japan must have some influence upon its price at the copper mines in Europe. The price of silver in Peru, or the quantity either of labour or of other goods which it will purchase there, must have some influence on its price, not only at the silver mines of Europe, but at those of China. After the discovery of the mines of Peru, the silver mines of Europe were, the greater part of them, abandoned. The value of silver was so much reduced that their produce could no longer pay the expense of working them, or replace, with a profit, the food, clothes, lodging, and other necessaries which were consumed in that operation. This was the case, too, with the mines of Cuba and St Domingo, and even with the ancient mines of Peru, after the discovery of those of Potosi.

The price of every metal at every mine, therefore, being regulated in some measure by its price at the most fertile mine in the world that is actually wrought, it can at the greater part of mines do very little more than pay the expense of working, and can seldom afford a very high rent to the landlord. Rent, accordingly, seems at the greater part of mines to have but a small share in the price of the coarse, and a still smaller in that of the precious metals. Labour and profit make up the greater part of both.

A sixth part of the gross produce may be reckoned the average rent of the tin mines of Cornwall, the most fertile that are known in the world, as we are told by the Reverend Mr Borlace, vice-warden of the stannaries. Some, he says, afford more, and some do not afford so much. A sixth part of the gross produce is the rent, too, of several very fertile lead mines in Scotland.

In the silver mines of Peru, we are told by Frezier and Ulloa, the proprietor frequently exacts no other acknowledgment from the undertaker of the mine, but that he will grind the ore at his mill, paying him the ordinary multure or price of grinding. Till 1736, indeed, the tax of the King of Spain amounted to one-fifth of the standard silver, which till then might be considered as the real rent of the greater part of the silver mines of Peru, the richest which have been known in the world. If there had been no tax this fifth would naturally have belonged to the landlord, and many mines might have been wrought which could not then be wrought, because they could not afford this tax. The tax of the Duke of Cornwall upon tin is supposed to amount to more than five per cent or one-twentieth part of the value; and whatever may be his proportion, it would naturally, too, belong to the proprietor of the mine, if tin was duty free. But if you add one-twentieth to one-sixth you will find that the whole average rent of the tin mines of Cornwall was to the whole average rent of the silver mines of Peru as thirteen to twelve. But the silver mines of Peru are not now able to pay even this low rent, and the tax upon silver was, in 1736, reduced from one-fifth to one-tenth. Even this tax upon silver, too, gives more temptation to smuggling than the tax of one-twentieth upon tin; and smuggling must be much easier in the precious than in the bulky commodity. The tax of the King of Spain accordingly is said to be very ill paid, and that of the Duke of Cornwall very well. Rent, therefore, it is probable, makes a greater part of the price of tin at the most fertile tin mines than it does of silver at the most fertile silver mines in the world. After replacing the stock employed in working those different mines, together with its ordinary profits, the residue which remains to the proprietor is greater, it seems, in the coarse than in the precious metal.

Neither are the profits of the undertakers of silver mines commonly very great in Peru. The same most respectable and well-informed authors acquaint us, that when any person undertakes to work a new mine in Peru, he is universally looked upon as a man destined to bankruptcy and ruin, and is upon that account shunned and avoided by everybody. Mining, it seems, is considered there in the same light as here, as a lottery, in which the prizes do not compensate the blanks, though the greatness of some tempts many adventurers to throw away their fortunes in such unprosperous projects.

As the sovereign, however, derives a considerable part of his revenue from the produce of silver mines, the law in Peru gives every possible encouragement to the discovery and working of new ones. Whoever discovers a new mine is entitled to measure off two hundred and forty-six feet in length according to what he supposes to be the direction of the vein, and half as much in breadth. He becomes proprietor of this portion of the mine, and can work it without paying any acknowledgement to the landlord. The interest of the Duke of Cornwall has given occasion to a regulation nearly of the same kind in that ancient duchy. In waste and unenclosed lands any person who discovers a tin mine may mark out its limits to a certain extent, which is called bounding a mine. The bounder becomes the real proprietor of the mine, and may either work it himself, or give it in lease to another, without the consent of the owner of the land, to whom, however, a very small acknowledgement must be paid upon working it. In both regulations the sacred rights of private property are sacrificed to the supposed interests of public revenue.

The same encouragement is given in Peru to the discovery and working of new gold mines; and in gold the king's tax amounts only to a twentieth part of the standard metal. It was once a fifth, and afterwards a tenth, as in silver; but it was found that the work could not bear even the lowest of these two taxes. If it is rare, however, say the same authors, Frezier and Ulloa, to find a person who has made his fortune by a silver, it is still much rarer to find one who had done so by a gold mine. This twentieth part seems to be the whole rent which is paid by the greater part of the gold mines in Chili and Peru. Gold, too, is much more liable to be smuggled than even silver; not only on account of the superior value of the metal in proportion to its bulk, but on account of the peculiar way in which nature produces it. Silver is very seldom found virgin, but, like most other metals, is generally mineralized with some other body, from which it is impossible to separate it in such quantities as will pay for the expense, but by a very laborious and tedious operation, which cannot well be carried on but in workhouses erected for the purpose, and therefore exposed to the inspection of the king's officers. Gold, on the contrary, is almost always found virgin. It is sometimes found in pieces of some bulk; and even when mixed in small and almost insensible particles with sand, earth, and other extraneous bodies, it can be separated from them by a very short and simple operation, which can be carried on in any private house by anybody who is possessed of a small quantity of mercury. If the king's tax, therefore, is but ill paid upon silver, it is likely to be much worse paid upon gold; and rent must make a much smaller part of the price of gold than even of that of silver.

The lowest price at which the precious metals can be sold, or the smallest quantity of other goods for which they can be exchanged during any considerable time, is regulated by the same principles which fix the lowest ordinary price of all other goods. The stock which must commonly be employed, the food, the clothes, and lodging which must commonly be consumed in bringing them from the mine to the market, determine it. It must at least be sufficient to replace that stock, with the ordinary profits.

Their highest price, however, seems not to be necessarily determined by anything but the actual scarcity or plenty of those metals themselves. It is not determined by that of any other commodity, in the same manner as the price of coals is by that of wood, beyond which no scarcity can ever raise it. Increase the scarcity of gold to a certain degree, and the smallest bit of it may become more precious than a diamond, and exchange for a greater quantity of other goods.

The demand for those metals arises partly from their utility and partly from their beauty. If you except iron, they are more useful than, perhaps, any other metal. As they are less liable to rust and impurity, they can more easily be kept clean, and the utensils either of the table or the kitchen are often upon that account more agreeable when made of them. A silver boiler is more cleanly than a lead, copper, or tin one; and the same quality would render a gold boiler still better than a silver one. Their principal merit, however, arises from their beauty, which renders them peculiarly fit for the ornaments of dress and furniture. No paint or dye can give so splendid a colour as gilding. The merit of their beauty is greatly enhanced by their scarcity. With the greater part of rich people, the chief enjoyment of riches consists in the parade of riches, which in their eye is never so complete as when they appear to possess those decisive marks of opulence which nobody can possess but themselves. In their eyes the merit of an object which is in any degree either useful or beautiful is greatly enhanced by its scarcity, or by the great labour which it requires to collect any considerable quantity of it, a labour which nobody can afford to pay but themselves. Such objects they are willing to purchase at a higher price than things much more beautiful and useful, but more common. These qualities of utility, beauty, and scarcity, are the original foundation of the high price of those metals, or of the great quantity of other goods for which they can everywhere be exchanged. This value was antecedent to and independent of their being employed as coin, and was the quality which fitted them for that employment. That employment, however, by occasioning a new demand, and by diminishing the quantity which could be employed in any other way, may have afterwards contributed to keep up or increase their value.

The demand for the precious stones arises altogether from their beauty. They are of no use but as ornaments; and the merit of their beauty is greatly enhanced by their scarcity, or by the difficulty and expense of getting them from the mine. Wages and profit accordingly make up, upon most occasions, almost the whole of their high price. Rent comes in but for a very small share; frequently for no share; and the most fertile mines only afford any considerable rent. When Tavernier, a jeweller, visited the diamond mines of Golconda and Visiapour, he was informed that the sovereign of the country, for whose benefit they were wrought, had ordered all of them to be shut up, except those which yield the largest and finest stones. The others, it seems, were to the proprietor not worth the working.

As the price both of the precious metals and of the precious stones is regulated all over the world by their price at the most fertile mine in it, the rent which a mine of either can afford to its proprietor is in proportion, not to its absolute, but to what may be called its relative fertility, or to its superiority over other mines of the same kind. If new mines were discovered as much superior to those of Potosi as they were superior to those of Europe, the value of silver might be so much degraded as to render even the mines of Potosi not worth the working. Before the discovery of the Spanish West Indies, the most fertile mines in Europe may have afforded as great a rent to their proprietor as the richest mines in Peru do at present. Though the quantity of silver was much less, it might have exchanged for an equal quantity of other goods, and the proprietor's share might have enabled him to purchase or command an equal quantity either of labour or of commodities. The value both of the produce and of the rent, the real revenue which they afforded both to the public and to the proprietor, might have been the same.

The most abundant mines either of the precious metals or of the precious stones could add little to the wealth of the world. A produce of which the value is principally derived from its scarcity, is necessarily degraded by its abundance. A service of plate, and the other frivolous ornaments of dress and furniture, could be purchased for a smaller quantity of labour, or for a smaller quantity of commodities; and in this would consist the sole advantage which the world could derive from that abundance.

It is otherwise in estates above ground. The value both of their produce and of their rent is in proportion to their absolute, and not to their relative fertility. The land which produces a certain quantity of food, clothes, and lodging, can always feed, clothe, and lodge a certain number of people; and whatever may be the proportion of the landlord, it will always give him a proportionable command of the labour of those people, and of the commodities with which that labour can supply him. The value of the most barren lands is not diminished by the neighbourhood of the most fertile. On the contrary, it is generally increased by it. The great number of people maintained by the fertile lands afford a market to many parts of the produce of the barren,

THE RENT OF LAND

which they could never have found among those whom their own produce could maintain.

Whatever increases the fertility of land in producing food increases not only the value of the lands upon which the improvement is bestowed, but contributes likewise to increase that of many other lands by creating a new demand for their produce. That abundance of food, of which, in consequence of the improvement of land, many people have the disposal beyond what they themselves can consume, is the great cause of the demand both for the precious metals and the precious stones, as well as for every other conveniency and ornament of dress, lodging, household furniture, and equipage. Food not only constitutes the principal part of the riches of the world, but it is the abundance of food which gives the principal part of their value to many other sorts of riches. The poor inhabitants of Cuba and St Domingo, when they were first discovered by the Spaniards, used to wear little bits of gold as ornaments in their hair and other parts of their dress. They seemed to value them as we would do any little pebbles of somewhat more than ordinary beauty, and to consider them as just worth the picking up, but not worth the refusing to anybody who asked them. They gave them to their new guests at the first request, without seeming to think that they had made them any very valuable present. They were astonished to observe the rage of the Spaniards to obtain them; and had no notion that there could anywhere be a country in which many people had the disposal of so great a superfluity of food, so scanty always among themselves, that for a very small quantity of those glittering baubles they would willingly give as much as might maintain a whole family for many years. Could they have been made to understand this, the passion of the Spaniards would not have surprised them.

PART III

*Of the Variations in the Proportion between the respective
Values of that Sort of Produce which always affords Rent, and of
that which sometimes does and sometimes does not afford Rent*

The increasing abundance of food, in consequence of increasing
improvement and cultivation, must necessarily increase the demand for every part of the produce of land which is not food,
and which can be applied either to use or to ornament. In the
whole progress of improvement, it might therefore be expected,
there should be only one variation in the comparative values of
those two different sorts of produce. The value of that sort
which sometimes does and sometimes does not afford rent,
should constantly rise in proportion to that which always
affords some rent. As art and industry advance, the materials of
clothing and lodging, the useful fossils and minerals of the
earth, the precious metals and the precious stones should gradually come to be more and more in demand, should gradually exchange for a greater and a greater quantity of food, or in other
words, should gradually become dearer and dearer. This accordingly has been the case with most of these things upon most
occasions, and would have been the case with all of them upon
all occasions, if particular accidents had not upon some occasions increased the supply of some of them in a still greater
proportion than the demand.

The value of a free-stone quarry, for example, will necessarily
increase with the increasing improvement and population of the
country round about it, especially if it should be the only one in
the neighbourhood. But the value of a silver mine, even though
there should not be another within a thousand miles of it, will
not necessarily increase with the improvement of the country in
which it is situated. The market for the produce of a free-stone
quarry can seldom extend more than a few miles round about it,
and the demand must generally be in proportion to the improvement and population of that small district. But the market
for the produce of a silver mine may extend over the whole
known world. Unless the world in general, therefore, be advancing in improvement and population, the demand for silver

might not be at all increased by the improvement even of a large country in the neighbourhood of the mine. Even though the world in general were improving, yet if, in the course of its improvement, new mines should be discovered, much more fertile than any which had been known before, though the demand for silver would necessarily increase, yet the supply might increase in so much a greater proportion that the real price of that metal might gradually fall; that is, any given quantity, a pound weight of it, for example, might gradually purchase or command a smaller and a smaller quantity of labour, or exchange for a smaller and a smaller quantity of corn, the principal part of the subsistence of the labourer.

The great market for silver is the commercial and civilized part of the world.

If by the general progress of improvement the demand of this market should increase, while at the same time the supply did not increase in the same proportion, the value of silver would gradually rise in proportion to that of corn. Any given quantity of silver would exchange for a greater and a greater quantity of corn; or, in other words, the average money price of corn would gradually become cheaper and cheaper.

If, on the contrary, the supply by some accident should increase for many years together in a greater proportion than the demand, that metal would gradually become cheaper and cheaper; or, in other words, the average money price of corn would, in spite of all improvements, gradually become dearer and dearer.

But if, on the other hand, the supply of the metal should increase nearly in the same proportion as the demand, it would continue to purchase or exchange for nearly the same quantity of corn, and the average money price of corn would, in spite of all improvements, continue very nearly the same.

These three seem to exhaust all the possible combinations of events which can happen in the progress of improvement; and during the course of the four centuries preceding the present, if we may judge by what has happened both in France and Great Britain, each of those three different combinations seem to have taken place in the European market, and nearly in the same order, too, in which I have here set them down.

DIGRESSION CONCERNING THE VARIATIONS
IN THE VALUE OF SILVER DURING THE COURSE
OF THE LAST FOUR CENTURIES

First Period

In 1350, and for some time before, the average price of the quarter of wheat in England seems not to have been estimated lower than four ounces of silver, Tower-weight, equal to about twenty shillings of our present money. From this price it seems to have fallen gradually to two ounces of silver, equal to about ten shillings of our present money, the price at which we find it estimated in the beginning of the sixteenth century, and at which it seems to have continued to be estimated till about 1570.

In 1350, being the 25th of Edward III, was enacted what is called, *The Statute of Labourers*. In the preamble it complains much of the insolence of servants, who endeavoured to raise their wages upon their masters. It therefore ordains that all servants and labourers should for the future be contented with the same wages and liveries (liveries in those times signified not only clothes but provisions) which they had been accustomed to receive in the 20th year of the king, and the four preceding years; that upon this account their livery wheat should nowhere be estimated higher than tenpence a bushel, and that it should always be in the option of the master to deliver them either the wheat or the money. Tenpence a bushel, therefore, had, in the 25th of Edward III, been reckoned a very moderate price of wheat, since it required a particular statute to oblige servants to accept of it in exchange for their usual livery of provisions; and it had been reckoned a reasonable price ten years before that, or in the 16th year of the king, the term to which the statute refers. But in the 16th year of Edward III, tenpence contained about half an ounce of silver, Tower-weight, and was nearly equal to half-a-crown of our present money. Four ounces of silver, Tower-weight, therefore, equal to six shillings and eightpence of the money of those times, and to near twenty shillings of that of the present, must have been reckoned a moderate price for the quarter of eight bushels.

This statute is surely a better evidence of what was reckoned in those times a moderate price of grain than the prices of some particular years which have generally been recorded by historians and other writers on account of their extraordinary dearness or cheapness, and from which, therefore, it is difficult to form any judgement concerning what may have been the ordinary price. There are, besides, other reasons for believing that in the beginning of the fourteenth century, and for some time before, the common price of wheat was not less than four ounces of silver the quarter, and that of other grain in proportion.

In 1309, Ralph de Born, prior of St Augustine's, Canterbury, gave a feast upon his installation-day, of which William Thorn has preserved not only the bill of fare but the prices of many particulars. In that feast were consumed, first, fifty-three quarters of wheat, which cost nineteen pounds, or seven shillings and twopence a quarter, equal to about one-and-twenty shillings and sixpence of our present money; secondly, fifty-eight quarters of malt, which cost seventeen pounds ten shillings, or six shillings a quarter, equal to about eighteen shillings of our present money; thirdly, twenty quarters of oats, which cost four pounds, or four shillings a quarter, equal to about twelve shillings of our present money. The prices of malt and oats seem here to be higher than their ordinary proportion to the price of wheat.

These prices are not recorded on account of their extraordinary dearness or cheapness, but are mentioned accidentally as the prices actually paid for large quantities of grain consumed at a feast which was famous for its magnificence.

In 1262, being the 51st of Henry III, was revived an ancient statute called, *The Assize of Bread and Ale*, which the king says in the preamble had been made in the times of his progenitors sometime kings of England. It is probably, therefore, as old at least as the time of his grandfather Henry II, and may have been as old as the conquest. It regulates the price of bread according as the prices of wheat may happen to be, from one shilling to twenty shillings the quarter of the money of those times. But statutes of this kind are generally presumed to provide with equal care for all deviations from the middle price, for

those below it as well as for those above it. Ten shillings, therefore, containing six ounces of silver, Tower-weight, and equal
to about thirty shillings of our present money, must, upon this
supposition, have been reckoned the middle price of the quarter
of wheat when this statute was first enacted, and must have
continued to be so in the 51st of Henry III. We cannot therefore
be very wrong in supposing that the middle price was not less
than one-third of the highest price at which this statute regulates the price of bread, or than six shillings and eightpence of
the money of those times, containing four ounces of silver,
Tower-weight.

From these different facts, therefore, we seem to have some
reason to conclude that, about the middle of the fourteenth
century, and for a considerable time before, the average or
ordinary price of the quarter of wheat was not supposed to be
less than four ounces of silver, Tower-weight.

From about the middle of the fourteenth to the beginning of
the sixteenth century, what was reckoned the reasonable and
moderate, that is the ordinary or average price of wheat, seems
to have sunk gradually to about one-half of this price; so as at
last to have fallen to about two ounces of silver, Tower-weight,
equal to about ten shillings of our present money. It continued
to be estimated at this price till about 1570.

In the household book of Henry, the fifth Earl of Northumberland, drawn up in 1512, there are two different estimations
of wheat. In one of them it is computed at six shillings and
eightpence the quarter, in the other at five shillings and eightpence only. In 1512, six shillings and eightpence contained only
two ounces of silver, Tower-weight, and were equal to about
ten shillings of our present money.

From the 25th of Edward III to the beginning of the reign of
Elizabeth, during the space of more than two hundred years, six
shillings and eightpence, it appears from several different
statutes, had continued to be considered as what is called the
moderate and reasonable, that is the ordinary average price of
wheat. The quantity of silver, however, contained in that nominal sum was, during the course of this period, continually
diminishing, in consequence of some alterations which were
made in the coin. But the increase of the value of silver had, it

seems, so far compensated the diminution of the quantity of it contained in the same nominal sum that the legislature did not think it worth while to attend to this circumstance.

Thus in 1436 it was enacted, that wheat might be exported without a licence when the price was so low as six shillings and eightpence; and in 1463 it was enacted, that no wheat should be imported if the price was not above six shillings and eightpence the quarter. The legislature had imagined that when the price was so low there could be no inconveniency in exportation, but that when it rose higher it became prudent to allow of importation. Six shillings and eightpence, therefore, containing about the same quantity of silver as thirteen shillings and fourpence of our present money (one third part less than the same nominal sum contained in the time of Edward III), had in those times been considered as what is called the moderate and reasonable price of wheat.

In 1554, by the 1st and 2nd of Philip and Mary; and in 1558, by the 1st of Elizabeth, the exportation of wheat was in the some manner prohibited, whenever the price of the quarter should exceed six shillings and eightpence, which did not then contain two pennyworth more silver than the same nominal sum does at present. But it had soon been found that to restrain the exportation of wheat till the price was so very low was, in reality, to prohibit it altogether. In 1562, therefore, by the 5th of Elizabeth, the exportation of wheat was allowed from certain ports whenever the price of the quarter should not exceed ten shillings, containing nearly the same quantity of silver as the like nominal sum does at present. This price had at this time, therefore, been considered as what is called the moderate and reasonable price of wheat. It agrees nearly with the estimation of the Northumberland book in 1512.

That in France the average price of grain was, in the same manner, much lower in the end of the fifteenth and beginning of the sixteenth century than in the two centuries preceeding, has been observed both by Mr Duprè de St Maur, and by the elegant author of the Essay on the police of grain. Its price, during the same period, had probably sunk in the same manner through the greater part of Europe.

This rise in the value of silver in proportion to that of corn, may either have been owing altogether to the increase of the demand for that metal, in consequence of increasing improvement and cultivation, the supply in the meantime continuing the same as before; or, the demand continuing the same as before, it may have been owing altogether to the gradual diminution of the supply; the greater part of the mines which were then known in the world being much exhausted, and consequently the expense of working them much increased; or it may have been owing partly to the one and partly to the other of those two circumstances. In the end of the fifteenth and beginning of the sixteenth centuries, the greater part of Europe was approaching towards a more settled form of government than it had enjoyed for several ages before. The increase of security would naturally increase industry and improvement; and the demand for the precious metals, as well as for every other luxury and ornament, would naturally increase with the increase of riches. A greater annual produce would require a greater quantity of coin to circulate it; and a greater number of rich people would require a greater quantity of plate and other ornaments of silver. It is natural to suppose, too, that the greater part of the mines which then supplied the European market with silver might be a good deal exhausted, and have become more expensive in the working. They had been wrought many of them from the time of the Romans.

It has been the opinion, however, of the greater part of those who have written upon the prices of commodities in ancient times that, from the Conquest, perhaps from the invasion of Julius Caesar, till the discovery of the mines of America, the value of silver was continually diminishing. This opinion they seem to have been led into, partly by the observations which they had occasion to make upon the prices both of corn and of some other parts of the rude produce of land; and partly by the popular notion that as the quantity of silver naturally increases in every country with the increase of wealth, so its value diminishes as its quantity increases.

In their observations upon the prices of corn, three different circumstances seem frequently to have misled them.

First, in ancient times almost all rents were paid in kind; in a certain quantity of corn, cattle, poultry, etc. It sometimes hap-

pened, however, that the landlord would stipulate that he
should be at liberty to demand of the tenant, either the annual
payment in kind, or a certain sum of money instead of it. The
price at which the payment in kind was in this manner exchanged for a certain sum of money is in Scotland called the
conversion price. As the option is always in the landlord to take
either the substance or the price, it is necessary for the safety of
the tenant, that the conversion price should rather be below than
above the average market price. In many places, accordingly, it
is not much above one-half of this price. Through the greater
part of Scotland this custom still continues with regard to
poultry, and in some places with regard to cattle. It might probably have continued to take place, too, with regard to corn, had
not the institution of the public fiars put an end to it. These are
annual valuations, according to the judgement of an assize, of
the average price of all the different sorts of grain, and of all the
different qualities of each, according to the actual market price
in every different county. This institution rendered it sufficiently safe for the tenant, and much more convenient for the
landlord, to convert, as they call it, the corn rent, rather at what
should happen to be the price of the fiars of each year, than at
any certain fixed price. But the writers who have collected the
prices of corn in ancient times seem frequently to have mistaken
what is called in Scotland the conversion price for the actual
market price. Fleetwood acknowledges, upon one occasion, that
he had made this mistake. As he wrote his book, however, for a
particular purpose, he does not think proper to make this
acknowledgement till after transcribing this conversion price
fifteen times. The price is eight shillings the quarter of wheat.
This sum in 1423, the year at which he begins with it, contained
the same quantity of silver as sixteen shillings of our present
money. But in 1562, the year at which he ends with it, it contained no more than the same nominal sum does at present.

Secondly, they have been misled by the slovenly manner in
which some ancient statutes of assize had been sometimes
transcribed by lazy copiers; and sometimes perhaps actually
composed by the legislature.

The ancient statutes of assize seem to have begun always with
determining what ought to be the price of bread and ale when

the price of wheat and barley were at the lowest, and to have proceeded gradually to determine what it ought to be, according as the prices of those two sorts of grain should gradually rise above this lowest price. But the transcribers of those statutes seem frequently to have thought it sufficient to copy the regulation as far as the three or four first and lowest prices, saving in this manner their own labour, and judging, I suppose, that this was enough to show what proportion ought to be observed in all higher prices.

Thus in the assize of bread and ale, of the 51st of Henry III, the price of bread was regulated according to the different prices of wheat, from one shilling to twenty shillings the quarter, of the money of those times. But in the manuscripts from which all the different editions of the statutes, preceding that of Mr Ruffhead, were printed, the copiers had never transcribed this regulation beyond the price of twelve shillings. Several writers, therefore, being misled by this faulty transcription, very naturally concluded that the middle price, or six shillings the quarter, equal to about eighteen shillings of our present money, was the ordinary or average price of wheat at that time.

In the statute of Tumbrel and Pillory, enacted nearly about the same time, the price of ale is regulated according to every sixpence rise in the price of barley, from two shillings to four shillings the quarter. That four shillings, however, was not considered as the highest price to which barley might frequently rise in those times, and that these prices were only given as an example of the proportion which ought to be observed in all other prices, whether higher or lower, we may infer from the last words of the statute; 'et sic deinceps crescetur vel diminuetur per sex denarios.' The expression is very slovenly, but the meaning is plain enough : 'That the price of ale is in this manner to be increased or diminished according to every sixpence rise or fall in the price of barley.' In the composition of this statute the legislature itself seems to have been as negligent as the copiers were in the transcription of the others.

In an ancient manuscript of the Regiam Majestatem, an old Scotch law book, there is a statute of assize in which the price of bread is regulated according to all the different prices of wheat, from tenpence to three shillings the Scotch boll, equal to about half an English quarter. Three shillings Scotch, at the time when this assize is supposed to have been enacted, were equal to about nine shillings sterling of our present money. Mr Ruddiman seems to conclude from this, that three shillings was the highest price to which wheat ever rose in those times, and that tenpence, a shilling, or at most two shillings, were the ordinary prices. Upon consulting the manuscript, however, it appears evidently[1] that all these prices are only set down as examples of the proportion which ought to be observed between the respective prices of wheat and bread. The last words of the statute are, 'reliqua judicabis secundum præscripta habendo respectum ad pretium bladi.' 'You shall judge of the remaining cases according to what is above written, having a respect to the price of corn.'

Thirdly, they seem to have been misled, too, by the very low price at which wheat was sometimes sold in very ancient times; and to have imagined that as its lowest price was then much lower than in later times, its ordinary price must likewise have been much lower. They might have found, however, that in those ancient times its highest price was fully as much above, as its lowest price was below anything that had ever been known in later times. Thus in 1270, Fleetwood gives us two prices of the quarter of wheat. The one is four pounds sixteen shillings of the money of those times, equal to fourteen pounds eight shillings of that of the present; the other is six pounds eight shillings, equal to nineteen pounds four shillings of our present money. No price can be found in the end of the fifteenth, or beginning of the sixteenth century, which approaches to the extravagance of these. The price of corn, though at all times liable to variation, varies most in those turbulent and disorderly societies, in which the interruption of all commerce and communication hinders the plenty of one part of the country from relieving the scarcity of another. In the disorderly state of England under the Plantagenets, who governed it from about the middle of the twelfth till towards the end of the fifteenth century, one district might be in plenty, while another at no great distance, by having its crop destroyed either by some

1. See his preface to Anderson's *Diplomata Scotiae*.

accident of the seasons, or by the incursion of some neighbouring baron, might be suffering all the horrors of a famine; and
yet if the lands of some hostile lord were interposed between
them, the one might not be able to give the least assistance to
the other. Under the vigorous administration of the Tudors,
who governed England during the latter part of the fifteenth
and through the whole of the sixteenth century, no baron was
powerful enough to dare to disturb the public security.

The reader will find at the end of this chapter all the prices of
wheat which have been collected by Fleetwood from 1202 to
1597, both inclusive, reduced to the money of the present times,
and digested according to the order of time, into seven divisions
of twelve years each. At the end of each division, too, he will
find the average price of the twelve years of which it consists. In
that long period of time, Fleetwood has been able to collect the
prices of no more than eighty years, so that four years are wanting to make out the last twelve years. I have added, therefore,
from the accounts of Eton college, the prices of 1598, 1599, 1600,
and 1601. It is the only addition which I have made. The reader
will see that from the beginning of the thirteenth, till after the
middle of the sixteenth century, the average price of each twelve
years grows gradually lower and lower; and that towards the
end of the sixteenth century it begins to rise again. The prices,
indeed, which Fleetwood has been able to collect, seem to have
been those chiefly which were remarkable for extraordinary
dearness or cheapness; and I do not pretend that any very certain conclusion can be drawn from them. So far, however, as
they prove anything at all, they confirm the account which I
have been endeavouring to give. Fleetwood himself, however,
seems, with most other writers, to have believed that during all
this period the value of silver, in consequence of its increasing
abundance, was continually diminishing. The prices of corn
which he himself has collected certainly do not agree with this
opinion. They agree perfectly with that of Mr Duprè de St
Maur, and with that which I have been endeavouring to explain. Bishop Fleetwood and Mr Duprè de St Maur are the two
authors who seem to have collected with the greatest diligence
and fidelity, the prices of things in ancient times. It is somewhat
curious that, though their opinions are so very different, their

facts, so far as they relate to the price of corn at least, should coincide so very exactly.

It is not, however, so much from the low price of corn as from that of some other parts of the rude produce of land that the most judicious writers have inferred the great value of silver in those very ancient times. Corn, it has been said, being a sort of manufacture, was, in those rude ages, much dearer in proportion than the greater part of other commodities; it is meant, I suppose, than the greater part of unmanufactured commodities, such as cattle, poultry, game of all kinds, etc. That in those times of poverty and barbarism these were proportionably much cheaper than corn is undoubtedly true. But this cheapness was not the effect of the high value of silver, but of the low value of those commodities. It was not because silver would in such times purchase or represent a greater quantity of labour, but because such commodities would purchase or represent a much smaller quantity than in times of more opulence and improvement. Silver must certainly be cheaper in Spanish America than in Europe; in the country where it is produced than in the country to which it is brought, at the expense of a long carriage both by land and by sea, of a freight and an insurance. One-and-twenty pence halfpenny sterling, however, we are told by Ulloa, was, not many years ago, at Buenos Ayres, the price of an ox chosen from a herd of three or four hundred. Sixteen shillings sterling, we are told by Mr Byron, was the price of a good horse in the capital of Chili. In a country naturally fertile, but of which the far greater part is altogether uncultivated, cattle, poultry, game of all kinds, etc., as they can be acquired with a very small quantity of labour, so they will purchase or command but a very small quantity. The low money price for which they may be sold is no proof that the real value of silver is there very high, but the real value of those commodities is very low.

Labour, it must always be remembered, and not any particular commodity or set of commodities, is the real measure of the value both of silver and of all other commodities.

But in countries almost waste, or but thinly inhabited, cattle, poultry, game of all kinds, etc., as they are the spontaneous productions of nature, so she frequently produces them in much greater quantities than the consumption of the inhabitants requires. In such a state of things the supply commonly exceeds the demand. In different states of society, in different stages of improvement, therefore, such commodities will represent or be equivalent to, very different quantities of labour.

In every state of society, in every stage of improvement, corn is the production of human industry. But the average produce of every sort of industry is always suited, more or less exactly, to the average consumption; the average supply to the average demand. In every different stage of improvement, besides, the raising of equal quantities of corn in the same soil and climate will, at an average, require nearly equal quantities of labour; or what comes to the same thing, the price of nearly equal quantities; the continual increase of the productive powers of labour in an improving state of cultivation being more or less counterbalanced by the continually increasing price of cattle, the principal instruments of agriculture. Upon all these accounts, therefore, we may rest assured that equal quantities of corn will, in every state of society, in every stage of improvement, more nearly represent, or be equivalent to, equal quantities of labour than equal quantities of any other part of the rude produce of land. Corn, accordingly, it has already been observed, is, in all the different stages of wealth and improvement, a more accurate measure of value than any other commodity or set of commodities. In all those different stages, therefore, we can judge better of the real value of silver by comparing it with corn than by comparing it with any other commodity or set of commodities.

Corn, besides, or whatever else is the common and favourite vegetable food of the people, constitutes, in every civilized country, the principal part of the subsistence of the labourer. In consequence of the extension of agriculture, the land of every country produces a much greater quantity of vegetable than of animal food, and the labourer everywhere lives chiefly upon the wholesome food that is cheapest and most abundant. Butcher's meat, except in the most thriving countries, or where labour is most highly rewarded, makes but an insignificant part of his subsistence; poultry makes a still smaller part of it, and game no part of it. In France, and even in Scotland, where labour is somewhat better rewarded than in France, the labouring poor seldom eat butcher's meat, except upon holidays, and other extraordinary occasions. The money price of labour, therefore, depends much more upon the average money price of corn, the subsistence of the labourer, than upon that of butcher's meat, or of any other part of the rude produce of land. The real value of gold and silver, therefore, the real quantity of labour which they can purchase or command, depends much more upon the quantity of corn which they can purchase or command than upon that of butcher's meat, or any other part of the rude produce of land.

Such slight observations, however, upon the prices either of corn or of other commodities, would not probably have misled so many intelligent authors had they not been influenced, at the same time, by the popular notion, that as the quantity of silver naturally increases in every country with the increase of wealth, so its value diminishes as its quantity increases. This notion, however, seems to be altogether groundless.

The quantity of the precious metals may increase in any country from two different causes: either, first, from the increased abundance of the mines which supply it; or, secondly, from the increased wealth of the people, from the increased produce of their annual labour. The first of these causes is no doubt necessarily connected with the diminution of the value of the precious metals, but the second is not.

When more abundant mines are discovered, a greater quantity of the precious metals is brought to market, and the quantity of the necessaries and conveniences of life for which they must be exchanged being the same as before, equal quantities of the metals must be exchanged for smaller quantities of commodities. So far, therefore, as the increase of the quantity of the precious metals in any country arises from the increased abundance of the mines, it is necessarily connected with some diminution of their value.

When, on the contrary, the wealth of any country increases, when the annual produce of its labour becomes gradually greater and greater, a greater quantity of coin becomes necessary in order to circulate a greater quantity of commodities; and the people, as they can afford it, as they have more commodities to give for it, will naturally purchase a greater and a greater quantity of plate. The quantity of their coin will increase from necessity; the quantity of their plate from vanity and ostentation, or from the same reason that the quantity of fine statues, pictures, and of every other luxury and curiosity, is likely to increase among them. But as statuaries and painters are not likely to be worse rewarded in times of wealth and prosperity than in times of poverty and depression, so gold and silver are not likely to be worse paid for.

The price of gold and silver, when the accidental discovery of more abundant mines does not keep it down, as it naturally rises with the wealth of every country, so, whatever be the state of the mines, it is at all times naturally higher in a rich than in a poor country. Gold and silver, like all other commodities, naturally seek the market where the best price is given for them, and the best price is commonly given for every thing in the country which can best afford it. Labour, it must be remembered, is the ultimate price which is paid for everything, and in countries where labour is equally well rewarded, the money price of labour will be in proportion to that of the subsistence of the labourer. But gold and silver will naturally exchange for a greater quantity of subsistence in a rich than in a poor country, in a country which abounds with subsistence than in one which is but indifferently supplied with it. If the two countries are at a great distance, the difference may be very great; because though the metals naturally fly from the worse to the better market, yet it may be difficult to transport them in such quantities as to bring their price nearly to a level in both. If the countries are near, the difference will be smaller, and may sometimes be scarce perceptible; because in this case the transportation will be easy. China is a much richer country than any part of Europe, and the difference between the price of subsistence in China and in Europe is very great. Rice in China is much cheaper than wheat is anywhere in Europe. England is a much richer country than Scotland; but the difference between the money-price of corn in those two countries is much smaller, and is but just perceptible. In proportion to the quantity or measure, Scotch corn generally appears to be a good deal cheaper than English; but in proportion to its quality, it is certainly somewhat dearer. Scotland receives almost every year very large supplies from England, and every commodity must commonly be somewhat dearer in the country to which it is brought than in that from which it comes. English corn, therefore, must be dearer in Scotland than in England, and yet in proportion to its quality, or to the quantity and goodness of the flour or meal which can be made from it, it cannot commonly be sold higher there than the Scotch corn which comes to market in competition with it.

The difference between the money price of labour in China and in Europe is still greater than that between the money price of subsistence; because the real recompense of labour is higher in Europe than in China, the greater part of Europe being in an improving state, while China seems to be standing still. The money price of labour is lower in Scotland than in England because the real recompense of labour is much lower; Scotland, though advancing to greater wealth, advancing much more slowly than England. The frequency of emigration from Scotland, and the rarity of it from England, sufficiently prove that the demand for labour is very different in the two countries. The proportion between the real recompense of labour in different countries, it must be remembered, is naturally regulated not by their actual wealth or poverty, but by their advancing, stationary, or declining condition.

Gold and silver, as they are naturally of the greatest value among the richest, so they are naturally of the least value among the poorest nations. Among savages, the poorest of all nations, they are of scarce any value.

In great towns corn is always dearer than in remote parts of the country. This, however, is the effect, not of the real cheapness of silver, but of the real dearness of corn. It does not cost less labour to bring silver to the great town than to the remote parts of the country; but it costs a great deal more to bring corn.

In some very rich and commercial countries, such as Holland and the territory of Genoa, corn is dear for the same reason that it is dear in great towns. They do not produce enough to maintain their inhabitants. They are rich in the industry and skill of their artificers and manufacturers; in every sort of machinery which can facilitate and abridge labour; in shipping, and in all the other instruments and means of carriage and commerce: but they are poor in corn, which, as it must be brought to them from distant countries, must, by an addition to its price, pay for the carriage from those countries. It does not cost less labour to bring silver to Amsterdam than to Dantzick; but it costs a great deal more to bring corn. The real cost of silver must be nearly the same in both places; but that of corn must be very different. Diminish the real opulence either of Holland or of the territory of Genoa, while the number of their inhabitants remains the same: diminish their power of supplying themselves from distant countries; and the price of corn, instead of sinking with that diminution in the quantity of their silver, which must necessarily accompany this declension either as its cause or as its effect, will rise to the price of a famine. When we are in want of necessaries we must part with all superfluities, of which the value, as it rises in times of opulence and prosperity, so it sinks in times of poverty and distress. It is otherwise with necessaries. Their real price, the quantity of labour which they can purchase or command, rises in times of poverty and distress, and sinks in times of opulence and prosperity, which are always times of great abundance; for they could not otherwise be times of opulence and prosperity. Corn is a necessary, silver is only a superfluity.

Whatever, therefore, may have been the increase in the quantity of the precious metals, which, during the period between the middle of the fourteenth and that of the sixteenth century, arose from the increase of wealth and improvement, it could have no tendency to diminish their value either in Great Britain or in any other part of Europe. If those who have collected the prices of things in ancient times, therefore, had, during this period, no reason to infer the diminution of the value of silver, from any observations which they had made upon the prices either of corn or of other commodities, they had still less reason to infer it from any supposed increase of wealth and improvement.

Second Period

But how various soever may have been the opinions of the learned concerning the progress of the value of silver during this first period, they are unanimous concerning it during the second.

From about 1570 to about 1640, during a period of about seventy years, the variation in the proportion between the value of silver and that of corn, held a quite opposite course. Silver sunk in its real value, or would exchange for a smaller quantity of labour than before; and corn rose in its nominal price, and instead of being commonly sold for about two ounces of silver the quarter, or about ten shillings of our present money, came to be sold for six and eight ounces of silver the quarter, or about thirty and forty shillings of our present money.

The discovery of the abundant mines of America seems to have been the sole cause of this diminution in the value of silver in proportion to that of corn. It is accounted for accordingly in the same manner by everybody; and there never has been any dispute either about the fact or about the cause of it. The greater part of Europe was, during this period, advancing in industry and improvement, and the demand for silver must consequently have been increasing. But the increase of the supply had, it seems, so far exceeded that of the demand, that the value of that metal sunk considerably. The discovery of the mines of America, it is to be observed, does not seem to have had any very sensible effect upon the prices of things in England till after 1570; though even the mines of Potosi had been discovered more than twenty years before.

From 1595 to 1620, both inclusive, the average price of the quarter of nine bushels of the best wheat at Windsor market appears, from the accounts of Eton College, to have been £2 1s. $6\frac{9}{13}d.$ From which sum, neglecting the fraction, and deducting a ninth, or 4s. $7\frac{1}{3}d.$ the price of the quarter of eight bushels comes out to have been £1 16s. $10\frac{2}{3}d.$ And from this sum, neglecting likewise the fraction, and deducting a ninth, or 4s. $1\frac{1}{9}d.$, for the difference between the price of the best wheat and that of the middle wheat, the price of the middle wheat comes out to have been about £1 12s. $8\frac{8}{9}d.$, or about six ounces and one-third of an ounce of silver.

From 1621 to 1636, both inclusive, the average price of the same measure of the best wheat at the same market appears, from the same accounts, to have been £2 10s.; from which making the like deductions as in the foregoing case, the average price of the quarter of eight bushels of middle wheat comes out to have been £1 19s. 6d., or about seven ounces and two-thirds of an ounce of silver.

Third Period

Between 1630 and 1640, or about 1636, the effect of the discovery of the mines of America in reducing the value of silver appears to have been completed, and the value of that metal seems never to have sunk lower in proportion to that of corn than it was about that time. It seems to have risen somewhat in the course of the present century, and it had probably begun to do so even some time before the end of the last.

From 1637 to 1700, both inclusive, being the sixty-four last years of the last century, the average price of the quarter of nine bushels of the best wheat at Windsor market appears, from the same accounts, to have been £2 11s. 0⅓d., which is only 1s. 0⅓d. dearer than it had been during the sixteen years before. But in the course of these sixty-four years there happened two events which must have produced a much greater scarcity of corn than what the course of the seasons would otherwise have occasioned, and which, therefore, without supposing any further reduction in the value of silver, will much more than account for this very small enhancement of price.

The first of these events was the civil war, which, by discouraging tillage and interrupting commerce, must have raised the price of corn much above what the course of the seasons would otherwise have occasioned. It must have had this effect more or less at all the different markets in the kingdom, but particularly at those in the neighbourhood of London, which require to be supplied from the greatest distance. In 1648, accordingly, the price of the best wheat at Windsor market appears, from the same accounts, to have been £4 5s., and in 1649 to have been £4 the quarter of nine bushels. The excess of those two years above £2 10s. (the average price of the sixteen years preceding 1637) is £3 5s.; which divided among the sixty-four last years of the last century will alone very nearly account for that small enhancement of price which seems to have taken place in them. These, however, though the highest, are by no means the only high prices which seem to have been occasioned by the civil wars.

The second event was the bounty upon the exportation of corn granted in 1688. The bounty, it has been thought by many people, by encouraging tillage, may, in a long course of years, have occasioned a greater abundance, and consequently a greater cheapness of corn in the home-market than what would otherwise have taken place there. How far the bounty could produce this effect at any time, I shall examine hereafter; I shall only observe at present that, between 1688 and 1700, it had not time to produce any such effect. During this short period its only effect must have been, by encouraging the exportation of the surplus produce of every year, and thereby hindering the abundance of one year from compensating the scarcity of another, to raise the price in the home-market. The scarcity which prevailed in England from 1693 to 1699, both inclusive, though no doubt principally owing to the badness of the seasons, and, therefore, extending through a considerable part of Europe, must have been somewhat enhanced by the bounty. In 1699, accordingly, the further exportation of corn was prohibited for nine months.

There was a third event which occurred in the course of the same period, and which, though it could not occasion any scarcity of corn, nor, perhaps, any augmentation in the real quantity of silver which was usually paid for it, must necessarily have occasioned some augmentation in the nominal sum. This event was the great debasement of the silver coin, by clipping and wearing. This evil had begun in the reign of Charles II and had gone on continually increasing till 1695; at which time, as we may learn from Mr Lowndes, the current silver coin was, at an average, near five-and-twenty per cent below its standard value. But the nominal sum which constitutes the market price of every commodity is necessarily regulated, not so much by the quantity of silver, which, according to the standard, ought to be contained in it, as by that which, it is found by experience, actually is contained in it. This nominal sum, therefore, is necessarily higher when the coin is much debased by clipping and wearing than when near to its standard value.

In the course of the present century, the silver coin has not at any time been more below its standard weight than it is at present. But though very much defaced, its value has been kept up by that of the gold coin for which it is exchanged. For though before the late recoinage, the gold coin was a good deal defaced too, it was less so than the silver. In 1695, on the contrary, the value of the silver coin was not kept up by the gold coin; a guinea then commonly exchanging for thirty shillings of the worn and clipt silver. Before the late recoinage of the gold, the price of silver bullion was seldom higher than five shillings and sevenpence an ounce, which is but fivepence above the mint price. But in 1695, the common price of silver bullion was six shillings and fivepence an ounce,[1] which is fifteenpence above the mint price. Even before the late recoinage of the gold, therefore, the coin, gold and silver together, when compared with silver bullion, was not supposed to be more than eight per cent below its standard value. In 1695, on the contrary, it had been supposed to be near five-and-twenty per cent below that value. But in the beginning of the present century, that is, immediately after the great recoinage in King William's time, the greater part of the current silver coin must have been still nearer to its standard weight than it is at present. In the course of the present century, too, there has been no great public calamity, such as the civil war, which could either discourage tillage, or interrupt the interior commerce of the country. And though the bounty, which has taken place through the greater part of this century, must always raise the price of corn somewhat higher than it otherwise would be in the actual state of tillage; yet as, in the course of this century, the bounty has had full time to produce all the good effects commonly imputed to it, to encourage tillage, and thereby to increase the quantity of corn in the home market, it may, upon the principles of a system which I shall explain and examine hereafter, be supposed to have done something to lower the price of that commodity the one way, as well as to raise it the other. It is by many people supposed to have done more. In the sixty-four first years of the present century accordingly the average price of the quarter of nine bushels of the best wheat at Windsor market appears, by the accounts of

1. Lowndes's *Essay on the Silver Coin*, p. 68.

Eton College, to have been £2 0s. 6$\frac{9}{32}$d., which is about ten
shillings and sixpence, or more than five-and-twenty per cent,
cheaper than it had been during the sixty-four last years of the
last century; and about 9s. 6d. cheaper than it had been during
the sixteen years preceding 1636, when the discovery of the
abundant mines of America may be supposed to have produced
its full effect; and about one shilling cheaper than it had been in
the twenty-six years preceding 1620, before that discovery can
well be supposed to have produced its full effect. According to
this account, the average price of middle wheat, during these
sixty-four first years of the present century, comes out to have
been about thirty-two shillings the quarter of eight bushels.

The value of silver, therefore, seems to have risen somewhat
in proportion to that of corn during the course of the present
century, and it had probably begun to do so even some time
before the end of the last.

In 1687, the price of the quarter of nine bushels of the best
wheat at Windsor market was £1 5s. 2d., the lowest price at
which it had ever been from 1595.

In 1688, Mr Gregory King, a man famous for his knowledge
in matters of this kind, estimated the average price of wheat in
years of moderate plenty to be to the grower 3s. 6d. the bushel,
or eight-and-twenty shillings the quarter. The grower's price I
understand to be the same with what is sometimes called the
contract price, or the price at which a farmer contracts for a
certain number of years to deliver a certain quantity of corn to a
dealer. As a contract of this kind saves the farmer the expense
and trouble of marketing, the contract price is generally lower
than what is supposed to be the average market price. Mr King
had judged eight-and-twenty shillings the quarter to be at that
time the ordinary contract price in years of moderate plenty.
Before the scarcity occasioned by the late extraordinary course of
bad seasons, it was, I have been assured, the ordinary contract
price in all common years.

In 1688 was granted the parliamentary bounty upon the exportation of corn. The country gentlemen, who then composed
a still greater proportion of the legislature than they do at
present, had felt that the money price of corn was falling. The
bounty was an expedient to raise it artificially to the high price

at which it had frequently been sold in the times of Charles I and II. It was to take place, therefore, till wheat was so high as forty-eight shillings the quarter, that is, twenty shillings, or five-sevenths dearer than Mr King had in that very year estimated the grower's price to be in times of moderate plenty. If his calculations deserve any part of the reputation which they have obtained very universally, eight-and-forty shillings the quarter was a price which, without some such expedient as the bounty, could not at that time be expected, except in years of extra-ordinary scarcity. But the government of King William was not then fully settled. It was in no condition to refuse anything to the country gentlemen, from whom it was at that very time soliciting the first establishment of the annual land-tax.

The value of silver, therefore, in proportion to that of corn, had probably risen somewhat before the end of the last century; and it seems to have continued to do so during the course of the greater part of the present; though the necessary operation of the bounty must have hindered that rise from being so sensible as it otherwise would have been in the actual state of tillage.

In plentiful years the bounty, by occasioning an extraordinary exportation, necessarily raises the price of corn above what it otherwise would be in those years. To encourage tillage, by keeping up the price of corn even in the most plentiful years, was the avowed end of the institution.

In years of great scarcity, indeed, the bounty has generally been suspended. It must, however, have had some effect even upon the prices of many of those years. By the extraordinary exportation which it occasions in years of plenty, it must frequently hinder the plenty of one year from compensating the scarcity of another.

Both in years of plenty and in years of scarcity, therefore, the bounty raises the price of corn above what it naturally would be in the actual state of tillage. If, during the sixty-four first years of the present century, therefore, the average price has been lower than during the sixty-four last years of the last century, it must, in the same state of tillage, have been much more so, had it not been for this operation of the bounty.

But without the bounty, it may be said, the state of tillage would not have been the same. What may have been the effects of this institution upon the agriculture of the country, I shall endeavour to explain hereafter, when I come to treat particularly of bounties. I shall only observe at present that this rise in the value of silver, in proportion to that of corn, has not been peculiar to England. It has been observed to have taken place in France during the same period, and nearly in the same proportion too, by three very faithful, diligent, and laborious collectors of the prices of corn, Mr Duprè de St Maur, Mr Messance, and the author of the Essay on the police of grain. But in France, till 1764, the exportation of grain was by law prohibited; and it is somewhat difficult to suppose that nearly the same diminution of price which took place in one country, notwithstanding this prohibition, should in another be owing to the extraordinary encouragement given to exportation.

It would be more proper, perhaps, to consider this variation in the average money price of corn as the effect rather of some gradual rise in the real value of silver in the European market than of any fall in the real average value of corn. Corn, it has already been observed, is at distant periods of time a more accurate measure of value than either silver, or perhaps any other commodity. When, after the discovery of the abundant mines of America, corn rose to three and four times its former money price, this change was universally ascribed, not to any rise in the real value of corn, but to a fall in the real value of silver. If during the sixty-four first years of the present century, therefore, the average money price of corn has fallen somewhat below what it had been during the greater part of the last century, we should in the same manner impute this change, not to any fall in the real value of corn, but to some rise in the real value of silver in the European market.

The high price of corn during these ten or twelve years past, indeed, has occasioned a suspicion that the real value of silver still continues to fall in the European market. This high price of corn, however, seems evidently to have been the effect of the extraordinary unfavourableness of the seasons, and ought therefore to be regarded, not as a permanent, but as a transitory and occasional event. The seasons for these ten or twelve years past have been unfavourable through the greater part of Europe; and the disorders of Poland have much increased the scarcity in all those countries which, in dear years, used to be supplied from that market. So long a course of bad seasons, though not a very common event, is by no means a singular one; and whoever has inquired much into the history of the prices of corn in former times will be at no loss to recollect several other examples of the same kind. Ten years of extraordinary scarcity, besides, are not more wonderful than ten years of extraordinary plenty. The low price of corn from 1741 to 1750, both inclusive, may very well be set in opposition to its high price during these last eight or ten years. From 1741 to 1750, the average price of the quarter of nine bushels of the best wheat at Windsor market, it appears from the accounts of Eton College, was only £1 13s. 9⅘d., which is nearly 6s. 3d. below the average price of the sixty-four first years of the present century. The average price of the quarter of eight bushels of middle wheat comes out, according to this account, to have been, during these ten years, only £1 6s. 8d.

Between 1741 and 1750, however, the bounty must have hindered the price of corn from falling so low in the home market as it naturally would have done. During these ten years the quantity of all sorts of grain exported, it appears from the custom-house books, amounted to no less than eight millions twenty-nine thousand one hundred and fifty-six quarters one bushel. The bounty paid for this amounted to £1,514,962 17s. 4½d. In 1749 accordingly, Mr Pelham, at that time prime minister, observed to the House of Commons that for the three years preceding a very extraordinary sum had been paid as bounty for the exportation of corn. He had good reason to make this observation, and in the following year he might have had still better. In that single year the bounty paid amounted to no less than £324,176 10s. 6d.[1] It is unnecessary to observe how much this forced exportation must have raised the price of corn above what it otherwise would have been in the home market.

At the end of the accounts annexed to this chapter the reader will find the particular account of those ten years separated from the rest. He will find there, too, the particular account of the preceding ten years, of which the average is likewise below, though not so much below, the general average of the sixty-four

1. See *Tracts on the Corn Trade*, Tract 3.

first years of the century. The year 1740, however, was a year of extraordinary scarcity. These twenty years preceding 1750 may very well be set in opposition to the twenty preceding 1770. As the former were a good deal below the general average of the century, notwithstanding the intervention of one or two dear years; so the latter have been a good deal above it, notwithstanding the intervention of one or two cheap ones, of 1759, for example. If the former have not been so much below the general average as the latter have been above it, we ought probably to impute it to the bounty. The change has evidently been too sudden to be ascribed to any change in the value of silver, which is always slow and gradual. The suddenness of the effect can be accounted for only by a cause which can operate suddenly, the accidental variation of the seasons.

The money price of labour in Great Britain has, indeed, risen during the course of the present century. This, however, seems to be the effect, not so much of any diminution in the value of silver in the European market, as of an increase in the demand for labour in Great Britain, arising from the great, and almost universal prosperity of the country. In France, a country not altogether so prosperous, the money price of labour has, since the middle of the last century, been observed to sink gradually with the average money price of corn. Both in the last century and in the present the day-wages of common labour are there said to have been pretty uniformly about the twentieth part of the average price of the septier of wheat, a measure which contains a little more than four Winchester bushels. In Great Britain the real recompense of labour, it has already been shown, the real quantities of the necessaries and conveniences of life which are given to the labourer, has increased considerably during the course of the present century. The rise in its money price seems to have been the effect, not of any diminution of the value of silver in the general market of Europe, but of a rise in the real price of labour in the particular market of Great Britain, owing to the peculiarly happy circumstances of the country.

For some time after the first discovery of America, silver would continue to sell at its former, or not much below its former price. The profits of mining would for some time be very great, and much above their natural rate. Those who im-

ported that metal into Europe, however, would soon find that
the whole annual importation could not be disposed of at this
high price. Silver would gradually exchange for a smaller and a
smaller quantity of goods. Its price would sink gradually
lower and lower till it fell to its natural price, or to what was
just sufficient to pay, according to their natural rates, the wages
of the labour, the profits and the stock, and the rent of the land,
which must be paid in order to bring it from the mine to the
market. In the greater part of the silver mines of Peru, the tax
of the King of Spain, amounting to a tenth of the gross produce,
eats up, it has already been observed, the whole rent of the land.
This tax was originally a half; it soon afterwards fell to a third,
then to a fifth, and at last to a tenth, at which rate it still
continues. In the greater part of the silver mines of Peru this, it
seems, is all that remains after replacing the stock of the
undertaker of the work, together with its ordinary profits; and
it seems to be universally acknowledged that these profits,
which were once very high, are now as low as they can well be,
consistently with carrying on their works.

The tax of the King of Spain was reduced to a fifth part of
the registered silver in 1504,[1] one-and-forty years before 1545,
the date of the discovery of the mines of Potosi. In the course of
ninety years, or before 1636, these mines, the most fertile in all
America, had time sufficient to produce their full effect, or to
reduce the value of silver in the European market as low as it
could well fall, while it continued to pay this tax to the King of
Spain. Ninety years is time sufficient to reduce any commodity,
of which there is no monopoly, to its natural price, or to the
lowest price at which, while it pays a particular tax, it can continue to be sold for any considerable time together.

The price of silver in the European market might perhaps
have fallen still lower, and it might have become necessary
either to reduce the tax upon it, not only to one tenth, as in
1736, but to one twentieth, in the same manner as that upon
gold, or to give up working the greater part of the American
mines which are now wrought. The gradual increase of the
demand for silver, or the gradual enlargement of the market for
the produce of the silver mines of America, is probably the

1. *Solorzano*, vol. ii.

cause which has prevented this from happening, and which has not only kept up the value of silver in the European market, but has perhaps even raised it somewhat higher than it was about the middle of the last century.

Since the first discovery of America, the market for the produce of its silver mines has been growing gradually more and more extensive.

First, The market of Europe has become gradually more and more extensive. Since the discovery of America, the greater part of Europe has been much improved. England, Holland, France, and Germany; even Sweden, Denmark, and Russia have all advanced considerably both in agriculture and in manufactures. Italy seems not to have gone backwards. The fall of Italy preceded the conquest of Peru. Since that time it seems rather to have recovered a little. Spain and Portugal, indeed, are supposed to have gone backwards. Portugal, however, is but a very small part of Europe, and the declension of Spain is not, perhaps, so great as is commonly imagined. In the beginning of the sixteenth century, Spain was a very poor country, even in comparison with France, which has been so much improved since that time. It was the well-known remark of the Emperor Charles V, who had travelled so frequently through both countries, that everything abounded in France, but that everything was wanting in Spain. The increasing produce of the agriculture and manufactures of Europe must necessarily have required a gradual increase in the quantity of silver coin to circulate it; and the increasing number of wealthy individuals must have required the like increase in the quantity of their plate and other ornaments of silver.

Secondly, America is itself a new market for the produce of its own silver mines; and as its advances in agriculture, industry, and population are much more rapid than those of the most thriving countries in Europe, its demand must increase much more rapidly. The English colonies are altogether a new market, which partly for coin and partly for plate, requires a continually augmenting supply of silver through a great continent where there never was any demand before. The greater part, too, of the Spanish and Portuguese colonies are altogether new markets. New Granada, the Yucatan, Paraguay, and the

Brazils were, before discovery by the Europeans, inhabited by savage nations who had neither arts nor agriculture. A considerable degree of both has now been introduced into all of them. Even Mexico and Peru, though they cannot be considered as altogether new markets, are certainly much more extensive ones than they ever were before. After all the wonderful tales which have been published concerning the splendid state of those countries in ancient times, whoever reads, with any degree of sober judgement, the history of their first discovery and conquest, will evidently discern that, in arts, agriculture, and commerce, their inhabitants were much more ignorant than the Tartars of the Ukraine are at present. Even the Peruvians, the more civilized nation of the two, though they made use of gold and silver as ornaments, had no coined money of any kind. Their whole commerce was carried on by barter, and there was accordingly scarce any division of labour among them. Those who cultivated the ground were obliged to build their own houses, to make their own household furniture, their own clothes, shoes, and instruments of agriculture. The few artificers among them are said to have been all maintained by the sovereign, the nobles, and the priests, and were probably their servants or slaves. All the ancient arts of Mexico and Peru have never furnished one single manufacture to Europe. The Spanish armies, though they scarce ever exceeded five hundred men, and frequently did not amount to half that number, found almost everywhere great difficulty in procuring subsistence. The families which they are said to have occasioned almost wherever they went, in countries, too, which at the same time are represented as very populous and well cultivated sufficiently demonstrate that the story of this populousness and high cultivation is in a great measure fabulous. The Spanish colonies are under a government in many respects less favourable to agriculture, improvement, and population than that of the English colonies. They seem, however, to be advancing in all these much more rapidly than any country in Europe. In a fertile soil and happy climate, the great abundance and cheapness of land, a circumstance common to all new colonies, is, it seems, so great an advantage as to compensate many defects in civil government. Frezier, who visited Peru in 1713, represents Lima as containing between twenty-five and twenty-eight thousand inhabitants. Ulloa, who resided in the same country between 1740 and 1746, represents it as containing more than fifty thousand. The difference in their accounts of the populousness of several other principal towns in Chili and Peru is nearly the same; and as there seems to be no reason to doubt of the good information of either, it marks an increase which is scarce inferior to that of the English colonies. America, therefore, is a new market for the produce of its own silver mines, of which the demand must increase much more rapidly than that of the most thriving country in Europe.

Thirdly, the East Indies is another market for the produce of the silver mines of America, and a market which, from the time of the first discovery of those mines, has been continually taking off a greater and a greater quantity of silver. Since that time, the direct trade between America and the East Indies, which is carried on by means of the Acapulco ships, has been continually augmenting, and the indirect intercourse by the way of Europe has been augmenting in a still greater proportion. During the sixteenth century, the Portuguese were the only European nation who carried on any regular trade to the East Indies. In the last years of that century the Dutch began to encroach upon this monopoly, and in a few years expelled them from their principal settlements in India. During the greater part of the last century those two nations divided the most considerable part of the East India trade between them; the trade of the Dutch continually augmenting in a still greater proportion than that of the Portuguese declined. The English and French carried on some trade with India in the last century, but it has been greatly augmented in the course of the present. The East India trade of the Swedes and Danes began in the course of the present century. Even the Muscovites now trade regularly with China by a sort of caravans which go overland through Siberia and Tartary to Pekin. The East India trade of all these nations, if we except that of the French, which the last war had well nigh annihilated, has been almost continually augmenting. The increasing consumption of East India goods in Europe is, it seems, so great as to afford a gradual increase of employment to them all. Tea, for example, was a drug very little used in

Europe before the middle of the last century. At present the value of the tea annually imported by the English East India Company, for the use of their own countrymen, amounts to more than a million and a half a year; and even this is not enough; a great deal more being constantly smuggled into the country from the ports of Holland, from Gottenburg in Sweden, and from the coast of France too, as long as the French East India Company was in prosperity. The consumption of the porcelain of China, of the spiceries of the Moluccas, of the piece goods of Bengal, and of innumerable other articles, has increased very nearly in a like proportion. The tonnage accordingly of all the European shipping employed in the East India trade, at any one time during the last century, was not, perhaps, much greater than that of the English East India Company before the late reduction of their shipping.

But in the East Indies, particularly in China and Indostan, the value of the precious metals, when the Europeans first began to trade to those countries, was much higher than in Europe; and it still continues to be so. In rice countries, which generally yield two, sometimes three crops in the year each of them more plentiful than any common crop of corn, the abundance of food must be much greater than in any corn country of equal extent. Such countries are accordingly much more populous. In them, too, the rich, having a greater superabundance of food to dispose of beyond what they themselves can consume, have the means of purchasing a much greater quantity of the labour of other people. The retinue of a grandee in China or Indostan accordingly is, by all accounts, much more numerous and splendid than that of the richest subjects in Europe. The same superabundance of food, of which they have the disposal, enables them to give a greater quantity of it for all those singular and rare productions which nature furnishes but in very small quantities; such as the precious metals and the precious stones, the great objects of the competition of the rich. Though the mines, therefore, which supplied the Indian market had been as abundant as those which supplied the European, such commodities would naturally exchange for a greater quantity of food in India than in Europe. But the mines which supplied the Indian market with the precious metals seem to have been a good deal less abundant, and those which supplied it with the precious stones a good deal more so, than the mines which supplied the European. The precious metals, therefore, would naturally exchange in India for somewhat a greater quantity of the precious stones, and for a much greater quantity of food than in Europe. The money price of diamonds, the greatest of all superfluities, would be somewhat lower, and that of food, the first of all necessaries, a great deal lower in the one country than in the other. But the real price of labour, the real quantity of the necessaries of life which is given to the labourer, it has already been observed, is lower both in China and Indostan, the two great markets of India, than it is through the greater part of Europe. The wages of the labourer will there purchase a smaller quantity of food; and as the money price of food is much lower in India than in Europe, the money price of labour is there lower upon a double account; upon account both of the small quantity of food which it will purchase, and of the low price of that food. But in countries of equal art and industry the money price of the greater part of manufactures will be in proportion to the money price of labour; and in manufacturing art and industry, China and Indostan, though inferior, seem not to be much inferior to any part of Europe. The money price of the greater part of manufactures, therefore, will naturally be much lower in those great empires than it is anywhere in Europe. Through the greater part of Europe, too, the expense of land-carriage increases very much both the real and nominal price of most manufactures. It costs more labour, and therefore more money, to bring first the materials, and afterwards the complete manufacture to market. In China and Indostan the extent and variety of inland navigation save the greater part of this labour, and consequently of this money, and thereby reduce still lower both the real and nominal price of the greater part of their manufactures. Upon all those accounts the precious metals are a commodity which it always has been, and still continues to be, extremely advantageous to carry from Europe to India. There is scarce any commodity which brings a better price there; or which, in proportion to the quantity of labour and commodities which it costs in Europe, will purchase or command a greater quantity of labour and commodities in India. It is more advantageous, too, to carry silver thither than gold; because in China, and the greater part of the other markets of India, the proportion between fine silver and fine gold is but as ten, or at most as twelve, to one; whereas in Europe it is as fourteen or fifteen to one. In China, and the greater part of the other markets of India, ten, or at most twelve, ounces of silver will purchase an ounce of gold: in Europe it requires from fourteen to fifteen ounces. In the cargoes, therefore, of the greater part of European ships which sail to India, silver has generally been one of the most valuable articles. It is the most valuable article in the Acapulco ships which sail to Manilla. The silver of the new continent seems in this manner to be one of the principal commodities by which the commerce between the two extremities of the old one is carried on, and it is by means of it, in a great measure, that those distant parts of the world are connected with one another.

In order to supply so very widely extended a market, the quantity of silver annually brought from the mines must not only be sufficient to support that continual increase both of coin and of plate which is required in all thriving countries; but to repair that continual waste and consumption of silver which takes place in all countries where that metal is used.

The continual consumption of the precious metals in coin by wearing, and in plate both by wearing and cleaning, is very sensible, and in commodities of which the use is so very widely extended, would alone require a very great annual supply. The consumption of those metals in some particular manufactures, though it may not perhaps be greater upon the whole than this gradual consumption, is, however, much more sensible, as it is much more rapid. In the manufactures of Birmingham alone the quantity of gold and silver annually employed in gilding and plating, and thereby disqualified from ever afterwards appearing in the shape of those metals, is said to amount to more than fifty thousand pounds sterling. We may from thence form some notion how great must be the annual consumption in all the different parts of the world either in manufactures of the same kind with those of Birmingham, or in laces, embroideries, gold and silver stuffs, the gilding of books, furniture, etc. A considerable quantity, too, must be annually lost in transporting those metals from one place to another both by sea and by land. In the greater part of the governments of Asia, besides, the almost universal custom of concealing treasures in the bowels of the earth, of which the knowledge frequently dies with the person who makes the concealment, must occasion the loss of a still greater quantity.

The quantity of gold and silver imported at both Cadiz and Lisbon (including not only what comes under register, but what may be supposed to be smuggled) amounts, according to the best accounts, to about six millions sterling a year.

According to Mr. Meggens[1] the annual importation of the precious metals into Spain, at an average of six years, viz., from 1748 to 1753, both inclusive; and into Portugal, at an average of seven years, viz., from 1747 to 1753, both inclusive, amounted in silver to 1,101,107 pounds weight; and in gold to 49,940 pounds weight. The silver, at sixty-two shillings the pound Troy, amounts to £3,413,431 10s. sterling. The gold, at forty-four guineas and a half the pound Troy, amounts to £2,333,446 14s. sterling. Both together amount to £5,746,878 4s. sterling. The account of what was imported under register he assures us is exact. He gives us the detail of the particular places from which the gold and silver were brought, and of the particular quantity of each metal, which, according to the register, each of them afforded. He makes an allowance, too, for the quantity of each metal which he supposes may have been smuggled. The great experience of this judicious merchant renders his opinion of considerable weight.

According to the eloquent, and sometimes, well-informed author of the *Philosophical and Political History of the Establishment of the Europeans in the two Indies*, the annual importation of registered gold and silver into Spain, at an average of eleven years, viz., from 1754 to 1764, both inclusive, amounted to 13,984,185¾ piastres of ten reals. On account of what may have been smuggled, however, the whole annual importation, he supposes, may have amounted to seventeen millions of piastres, which, at 4s. 6d. the piastre, is equal to £3,825,000

1. Postscript to the *Universal Merchant*, pp. 15 and 16. This Postscript was not printed till 1756, three years after the publication of the book, which has never had a second edition. The Postscript is, therefore, to be found in few copies : It corrects several errors in the book.

sterling. He gives the detail, too, of the particular places from which the gold and silver were brought, and of the particular quantities of each metal which, according to the register, each of them afforded. He informs us, too, that if we were to judge of the quantity of gold annually imported from the Brazils into Lisbon by the amount of the tax paid to the King of Portugal, which it seems is one-fifth of the standard metal, we might value it at eighteen millions of cruzadoes, or forty-five millions of French livres, equal to about two millions sterling. On account of what may have been smuggled, however, we may safely, he says, add to the sum an eighth more, or £250,000 sterling, so that the whole will amount to £2,250,000 sterling. According to this account, therefore, the whole annual importation of the precious metals into both Spain and Portugal amounts to about £6,075,000 sterling.

Several other very well authenticated, though manuscript, accounts, I have been assured, agree in making this whole annual importation amount at an average to about six millions sterling; sometimes a little more, sometimes a little less.

The annual importation of the precious metals into Cadiz and Lisbon, indeed, is not equal to the whole annual produce of the mines of America. Some part is sent annually by the Acapulco ships to Manilla; some part is employed in the contraband trade which the Spanish colonies carry on with those of other European nations; and some part, no doubt, remains in the country. The mines of America, besides, are by no means the only gold and silver mines in the world. They are, however, by far the most abundant. The produce of all the other mines which are known is insignificant, it is acknowledged, in comparison with theirs; and the far greater part of their produce, it is likewise acknowledged, is annually imported into Cadiz and Lisbon. But the consumption of Birmingham alone, at the rate of fifty thousand pounds a year, is equal to the hundred-and-twentieth part of this annual importation at the rate of six millions a year. The whole annual consumption of gold and silver, therefore, in all the different countries of the world where those metals are used, may perhaps be nearly equal to the whole annual produce. The remainder may be no more than sufficient to supply the increasing demand of all thriving countries. It may even have fallen so far short of this demand as somewhat to raise the price of those metals in the European market.

The quantity of brass and iron annually brought from the mine to the market is out of all proportion greater than that of gold and silver. We do not, however, upon this account, imagine that those coarse metals are likely to multiply beyond the demand, or to become gradually cheaper and cheaper. Why should we imagine that the precious metals are likely to do so? The coarse metals, indeed, though harder, are put to much harder uses, and, as they are of less value, less care is employed in their preservation. The precious metals, however, are not necessarily immortal any more than they, but are liable, too, to be lost, wasted, and consumed in a great variety of ways.

The price of all metals, though liable to slow and gradual variations, varies less from year to year than that of almost any other part of the rude produce of land; and the price of the precious metals is even less liable to sudden variations than that of the coarse ones. The durableness of metals is the foundation of this extraordinary steadiness of price. The corn which was brought to market last year will be all or almost all consumed long before the end of this year. But some part of the iron which was brought from the mine two or three hundred years ago may be still in use, and perhaps some part of the gold which was brought from it two or three thousand years ago. The different masses of corn which in different years must supply the consumption of the world will always be nearly in proportion to the respective produce of those different years. But the proportion between the different masses of iron which may be in use in two different years will be very little affected by any accidental difference in the produce of the iron mines of those two years; and the proportion between the masses of gold will be still less affected by any such difference in the produce of the gold mines. Though the produce of the greater part of metallic mines, therefore, varies, perhaps, still more from year to year than that of the greater part of corn fields, those variations have not the same effect upon the price of the one species of commodities as upon that of the other.

VARIATIONS IN THE PROPORTION BETWEEN THE
RESPECTIVE VALUES OF GOLD AND SILVER

Before the discovery of the mines of America, the value of fine gold to fine silver was regulated in the different mints of Europe between the proportions of one to ten and one to twelve; that is, an ounce of fine gold was supposed to be worth from ten to twelve ounces of fine silver. About the middle of the last century it came to be regulated, between the proportions of one to fourteen and one to fifteen; that is, an ounce of fine gold came to be supposed worth between fourteen and fifteen ounces of fine silver. Gold rose in its nominal value, or in the quantity of silver which was given for it. Both metals sunk in their real value, or in the quantity of labour which they could purchase; but silver sunk more than gold. Though both the gold and silver mines of America exceeded in fertility all those which had ever been known before, the fertility of the silver mines had, it seems, been proportionately still greater than that of the gold ones.

The great quantities of silver carried annually from Europe to India have, in some of the English settlements, gradually reduced the value of that metal in proportion to gold. In the mint of Calcutta an ounce of fine gold is supposed to be worth fifteen ounces of fine silver, in the same manner as in Europe. It is in the mint perhaps rated too high for the value which it bears in the market of Bengal. In China, the proportion of gold to silver still continues as one to ten, or one to twelve. In Japan it is said to be as one to eight.

The proportion between the quantities of gold and silver annually imported into Europe, according to Mr Meggens's account, is as one to twenty-two nearly; that is, for one ounce of gold there are imported a little more than twenty-two ounces of silver. The great quantity of silver sent annually to the East Indies reduces, he supposes, the quantities of those metals which remain in Europe to the proportion of one to fourteen or fifteen, the proportion of their values. The proportion between their values, he seems to think, must necessarily be the same as that between their quantities, and would therefore be as one to twenty-two, were it not for this greater exportation of silver.

But the ordinary proportion between the respective values of two commodities is not necessarily the same as that between the quantities of them which are commonly in the market. The price of an ox, reckoned at ten guineas, is about threescore times the price of a lamb, reckoned at 3s. 6d. It would be absurd, however, to infer from thence that there are commonly in the market threescore lambs for one ox: and it would be just as absurd to infer, because an ounce of gold will commonly purchase from fourteen to fifteen ounces of silver, that there are commonly in the market only fourteen or fifteen ounces of silver for one ounce of gold.

The quantity of silver commonly in the market, it is probable, is much greater in proportion to that of gold than the value of a certain quantity of gold is to that of an equal quantity of silver. The whole quantity of a cheap commodity brought to market is commonly not only greater, but of greater value, than the whole quantity of a dear one. The whole quantity of bread annually brought to market is not only greater, but of greater value than the whole quantity of butcher's meat; the whole quantity of butcher's meat, than the whole quantity of poultry; and the whole quantity of poultry, than the whole quantity of wild fowl. There are so many more purchasers for the cheap than for the dear commodity that not only a greater quantity of it, but a greater value, can commonly be disposed of. The whole quantity, therefore, of the cheap commodity must commonly be greater in proportion to the whole quantity of the dear one than the value of a certain quantity of the dear one is to the value of an equal quantity of the cheap one. When we compare the precious metals with one another, silver is a cheap and gold a dear commodity. We ought naturally to expect, therefore, that there should always be in the market not only a greater quantity, but a greater value of silver than of gold. Let any man who has a little of both compare his own silver with his gold plate, and he will probably find that, not only the quantity, but the value of the former greatly exceeds that of the latter. Many people, besides, have a good deal of silver who have no gold plate, which, even with those who have it, is generally confined to watch-cases, snuff-boxes, and such like trinkets, of which the whole amount is seldom of great value. In the British coin, indeed, the value of the gold preponderates greatly, but it is not so in that of all countries. In the coin of some countries the value of the two metals is nearly equal. In the Scotch coin, before the union with England, the gold preponderated very little, though it did somewhat,[1] as it appears by the accounts of the mint. In the coin of many countries the silver preponderates. In France, the largest sums are commonly paid in that metal, and it is there difficult to get more gold than what is necessary to carry about in your pocket. The superior value, however, of the silver plate above that of the gold, which takes place in all countries, will much more than compensate the preponderancy of the gold coin above the silver, which takes place only in some countries.

Though, in one sense of the word, silver always has been, and probably always will be, much cheaper than gold; yet in another sense gold may, perhaps, in the present state of the Spanish market, be said to be somewhat cheaper than silver. A commodity may be said to be dear or cheap, not only according to the absolute greatness or smallness of its usual price, but according as that price is more or less above the lowest for which it is possible to bring it to market for any considerable time together. This lowest price is that which barely replaces, with a moderate profit, the stock which must be employed in bringing the commodity thither. It is the price which affords nothing to the landlord, of which rent makes not any component part, but which resolves itself altogether into wages and profit. But, in the present state of the Spanish market, gold is certainly somewhat nearer to this lowest price than silver. The tax of the King of Spain upon gold is only one-twentieth part of the standard metal, or five per cent; whereas his tax upon silver amounts to one-tenth part of it, or to ten per cent. In these taxes too, it has already been observed, consists the whole rent of the greater part of the gold and silver mines of Spanish America; and that upon gold is still worse paid than that upon silver. The profits of the undertakers of gold mines too, as they more rarely make a fortune, must, in general, be still more moderate than those of the undertakers of silver mines. The price of Spanish gold, therefore, as it affords both less rent and less profit, must, in the

1. See Ruddiman's Preface to Anderson's *Diplomata, etc., Scotiae.*

Spanish market, be somewhat nearer to the lowest price for which it is possible to bring it thither than the price of Spanish silver. When all expenses are computed, the whole quantity of the one metal, it would seem, cannot, in the Spanish market, be disposed of so advantageously as the whole quantity of the other. The tax, indeed, of the King of Portugal upon the gold of the Brazils is the same with the ancient tax of the King of Spain upon the silver of Mexico and Peru; or one-fifth part of the standard metal. It may, therefore, be uncertain whether to the general market of Europe the whole mass of American gold comes at a price nearer to the lowest for which it is possible to bring it thither than the whole mass of American silver.

The price of diamonds and other precious stones may, perhaps, be still nearer to the lowest price at which it is possible to bring them to market than even the price of gold.

Though it is not very probable that any part of a tax, which is not only imposed upon one of the most proper subjects of taxation, a mere luxury and superfluity, but which affords so very important a revenue as the tax upon silver, will ever be given up as long as it is possible to pay it; yet the same impossibility of paying it, which in 1736 made it necessary to reduce it from one-fifth to one-tenth, may in time make it necessary to reduce it still further; in the same manner as it made it necessary to reduce the tax upon gold to one-twentieth. That the silver mines of Spanish America, like all other mines, become gradually more expensive in the working, on account of the greater depths at which it is necessary to carry on the works, and of the greater expense of drawing out the water and of supplying them with fresh air at those depths, is acknowledged by everybody who has inquired into the state of those mines.

These causes, which are equivalent to a growing scarcity of silver (for a commodity may be said to grow scarcer when it becomes more difficult and expensive to collect a certain quantity of it) must, in time, produce one or other of the three following events. The increase of expense must either, first, be compensated altogether by a proportionable increase in the price of the metal; or, secondly, it must be compensated altogether by a proportionable diminution of the tax upon silver; or, thirdly, it must be compensated partly by the one, and partly by the other of those two expedients. This third event is very possible. As gold rose in its price in proportion to silver, notwithstanding a great diminution of the tax upon gold, so silver might rise in its price in proportion to labour and commodities, notwithstanding an equal diminution of the tax upon silver.

Such successive reductions of the tax, however, though they may not prevent altogether, must certainly retard, more or less, the rise in the value of silver in the European market. In consequence of such reductions many mines may be wrought which could not be wrought before, because they could not afford to pay the old tax; and the quantity of silver annually brought to market must always be somewhat greater, and, therefore, the value of any given quantity somewhat less, than it otherwise would have been. In consequence of the reduction in 1736, the value of silver in the European market, though it may not at this day be lower than before that reduction, is, probably, at least ten per cent lower than it would have been had the Court of Spain continued to exact the old tax.

That, notwithstanding this reduction, the value of silver has, during the course of the present century, begun to rise somewhat in the European market, the facts and arguments which have been alleged above dispose me to believe, or more properly to suspect and conjecture; for the best opinion which I can form upon this subject scarce, perhaps, deserves the name of belief. The rise, indeed, supposing there has been any, has hitherto been so very small that after all that has been said it may, perhaps, appear to many people uncertain, not only whether this event has actually taken place; but whether the contrary may not have taken place, or whether the value of silver may not still continue to fall in the European market.

It must be observed, however, that whatever may be the supposed annual importation of gold and silver, there must be a certain period at which the annual consumption of those metals will be equal to that annual importation. Their consumption must increase as their mass increases, or rather in a much greater proportion. As their mass increases, their value diminishes. They are more used and less cared for, and their consumption consequently increases in a greater proportion than their mass. After a certain period, therefore, the annual consumption of those metals must, in this manner, become equal to their annual importation, provided that importation is not continually increasing; which, in the present times, is not supposed to be the case.

If, when the annual consumption has become equal to the annual importation, the annual importation should gradually diminish, the annual consumption may, for some time, exceed the annual importation. The mass of those metals may gradually and insensibly diminish, and their value gradually and insensibly rise, till the annual importation becoming again stationary, the annual consumption will gradually and insensibly accommodate itself to what that annual importation can maintain.

GROUNDS OF THE SUSPICION THAT THE VALUE OF SILVER STILL CONTINUES TO DECREASE

The increase of the wealth of Europe, and the popular notion that, as the quantity of the precious metals naturally increases with the increase of wealth so their value diminishes as their quantity increases, may, perhaps, dispose many people to believe that their value still continues to fall in the European market; and the still gradually increasing price of many parts of the rude produce of land may confirm them still further in this opinion.

That that increase in the quantity of the precious metals, which arises in any country from the increase of wealth, has no tendency to diminish their value, I have endeavoured to show already. Gold and silver naturally resort to a rich country, for the same reason that all sorts of luxuries and curiosities resort to it; not because they are cheaper there than in poorer countries, but because they are dearer, or because a better price is given for them. It is the superiority of price which attracts them, and as soon as that superiority ceases, they necessarily cease to go thither.

If you except corn and such other vegetables as are raised altogether by human industry, that all other sorts of rude produce, cattle, poultry, game of all kinds, the useful fossils and minerals of the earth, etc., naturally grow dearer as the society advances in wealth and improvement, I have endeavoured to show already. Though such commodities, therefore, come to exchange for a greater quantity of silver than before, it will not from thence follow that silver has become really cheaper, or will purchase less labour than before, but that such commodities have become really dearer, or will purchase more labour than before. It is not their nominal price only, but their real price which rises in the progress of improvement. The rise of their nominal price is the effect, not of any degradation of the value of silver, but of the rise in their real price.

DIFFERENT EFFECTS OF THE PROGRESS OF IMPROVEMENT UPON THREE DIFFERENT SORTS OF RUDE PRODUCE

These different sorts of rude produce may be divided into three classes. The first comprehends those which it is scarce in the power of human industry to multiply at all. The second, those which it can multiply in proportion to the demand. The third, those in which the efficacy of industry is either limited or uncertain. In the progress of wealth and improvement, the real price of the first may rise to any degree of extravagance, and seems not to be limited by any certain boundary. That of the second, though it may rise greatly, has, however, a certain boundary beyond which it cannot well pass for any considerable time together. That of the third, though its natural tendency is to rise in the progress of improvement, yet in the same degree of improvement it may sometimes happen even to fall, sometimes to continue the same, and sometimes to rise more or less, according as different accidents render the efforts of human industry, in multiplying this sort of rude produce, more or less successful.

First Sort

The first sort of rude produce of which the price rises in the progress of improvement is that which it is scarce in the power of human industry to multiply at all. It consists in those things which nature produces only in certain quantities, and which, being of a very perishable nature, it is impossible to accumulate together the produce of many different seasons. Such are the greater part of rare and singular birds and fishes, many different sorts of game, almost all wild-fowl, all birds of passage in particular, as well as many other things. When wealth and the luxury which accompanies it increase, the demand for these is likely to increase with them, and no effort of human industry may be able to increase the supply much beyond what it was before this increase of the demand. The quantity of such commodities, therefore, remaining the same, or nearly the same, while the competition to purchase them is continually increasing, their price may rise to any degree of extravagance, and seems not to be limited by any certain boundary. If woodcocks should become so fashionable as to sell for twenty guineas a-piece, no effort of human industry could increase the number of those brought to market much beyond what it is at present. The high price paid by the Romans, in the time of their greatest grandeur, for rare birds and fishes, may in this manner easily be accounted for. These prices were not the effects of the low value of silver in those times, but of the high value of such rarities and curiosities as human industry could not multiply at pleasure. The real value of silver was higher at Rome, for some time before and after the fall of the republic, than it is through the greater part of Europe at present. Three sestertii, equal to about sixpence sterling, was the price which the republic paid for the modius or peck of the tithe wheat of Sicily. This price, however, was probably below the average market price, the obligation to deliver their wheat at this rate being considered as a tax upon the Sicilian farmers. When the Romans, therefore, had occasion to order more corn than the tithe of wheat amounted to, they were bound by capitulation to pay for the surplus at the rate of four sestertii, or eightpence sterling, the peck; and this had probably been reckoned the moderate and reasonable, that is, the ordinary or average contract price of those times; it is equal to about one and twenty shillings the quarter. Eight-and-twenty shillings the quarter was, before the late years of scarcity, the ordinary contract price of English wheat, which in quality is inferior to the Sicilian, and generally sells for a lower price in the European market. The value of silver, therefore, in those ancient times, must have been to its value in the present as three to four inversely; that is, three ounces of silver would then have purchased the same quantity of labour and commodities which four ounces will do at present. When we read in Pliny, therefore, that Seius[1] bought a white nightingale, as a present for the Empress Agrippina, at the price of six thousand sestertii, equal to about fifty pounds of our present money; and that Asinius Celer[2] purchased a surmullet at the price of eight thousand sestertii, equal to about sixty-six pounds thirteen shillings and fourpence of our present money, the extravagance of those prices, how much soever it may surprise us, is apt, notwithstanding, to appear to us about one-third less than it really was. Their real price, the quantity of labour and subsistence which was given away for them, was about one-third more than their nominal price is apt to express to us in the present times. Seius gave for the nightingale the command of a quantity of labour and subsistence equal to what £66 13s. 4d. would purchase in the present times; and Asinius Celer gave for the surmullet the command of a quantity equal to what £88 17s. 9½d. would purchase. What occasioned the extravagance of those high prices was, not so much the abundance of silver as the abundance of labour and subsistence of which those Romans had the disposal beyond what was necessary for their own use. The quantity of silver of which they had the disposal was a good deal less than what the command of the same quantity of labour and subsistence would have procured to them in the present times.

Second Sort

The second sort of rude produce of which the price rises in the progress of improvement is that which human industry can multiply in proportion to the demand. It consists in those useful plants and animals which, in uncultivated countries, nature produces with such profuse abundance that they are of little or no value, and which, as cultivation advances are therefore forced to give place to some more profitable produce. During a long period in the progress of improvement, the quantity of

1. Lib. x. c. 29.   2. Lib. ix. c. 17.

these is continually diminishing, while at the same time the demand for them is continually increasing. Their real value, therefore, the real quantity of labour which they will purchase or command, gradually rises, till at last it gets so high as to render them as profitable a produce as anything else which human industry can raise upon the most fertile and best culti- vated land. When it has got so high it cannot well go higher. If it did, more land and more industry would soon be employed to increase their quantity.

When the price of cattle, for example, rises so high that it is as profitable to cultivate land in order to raise food for them as in order to raise food for man, it cannot well go higher. If it did, more corn land would soon be turned into pasture. The extension of tillage, by diminishing the quantity of wild pas- ture, diminishes the quantity of butcher's meat which the country naturally produces without labour or cultivation, and by increasing the number of those who have either corn, or, what comes to the same thing, the price of corn, to give in exchange for it, increases the demand. The price of butcher's meat, therefore, and consequently of cattle, must gradually rise till it gets so high that it becomes as profitable to employ the most fertile and best cultivated lands in raising food for them as in raising corn. But it must always be late in the progress of improvement before tillage can be so far extended as to raise the price of cattle to this height; and till it has got to this height, if the country is advancing at all, their price must be continually rising. There are, perhaps, some parts of Europe in which the price of cattle has not yet got to this height. It had not got to this height in any part of Scotland before the union. Had the Scotch cattle been always confined to the market of Scotland, in a country in which the quantity of land which can be applied to no other purpose but the feeding of cattle is so great in propor- tion to what can be applied to other purposes, it is scarce pos- sible, perhaps, that their price could ever have risen so high as to render it profitable to cultivate land for the sake of feeding them. In England, the price of cattle, it has already been ob- served, seems, in the neighbourhood of London, to have got to this height about the beginning of the last century; but it was much later probably before it got to it through the greater part of the remoter counties; in some of which, perhaps, it may scarce yet have got to it. Of all the different substances, however, which compose this second sort of rude produce, cattle is, perhaps, that of which the price, in the progress of improvement, first rises to this height.

Till the price of cattle, indeed, has got to this height, it seems scarce possible that the greater part, even of those lands which are capable of the highest cultivation, can be completely cultivated. In all farms too distant from any town to carry manure from it, that is, in the far greater part of those of every extensive country, the quantity of well-cultivated land must be in proportion to the quantity of manure which the farm itself produces; and this again must be in proportion to the stock of cattle which are maintained upon it. The land is manured either by pasturing the cattle upon it, or by feeding them in the stable, and from thence carrying out their dung to it. But unless the price of the cattle be sufficient to pay both the rent and profit of cultivated land, the farmer cannot afford to pasture them upon it; and he can still less afford to feed them in the stable. It is with the produce of improved and cultivated land only that the cattle can be fed in the stable; because to collect the scanty and scattered produce of waste and unimproved lands would require too much labour and be too expensive. If the price of the cattle, therefore, is not sufficient to pay for the produce of improved and cultivated land, when they are allowed to pasture it, that price will be still less sufficient to pay for that produce when it must be collected with a good deal of additional labour, and brought into the stable to them. In these circumstances, therefore, no more cattle can, with profit, be fed in the stable than what are necessary for tillage. But these can never afford manure enough for keeping constantly in good condition all the lands which they are capable of cultivating. What they afford being insufficient for the whole farm will naturally be reserved for the lands to which it can be most advantageously or conveniently applied; the most fertile, or those, perhaps, in the neighbourhood of the farmyard. These, therefore, will be kept constantly in good condition and fit for tillage. The rest will, the greater part of them, be allowed to lie waste, producing scarce anything but some miserable pasture, just sufficient to keep

alive a few straggling, half-starved cattle; the farm, though
much understocked in proportion to what would be necessary
for its complete cultivation, being very frequently overstocked
in proportion to its actual produce. A portion of this waste land,
however, after having been pastured in this wretched manner
for six or seven years together, may be ploughed up, when it
will yield, perhaps, a poor crop or two of bad oats, or of some
other coarse grain, and then, being entirely exhausted, it must
be rested and pastured again as before and another portion
ploughed up to be in the same manner exhausted and rested
again in its turn. Such accordingly was the general system of
management all over the low country of Scotland before the
union. The lands which were kept constantly well manured and
in good condition seldom exceeded a third or a fourth part of
the whole farm, and sometimes did not amount to a fifth or a
sixth part of it. The rest were never manured, but a certain
portion of them was in its turn, notwithstanding, regularly
cultivated and exhausted. Under this system of management, it
is evident, even that part of the land of Scotland which is capable of good cultivation could produce but little in comparison
of what it may be capable of producing. But how disadvantageous soever this system may appear, yet before the union the
low price of cattle seems to have rendered it almost unavoidable.
If, notwithstanding a great rise in their price, it still continues
to prevail through a considerable part of the country, it is
owing, in many places, no doubt, to ignorance and attachment
to old customs, but in most places to the unavoidable obstructions which the natural course of things opposes to the immediate or speedy establishment of a better system: first, to the
poverty of the tenants, to their not having yet had time to
acquire a stock of cattle sufficient to cultivate their lands more
completely, the same rise of price which would render it
advantageous for them to maintain a greater stock rendering it
more difficult for them to acquire it; and, secondly, to their not
having yet had time to put their lands in condition to maintain
this greater stock properly, supposing they were capable of
acquiring it. The increase of stock and the improvement of land
are two events which must go hand in hand, and of which the
one can nowhere much out-run the other. Without some in-

crease of stock there can be scarce any improvement of land, but
there can be no considerable increase of stock but in consequence
of a considerable improvement of land; because otherwise the
land could not maintain it. These natural obstructions to the
establishment of a better system cannot be removed but by a
long course of frugality and industry; and half a century or a
century more, perhaps, must pass away before the old system,
which is wearing out gradually, can be completely abolished
through all the different parts of the country. Of all the commercial advantages, however, which Scotland has derived from
the union with England, this rise in the price of cattle is, perhaps, the greatest. It has not only raised the value of all highland estates, but it has, perhaps, been the principal cause of the
improvement of the low country.

In all new colonies the great quantity of waste land, which
can for many years be applied to no other purpose but the feeding of cattle, soon renders them extremely abundant, and in
everything great cheapness is the necessary consequence of great
abundance. Though all the cattle of the European colonies in
America were originally carried from Europe, they soon multiplied so much there, and became of so little value that even
horses were allowed to run wild in the woods without any
owner thinking it worth while to claim them. It must be a long
time, after the first establishment of such colonies, before it can
become profitable to feed cattle upon the produce of cultivated
land. The same causes, therefore, the want of manure, and the
disproportion between the stock employed in cultivation, and
the land which it is destined to cultivate, are likely to introduce
there a system of husbandry not unlike that which still continues to take place in so many parts of Scotland. Mr Kalm, the
Swedish traveller, when he gives an account of the husbandry of
some of the English colonies in North America, as he found it
in 1749, observes, accordingly, that he can with difficulty discover there the character of the English nation, so well skilled in
all the different branches of agriculture. They make scarce any
manure for their corn fields, he says; but when one piece of
ground has been exhausted by continual cropping, they clear
and cultivate another piece of fresh land; and when that is exhausted, proceed to a third. Their cattle are allowed to wander

through the woods and other uncultivated grounds, where they are half-starved; having long ago extirpated almost all the annual grasses by cropping them too early in the spring, before they had time to form their flowers, or to shed their seeds.[1] The annual grasses were, it seems, the best natural grasses in that part of North America; and when the Europeans first settled there, they used to grow very thick, and to rise three or four feet high. A piece of ground which, when he wrote, could not maintain one cow, would in former times, he was assured, have maintained four, each of which would have given four times the quantity of milk which that one was capable of giving. The poorness of the pasture had, in his opinion, occasioned the degradation of their cattle, which degenerated sensibly from one generation to another. They were probably not unlike that stunted breed which was common all over Scotland thirty or forty years ago, and which is now so much mended through the greater part of the low country, not so much by a change of the breed, though that expedient has been employed in some places, as by a more plentiful method of feeding them.

Though it is late, therefore, in the progress of improvement before cattle can bring such a price as to render it profitable to cultivate land for the sake of feeding them; yet of all the different parts which composed this second sort of rude produce, they are perhaps the first which bring this price; because till they bring it, it seems impossible that improvement can be brought near even to that degree of perfection to which it has arrived in many parts of Europe.

As cattle are among the first, so perhaps venison is among the last parts of this sort of rude produce which bring this price. The price of venison in Great Britain, how extravagant soever it may appear, is not near sufficient to compensate the expense of a deer park, as is well known to all those who have had any experience in the feeding of deer. If it was otherwise, the feeding of deer would soon become an article of common farming, in the same manner as the feeding of those small birds called Turdi was among the ancient Romans. Varro and Columella assure us that it was a most profitable article. The fattening of ortolans, birds of passage which arrive lean in the country, is

1. Kalm's *Travels*, vol. i. pp. 343, 344.

said to be so in some parts of France. If venison continues in fashion, and the wealth and luxury of Great Britain increase as they have done for some time past, its price may very probably rise still higher than it is at present.

Between that period in the progress of improvement which brings to its height the price of so necessary an article as cattle, and that which brings to it the price of such a superfluity as venison, there is a very long interval, in the course of which many other sorts of rude produce gradually arrived at their highest price, some sooner and some later, according to different circumstances.

Thus in every farm the offals of the barn and stables will maintain a certain number of poultry. These, as they are fed with what would otherwise be lost, are a mere save-all; and as they cost the farmer scarce anything, so he can afford to sell them for very little. Almost all that he gets is pure gain, and their price can scarce be so low as to discourage him from feeding this number. But in countries ill cultivated, and therefore but thinly inhabited, the poultry, which are thus raised without expense, are often fully sufficient to supply the whole demand. In this state of things, therefore, they are often as cheap as butcher's meat, or any other sort of animal food. But the whole quantity of poultry, which the farm in this manner produces without expense, must always be much smaller than the whole quantity of butcher's meat which is reared upon it; and in times of wealth and luxury what is rare, with only nearly equal merit, is always preferred to what is common. As wealth and luxury increase, therefore, in consequence of improvement and cultivation, the price of poultry gradually rises above that of butcher's meat, till at last it gets so high that it becomes profitable to cultivate land for the sake of feeding them. When it has got to this height it cannot well go higher. If it did, more land would soon be turned to this purpose. In several provinces of France, the feeding of poultry is considered as a very important article in rural economy, and sufficiently profitable to encourage the farmer to raise a considerable quantity of Indian corn and buckwheat for this purpose. A middling farmer will there sometimes have four hundred fowls in his yard. The feeding of poultry seems scarce yet to be generally considered as a matter of so much importance in England. They are certainly, however, dearer in England than in France, as England receives consider- able supplies from France. In the progress of improvement, the period at which every particular sort of animal food is dearest must naturally be that which immediately precedes the general practice of cultivating land for the sake of raising it. For some time before this practice becomes general, the scarcity must necessarily raise the price. After it has become general, new methods of feeding are commonly fallen upon, which enable the farmer to raise upon the same quantity of ground a much greater quantity of that particular sort of animal food. The plenty not only obliges him to sell cheaper, but in consequence of these improvements he can afford to sell cheaper; for if he could not afford it, the plenty would not be of long continuance. It has been probably in this manner that the introduction of clover, turnips, carrots, cabbages, etc., has contributed to sink the common price of butcher's meat in the London market somewhat below what it was about the beginning of the last century.

The hog, that finds his food among ordure and greedily devours many things rejected by every other useful animal, is, like poultry, originally kept as a save-all. As long as the number of such animals, which can thus be reared at little or no ex- pense, is fully sufficient to supply the demand, this sort of butcher's meat comes to market at a much lower price than any other. But when the demand rises beyond what this quantity can supply, when it becomes necessary to raise food on purpose for feeding and fattening hogs, in the same manner as for feed- ing and fattening other cattle, the price necessarily rises, and becomes proportionably either higher or lower than that of other butcher's meat, according as the nature of the country, and the state of its agriculture, happen to render the feeding of hogs more or less expensive than that of other cattle. In France, according to Mr Buffon, the price of pork is nearly equal to that of beef. In most parts of Great Britain it is at present somewhat higher.

The great rise in the price both of hogs and poultry has in Great Britain been frequently imputed to the diminution of the number of cottagers and other small occupiers of land; an event

which has in every part of Europe been the immediate forerunner of improvement and better cultivation, but which at the
same time may have contributed to raise the price of those
articles both somewhat sooner and somewhat faster than it
would otherwise have risen. As the poorest family can often
maintain a cat or a dog without any expense, so the poorest
occupiers of land can commonly maintain a few poultry, or a
sow and a few pigs, at very little. The little offals of their own
table, their whey, skimmed milk, and butter-milk, supply those
animals with a part of their food, and they find the rest in the
neighbouring fields without doing any sensible damage to anybody. By diminishing the number of those small occupiers,
therefore, the quantity of this sort of provisions, which is thus
produced at little or no expense, must certainly have been a
good deal diminished, and their price must consequently have
been raised both sooner and faster than it would otherwise have
risen. Sooner or later, however, in the progress of improvement,
it must at any rate have risen to the utmost height to which it is
capable of rising; or to the price which pays the labour and
expense of cultivating the land which furnishes them with food
as well as these are paid upon the greater part of other cultivated land.

The business of the dairy, like the feeding of hogs and
poultry, is originally carried on as a save-all. The cattle necessarily kept upon the farm produce more milk than either the
rearing of their own young or the consumption of the farmer's
family requires; and they produce most at one particular season.
But of all the productions of land, milk is perhaps the most
perishable. In the warm season, when it is most abundant, it
will scarce keep four-and-twenty hours. The farmer, by making
it into fresh butter, stores a small part of it for a week: by
making it into salt butter, for a year: and by making it into
cheese, he stores a much greater part of it for several years.
Part of all these is reserved for the use of his own family. The
rest goes to market, in order to find the best price which is to be
had, and which can scarce be so low as to discourage him from
sending thither whatever is over and above the use of his own
family. If it is very low, indeed, he will be likely to manage his
dairy in a very slovenly and dirty manner, and will scarce

perhaps think it worth while to have a particular room or building on purpose for it, but will suffer the business to be carried on amidst the smoke, filth, and nastiness of his own kitchen; as was the case of almost all the farmers' dairies in Scotland thirty or forty years ago, and as is the case of many of them still. The same causes which gradually raise the price of butcher's meat, the increase of the demand, and, in consequence of the improvement of the country, the diminution of the quantity which can be fed at little or no expense, raise, in the same manner, that of the produce of the dairy, of which the price naturally connects with that of butcher's meat, or with the expense of feeding cattle. The increase of price pays for more labour, care, and cleanliness. The dairy becomes more worthy of the farmer's attention, and the quality of its produce gradually improves. The price at last gets so high that it becomes worth while to employ some of the most fertile and best cultivated lands in feeding cattle merely for the purpose of the dairy; and when it has got to this height, it cannot well go higher. If it did, more land would soon be turned to this purpose. It seems to have got to this height through the greater part of England, where much good land is commonly employed in this manner. If you except the neighbourhood of a few considerable towns, it seems not yet to have got to this height anywhere in Scotland, where common farmers seldom employ much good land in raising food for cattle merely for the purpose of the dairy. The price of the produce, though it has risen very considerably within these few years, is probably still too low to admit of it. The inferiority of the quality, indeed, compared with that of the produce of English dairies, is fully equal to that of the price. But this inferiority of quality is, perhaps, rather the effect of this lowness of price than the cause of it. Though the quality was much better, the greater part of what is brought to market could not, I apprehend, in the present circumstances of the country, be disposed of at a much better price; and the present price, it is probable, would not pay the expense of the land and labour necessary for producing a much better quality. Through the greater part of England, notwithstanding the superiority of price, the dairy is not reckoned a more profitable employment of land than the raising of corn, or the fattening of cattle, the two great objects of agriculture. Through the greater part of Scotland, therefore, it cannot yet be even so profitable.

The lands of no country, it is evident, can ever be completely cultivated and improved till once the price of every produce, which human industry is obliged to raise upon them, has got so high as to pay for the expense of complete improvement and cultivation. In order to do this, the price of each particular produce must be sufficient, first, to pay the rent of good corn land, as it is that which regulates the rent of the greater part of other cultivated land; and, secondly, to pay the labour and expense of the farmer as well as they are commonly paid upon good corn land; or, in other words, to replace with the ordinary profits the stock which he employs about it. This rise in the price of each particular produce must evidently be previous to the improvement and cultivation of the land which is destined for raising it. Gain is the end of all improvement, and nothing could deserve that name of which loss was to be the necessary consequence. But loss must be the necessary consequence of improving land for the sake of a produce of which the price could never bring back the expense. If the complete improvement and cultivation of the country be, as it most certainly is, the greatest of all public advantages, this rise in the price of all those different sorts of rude produce, instead of being considered as a public calamity, ought to be regarded as the necessary forerunner and attendant of the greatest of all public advantages.

This rise, too, in the nominal or money-price of all those different sorts of rude produce has been the effect, not of any degradation in the value of silver, but of a rise in their real price. They have become worth, not only a greater quantity of silver, but a greater quantity of labour and subsistence than before. As it costs a greater quantity of labour and subsistence to bring them to market, so when they are brought thither, they represent or are equivalent to a greater quantity.

Third Sort

The third and last sort of rude produce, of which the price naturally rises in the progress of improvement, is that in which the efficacy of human industry, in augmenting the quantity, is either limited or uncertain. Though the real price of this sort of rude produce, therefore, naturally tends to rise in the progress of improvement, yet, according as different accidents happen to render the efforts of human industry more or less successful in augmenting the quantity, it may happen sometimes even to fall, sometimes to continue the same in very different periods of improvement, and sometimes to rise more or less in the same period.

There are some sorts of rude produce which nature has rendered a kind of appendages to other sorts; so that the quantity of the one which any country can afford, is necessarily limited by that of the other. The quantity of wool or of raw hides, for example, which any country can afford is necessarily limited by the number of great and small cattle that are kept in it. The state of its improvement, and the nature of its agriculture, again necessarily determine this number.

The same causes which, in the progress of improvement, gradually raise the price of butcher's meat, should have the same effect, it may be thought, upon the prices of wool and raw hides, and raise them, too, nearly in the same proportion. It probably would be so if, in the rude beginnings of improvement, the market for the latter commodities was confined within as narrow bounds as that for the former. But the extent of their respective markets is commonly extremely different.

The market for butcher's meat is almost everywhere confined to the country which produces it. Ireland, and some part of British America indeed, carry on a considerable trade in salt provisions; but they are, I believe, the only countries in the commercial world which do so, or which export to other countries any considerable part of their butcher's meat.

The market for wool and raw hides, on the contrary, is in the rude beginnings of improvement very seldom confined to the country which produces them. They can easily be transported to distant countries, wool without any preparation, and raw hides with very little: and as they are the materials of many manufactures, the industry of other countries may occasion a demand for them, though that of the country which produces them might not occasion any.

In countries ill cultivated, and therefore but thinly inhabited,

the price of the wool and the hide bears always a much greater
proportion to that of the whole beast than in countries where,
improvement and population being further advanced, there is
more demand for butcher's meat. Mr Hume observes that in the
Saxon times the fleece was estimated at two-fifths of the value of
the whole sheep, and that this was much above the proportion
of its present estimation. In some provinces of Spain, I have
been assured, the sheep is frequently killed merely for the sake
of the fleece and the tallow. The carcase is often left to rot upon
the ground, or to be devoured by beasts and birds of prey. If
this sometimes happens even in Spain, it happens almost constantly in Chili, at Buenos Ayres, and in many other parts of
Spanish America, where the horned cattle are almost constantly
killed merely for the sake of the hide and the tallow. This, too,
used to happen almost constantly in Hispaniola, while it was
infested by the Buccaneers, and before the settlement, improvement, and populousness of the French plantations (which now
extend round the coast of almost the whole western half of the
island) had given some value to the cattle of the Spaniards, who
still continue to possess, not only the eastern part of the coast,
but the whole inland and mountainous part of the country.

Though in the progress of improvement and population the
price of the whole beast necessarily rises, yet the price of the
carcase is likely to be much more affected by this rise than that
of the wool and the hide. The market for the carcase, being in
the rude state of society confined always to the country which
produces it, must necessarily be extended in proportion to the
improvement and population of that country. But the market
for the wool and the hides even of a barbarous country often
extending to the whole commercial world, it can very seldom be
enlarged in the same proportion. The state of the whole commercial world can seldom be much affected by the improvement
of any particular country; and the market for such commodities
may remain the same, or very nearly the same after such improvements as before. It should, however, in the natural course
of things rather upon the whole be somewhat extended in consequence of them. If the manufactures, especially, of which
those commodities are the materials should ever come to flourish in the country, the market, though it might not be much

enlarged, would at least be brought much nearer to the place of growth than before; and the price of those materials might at least be increased by what had usually been the expense of transporting them to distant countries. Though it might not rise therefore in the same proportion as that of butcher's meat, it ought naturally to rise somewhat, and it ought certainly not to fall.

In England, however, notwithstanding the flourishing state of its woollen manufacture, the price of English wool has fallen very considerably since the time of Edward III. There are many authentic records which demonstrate that during the reign of that prince (towards the middle of the fourteenth century, or about 1339) what was reckoned the moderate and reasonable price of the tod, or twenty-eight pounds of English wool, was not less than ten shillings of the money of those times,[1] containing at the rate of twentypence the ounce, six ounces of silver Tower-weight, equal to about thirty shillings of our present money. In the present times, one-and-twenty shillings the tod may be reckoned a good price for very good English wool. The money-price of wool, therefore, in the time of Edward III, was to its money-price in the present times as ten to seven. The superiority of its real price was still greater. At the rate of six shillings and eightpence the quarter, ten shillings was in those ancient times the price of twelve bushels of wheat. At the rate of twenty-eight shillings the quarter, one-and-twenty shillings is in the present times the price of six bushels only. The proportion between the real prices of ancient and modern times, therefore, is as twelve to six, or as two to one. In those ancient times a tod of wool would have purchased twice the quantity of subsistence which it will purchase at present; and consequently twice the quantity of labour, if the real recompense of labour had been the same in both periods.

This degradation both in the real and nominal value of wool could never have happened in consequence of the natural course of things. It has accordingly been the effect of violence and artifice: first, of the absolute prohibition of exporting wool from England; secondly, of the permission of importing it from Spain duty free; thirdly, of the prohibition of exporting it from

1. See Smith's *Memoirs of Wool*, vol. i. c. 5, 6, and 7; also, vol. ii. c. 176.

Ireland to any other country but England. In consequence of these regulations the market for English wool, intead of being somewhat extended in consequence of the improvement of England, has been confined to the home market, where the wool of several other countries is allowed to come into competition with it, and where that of Ireland is forced into competition with it. As the woollen manufactures, too, of Ireland are fully as much discouraged as is consistent with just and fair dealing, the Irish can work up but a small part of their own wool at home, and are, therefore, obliged to send a greater proportion of it to Great Britain, the only market they are allowed.

I have not been able to find any such authentic records concerning the price of raw hides in ancient times. Wool was commonly paid as a subsidy to the king, and its valuation in that subsidy ascertains, at least in some degree, what was its ordinary price. But this seems not to have been the case with raw hides. Fleetwood, however, from an account in 1425, between the prior of Burcester Oxford and one of his canons, gives us their price, at least as it was stated upon that particular occasion, viz., five ox hides at twelve shillings; five cow hides at seven shillings and threepence; thirty-six sheep skins of two years old at nine shillings; sixteen calves skins at two shillings. In 1425, twelve shillings contained about the same quantity of silver as four-and-twenty shillings of our present money. An ox hide, therefore, was in this account valued at the same quantity of silver as 4s. four-fifths of our present money. Its nominal price was a good deal lower than at present. But at the rate of six shillings and eightpence the quarter, twelve shillings would in those times have purchased fourteen bushels and four-fifths of a bushel of wheat, which, at three and sixpence the bushel, would in the present times cost 51s. 4d. An ox hide, therefore, would in those times have purchased as much corn as ten shillings and threepence would purchase at present. Its real value was equal to ten shillings and threepence of our present money. In those ancient times when the cattle were half starved during the greater part of the winter, we cannot suppose that they were of a very large size. An ox hide which weighs four stone of sixteen pounds avoirdupois is not in the present times reckoned a bad one; and in those ancient times would probably have been reckoned a very good one. But at half-a-crown the stone, which at this moment (February 1773) I understand to be the common price, such a hide would at present cost only ten shillings. Though its nominal price, therefore, is higher in the present than it was in those ancient times, its real price, the real quantity of subsistence which it will purchase or command, is rather somewhat lower. The price of cow hides, as stated in the above account, is nearly in the common proportion to that of ox hides. That of sheep skins is a good deal above it. They had probably been sold with the wool. That of calves skins, on the contrary, is greatly below it. In countries where the price of cattle is very low, the calves, which are not intended to be reared in order to keep up the stock, are generally killed very young; as was the case in Scotland twenty or thirty years ago. It saves the milk, which their price would not pay for. Their skins, therefore, are commonly good for little.

The price of raw hides is a good deal lower at present than it was a few years ago, owing probably to the taking off the duty upon sealskins, and to the allowing, for a limited time, the importation of raw hides from Ireland and from the plantations duty free, which was done in 1769. Take the whole of the present century at an average, their real price has probably been somewhat higher than it was in those ancient times. The nature of the commodity renders it not quite so proper for being transported to distant markets as wool. It suffers more by keeping. A salted hide is reckoned inferior to a fresh one, and sells for a lower price. This circumstance must necessarily have some tendency to sink the price of raw hides produced in a country which does not manufacture them, but is obliged to export them; and comparatively to raise that of those produced in a country which does manufacture them. It must have some tendency to sink their price in a barbarous, and to raise it in an improved and manufacturing country. It must have had some tendency, therefore, to sink it in ancient and to raise it in modern times. Our tanners, besides, have not been quite so successful as our clothiers in convincing the wisdom of the nation that the safety of the commonwealth depends upon the prosperity of their particular manufacture. They have accordingly been much less favoured. The exportation of raw hides has, indeed, been prohibited, and declared a nuisance; but their importation from foreign countries has been subjected to a duty; and though this duty has been taken off from those of Ireland and the plantations (for the limited time of five years only), yet Ireland has not been confined to the market of Great Britain for the sale of its surplus hides, or of those which are not manufactured at home. The hides of common cattle have but within these few years been put among the enumerated commodities which the plantations can send nowhere but to the mother country; neither has the commerce of Ireland been in this case oppressed hitherto in order to support the manufactures of Great Britain.

Whatever regulations tend to sink the price either of wool or of raw hides below what it naturally would be must, in an improved and cultivated country, have some tendency to raise the price of butcher's meat. The price both of the great and small cattle, which are fed on improved and cultivated land, must be sufficient to pay the rent which the landlord, and the profit which the farmer has reason to expect from improved and cultivated land. If it is not, they will soon cease to feed them. Whatever part of this price, therefore, is not paid by the wool and the hide must be paid by the carcase. The less there is paid for the one, the more must be paid for the other. In what manner this price is to be divided upon the different parts of the beast is indifferent to the landlords and farmers, provided it is all paid to them. In an improved and cultivated country, therefore, their interest as landlords and farmers cannot be much affected by such regulations, though their interest as consumers may, by the rise in the price of provisions. It would be quite otherwise, however, in an unimproved and uncultivated country, where the greater part of the lands could be applied to no other purpose but the feeding of cattle, and where the wool and the hide made the principal part of the value of those cattle. Their interest as landlords and farmers would in this case be very deeply affected by such regulations, and their interest as consumers very little. The fall in the price of the wool and the hide would not in this case raise the price of the carcase, because the greater part of the lands of the country being applicable to no other purpose but the feeding of cattle, the same number would still continue to be fed. The same quantity of butcher's meat would still come to market. The demand for it would be no greater than before. Its price, therefore, would be the same as before. The whole price of cattle would fall, and along with it both the rent and the profit of all those lands of which cattle was the principal produce, that is, of the greater part of the lands of the country. The perpetual prohibition of the exportation of wool, which is commonly, but very falsely, ascribed to Edward III, would, in the then circumstances of the country, have been the most destructive regulation which could well have been thought of. It would not only have reduced the actual value of the greater part of the lands of the kingdom, but by reducing the price of the most important species of small cattle, it would have retarded very much its subsequent improvement.

The wool of Scotland fell very considerably in its price in consequence of the union with England, by which it was excluded from the great market of Europe, and confined to the narrow one of Great Britain. The value of the greater part of the lands in the southern counties of Scotland, which are chiefly a sheep country, would have been very deeply affected by this event, had not the rise in the price of butcher's meat fully compensated the fall in the price of wool.

As the efficacy of human industry, in increasing the quantity either of wool or of raw hides, is limited, so far as it depends upon the produce of the country where it is exerted; so it is uncertain so far as it depends upon the produce of other countries. It so far depends, not so much upon the quantity which they produce, as upon that which they do not manufacture; and upon the restraints which they may or may not think proper to impose upon the exportation of this sort of rude produce. These circumstances, as they are altogether independent of domestic industry, so they necessarily render the efficacy of its efforts more or less uncertain. In multiplying this sort of rude produce, therefore, the efficacy of human industry is not only limited, but uncertain.

In multiplying another very important sort of rude produce, the quantity of fish that is brought to market, it is likewise both limited and uncertain. It is limited by the local situation of the country, by the proximity or distance of its different provinces from the sea, by the number of its lakes and rivers, and by what may be called the fertility or barrenness of those seas, lakes, and rivers, as to this sort of rude produce. As population increases, as the annual produce of the land and labour of the country grows greater and greater, there come to be more buyers of fish, and those buyers, too, have a greater quantity and variety of other goods, or, what is the same thing, the price of a greater quantity and variety of other goods to buy with. But it will generally be impossible to supply the great and extended market without employing a quantity of labour greater than in proportion to what had been requisite for supplying the narrow and confined one. A market which, from requiring only one thousand, comes to require annually ten thousand tons of fish, can seldom be supplied without employing more than ten times the quantity of labour which had before been sufficient to supply it. The fish must generally be sought for at a greater distance, larger vessels must be employed, and more expensive machinery of every kind made use of. The real price of this commodity, therefore, naturally rises in the progress of improvement. It has accordingly done so, I believe, more or less in every country.

Though the success of a particular day's fishing may be a very uncertain matter, yet, the local situation of the country being supposed, the general efficacy of industry in bringing a certain quantity of fish to market, taking the course of a year, or of several years together, it may perhaps be thought, is certain enough; and it, no doubt, is so. As it depends more, however, upon the local situation of the country than upon the state of its wealth and industry; as upon this account it may in different countries be the same in very different periods of improvement, and very different in the same period; its connexion with the state of improvement is uncertain, and it is of this sort of uncertainty that I am here speaking.

In increasing the quantity of the different minerals and metals which are drawn from the bowels of the earth, that of the more precious ones particularly, the efficacy of human industry seems not to be limited, but to be altogether uncertain.

The quantity of the precious metals which is to be found in any country is not limited by anything in its local situation, such as the fertility or barrenness of its own mines. Those metals frequently abound in countries which possess no mines. Their quantity in every particular country seems to depend upon two different circumstances; first, upon its power of purchasing, upon the state of its industry, upon the annual produce of its land and labour, in consequence of which it can afford to employ a greater or a smaller quantity of labour and subsistence in bringing or purchasing such superfluities as gold and silver, either from its own mines or from those of other countries; and, secondly, upon the fertility or barrenness of the mines which may happen at any particular time to supply the commercial world with those metals. The quantity of those metals in the countries most remote from the mines must be more or less affected by this fertility or barrenness, on account of the easy and cheap transportation of those metals, of their small bulk and great value. Their quantity in China and Indostan must have been more or less affected by the abundance of the mines of America.

So far as their quantity in any particular country depends upon the former of those two circumstances (the power of purchasing), their real price, like that of all other luxuries and superfluities, is likely to rise with the wealth and improvement of the country, and to fall with its poverty and depression. Countries which have a great quantity of labour and subsistence to spare can afford to purchase any particular quantity of those metals at the expense of a greater quantity of labour and subsistence than countries which have less to spare.

So far as their quantity in any particular country depends upon the latter of those two circumstances (the fertility or barrenness of the mines which happen to supply the commercial world), their real price, the real quantity of labour and subsistence which they will purchase or exchange for, will, no doubt, sink more or less in proportion to the fertility, and rise in proportion to the barrenness of those mines.

The fertility or barrenness of the mines, however, which may happen at any particular time to supply the commercial world, is a circumstance which, it is evident, may have no sort of connexion with the state of industry in a particular country. It seems even to have no very necessary connexion with that of the world in general. As arts and commerce, indeed, gradually spread themselves over a greater and greater part of the earth, the search for new mines, being extended over a wider surface, may have somewhat a better chance for being successful than when confined within narrower bounds. The discovery of new mines, however, as the old ones come to be gradually exhausted, is a matter of the greatest uncertainty, and such as no human skill or industry can ensure. All indications, it is acknowledged, are doubtful, and the actual discovery and successful working of a new mine can alone ascertain the reality of its value, or even of its existence. In this search there seem to be no certain limits either to the possible success or to the possible disappointment of human industry. In the course of a century or two, it is possible that new mines may be discovered more fertile than any that have ever yet been known; and it is just equally possible that the most fertile mine then known may be more barren than any that was wrought before the discovery of the mines of America. Whether the one or the other of those two events may happen to take place is of very little importance to the real wealth and prosperity of the world, to the real value of the annual produce of the land and labour of mankind. Its nominal value, the quantity of gold and silver by which this annual produce could be expressed or represented, would, no doubt, be very different; but its real value, the real quantity of labour which it could purchase or command, would be precisely the same. A shilling might in the one case represent no more labour than a penny does at present; and a penny in the other might represent as much as a shilling does now. But in the one case he who had a shilling in his pocket would be no richer than he who has a penny at present; and in the other he who had a penny would be just as rich as he who has a shilling now. The cheapness and abundance of gold and silver plate would be the sole advantage which the world could derive from the one event, and the dearness and scarcity of those trifling superfluities the only inconveniency if could suffer from the other.

CONCLUSION OF THE DIGRESSION CONCERNING THE
VARIATIONS IN THE VALUE OF SILVER

The greater part of the writers who have collected the money prices of things in ancient times seem to have considered the low money-price of corn, and of goods in general, or, in other words, the high value of gold and silver, as a proof, not only of the scarcity of those metals, but of the poverty and barbarism of the country at the time when it took place. This notion is connected with the system of political economy which represents national wealth as consisting in the abundance, and national poverty in the scarcity, of gold and silver; a system which I shall endeavour to explain and examine at great length in the fourth book of this inquiry. I shall only observe at present that the high value of the precious metals can be no proof of the poverty or barbarism of any particular country at the time when it took place. It is a proof only of the barrenness of the mines which happened at that time to supply the commercial world. A poor country, as it cannot afford to buy more, so it can as little afford to pay dearer for gold and silver than a rich one; and the value of those metals, therefore, is not likely to be higher in the former than in the latter. In China, a country much richer than any part of Europe, the value of the precious metals is much higher than in any part of Europe. As the wealth of Europe, indeed, has increased greatly since the discovery of the mines of America, so the value of gold and silver has gradually diminished. This diminution of their value, however, has not been owing to the increase of the real wealth of Europe, of the annual produce of its land and labour, but to the accidental discovery of more abundant mines than any that were known before. The increase in the quantity of gold and silver in Europe, and the increase of its manufactures and agriculture, are two events which, though they have happened nearly about the same time, yet have arisen from very different causes, and have scarce any natural connection with one another. The one has arisen from a mere accident, in which neither prudence nor policy either had or could have any share. The other from the fall of the feudal system, and from the establishment of a government which afforded to industry the only encouragement which it requires, some tolerable security that it shall enjoy the fruits of its own labour. Poland, where the feudal system still continues to take place, is at this day as beggarly a country as it was before the discovery of America. The money price of corn, however, has risen; the real value of the precious metals has fallen in Poland, in the same manner as in other parts of Europe. Their quantity, therefore, must have increased there as in other places, and nearly in the same proportion to the annual produce of its land and labour. This increase of the quantity of those metals, however, has not, it seems, increased that annual produce, has neither improved the manufactures and agriculture of the country, nor mended the circumstances of its inhabitants. Spain and Portugal, the countries which possess the mines, are, after Poland, perhaps, the two most beggarly countries in Europe. The value of the precious metals, however, must be lower in Spain and Portugal than in any other part of Europe; as they come from those countries to all other parts of Europe, loaded, not only with a freight and an insurance, but with the expense of smuggling, their exportation being either prohibited, or subjected to a duty. In proportion to the annual produce of the land and labour, therefore, their quantity must be greater in those countries than in any other part of Europe. Those countries, however, are poorer than the greater part of Europe. Though the feudal system has been abolished in Spain and Portugal, it has not been succeeded by a much better.

As the low value of gold and silver, therefore, is no proof of the wealth and flourishing state of the country where it takes place; so neither is their high value, or the low money price either of goods in general, or of corn in particular, any proof of its poverty and barbarism.

But though the low money price either of goods in general, or of corn in particular, be no proof of the poverty or barbarism of the times, the low money price of some particular sorts of goods, such as cattle, poultry, game of all kinds, etc., in proportion to that of corn, is a most decisive one. It clearly demonstrates, first, their great abundance in proportion to that of corn, and consequently the great extent of the land which they occupied in proportion to what was occupied by corn; and, secondly, the low value of this land in proportion to that of corn land, and consequently the uncultivated and unimproved state of the far greater part of the lands of the country. It clearly demonstrates that the stock and population of the country did not bear the same proportion to the extent of its territory which they commonly do in civilized countries, and that society was at that time, and in that country, but in its infancy. From the high or low money price either of goods in general, or of corn in particular, we can infer only that the mines which at that time happened to supply the commercial world with gold and silver were fertile or barren, not that the country was rich or poor. But from the high or low money price of some sorts of goods in proportion to that of others, we can infer, with a degree of probability that approaches almost to certainty, that it was rich or poor, that the greater part of its lands were improved or unimproved, and that it was either in a more or less barbarous state, or in a more or less civilized one.

Any rise in the money price of goods which proceeded altogether from the degradation of the value of silver would affect all sorts of goods equally, and raise their price universally a third, or a fourth, or a fifth part higher, according as silver happened to lose a third, or a fourth, or a fifth part of its former value. But the rise in the price of provisions, which has been the subject of so much reasoning and conversation, does not affect all sorts of provisions equally. Taking the course of the present century at an average, the price of corn, it is acknowledged, even by those who account for this rise by the degradation of the value of silver, has risen much less than that of some other sorts of provisions. The rise in the price of those other sorts of provisions, therefore, cannot be owing altogether to the degradation of the value of silver. Some other causes must be taken into the account, and those which have been above assigned will, perhaps, without having recourse to the supposed degradation of the value of silver, sufficiently explain this rise in those particular sorts of provisions of which the price has actually risen in proportion to that of corn.

As to the price of corn itself, it has, during the sixty-four first years of the present century, and before the late extraordinary course of bad seasons, been somewhat lower than it was during the sixty-four last years of the preceding century. This fact is attested, not only by the accounts of Windsor market, but by the public fiars of all the different counties of Scotland, and by the accounts of several different markets in France, which have been collected with great diligence and fidelity by Mr Messance and Mr Duprè St Maur. The evidence is more complete than could well have been expected in a matter which is naturally so very difficult to be ascertained.

As to the high price of corn during these last ten or twelve years, it can be sufficiently accounted for from the badness of the seasons, without supposing any degradation in the value of silver. The opinion, therefore, that silver is continually sinking in its value, seems not to be founded upon any good observations, either upon the prices of corn, or upon those of other provisions.

The same quantity of silver, it may, perhaps, be said, will in the present times, even according to the account which has been here given, purchase a much smaller quantity of several sorts of provisions than it would have done during some part of the last century; and to ascertain whether this change be owing to a rise in the value of those goods, or to a fall in the value of silver, is only to establish a vain and useless distinction, which can be of no sort of service to the man who has only a certain quantity of silver to go to market with, or a certain fixed revenue in money. I certainly do not pretend that the knowledge of this distinction will enable him to buy cheaper. It may not, however, upon that account be altogether useless.

It may be of some use to the public by affording an easy proof of the prosperous condition of the country. If the rise in the price of some sorts of provisions be owing altogether to a fall in the value of silver, it is owing to a circumstance from which nothing can be inferred but the fertility of the American mines. The real wealth of the country, the annual produce of its land and labour, may, notwithstanding this circumstance, be either gradually declining, as in Portugal and Poland; or gradually advancing, as in most other parts of Europe. But if this rise in the price of some sorts of provisions be owing to a rise in the real value of the land which produces them, to its increased fertility, or, in consequence of more extended improvement and good cultivation, to its having been rendered fit for producing corn; it is owing to a circumstance which indicates in the clearest manner the prosperous and advancing state of the country. The land constitutes by far the greatest, the most important, and the most durable part of the wealth of every extensive country. It may surely be of some use, or, at least, it may give some satisfaction to the public, to have so decisive a proof of the increasing value of by far the greatest, the most important, and the most durable part of its wealth.

It may, too, be of some use to the public in regulating the pecuniary reward of some of its inferior servants. If this rise in the price of some sorts of provisions be owing to a fall in the value of silver, their pecuniary reward, provided it was not too large before, ought certainly to be augmented in proportion to the extent of this fall. If it is not augmented, their real recompense will evidently be so much diminished. But if this rise of price is owing to the increased value, in consequence of the improved fertility of the land which produces such provisions, it becomes a much nicer matter to judge either in what proportion any pecuniary reward ought to be augmented, or whether it ought to be augmented at all. The extension of improvement and cultivation, as it necessarily raises more or less, in proportion to the price of corn, that of every sort of animal food, so it as necessarily lowers that of, I believe, every sort of vegetable food. It raises the price of animal food; because a great part of the land which produces it, being rendered fit for producing corn, must afford to the landlord and farmer the rent and profit of corn-land. It lowers the price of vegetable food; because, by increasing the fertility of the land, it increases its abundance. The improvements of agriculture, too, introduce many sorts of vegetable food, which, requiring less land and not more labour than corn, come much cheaper to market. Such are potatoes and maize, or what is called Indian corn, the two most important improvements which the agriculture of Europe, perhaps, which Europe itself has received from the great extension of its commerce and navigation. Many sorts of vegetable food, besides, which in the rude state of agriculture are confined to the kitchen-garden, and raised only by the spade, come in its improved state to be introduced into common fields, and to be raised by the plough: such as turnips, carrots, cabbages, etc. If in the progress of improvement, therefore, the real price of one species of food necessarily rises, that of another as necessarily falls, and it becomes a matter of more nicety to judge how far the rise in the one may be compensated by the fall in the other. When the real price of butcher's meat has once got to its height (which, with regard to every sort, except, perhaps, that of hogs' flesh, it seems to have done through a great part of England more than a century ago), any rise which can afterwards happen in that of any other sort of animal food cannot much affect the circumstances of the inferior ranks of people. The circumstances of the poor through a great part of England cannot surely be so much distressed by any rise in the price of poultry, fish, wild-fowl, or venison, as they must be relieved by the fall in that of potatoes.

In the present season of scarcity the high price of corn no doubt distresses the poor. But in time of moderate plenty, when corn is at its ordinary or average price, the natural rise in the price of any other sort of rude produce cannot much affect them. They suffer more, perhaps, by the artificial rise which has been occasioned by taxes in the price of some manufactured commodities; as of salt, soap, leather, candles, malt, beer, and ale, etc.

EFFECTS OF THE PROGRESS OF IMPROVEMENT UPON THE REAL PRICE OF MANUFACTURES

It is the natural effect of improvement, however, to diminish gradually the real price of almost all manufactures. That of the manufacturing workmanship diminishes, perhaps, in all of them without exception. In consequence of better machinery, of greater dexterity, and of a more proper division and distribution of work, all of which are the natural effects of improvement, a much smaller quantity of labour becomes requisite for executing any particular piece of work, and though, in consequence of the flourishing circumstances of the society, the real price of labour should rise very considerably, yet the great diminution of the quantity will generally much more than compensate the greatest rise which can happen in the price.

There are, indeed, a few manufactures in which the necessary rise in the real price of the rude materials will more than compensate all the advantages which improvement can introduce into the execution of the work. In carpenters' and joiners' work, and in the coarser sort of cabinet work, the necessary rise in the real price of barren timber, in consequence of the improvement of land, will more than compensate all the advantages which can be derived from the best machinery, the greatest dexterity, and the most proper division and distribution of work.

But in all cases in which the real price of the rude materials either does not rise at all, or does not rise very much, that of the manufactured commodity sinks very considerably.

This diminution of price has, in the course of the present and preceding century, been most remarkable in those manufactures of which the materials are the coarser metals. A better movement of a watch, than about the middle of the last century could have been bought for twenty pounds, may now perhaps be had for twenty shillings. In the work of cutlers and locksmiths, in all the toys which are made of the coarser metals, and in all those goods which are commonly known by the name of Birmingham and Sheffield ware, there has been, during the same period, a very great reduction of price, though not altogether so great as in watch-work. It has, however, been sufficient to astonish the workmen of every other part of Europe, who in many cases acknowledge that they can produce no work of equal goodness for double, or even for triple the price. There are perhaps no manufactures in which the division of labour can be carried further, or in which the machinery employed admits of a greater variety of improvements, than those of which the materials are the coarser metals.

In the clothing manufacture there has, during the same period, been no such sensible reduction of price. The price of superfine cloth, I have been assured, on the contrary, has, within these five-and-twenty or thirty years, risen somewhat in proportion to its quality; owing, it was said, to a considerable rise in the price of the material, which consists altogether of Spanish wool. That of the Yorkshire cloth, which is made altogether of English wool, is said indeed, during the course of the present century, to have fallen a good deal in proportion to its quality. Quality, however, is so very disputable a matter that I look upon all information of this kind as somewhat uncertain. In the clothing manufacture, the division of labour is nearly the same now as it was a century ago, and the machinery employed is not very different. There may, however, have been some small improvements in both, which may have occasioned some reduction of price.

But the reduction will appear much more sensible and undeniable if we compare the price of this manufacture in the present times with what it was in a much remoter period, towards the end of the fifteenth century, when the labour was probably much less subdivided, and the machinery employed much more imperfect, than it is at present.

In 1487, being the 4th of Henry VII, it was enacted that 'whosoever shall sell by retail a broad yard of the finest scarlet grained, or of other grained cloth of the finest making, above sixteen shillings, shall forfeit forty shillings for every yard so sold.' Sixteen shillings, therefore, containing about the same quantity of silver as four-and-twenty shillings of our present money, was, at that time, reckoned not an unreasonable price for a yard of the finest cloth; and as this is a sumptuary law, such cloth, it is probable, had usually been sold somewhat dearer. A guinea may be reckoned the highest price in the present times. Even though the quality of the cloths, therefore, should be supposed equal, and that of the present times is most probably much superior, yet, even upon this supposition, the money price of the finest cloth appears to have been considerably reduced since the end of the fifteenth century. But its real price has been much more reduced. Six shillings and eightpence was then, and long afterwards, reckoned the average price of a quarter of wheat. Sixteen shillings, therefore, was the price of two quarters and more than three bushels of wheat. Valuing a quarter of wheat in the present times at eight-and-twenty shillings, the real price of a yard of fine cloth must, in those times, have been equal to at least three pounds six shillings and sixpence of our present money. The man who bought it must have parted with the command of a quantity of labour and subsistence equal to what that sum would purchase in the present times.

The reduction in the real price of the coarse manufacture, though considerable, has not been so great as in that of the fine.

In 1463, being the 3rd of Edward IV, it was enacted that 'no servant in husbandry, nor common labourer, nor servant to any artificer inhabiting out of a city or burgh shall use or wear in their clothing any cloth above two shillings the broad yard.' In the 3rd of Edward IV, two shillings contained very nearly the same quantity of silver as four of our present money. But the Yorkshire cloth which is now sold at four shillings the yard is probably much superior to any that was then made for the wearing of the very poorest order of common servants. Even the money price of their clothing, therefore, may, in proportion to the quality, be somewhat cheaper in the present than it was in those ancient times. The real price is certainly a good deal cheaper. Tenpence was then reckoned what is called the moderate and reasonable price of a bushel of wheat. Two shillings, therefore, was the price of two bushels and near two pecks of wheat, which in the present times, at three shillings and sixpence the bushel, would be worth eight shillings and ninepence. For a yard of this cloth the poor servant must have parted with the power of purchasing a quantity of subsistence equal to what eight shillings and ninepence would purchase in the present times. This is a sumptuary law too, restraining the luxury and extravagance of the poor. Their clothing, therefore, had commonly been much more expensive.

The same order of people are, by the same law, prohibited from wearing hose, of which the price should exceed fourteenpence the pair, equal to about eight-and-twentypence of our present money. But fourteenpence was in those times the price of a bushel and near two pecks of wheat, which, in the present times, at three and sixpence the bushel, would cost five shillings and threepence. We should in the present times consider this as a very high price for a pair of stockings to a servant of the poorest and lowest order. He must, however, in those times have paid what was really equivalent to this price for them.

In the time of Edward IV the art of knitting stockings was probably not known in any part of Europe. Their hose were made of common cloth, which may have been one of the causes of their dearness. The first person that wore stockings in England is said to have been Queen Elizabeth. She received them as a present from the Spanish ambassador.

Both in the coarse and in the fine woollen manufacture, the machinery employed was much more imperfect in those ancient than it is in the present times. It has since received three very capital improvements, besides, probably, many smaller ones of which it may be difficult to ascertain either the number or the importance. The three capital improvements are: first, the exchange of the rock and spindle for the spinning-wheel, which, with the same quantity of labour, will perform more than double the quantity of work. Secondly, the use of several very ingenious machines which facilitate and abridge in a still greater proportion the winding of the worsted and woollen yarn, or the proper arrangements of the warp and woof before they are put into the loom; an operation which, previous to the invention of those machines, must have been extremely tedious and troublesome. Thirdly, the employment of the fulling mill for thickening the cloth, instead of treading it in water. Neither wind nor water mills of any kind were known in England so early as the beginning of the sixteenth century, nor, so far as I know, in any other part of Europe north of the Alps. They had been introduced into Italy some time before.

The consideration of these circumstances may, perhaps, in some measure explain to us why the real price both of the coarse and of the fine manufacture was so much higher in those ancient than it is in the present times. It cost a greater quantity of labour to bring the goods to market. When they were brought thither, therefore, they must have purchased or exchanged for the price of a greater quantity.

The coarse manufacture probably was, in those ancient times, carried on in England, in the same manner as it always has been in countries where arts and manufactures are in their infancy. It was probably a household manufacture, in which every different part of the work was occasionally performed by all the different members of almost every private family; but so as to be their work only when they had nothing else to do, and not to be the principal business from which any of them derived the greater part of their subsistence. The work which is performed in this manner, it has already been observed, comes always much cheaper to market than that which is the principal or sole fund of the workman's subsistence. The fine manufacture, on the other hand, was not in those times carried on in England, but in the rich and commercial country of Flanders; and it was probably conducted then, in the same manner as now, by people who derived the whole, or the principal part of their subsistence from it. It was, besides, a foreign manufacture, and must have paid some duty, the ancient custom of tonnage and poundage at least, to the king. This duty, indeed, would not probably be very great. It was not then the policy of Europe to restrain, by high duties, the importation of foreign manufactures, but rather to encourage it, in order that merchants might be enabled to supply, at as easy a rate as possible, the great men with the conveniences and luxuries which they wanted, and which the industry of their own country could not afford them.

The consideration of these circumstances may perhaps in some measure explain to us why, in those ancient times, the real price of the coarse manufacture was, in proportion to that of the fine, so much lower than in the present times.

CONCLUSION OF THE CHAPTER

I shall conclude this very long chapter with observing that every improvement in the circumstances of the society tends either directly or indirectly to raise the real rent of land, to increase the real wealth of the landlord, his power of purchasing the labour, or the produce of the labour of other people.

The extension of improvement and cultivation tends to raise it directly. The landlord's share of the produce necessarily increases with the increase of the produce.

That rise in the real price of those parts of the rude produce of land, which is first the effect of extended improvement and cultivation, and afterwards the cause of their being still further extended, the rise in the price of cattle, for example, tends too to raise the rent of land directly, and in a still greater proportion. The real value of the landlord's share, his real command of the labour of other people, not only rises with the real value of the produce, but the proportion of his share to the whole produce rises with it. That produce, after the rise in its real price, requires no more labour to collect it than before. A smaller proportion of it will, therefore, be sufficient to replace, with the ordinary profit, the stock which employs that labour. A greater proportion of it must, consequently, belong to the landlord.

All those improvements in the productive powers of labour, which tend directly to reduce the real price of manufactures, tend indirectly to raise the real rent of land. The landlord exchanges that part of his rude produce, which is over and above his own consumption, or what comes to the same thing, the price of that part of it, for manufactured produce. Whatever reduces the real price of the latter, raises that of the former. An equal quantity of the former becomes thereby equivalent to a greater quantity of the latter; and the landlord is enabled to purchase a greater quantity of the conveniences, ornaments, or luxuries, which he has occasion for.

Every increase in the real wealth of the society, every increase in the quantity of useful labour employed within it, tends indirectly to raise the real rent of land. A certain proportion of this labour naturally goes to the land. A greater number of men and cattle are employed in its cultivation, the produce increases with the increase of the stock which is thus employed in raising it, and the rent increases with the produce.

The contrary circumstances, the neglect of cultivation and improvement, the fall in the real price of any part of the rude produce of land, the rise in the real price of manufactures from the decay of manufacturing art and industry, the declension of the real wealth of the society, all tend, on the other hand, to lower the real rent of land, to reduce the real wealth of the landlord, to diminish his power of purchasing either the labour, or the produce of the labour of other people.

The whole annual produce of the land and labour of every country, or what comes to the same thing, the whole price of that annual produce, naturally divides itself, it has already been observed, into three parts; the rent of land, the wages of labour, and the profits of stock; and constitutes a revenue to three different orders of people; to those who live by rent, to those who live by wages, and to those who live by profit. These are the three great, original, and constituent orders of every civilized society, from whose revenue that of every other order is ultimately derived.

The interest of the first of those three great orders, it appears from what has been just now said, is strictly and inseparably connected with the general interest of the society. Whatever either promotes or obstructs the one, necessarily promotes or obstructs the other. When the public deliberates concerning any regulation of commerce or police, the proprietors of land never can mislead it, with a view to promote the interest of their own particular order; at least, if they have any tolerable knowledge of that interest. They are, indeed, too often defective in this tolerable knowledge. They are the only one of the three orders whose revenue costs them neither labour nor care, but comes to them, as it were, of its own accord, and independent of any plan or project of their own. That indolence, which is the natural effect of the ease and security of their situation, renders them too often, not only ignorant, but incapable of that application of mind which is necessary in order to foresee and understand the consequences of any public regulation.

The interest of the second order, that of those who live by wages, is as strictly connected with the interest of the society as that of the first. The wages of the labourer, it has already been shown, are never so high as when the demand for labour is continually rising, or when the quantity employed is every year increasing considerably. When this real wealth of the society becomes stationary, his wages are soon reduced to what is barely enough to enable him to bring up a family, or to continue the race of labourers. When the society declines, they fall even below this. The order of proprietors may, perhaps, gain more by the prosperity of the society than that of labourers: but there is no order that suffers so cruelly from its decline. But though the interest of the labourer is strictly connected with that of the society, he is incapable either of comprehending that interest or of understanding its connexion with his own. His condition leaves him no time to receive the necessary information, and his education and habits are commonly such as to render him unfit to judge even though he was fully informed. In the public deliberations, therefore, his voice is little heard and less regarded, except upon some particular occasions, when his clamour is animated, set on, and supported by his employers, not for his, but their own particular purposes.

His employers constitute the third order, that of those who live by profit. It is the stock that is employed for the sake of profit which puts into motion the greater part of the useful

labour of every society. The plans and projects of the employers
of stock regulate and direct all the most important operations of
labour, and profit is the end proposed by all those plans and
projects. But the rate of profit does not, like rent and wages, rise
with the prosperity and fall with the declension of the society.
On the contrary, it is naturally low in rich and high in poor
countries, and it is always highest in the countries which are
going fastest to ruin. The interest of this third order, therefore,
has not the same connexion with the general interest of the
society as that of the other two. Merchants and master manufacturers are, in this order, the two classes of people who commonly employ the largest capitals, and who by their wealth
draw to themselves the greatest share of the public consideration. As during their whole lives they are engaged in plans and
projects, they have frequently more acuteness of understanding
than the greater part of country gentlemen. As their thoughts,
however, are commonly exercised rather about the interest of
their own particular branch of business, than about that of the
society, their judgement, even when given with the greatest
candour (which it has not been upon every occasion) is much
more to be depended upon with regard to the former of those
two objects than with regard to the latter. Their superiority
over the country gentleman is not so much in their knowledge
of the public interest, as in their having a better knowledge of
their own interest than he has of his. It is by this superior
knowledge of their own interest that they have frequently imposed upon his generosity, and persuaded him to give up both
his own interest and that of the public, from a very simple but
honest conviction that their interest, and not his, was the interest of the public. The interest of the dealers, however, in any
particular branch of trade or manufactures, is always in some
respects different from, and even opposite to, that of the public.
To widen the market and to narrow the competition, is always
the interest of the dealers. To widen the market may frequently
be agreeable enough to the interest of the public; but to narrow
the competition must always be against it, and can serve only
to enable the dealers, by raising their profits above what they
naturally would be, to levy, for their own benefit, an absurd tax
upon the rest of their fellow-citizens. The proposal of any new

law or regulation of commerce which comes from this order ought always to be listened to with great precaution, and ought never to be adopted till after having been long and carefully examined, not only with the most scrupulous, but with the most suspicious attention. It comes from an order of men whose interest is never exactly the same with that of the public, who have generally an interest to deceive and even to oppress the public, and who accordingly have upon many occasions, both deceived and oppressed it.

Years XII	Price of the quarter of wheat each year	Average of the different prices of the same year	The average price of each year in money of the present times
	£ s. d.	£ s. d.	£ s. d.
1202	− 12 −	− − −	1 16 −
1205	⎰ − 12 − ⎱ ⎱ − 13 4 ⎰ ⎰ − 15 − ⎱	− 13 5	2 − 3
1223	− 12 −	− − −	1 16 −
1237	− 3 4	− − −	− 10 −
1243	− 2 −	− − −	− 6 −
1244	− 2 −	− − −	− 6 −
1246	− 16 −	− − −	2 8 −
1247	− 13 4	− − −	2 − −
1257	1 4 −	− − −	3 12 −
1258	⎰ 1 − − ⎱ ⎱ − 15 − ⎰ ⎰ − 16 − ⎱	− 17 −	2 11 −
1270	⎰ 4 16 − ⎱ ⎱ 6 8 − ⎰	5 12 −	16 16 −
1286	⎰ − 2 8 ⎱ ⎱ − 16 − ⎰	− 9 4	1 8 −

Total	£35 9 3
Average Price	£2 19 1¼

Years XII	Price of the quarter of wheat each year			Average of the different prices of the same year			The average price of each year in money of the present times		
	£	s.	d.	£	s.	d.	£	s.	d.
1287	–	3	4	–	–	–	–	10	–
1288	–	–	8	–	3	$\frac{1}{4}$	–	9	$\frac{3}{4}$
	–	1	–						
	–	1	4						
	–	1	6						
	–	1	8						
	–	2	–						
	–	3	4						
	–	9	4						
1289	–	12	–	–	10	$1\frac{3}{4}$	1	10	$4\frac{3}{4}$
	–	6	–						
	–	2	–						
	–	10	8						
	1	–	–						
1290	–	16	–	–	–	–	2	8	–
1294	–	16	–	–	–	–	2	8	–
1302	–	4	–	–	–	–	–	12	–
1309	–	7	2	–	–	–	1	1	6
1315	1	–	–	–	–	–	3	–	–
1316	1	–	–	1	10	6	4	11	6
	1	10	–						
	1	12	–						
	2	–	–						
1317	2	4	–	1	19	6	5	18	6
	–	14	–						
	2	13	–						
	4	–	–						
	–	6	8						
1336	–	2	–	–	–	–	–	6	–
1338	–	3	4	–	–	–	–	10	–

Total   £23 4 $11\frac{1}{4}$

Average Price   £1 18 8

Years XII	Price of the quarter of wheat each year			Average of the different prices of the same year			The average price of each year in money of the present times		
	£	s.	d.	£	s.	d.	£	s.	d.
1339	–	9	–	–	–	–	1	7	–
1349	–	2	–	–	–	–	–	5	2
1359	1	6	8	–	–	–	3	2	2
1361	–	2	–	–	–	–	–	4	8
1363	–	15	–	–	–	–	1	15	–
1369	{1 – – / 1 4 –}			1	2	–	2	9	4
1379	–	4	–	–	–	–	–	9	4
1387	–	2	–	–	–	–	–	4	8
1390	{– 13 4 / – 14 – / – 16 –}			–	14	5	1	13	7
1401	–	16	–	–	–	–	1	17	4
1407	{– 4 4¼ / – 3 4}			–	3	10	–	8	11
1416	–	16	–	–	–	–	1	12	–
			Total				£15	9	4
			Average Price				£1	5	9⅓

	£	s.	d.	£	s.	d.	£	s.	d.
1423	–	8	–	–	–	–	–	16	–
1425	–	4	–	–	–	–	–	8	–
1434	1	6	8	–	–	–	2	13	4
1435	–	5	4	–	–	–	–	10	8
1439	{1 – – / 1 6 8}			1	3	4	2	6	8
1440	1	4	–	–	–	–	2	8	–
1444	{– 4 4 / – 4 –}			–	4	2	–	8	4
1445	–	4	6	–	–	–	–	9	–
1447	–	8	–	–	–	–	–	16	–
1448	–	6	8	–	–	–	–	13	4
1449	–	5	–	–	–	–	–	10	–
1451	–	8	–	–	–	–	–	16	–
			Total				£12	15	4
			Average Price				£1	1	3½

Years XII	Price of the quarter of wheat each year			Average of the different prices of the same year			The average price of each year in money of the present times		
	£	s.	d.	£	s.	d.	£	s.	d.
1453	–	5	4	–	–	–	–	10	8
1455	–	1	2	–	–	–	–	2	4
1457	–	7	8	–	–	–	–	15	4
1459	–	5	–	–	–	–	–	10	–
1460	–	8	–	–	–	–	–	16	–
1463	{ – 2 – / – 1 8 }			–	1	10	–	3	8
1464	–	6	8	–	–	–	–	10	–
1486	1	4	–	–	–	–	1	17	–
1491	–	14	8	–	–	–	1	2	–
1494	–	4	–	–	–	–	–	6	–
1495	–	3	4	–	–	–	–	5	–
1497	1	–	–	–	–	–	1	11	–
					Total		£8	9	–
					Average Price		–	14	1

	£	s.	d.	£	s.	d.	£	s.	d.
1499	–	4	–	–	–	–	–	6	–
1504	–	5	8	–	–	–	–	8	6
1521	1	–	–	–	–	–	1	10	–
1551	–	8	–	–	–	–	–	2	–
1553	–	8	–	–	–	–	–	8	–
1554	–	8	–	–	–	–	–	8	–
1555	–	8	–	–	–	–	–	8	–
1556	–	8	–	–	–	–	–	8	–
1557	{ – 4 – / – 5 – / – 8 – / 2 13 4 }			–	17	8½	–	17	8½
1558	–	8	–	–	–	–	–	8	–
1559	–	8	–	–	–	–	–	8	–
1560	–	8	–	–	–	–	–	8	–
					Total		£6	0	2½
					Average Price		–	10	−5/12

Years XII	Price of the quarter of wheat each year			Average of the different prices of the same year			The average price of each year in money of the present times		
	£	s.	d.	£	s.	d.	£	s.	d.
1561	–	8	–	–	–	–	–	8	–
1562	–	8	–	–	–	–	–	8	–
1574	{ 2	16	–	2	–	–	2	–	–
	1	4	– }						
1587	3	4	–	–	–	–	3	4	–
1594	2	16	–	–	–	–	2	16	–
1595	2	13	–	–	–	–	2	13	–
1596	4	–	–	–	–	–	4	–	–
1597	{ 5	4	–	4	12	–	4	12	–
	4	–	– }						
1598	2	16	8	–	–	–	2	16	8
1599	1	19	2	–	–	–	1	19	2
1600	1	17	8	–	–	–	1	17	8
1601	1	14	10	–	–	–	1	14	10

Total   £28   9   4

Average Price   £2   7   5⅓

Prices of the quarter of nine bushels of the best or highest priced wheat at Windsor Market, on Lady-day and Michaelmas, from 1595 to 1764, both inclusive; the price of each year being the medium between the highest prices of those two market days

Years	£	s.	d.	Years	£	s.	d.
1595	2	0	0	1621	1	10	4
1596	2	8	0	1622	2	18	8
1597	3	9	6	1623	2	12	0
1598	2	16	8	1624	2	8	0
1599	1	19	2	1625	2	12	0
1600	1	17	8	1626	2	9	4
1601	1	14	10	1627	1	16	0
1602	1	9	4	1628	1	8	0
1603	1	15	4	1629	2	2	0
1604	1	10	8	1630	2	15	8
1605	1	15	10	1631	3	8	0
1606	1	13	0	1632	2	13	4
1607	1	16	8	1633	2	18	0
1608	2	16	8	1634	2	16	0
1609	2	10	0	1635	2	16	0
1610	1	15	10	1636	2	16	8
1611	1	18	8				
1612	2	2	4	16)40	0	0	
1613	2	8	8				
1614	2	1	8½	£2	10	0	
1615	1	18	8				
1616	2	0	4				
1617	2	8	8				
1618	2	6	8				
1619	1	15	4				
1620	1	10	4				

26)54 0 6½

£2 1 6 9/13

	Wheat per quarter				Wheat per quarter		
Years	£	s.	d.	Years	£	s.	d.
1637	2	13	0	Brought over	79	14	10
1638	2	17	4	1671	2	2	0
1639	2	4	10	1672	2	1	0
1640	2	4	8	1673	2	6	8
1641	2	8	0	1674	3	8	8
1642[1]	0	0	0	1675	3	4	8
1643	0	0	0	1676	1	18	0
1644	0	0	0	1677	2	2	0
1645	0	0	0	1678	2	19	0
1646	2	8	0	1679	3	0	0
1647	3	13	8	1680	2	5	0
1648	4	5	0	1681	2	6	8
1649	4	0	0	1682	2	4	0
1650	3	16	8	1683	2	0	0
1651	3	13	4	1684	2	4	0
1652	2	9	6	1685	2	6	8
1653	1	15	6	1686	1	14	0
1654	1	6	0	1687	1	5	2
1655	1	13	4	1688	2	6	0
1656	2	3	0	1689	1	10	0
1657	2	6	8	1690	1	14	8
1658	3	5	0	1691	1	14	0
1659	3	6	0	1692	2	6	8
1660	2	16	6	1693	3	7	8
1661	3	10	0	1694	3	4	0
1662	3	14	0	1695	2	13	0
1663	2	17	0	1696	3	11	0
1664	2	0	6	1697	3	0	0
1665	2	9	4	1698	3	8	4
1666	1	16	0	1699	3	4	0
1667	1	16	0	1700	2	0	0
1668	2	0	0				
1669	2	4	4	60)153	1	8	
1670	2	1	8	£2	11	0⅓	

Carry over £79 14 10

1. Wanting in the account. The year 1646 supplied by Bishop Fleetwood.

	Wheat per quarter				Wheat per quarter		
Years	£	s.	d.	Years	£	s.	d.
1701	1	17	8	Brought over	69	8	8
1702	1	9	6	1734	1	18	10
1703	1	16	0	1735	2	3	0
1704	2	6	6	1736	2	0	4
1705	1	10	0	1737	1	18	0
1706	1	6	0	1738	1	15	6
1707	1	8	6	1739	1	18	6
1708	2	1	6	1740	2	10	8
1709	3	18	6	1741	2	6	8
1710	3	18	0	1742	1	14	0
1711	2	14	0	1743	1	4	10
1712	2	6	4	1744	1	4	10
1713	2	11	0	1745	1	7	6
1714	2	10	4	1746	1	19	0
1715	2	3	0	1747	1	14	10
1716	2	8	0	1748	1	17	0
1717	2	5	8	1749	1	17	0
1718	1	18	10	1750	1	12	6
1719	1	15	0	1751	1	18	6
1720	1	17	0	1752	2	1	10
1721	1	17	6	1753	2	4	8
1722	1	16	0	1754	1	14	8
1723	1	14	8	1755	1	13	10
1724	1	17	0	1756	2	5	3
1725	2	8	6	1757	3	0	0
1726	2	6	0	1758	2	10	0
1727	2	2	0	1759	1	19	10
1728	2	14	6	1760	1	16	6
1729	2	6	10	1761	1	10	3
1730	1	16	6	1762	1	19	0
1731	1	12	10	1763	2	0	9
1732	1	6	8	1764	2	6	9
1733	1	8	4				
					64)129	13	6
Carry over	£69	8	8				

$$£2 \quad 0 \quad 6\tfrac{19}{32}$$

	Wheat per quarter				Wheat per quarter		
Years	£	s.	d.	Years	£	s.	d.
1731	1	12	10	1741	2	6	8
1732	1	6	8	1742	1	14	0
1733	1	8	4	1743	1	4	10
1734	1	18	10	1744	1	4	10
1735	2	3	0	1745	1	7	6
1736	2	0	4	1746	1	19	0
1737	1	18	0	1747	1	14	10
1738	1	15	6	1748	1	17	0
1739	1	18	6	1749	1	17	0
1740	2	10	8	1750	1	12	6
	10)18	12	8		10)16	18	2
	£1	17	3$\frac{1}{3}$		£1	13	9$\frac{4}{5}$

BOOK TWO

*Of the Nature, Accumulation, and
Employment of Stock*

INTRODUCTION

IN that rude state of society in which there is no division of labour, in which exchanges are seldom made, and in which every man provides everything for himself, it is not necessary that any stock should be accumulated or stored up beforehand in order to carry on the business of the society. Every man endeavours to supply by his own industry his own occasional wants as they occur. When he is hungry, he goes to the forest to hunt; when his coat is worn out, he clothes himself with the skin of the first large animal he kills: and when his hut begins to go to ruin, he repairs it, as well as he can, with the trees and the turf that are nearest it.

But when the division of labour has once been thoroughly introduced, the produce of a man's own labour can supply but a very small part of his occasional wants. The far greater part of them are supplied by the produce of other men's labour, which he purchases with the produce, or, what is the same thing, with the price of the produce of his own. But this purchase cannot be made till such time as the produce of his own labour has not only been completed, but sold. A stock of goods of different kinds, therefore, must be stored up somewhere sufficient to maintain him, and to supply him with the materials and tools of his work till such time, at least, as both these events can be brought about. A weaver cannot apply himself entirely to his peculiar business, unless there is beforehand stored up somewhere, either in his own possession or in that of some other person, a stock sufficient to maintain him, and to supply him with the materials and tools of his work, till he has not only completed, but sold his web. This accumulation must, evidently, be previous to his applying his industry for so long a time to such a peculiar business.

As the accumulation of stock must, in the nature of things, be previous to the division of labour, so labour can be more and more subdivided in proportion only as stock is previously more and more accumulated. The quantity of materials which the same number of people can work up, increases in a great proportion as labour comes to be more and more subdivided; and as the operations of each workman are gradually reduced to a greater degree of simplicity, a variety of new machines come to be invented for facilitating and abridging those operations. As the division of labour advances, therefore, in order to give constant employment to an equal number of workmen, an equal stock of provisions, and a greater stock of materials and tools than what would have been necessary in a ruder state of things, must be accumulated beforehand. But the number of workmen in every branch of business generally increases with the division of labour in that branch, or rather it is the increase of their number which enables them to class and subdivide themselves in this manner.

As the accumulation of stock is previously necessary for carrying on this great improvement in the productive powers of labour, so that accumulation naturally leads to this improvement. The person who employs his stock in maintaining labour, necessarily wishes to employ it in such a manner as to produce as great a quantity of work as possible. He endeavours, therefore, both to make among his workmen the most proper distribution of employment, and to furnish them with the best machines which he can either invent or afford to purchase. His abilities in both these respects are generally in proportion to the extent of his stock, or to the number of people whom it can employ. The quantity of industry, therefore, not only increases in every country with the increase of the stock which employs it, but, in consequence of that increase, the same quantity of industry produces a much greater quantity of work.

Such are in general the effects of the increase of stock upon industry and its productive powers.

In the following book I have endeavoured to explain the nature of stock, the effects of its accumulation into capitals of different kinds, and the effects of the different employments of those capitals. This book is divided into five chapters. In the first chapter, I have endeavoured to show what are the different parts or branches into which the stock, either of an individual, or of a great society, naturally divides itself. In the second, I have endeavoured to explain the nature and operation of money considered as a particular branch of the general stock of the society. The stock which is accumulated into a capital, may either be employed by the person to whom it belongs, or it may be lent to some other person. In the third and fourth chapters, I have endeavoured to examine the manner in which it operates in both these situations. The fifth and last chapter treats of the different effects which the different employments of capital immediately produce upon the quantity both of national industry, and of the annual produce of land and labour.

CHAPTER I

OF THE DIVISION OF STOCK

WHEN the stock which a man possesses is no more than sufficient to maintain him for a few days or a few weeks, he seldom thinks of deriving any revenue from it. He consumes it as sparingly as he can, and endeavours by his labour to acquire something which may supply its place before it be consumed altogether. His revenue is, in this case, derived from his labour only. This is the state of the greater part of the labouring poor in all countries.

But when he possesses stock sufficient to maintain him for months or years, he naturally endeavours to derive a revenue from the greater part of it; reserving only so much for his immediate consumption as may maintain him till this revenue begins to come in. His whole stock, therefore, is distinguished into two parts. That part which, he expects, is to afford him this revenue, is called his capital. The other is that which supplies his immediate consumption; and which consists either, first, in that portion of his whole stock which was originally reserved for this purpose; or secondly, in his revenue, from whatever source derived, as it gradually comes in; or, thirdly, in such things as had been purchased by either of these in former years, and which are not yet entirely consumed; such as a stock of clothes, household furniture, and the like. In one, or other, or all these three articles, consists the stock which men commonly reserve for their own immediate consumption.

There are two different ways in which a capital may be employed so as to yield a revenue or profit to its employer.

First, it may be employed in raising, manufacturing, or purchasing goods, and selling them again with a profit. The capital employed in this manner yields no revenue or profit to its employer, while it either remains in his possession, or continues in the same shape. The goods of the merchant yield him no revenue or profit till he sells them for money, and the money yields him as little till it is again exchanged for goods. His capital is continually going from him in one shape, and returning to him in another, and it is only by means of such circulation, or successive exchanges, that it can yield him any profit. Such capitals, therefore, may very properly be called circulating capitals.

Secondly, it may be employed in the improvement of land, in the purchase of useful machines and instruments of trade, or in such-like things as yield a revenue or profit without changing masters, or circulating any further. Such capitals, therefore, may very properly be called fixed capitals.

Different occupations require very different proportions between the fixed and circulating capitals employed in them.

The capital of a merchant, for example, is altogether a circulating capital. He has occasion for no machines or instruments of trade, unless his shop, or warehouse, be considered as such.

Some part of the capital of every master artificer or manufacturer must be fixed in the instruments of his trade. This part, however, is very small in some, and very great in others. A master tailor requires no other instruments of trade but a parcel of needles. Those of the master shoemaker are a little, though but a very little, more expensive. Those of the weaver rise a good deal above those of the shoemaker. The far greater part of the capital of all such master artificers, however, is circulated, either in the wages of their workmen, or in the price of their materials, and repaid with a profit by the price of the work.

In other works a much greater fixed capital is required. In a great iron-work, for example, the furnace for melting the ore, the forge, the slitt-mill, are instruments of trade which cannot be erected without a very great expense. In coal-works and mines of every kind, the machinery necessary both for drawing out the water and for other purposes is frequently still more expensive.

That part of the capital of the farmer which is employed in the instruments of agriculture is a fixed, that which is employed in the wages and maintenance of his labouring servants, is a circulating capital. He makes a profit of the one by keeping it in his own possession, and of the other by parting with it. The price or value of his labouring cattle is a fixed capital in the same manner as that of the instruments of husbandry. Their maintenance is a circulating capital in the same manner as that of the labouring servants. The farmer makes his profit by keeping the labouring cattle, and by parting with their maintenance. Both the price and the maintenance of the cattle which are brought in and fattened, not for labour, but for sale, are a circulating capital. The farmer makes his profit by parting with them. A flock of sheep or a herd of cattle that, in a breeding country, is bought in, neither for labour, nor for sale, but in order to make a profit by their wool, by their milk, and by their increase, is a fixed capital. The profit is made by keeping them. Their maintenance is a circulating capital. The profit is made by parting with it; and it comes back with both its own profit and the profit upon the whole price of the cattle, in the price of the wool, the milk, and the increase. The whole value of the seed, too, is properly a fixed capital. Though it goes backwards and forwards between the ground and the granary, it never changes masters, and therefore does not properly circulate. The farmer makes his profit, not by its sale, but by its increase.

The general stock of any country or society is the same with that of all its inhabitants or members, and therefore naturally divides itself into the same three portions, each of which has a distinct function or office.

The first is that portion which is reserved for immediate consumption, and of which the characteristic is, that it affords no revenue or profit. It consists in the stock of food, clothes, household furniture, etc., which have been purchased by their proper consumers, but which are not yet entirely consumed. The whole stock of mere dwelling-houses too, subsisting at any one time in the country, make a part of this first portion. The stock that is laid out in a house, if it is to be the dwelling-house of the proprietor, ceases from that moment to serve in the function of a capital, or to afford any revenue to its owner. A dwelling-house, as such, contributes nothing to the revenue of its inhabitant; and though it is, no doubt, extremely useful to him, it is as his clothes and household furniture are useful to him, which, however, make a part of his expense, and not of his revenue. If is to be let to a tenant for rent, as the house itself can produce nothing, the tenant must always pay the rent out of some other revenue which he derives either from labour, or stock, or land. Though a house, therefore, may yield a revenue to its proprietor, and thereby serve in the function of a capital to him, it cannot yield any to the public, nor serve in the function of a capital to it, and the revenue of the whole body of the people can never be in the smallest degree increased by it. Clothes, and household furniture, in the same manner, sometimes yield a revenue, and thereby serve in the function of a capital to particular persons. In countries where masquerades are common, it is a trade to let out masquerade dresses for a night. Upholsterers frequently let furniture by the month or by the year. Undertakers let the furniture of funerals by the day and by the week. Many people let furnished houses, and get a rent, not only for the use of the house, but for that of the furniture. The revenue, however, which is derived from such things must always be ultimately drawn from some other source of revenue. Of all parts of the stock, either of an individual, or of a society, reserved for immediate consumption, what is laid out in houses is most slowly consumed. A stock of clothes may last several years: a stock of furniture half a century or a century: but a stock of houses, well built and properly taken care of, may last many centuries. Though the period of their total consumption, however, is more distant, they are still as really a stock reserved for immediate consumption as either clothes or household furniture.

The second of the three portions into which the general stock of the society divides itself, is the fixed capital, of which the characteristic is, that it affords a revenue or profit without circulating or changing masters. It consists chiefly of the four following articles:

First, of all useful machines and instruments of trade which facilitate and abridge labour:

Secondly, of all those profitable buildings which are the means of procuring a revenue, not only to their proprietor who lets them for a rent, but to the person who possesses them and pays that rent for them; such as shops, warehouses, workhouses, farmhouses, with all their necessary buildings; stables, granaries, etc. These are very different from mere dwelling houses. They are a sort of instruments of trade, and may be considered in the same light:

Thirdly, of the improvements of land, of what has been profitably laid out in clearing, draining, enclosing, manuring, and reducing it into the condition most proper for tillage and culture. An improved farm may very justly be regarded in the same light as those useful machines which facilitate and abridge labour, and by means of which an equal circulating capital can afford a much greater revenue to its employer. An improved farm is equally advantageous and more durable than any of those machines, frequently requiring no other repairs than the most profitable application of the farmer's capital employed in cultivating it:

Fourthly, of the acquired and useful abilities of all the inhabitants or members of the society. The acquisition of such talents, by the maintenance of the acquirer during his education, study, or apprenticeship, always costs a real expense, which is a capital fixed and realized, as it were, in his person. Those talents, as they make a part of his fortune, so do they likewise of that of the society to which he belongs. The improved dexterity of a workman may be considered in the same light as a machine or instrument of trade which facilitates and abridges labour, and which, though it costs a certain expense, repays that expense with a profit.

The third and last of the three portions into which the general stock of the society naturally divides itself, is the circulating capital; of which the characteristic is, that it affords a revenue only by circulating or changing masters. It is composed likewise of four parts:

First, of the money by means of which all the other three are circulated and distributed to their proper consumers:

Secondly, of the stock and provisions which are in the possession of the butcher, the grazier, the farmer, the corn-merchant, the brewer, etc., and from the sale of which they expect to derive a profit:

Thirdly, of the materials, whether altogether rude, or more or less manufactured, of clothes, furniture, and building, which are not yet made up into any of those three shapes, but which remain in the hands of the growers, the manufacturers, the mercers and drapers, the timber merchants, the carpenters and joiners, the brickmakers, etc.:

Fourthly, and lastly, of the work which is made up and completed, but which is still in the hands of the merchant or manufacturer, and not yet disposed of or distributed to the proper consumers; such as the finished work which we frequently find ready-made in the shops of the smith, the cabinet-maker, the goldsmith, the jeweller, the china-merchant, etc. The circulating capital consists in this manner, of the provisions, materials, and finished work of all kinds that are in the hands of their respective dealers, and of the money that is necessary for circulating and distributing them to those who are finally to use or to consume them.

Of these four parts, three – provisions, materials, and finished work – are, either annually, or in a longer or shorter period, regularly withdrawn from it, and placed either in the fixed capital or in the stock reserved for immediate consumption.

Every fixed capital is both originally derived from, and requires to be continually supported by a circulating capital. All useful machines and instruments of trade are originally derived from a circulating capital, which furnishes the materials of which they are made, and the maintenance of the workmen who make them. They require, too, a capital of the same kind to keep them in constant repair.

No fixed capital can yield any revenue but by means of a circulating capital. The most useful machines and instruments of trade will produce nothing without the circulating capital which affords the materials they are employed upon, and the maintenance of the workmen who employ them. Land, however improved, will yield no revenue without a circulating capital, which maintains the labourers who cultivate and collect its produce.

To maintain and augment the stock which may be reserved for immediate consumption is the sole end and purpose both of the fixed and circulating capitals. It is this stock which feeds, clothes, and lodges the people. Their riches or poverty depend upon the abundant or sparing supplies which those two capitals can afford to the stock reserved for immediate consumption.

So great a part of the circulating capital being continually withdrawn from it, in order to be placed in the other two branches of the general stock of the society; it must in its turn require continual supplies, without which it would soon cease to exist. These supplies are principally drawn from three sources, the produce of land, of mines, and of fisheries. These afford continual supplies of provisions and materials, of which part is afterwards wrought up into finished work, and by which are replaced the provisions, materials, and finished work continually withdrawn from the circulating capital. From mines, too, is drawn what is necessary for maintaining and augmenting that part of it which consists in money. For though, in the ordinary course of business, this part is not, like the other three, necessarily withdrawn from it, in order to be placed in the other two branches of the general stock of the society, it must, however, like all other things, be wasted and worn out at last, and sometimes, too, be either lost or sent abroad, and must, therefore, require continual, though, no doubt, much smaller supplies.

Land, mines, and fisheries, require all both a fixed and a circulating capital to cultivate them; and their produce replaces with a profit, not only those capitals, but all the others in the society. Thus the farmer annually replaces to the manufacturer the provisions which he had consumed and the materials which he had wrought up the year before; and the manufacturer replaces to the farmer the finished work which he had wasted and worn out in the same time. This is the real exchange that is annually made between those two orders of people, though it

seldom happens that the rude produce of the one and the manufactured produce of the other, are directly bartered for one another; because it seldom happens that the farmer sells his corn
and his cattle, his flax and his wool, to the very same person of
whom he chooses to purchase the clothes, furniture, and instruments of trade which he wants. He sells, therefore, his rude
produce for money, with which he can purchase, wherever it is
to be had, the manufactured produce he has occasion for. Land
even replaces, in part at least, the capitals with which fisheries
and mines are cultivated. It is the produce of land which draws
the fish from the waters; and it is the produce of the surface of
the earth which extracts the minerals from its bowels.

The produce of land, mines, and fisheries, when their natural
fertility is equal, is in proportion to the extent and proper
application of the capitals employed about them. When the
capitals are equal and equally well applied, it is in proportion to
their natural fertility.

In all countries where there is tolerable security, every man of
common understanding will endeavour to employ whatever
stock he can command in procuring either present enjoyment or
future profit. If it is employed in procuring present enjoyment,
it is a stock reserved for immediate consumption. If it is employed in procuring future profit, it must procure this profit
either by staying with him, or by going from him. In the one
case it is a fixed, in the other it is a circulating capital. A man
must be perfectly crazy who, where there is tolerable security,
does not employ all the stock which he commands, whether it
be his own or borrowed of other people, in some one or other of
those three ways.

In those unfortunate countries, indeed, where men are continually afraid of the violence of their superiors, they frequently
bury and conceal a great part of their stock, in order to have it
always at hand to carry with them to some place of safety, in
case of their being threatened with any of those disasters to
which they consider themselves as at all times exposed. This is
said to be a common practice in Turkey, in Indostan, and, I
believe, in most other governments of Asia. It seems to have
been a common practice among our ancestors during the violence of the feudal government. Treasure-trove was in those

times considered as no contemptible part of the revenue of the
greatest sovereigns in Europe. It consisted in such treasure as
was found concealed in the earth, and to which no particular
person could prove any right. This was regarded in those times
as so important an object, that it was always considered as belonging to the sovereign, and neither to the finder nor to the
proprietor of the land, unless the right to it had been conveyed
to the latter by an express clause in his charter. It was put upon
the same footing with gold and silver mines, which, without a
special clause in the charter, were never supposed to be com-
prehended in the general grant of the lands, though mines of
lead, copper, tin, and coal were, as things of small consequence.

CHAPTER II

OF MONEY CONSIDERED AS A PARTICULAR
BRANCH OF THE GENERAL STOCK OF THE SOCIETY,
OR OF THE EXPENSE OF MAINTAINING THE
NATIONAL CAPITAL

IT has been shown in the first Book, that the price of the greater
part of commodities resolves itself into three parts, of which one
pays the wages of the labour, another the profits of the stock,
and a third the rent of the land which had been employed in
producing and bringing them to market : that there are, indeed,
some commodities of which the price is made up of two of those
parts only, the wages of labour, and the profits of stock : and a
very few in which it consists altogether in one, the wages of
labour : but that the price of every commodity necessarily resolves itself into some one, or other, or all of these three parts;
every part of it which goes neither to rent nor to wages, being
necessarily profit to somebody.

Since this is the case, it has been observed, with regard to
every particular commodity, taken separately, it must be so with
regard to all the commodities which compose the whole annual
produce of the land and labour of every country, taken complexly. The whole price or exchangeable value of that annual

produce must resolve itself into the same three parts, and be parcelled out among the different inhabitants of the country, either as the wages of their labour, the profits of their stock, or the rent of their land.

But though the whole value of the annual produce of the land and labour of every country is thus divided among and constitutes a revenue to its different inhabitants, yet as in the rent of a private estate we distinguish between the gross rent and the net rent, so may we likewise in the revenue of all the inhabitants of a great country.

The gross rent of a private estate comprehends whatever is paid by the farmer; the net rent, what remains free to the landlord, after deducting the expense of management, of repairs, and all other necessary charges; or what, without hurting his estate, he can afford to place his stock reserved for immediate consumption, or to spend upon his table, equipage, the ornaments of his house and furniture, his private enjoyments and amusements. His real wealth is in proportion, not to his gross, but to his net rent.

The gross revenue of all the inhabitants of a great country comprehends the whole annual produce of their land and labour; the net revenue, what remains free to them after deducting the expense of maintaining – first, their fixed, and, secondly, their circulating capital; or what, without encroaching upon their capital, they can place in their stock reserved for immediate consumption, or spend upon their subsistence, conveniencies, and amusements. Their real wealth, too, is in proportion, not to their gross, but to their net revenue.

The whole expense of maintaining the fixed capital must evidently be excluded from the net revenue of the society. Neither the materials necessary for supporting their useful machines and instruments of trade, their profitable buildings, etc., nor the produce of the labour necessary for fashioning those materials into the proper form, can ever make any part of it. The price of that labour may indeed make a part of it; as the workmen so employed may place the whole value of their wages in their stock reserved for immediate consumption. But in other sorts of labour, both the price and the produce go to this stock, the price to that of the workmen, the produce to that of other

MONEY A BRANCH OF THE GENERAL STOCK

people, whose subsistence, conveniences, and amusements, are augmented by the labour of those workmen.

The intention of the fixed capital is to increase the productive powers of labour, or to enable the same number of labourers to perform a much greater quantity of work. In a farm where all the necessary buildings, fences, drains, communications, etc., are in the most perfect good order, the same number of labourers and labouring cattle will raise a much greater produce than in one of equal extent and equally good ground, but not furnished with equal conveniences. In manufactures the same number of hands, assisted with the best machinery, will work up a much greater quantity of goods than with more imperfect instruments of trade. The expense which is properly laid out upon a fixed capital of any kind, is always repaid with great profit, and increases the annual produce by a much greater value than that of the support which such improvements require. This support, however, still requires a certain portion of that produce. A certain quantity of materials, and the labour of a certain number of workmen, both of which might have been immediately employed to augment the food, clothing and lodging, the subsistence and conveniences of the society, are thus diverted to another employment, highly advantageous indeed, but still different from this one. It is upon this account that all such improvements in mechanics, as enable the same number of workmen to perform an equal quantity of work, with cheaper and simpler machinery than had been usual before, are always regarded as advantageous to every society. A certain quantity of materials, and the labour of a certain number of workmen, which had before been employed in supporting a more complex and expensive machinery, can afterwards be applied to augment the quantity of work which that or any other machinery is useful only for performing. The undertaker of some great manufactory who employed a thousand a-year in the maintenance of his machinery, if he can reduce this expense to five hundred, he will naturally employ the other five hundred in purchasing an additional quantity of materials to be wrought up by an additional number of workmen. The quantity of that work, therefore, which his machinery was useful only for performing, will naturally be augmented, and with it all the advantage and conveniency which the society can derive from that work.

The expense of maintaining the fixed capital in a great country may very properly be compared to that of repairs in a private estate. The expense of repairs may frequently be necessary, for supporting the produce of the estate, and consequently both the gross and the net rent of the landlord. When by a more proper direction, however, it can be diminished without occasioning any diminution of produce, the gross rent remains at least the same as before, and the net rent is necessarily augmented.

But though the whole expense of maintaining the fixed capital is thus necessarily excluded from the net revenue of the society, it is not the same case with that of maintaining the circulating capital. Of the four parts of which this latter capital is composed – money, provisions, materials, and finished work – the three last, it has already been observed, are regularly withdrawn from it, and placed either in the fixed capital of the society, or in their stock reserved for immediate consumption. Whatever portion of those consumable goods is not employed in maintaining the former, goes all to the latter, and makes a part of the net revenue of the society. The maintenance of those three parts of the circulating capital, therefore, withdraws no portion of the annual produce from the net revenue of the society, besides what is necessary for maintaining the fixed capital.

The circulating capital of a society is in this respect different from that of an individual. That of an individual is totally excluded from making any part of his net revenue, which must consist altogether in his profits. But though the circulating capital of every individual makes a part of that of the society to which he belongs, it is not upon that account totally excluded from making a part likewise of their net revenue. Though the whole goods in a merchant's shop must by no means be placed in his own stock reserved for immediate consumption, they may in that of other people, who, from a revenue derived from other funds, may regularly replace their value to him, together with its profits, without occasioning any diminution either of his capital or of theirs.

Money, therefore, is the only part of the circulating capital of a society, of which the maintenance can occasion any diminution in their net revenue.

The fixed capital, and that part of the circulating capital which consists in money, so far as they affect the revenue of the society, bear a very great resemblance to one another.

First, as those machines and instruments of trade, etc., require a certain expense, first to erect them, and afterwards to support them, both which expenses, though they make a part of the gross, are deductions from the net revenue of the society; so the stock of money which circulates in any country must require a certain expense, first to collect it, and afterwards to support it, both which expenses, though they make a part of the gross, are, in the same manner, deductions from the net revenue of the society. A certain quantity of very valuable materials, gold and silver, and of very curious labour, instead of augmenting the stock reserved for immediate consumption, the subsistence, conveniences, and amusements of individuals, is employed in supporting that great but expensive instrument of commerce, by means of which every individual in the society has his subsistence, conveniences, and amusements regularly distributed to him in their proper proportion.

Secondly, as the machines and instruments of trade, etc., which compose the fixed capital either of an individual or of a society, make no part either of the gross or of the net revenue of either; so money, by means of which the whole revenue of the society is regularly distributed among all its different members, makes itself no part of that revenue. The great wheel of circulation is altogether different from the goods which are circulated by means of it. The revenue of the society consists altogether in those goods, and not in the wheel which circulates them. In computing either the gross or the net revenue of any society, we must always, from their whole annual circulation of money and goods, deduct the whole value of the money, of which not a single farthing can ever make any part of either.

It is the ambiguity of language only which can make this proposition appear either doubtful or paradoxical. When properly explained and understood, it is almost self-evident.

When we talk of any particular sum of money, we sometimes

mean nothing but the metal pieces of which it is composed; and sometimes we include in our meaning some obscure reference to the goods which can be had in exchange for it, or to the power of purchasing which the possession of it conveys. Thus when we say that the circulating money of England has been computed at eighteen millions, we mean only to express the amount of the metal pieces, which some writers have computed, or rather have supposed to circulate in that country. But when we say that a man is worth fifty or a hundred pounds a-year, we mean commonly to express not only the amount of the metal pieces which are annually paid to him, but the value of the goods which we can annually purchase or consume. We mean commonly to ascertain what is or ought to be this way of living, or the quantity and quality of the necessaries and conveniencies of life in which he can with propriety indulge himself.

When, by any particular sum of money, we mean not only to express the amount of the metal pieces of which it is composed, but to include in its signification some obscure reference to the goods which can be had in exchange for them, the wealth or revenue which it in this case denotes, is equal only to one of the two values which are thus intimated somewhat ambiguously by the same word, and to the latter more properly than to the former, to the money's worth more properly than to the money.

Thus if a guinea be the weekly pension of a particular person, he can in the course of the week purchase with it a certain quantity of subsistence, conveniencies, and amusements. In proportion as this quantity is great or small, so are his real riches, his real weekly revenue. His weekly revenue is certainly not equal both to the guinea, and to what can be purchased with it, but only to one or other of those two equal values; and to the latter more properly than to the former, to the guinea's worth rather than to the guinea.

If the pension of such a person was paid to him, not in gold, but in a weekly bill for a guinea, his revenue surely would not so properly consist in the piece of paper, as in what he could get for it. A guinea may be considered as a bill for a certain quantity of necessaries and conveniencies upon all the tradesmen in the neighbourhood. The revenue of the person to whom it is paid, does not so properly consist in the piece of gold, as in what he can get for it, or in what he can exchange it for. If it could be exchanged for nothing, it would, like a bill upon a bankrupt, be of no more value than the most useless piece of paper.

Though the weekly or yearly revenue of all the different inhabitants of any country, in the same manner, may be, and in reality frequently is paid to them in money, their real riches, however, the real weekly or yearly revenue of all of them taken together, must always be great or small in proportion to the quantity of consumable goods which they can all of them purchase with this money. The whole revenue of all of them taken together is evidently not equal to both the money and the consumable goods; but only to one or other of those two values, and to the latter more properly than to the former.

Though we frequently, therefore, express a person's revenue by the metal pieces which are annually paid to him, it is because the amount of those pieces regulates the extent of his power of purchasing, or the value of the goods which he can annually afford to consume. We still consider his revenue as consisting in this power of purchasing or consuming, and not in the pieces which convey it.

But if this is sufficiently evident even with regard to an individual, it is still more so with regard to a society. The amount of the metal pieces which are annually paid to an individual, is often precisely equal to his revenue, and is upon that account the shortest and best expression of its value. But the amount of the metal pieces which circulate in a society can never be equal to the revenue of all its members. As the same guinea which pays the weekly pension of one man today, may pay that of another tomorrow, and that of a third the day thereafter, the amount of the metal pieces which annually circulate in any country must always be of much less value than the whole money pensions annually paid with them. But the power of purchasing, or the goods which can successively be bought with the whole of those money pensions as they are successively paid, must always be precisely of the same value with those pensions; as must likewise be the revenue of the different persons to whom they are paid. That revenue, therefore, cannot consist in those metal pieces, of which the amount is so much inferior to its value, but in the power of purchasing, in the goods which can successively be bought with them as they circulate from hand to hand.

Money, therefore, the great wheel of circulation, the great instrument of commerce, like all other instruments of trade, though it makes a part and a very valuable part of the capital, makes no part of the revenue of the society to which it belongs; and though the metal pieces of which it is composed, in the course of their annual circulation, distribute to every man the revenue which properly belongs to him, they make themselves no part of that revenue.

Thirdly, and lastly, the machines and instruments of trade, etc., which compose the fixed capital, bear this further resemblance to that part of the circulating capital which consists in money; that as every saving in the expense of erecting and supporting those machines, which does not diminish the productive powers of labour, is an improvement of the net revenue of the society, so every saving in the expense of collecting and supporting that part of the circulating capital which consists in money, is an improvement of exactly the same kind.

It is sufficiently obvious, and it has partly, too, been explained already, in what manner every saving in the expense of supporting the fixed capital is an improvement of the net revenue of the society. The whole capital of the undertaker of every work is necessarily divided between his fixed and his circulating capital. While his whole capital remains the same, the smaller the one part, the greater must necessarily be the other. It is the circulating capital which furnishes the materials and wages of labour, and puts industry into motion. Every saving, therefore, in the expense of maintaining the fixed capital, which does not diminish the productive powers of labour, must increase the fund which puts industry into motion, and consequently the annual produce of land and labour, the real revenue of every society.

The substitution of paper in the room of gold and silver money, replaces a very expensive instrument of commerce with one much less costly, and sometimes equally convenient. Circulation comes to be carried on by a new wheel, which it costs less both to erect and to maintain than the old one. But in what manner this operation is performed, and in what manner it tends to increase either the gross or the net revenue of the society, is not altogether so obvious, and may therefore require some further explication.

There are several different sorts of paper money; but the circulating notes of banks and bankers are the species which is best known, and which seems best adapted for this purpose.

When the people of any particular country have such confidence in the fortune, probity, and prudence of a particular banker, as to believe that he is always ready to pay upon demand such of his promissory notes as are likely to be at any time presented to him; those notes come to have the same currency as gold and silver money, from the confidence that such money can at any time be had for them.

A particular banker lends among his customers his own promissory notes, to the extent, we shall suppose, of a hundred thousand pounds. As those notes serve all the purposes of money, his debtors pay him the same interest as if he had lent them so much money. This interest is the source of his gain. Though some of those notes are continually coming back upon him for payment, part of them continue to circulate for months and years together. Though he has generally in circulation, therefore, notes to the extent of a hundred thousand pounds, twenty thousand pounds in gold and silver may, frequently, be a sufficient provision for answering occasional demands. By this operation, therefore, twenty thousand pounds in gold and silver perform all the functions which a hundred thousand could otherwise have performed. The same exchanges may be made, the same quantity of consumable goods may be circulated and distributed to their proper consumers, by means of his promissory notes, to the value of a hundred thousand pounds, as by an equal value of gold and silver money. Eighty thousand pounds of gold and silver, therefore, can, in this manner, be spared from the circulation of the country; and if different operations of the same kind should, at the same time, be carried on by many different banks and bankers, the whole circulation may thus be conducted with a fifth part only of the gold and silver which would otherwise have been requisite.

Let us suppose, for example, that the whole circulating money of some particular country amounted, at a particular time, to one million sterling, that sum being then sufficient for circulating the whole annual produce of their land and labour. Let us suppose, too, that some time thereafter, different banks and bankers issued promissory notes, payable to the bearer, to the extent of one million, reserving in their different coffers two hundred thousand pounds for answering occasional demands. There would remain, therefore, in circulation, eight hundred thousand pounds in gold and silver, and a million of bank notes, or eighteen hundred thousand pounds of paper and money together. But the annual produce of the land and labour of the country had before required only one million to circulate and distribute it to its proper consumers, and that annual produce cannot be immediately augmented by those operations of banking. One million, therefore, will be sufficient to circulate it after them. The goods to be bought and sold being precisely the same as before, the same quantity of money will be sufficient for buying and selling them. The channel of circulation, if I may be allowed such an expression, will remain precisely the same as before. One million we have supposed sufficient to fill that channel. Whatever, therefore, is poured into it beyond this sum cannot run in it, but must overflow. One million eight hundred thousand pounds are poured into it. Eight hundred thousand pounds, therefore, must overflow, that sum being over and above what can be employed in the circulation of the country. But though this sum cannot be employed at home, it is too valuable to be allowed to lie idle. It will, therefore, be sent abroad, in order to seek that profitable employment which it cannot find at home. But the paper cannot go abroad; because at a distance from the banks which issue it, and from the country in which payment of it can be exacted by law, it will not be received in common payments. Gold and silver, therefore, to the amount of eight hundred thousand pounds will be sent abroad, and the channel of home circulation will remain filled with a million of paper, instead of the million of those metals which filled it before.

But though so great a quantity of gold and silver is thus sent abroad, we must not imagine that it is sent abroad for nothing, or that its proprietors make a present of it to foreign nations. They will exchange it for foreign goods of some kind or

another, in order to supply the consumption either of some
other foreign country or of their own.

If they employ it in purchasing goods in one foreign country
in order to supply the consumption of another, or in what is
called the carrying trade, whatever profit they make will be an
addition to the net revenue of their own country. It is like a new
fund, created for carrying on a new trade; domestic business
being now transacted by paper, and the gold and silver being
converted into a fund for this new trade.

If they employ it in purchasing foreign goods for home consumption, they may either, first, purchase such goods as are
likely to be consumed by idle people who produce nothing, such
as foreign wines, foreign silks, etc; or, secondly, they may purchase an additional stock of materials, tools, and provisions, in
order to maintain and employ an additional number of industrious people, who re-produce, with a profit, the value of their
annual consumption.

So far as it is employed in the first way, it promotes prodigality, increases expense and consumption without increasing
production, or establishing any permanent fund for supporting
that expense, and is in every respect hurtful to the society.

So far as it is employed in the second way, it promotes industry; and though it increases the consumption of the society,
it provides a permanent fund for supporting that consumption,
the people who consume re-producing, with a profit, the whole
value of their annual consumption. The gross revenue of the
society, the annual produce of their land and labour, is increased by the whole value which the labour of those workmen
adds to the materials upon which they are employed; and their
net revenue by what remains of this value, after deducting what
is necessary for supporting the tools and instruments of their
trade.

That the greater part of the gold and silver which, being
forced abroad by those operations of banking, is employed in
purchasing foreign goods for home consumption, is and must
be employed in purchasing those of this second kind, seems not
only probable but almost unavoidable. Though some particular
men may sometimes increase their expense very considerably
though their revenue does not increase at all, we may be assured

that no class or order of men ever does so; because, though the principles of common prudence do not always govern the conduct of every individual, they always influence that of the majority of every class or order. But the revenue of idle people, considered as a class or order, cannot, in the smallest degree, be increased by those operations of banking. Their expense in general, therefore, cannot be much increased by them, though that of a few individuals among them may, and in reality sometimes is. The demand of idle people, therefore, for foreign goods being the same, or very nearly the same, as before, a very small part of the money, which being forced abroad by those operations of banking, is employed in purchasing foreign goods for home consumption, is likely to be employed in purchasing those for their use. The greater part of it will naturally be destined for the employment of industry, and not for the maintenance of idleness.

When we compute the quantity of industry which the circulating capital of any society can employ, we must always have regard to those parts of it only which consist in provisions, materials, and finished work : the other, which consists in money, and which serves only to circulate those three, must always be deducted. In order to put industry into motion, three things are requisite; materials to work upon, tools to work with, and the wages or recompence for the sake of which the work is done. Money is neither a material to work upon, nor a tool to work with; and though the wages of the workman are commonly paid to him in money, his real revenue, like that of all other men, consists, not in the money, but in the money's worth; not in the metal pieces, but in what can be got for them.

The quantity of industry which any capital can employ must, evidently, be equal to the number of workmen whom it can supply with materials, tools, and a maintenance suitable to the nature of the work. Money may be requisite for purchasing the materials and tools of the work, as well as the maintenance of the workmen. But the quantity of industry which the whole capital can employ is certainly not equal both to the money which purchases, and to the materials, tools, and maintenance, which are purchased with it; but only to one or other of those two values, and to the latter more properly than to the former.

When paper is substituted in the room of gold and silver money, the quantity of the materials, tools, and maintenance, which the whole circulating capital can supply, may be increased by the whole value of gold and silver which used to be employed in purchasing them. The whole value of the great wheel of circulation and distribution, is added to the goods which are circulated and distributed by means of it. The operation, in some measure, resembles that of the undertaker of some great work, who, in consequence of some improvement in mechanics, takes down his old machinery, and adds the difference between its price and that of the new to his circulating capital, to the fund from which he furnishes materials and wages to his workmen.

What is the proportion which the circulating money of any country bears to the whole value of the annual produce circulated by means of it, it is, perhaps, impossible to determine. It has been computed by different authors at a fifth, at a tenth, at a twentieth, and at a thirtieth part of that value. But how small soever the proportion which the circulating money may bear to the whole value of the annual produce, as but a part, and frequently but a small part, of that produce, is ever destined for the maintenance of industry, it must always bear a very considerable proportion to that part. When, therefore, by the substitution of paper, the gold and silver necessary for circulation is reduced to, perhaps, a fifth part of the former quantity, if the value of only the greater part of the other four-fifths be added to the funds which are destined for the maintenance of industry, it must make a very considerable addition to the quantity of that industry, and, consequently, to the value of the annual produce of land and labour.

An operation of this kind has, within these five-and-twenty or thirty years, been performed in Scotland, by the erection of new banking companies in almost every considerable town, and even in some country villages. The effects of it have been precisely those above described. The business of the country is almost entirely carried on by means of the paper of those different banking companies, with which purchases and payments of all kinds are commonly made. Silver very seldom appears ex-

cept in the change of a twenty shillings bank note, and gold still
seldomer. But though the conduct of all those different companies has not been unexceptionable, and has accordingly required an act of parliament to regulate it, the country, notwithstanding, has evidently derived great benefit from their trade. I
have heard it asserted, that the trade of the city of Glasgow
doubled in about fifteen years after the first erection of the
banks there; and that the trade of Scotland has more than quadrupled since the first erection of the two public banks at Edinburgh, of which the one, called the Bank of Scotland, was
established by act of parliament in 1695; the other, called the
Royal Bank, by royal charter in 1727. Whether the trade, either
of Scotland in general, or of the city of Glasgow in particular,
has really increased in so great a proportion, during so short a
period, I do not pretend to know. If either of them has increased in this proportion, it seems to be an effect too great to be
accounted for by the sole operation of this cause. That the trade
and industry of Scotland, however, have increased very considerably during this period, and that the banks have contributed a good deal to this increase, cannot be doubted.

The value of the silver money which circulated in Scotland
before the union, in 1707, and which, immediately after it, was
brought into the Bank of Scotland in order to be re-coined,
amounted to £411,117 10s. 9d. sterling. No account has been got
of the gold coin; but it appears from the ancient accounts of the
mint of Scotland, that the value of the gold annually coined
somewhat exceeded that of the silver.[1] There were a good many
people, too, upon this occasion, who, from a diffidence of re-
payment, did not bring their silver into the Bank of Scotland :
and there was, besides, some English coin which was not called
in. The whole value of the gold and silver, therefore, which
circulated in Scotland before the union, cannot be estimated at
less than a million sterling. It seems to have constituted almost
the whole circulation of that country; for though the circulation
of the Bank of Scotland, which had then no rival, was considerable, it seems to have made but a very small part of the whole.
In the present times the whole circulation of Scotland cannot be
estimated at less than two millions, of which that part which

1. See Ruddiman's Preface to Anderson's *Diplomata Scotiae*.

consists in gold and silver most probably does not amount to half a million. But though the circulating gold and silver of Scotland have suffered so great a diminution during this period, its real riches and prosperity do not appear to have suffered any. Its agriculture, manufactures, and trade, on the contrary, the annual produce of its land and labour, have evidently been augmented.

It is chiefly by discounting bills of exchange, that is, by advancing money upon them before they are due, that the greater part of banks and bankers issue their promissory notes. They deduct always, upon whatever sum they advance, the legal interest till the bill shall become due. The payment of the bill, when it becomes due, replaces to the bank the value of what had been advanced, together with a clear profit of the interest. The banker who advances to the merchant whose bill he discounts, not gold and silver, but his own promissory notes, has the advantage of being able to discount to a greater amount, by the whole value of his promissory notes, which he finds by experience are commonly in circulation. He is thereby enabled to make his clear gain of interest on so much a larger sum.

The commerce of Scotland, which at present is not very great, was still more inconsiderable when the two first banking companies were established, and those companies would have had but little trade had they confined their business to the discounting of bills of exchange. They invented, therefore, another method of issuing their promissory notes; by granting what they called cash accounts, that is by giving credit to the extent of a certain sum (two or three thousand pounds, for example) to any individual who could procure two persons of undoubted credit and good landed estate to become surety for him, that whatever money should be advanced to him, within the sum for which the credit had been given, should be repaid upon demand, together with the legal interest. Credits of this kind are, I believe, commonly granted by banks and bankers in all different parts of the world. But the easy terms upon which the Scotch banking companies accept of re-payment are, so far as I know, peculiar to them, and have, perhaps, been the principal cause, both of the great trade of those companies and of the benefit which the country has received from it.

Whoever has a credit of this kind with one of those companies, and borrows a thousand pounds upon it, for example, may repay this sum piecemeal, by twenty and thirty pounds at a time, the company discounting a proportionate part of the interest of the great sum from the day on which each of those small sums is paid in, till the whole be in this manner repaid. All merchants, therefore, and almost all men of business, find it convenient to keep such cash accounts with them, and are thereby interested to promote the trade of those companies, by readily receiving their notes in all payments, and by encouraging all those with whom they have any influence to do the same. The banks, when their customers apply to them for money, generally advance it to them in their own promissory notes. These the merchants pay away to the manufacturers for goods, the manufacturers to the farmers for materials and provisions, the farmers to their landlords for rent, the landlords repay them to the merchants for the conveniences and luxuries with which they supply them, and the merchants again return them to the banks in order to balance their cash accounts, or to replace what they may have borrowed of them; and thus almost the whole money business of the country is transacted by means of them. Hence the great trade of those companies.

By means of those cash accounts every merchant can, without imprudence, carry on a greater trade than he otherwise could do. If there are two merchants, one in London and the other in Edinburgh, who employ equal stocks in the same branch of trade, the Edinburgh merchant can, without imprudence, carry on a greater trade and give employment to a greater number of people than the London merchant. The London merchant must always keep by him a considerable sum of money, either in his own coffers, or in those of his banker, who gives him no interest for it, in order to answer the demands continually coming upon him for payment of the goods which he purchases upon credit. Let the ordinary amount of this sum be supposed five hundred pounds. The value of the goods in his warehouse must always be less by five hundred pounds than it would have been had he not been obliged to keep such a sum unemployed. Let us suppose that he generally disposes of his whole stock upon hand, or of goods to the value of his whole stock upon hand, once in the year. By being obliged to keep so great a sum unemployed, he must sell in a year five hundred pounds' worth less goods than he might otherwise have done. His annual profits must be less by all that he could have made by the sale of five hundred pounds' worth more goods; and the number of people employed in preparing his goods for the market must be less by all those that five hundred pounds more stock could have employed. The merchant in Edinburgh, on the other hand, keeps no money unemployed for answering such occasional demands. When they actually come upon him, he satisfies them from his cash account with the bank, and gradually replaces the sum borrowed with the money or paper which comes in from the occasional sales of his goods. With the same stock, therefore, he can, without imprudence, have at all times in his warehouse a larger quantity of goods than the London merchant; and can thereby both make a greater profit himself, and give constant employment to a greater number of industrious people who prepare those goods for the market. Hence the great benefit which the country has derived from this trade.

The facility of discounting bills of exchange, it may be thought indeed, gives the English merchants a conveniency equivalent to the cash accounts of the Scotch merchants. But the Scotch merchants, it must be remembered, can discount their bills of exchange as easily as the English merchants; and have, besides, the additional conveniency of their cash accounts.

The whole paper money of every kind which can easily circulate in any country never can exceed the value of the gold and silver, of which it supplies the place, or which (the commerce being supposed the same) would circulate there, if there was no paper money. If twenty shilling notes, for example, are the lowest paper money current in Scotland, the whole of that currency which can easily circulate there cannot exceed the sum of gold and silver which would be necessary for transacting the annual exchanges of twenty shillings' value and upwards usually transacted within that country. Should the circulating paper at any time exceed that sum, as the excess could neither be sent abroad nor be employed in the circulation of the country, it must immediately return upon the banks to be exchanged for gold and silver. Many people would immediately perceive that

they had more of this paper than was necessary for transacting
their business at home, and as they could not send it abroad,
they would immediately demand payment of it from the banks.
When this superfluous paper was converted into gold and
silver, they could easily find a use for it by sending it abroad;
but they could find none while it remained in the shape of
paper. There would immediately, therefore, be a run upon the
banks to the whole extent of this superfluous paper, and, if they
showed any difficulty or backwardness in payment, to a much
greater extent; the alarm which this would occasion, necessarily
increasing the run.

Over and above the expenses which are common to every
branch of trade; such as the expense of house rent, the wages of
servants, clerks, accountants, etc.; the expenses peculiar to a
bank consist chiefly in two articles: first, in the expense of
keeping at all times in its coffers, for answering the occasional
demands of the holders of its notes, a large sum of money, of
which it loses the interest; and, secondly, in the expense of replenishing those coffers as fast as they are emptied by answering
such occasional demands.

A banking company, which issues more paper than can be
employed in the circulation of the country, and of which the
excess is continually returning upon them for payment, ought to
increase the quantity of gold and silver, which they keep at all
times in their coffers, not only in proportion to this excessive
increase of their circulation, but in a much greater proportion;
their notes returning upon them much faster in proportion to
the excess of their quantity. Such a company, therefore, ought
to increase the first article of their expense, not only in proportion to this forced increase of their business, but in a much
greater proportion.

The coffers of such a company too, though they ought to be
filled much fuller, yet must empty themselves much faster than
if their business was confined within more reasonable bounds,
and must require, not only a more violent, but a more constant
and uninterrupted exertion of expense in order to replenish
them. The coin too, which is thus continually drawn in such
large quantities from their coffers, cannot be employed in the
circulation of the country. It comes in place of a paper which is

over and above what can be employed in that circulation, and is therefore over and above what can be employed in it too. But as that coin will not be allowed to lie idle, it must, in one shape or another, be sent abroad, in order to find that profitable employment which it cannot find at home; and this continual exportation of gold and silver, by enhancing the difficulty, must necessarily enhance still further the expense of the bank, in finding new gold and silver in order to replenish those coffers, which empty themselves so very rapidly. Such a company, therefore, must, in proportion to this forced increase of their business, increase the second article of their expense still more than the first.

Let us suppose that all the paper for a particular bank, which the circulation of the country can easily absorb and employ, amounts exactly to forty thousand pounds; and that for answering occasional demands, this bank is obliged to keep at all times in its coffers ten thousand pounds in gold and silver. Should this bank attempt to circulate forty-four thousand pounds, the four thousand pounds which are over and above what the circulation can easily absorb and employ, will return upon it almost as fast as they are issued. For answering occasional demands, therefore, this bank ought to keep at all times in its coffers, not eleven thousand pounds only, but fourteen thousand pounds. It will thus gain nothing by the interest of the four thousand pounds' excessive circulation; and it will lose the whole expense of continually collecting four thousand pounds in gold and silver, which will be continually going out of its coffers as fast as they are brought into them.

Had every particular banking company always understood and attended to its own particular interest, the circulation never could have been overstocked with paper money. But every particular banking company has not always understood or attended to its own particular interest, and the circulation has frequently been overstocked with paper money.

By issuing too great a quantity of paper, of which the excess was continually returning, in order to be exchanged for gold and silver, the Bank of England was for many years together obliged to coin gold to the extent of between eight hundred thousand pounds and a million a year; or at an average, about eight hundred and fifty thousand pounds. For this great coinage the bank (in consequence of the worn and degraded state into which the gold coin had fallen a few years ago) was frequently obliged to purchase gold bullion at the high price of four pounds an ounce, which it soon after issued in coin at £3 17s. 10½d. an ounce, losing in this manner between two and a half and three per cent upon the coinage of so very large a sum. Though the bank therefore paid no seignorage, though the government was properly at the expense of the coinage, this liberality of government did not prevent altogether the expense of the bank.

The Scotch banks, in consequence of an excess of the same kind, were all obliged to employ constantly agents at London to collect money for them, at an expense which was seldom below one and a half or two per cent. This money was sent down by the waggon, and insured by the carriers at an additional expense of three quarters per cent or fifteen shillings on the hundred pounds. Those agents were not always able to replenish the coffers of their employers so fast as they were emptied. In this case the resource of the banks was to draw upon their correspondents in London bills of exchange to the extent of the sum which they wanted. When those correspondents afterwards drew upon them for the payment of this sum, together with the interest and a commission, some of those banks, from the distress into which their excessive circulation had thrown them, had sometimes no other means of satisfying this draught but by drawing a second set of bills either upon the same, or upon some other correspondents in London; and the same sum, or rather bills for the same sum, would in this manner make sometimes more than two or three journeys, the debtor bank, paying always the interest and commission upon the whole accumulated sum. Even those Scotch banks which never distinguished themselves by their extreme imprudence, were sometimes obliged to employ this ruinous resource.

The gold coin which was paid out either by the Bank of England, or by the Scotch banks, in exchange for that part of their paper which was over and above what could be employed in the circulation of the country, being likewise over and above what could be employed in that circulation, was sometimes sent abroad in the shape of coin, sometimes melted down and sent abroad in the shape of bullion, and sometimes melted down and sold to the Bank of England at the high price of four pounds an ounce. It was the newest, the heaviest, and the best pieces only which were carefully picked out of the whole coin, and either sent abroad or melted down. At home, and while they remained in the shape of coin, those heavy pieces were of no more value than the light. But they were of more value abroad, or when melted down into bullion, at home. The Bank of England, notwithstanding their great annual coinage, found to their astonishment that there was every year the same scarcity of coin as there had been the year before; and that notwithstanding the great quantity of good and new coin which was every year issued from the bank, the state of the coin, instead of growing better and better, became every year worse and worse. Every year they found themselves under the necessity of coining nearly the same quantity of gold as they had coined the year before, and from the continual rise in the price of gold bullion, in consequence of the continual wearing and clipping of the coin, the expense of this great annual coinage became every year greater and greater. The Bank of England, it is to be observed, by supplying its own coffers with coin, is indirectly obliged to supply the whole kingdom, into which coin is continually flowing from those coffers in a great variety of ways. Whatever coin therefore was wanted to support this excessive circulation both of Scotch and English paper money, whatever vacuities this excessive circulation occasioned in the necessary coin of the kingdom, the Bank of England was obliged to supply them. The Scotch banks, no doubt, paid all of them very dearly for their own imprudence and inattention. But the Bank of England paid very dearly, not only for its own imprudence, but for the much greater imprudence of almost all the Scotch banks.

The over-trading of some bold projectors in both parts of the united kingdom was the original cause of this excessive circulation of paper money.

What a bank can with propriety advance to a merchant or undertaker of any kind, is not either the whole capital with which he trades, or even any considerable part of that capital; but that part of it only which he would otherwise be obliged to keep by him unemployed, and in ready money for answering occasional demands. If the paper money which the bank advances never exceeds this value, it can never exceed the value of the gold and silver which would necessarily circulate in the country if there was no paper money; it can never exceed the quantity which the circulation of the country can easily absorb and employ.

When a bank discounts to a merchant a real bill of exchange drawn by a real creditor upon a real debtor, and which, as soon as it becomes due, is really paid by that debtor, it only advances to him a part of the value which he would otherwise be obliged to keep by him unemployed and in ready money for answering occasional demands. The payment of the bill, when it becomes due, replaces to the bank the value of what it had advanced, together with the interest. The coffers of the bank, so far as its dealings are confined to such customers, resemble a water pond, from which, though a stream is continually running out, yet another is continually running in, fully equal to that which runs out; so that, without any further care or attention, the pond keeps always equally, or very near equally full. Little or no expense can ever be necessary for replenishing the coffers of such a bank.

A merchant, without over-trading, may frequently have occasion for a sum of ready money, even when he has no bills to discount. When a bank, besides discounting his bills, advances him likewise upon such occasions such sums upon his cash account, and accepts of a piecemeal repayment as the money comes in from the occasional sale of his goods, upon the easy terms of the banking companies of Scotland; it dispenses him entirely from the necessity of keeping any part of his stock by him unemployed and in ready money for answering occasional demands. When such demands actually come upon him, he can answer them sufficiently from his cash account. The bank, however, in dealing with such customers, ought to observe with great attention, whether in the course of some short period (of four, five, six, or eight months, for example) the sum of the repayments which it commonly receives from them is, or is not, fully equal to that of the advances which it commonly makes to them. If, within the course of such short periods, the sum of the repayments from certain customers is, upon most occasions, fully equal to that of the advances, it may safely continue to deal with such customers. Though the stream which is in this case continually running out from its coffers may be very large, that which is continually running into them must be at least equally large; so that without any further care or attention those coffers are likely to be always equally or very near equally full; and scarce ever to require any extraordinary expense to replenish them. If, on the contrary, the sum of the repayments from certain other customers falls commonly very much short of the advances which it makes to them, it cannot with any safety continue to deal with such customers, at least if they continue to deal with it in this manner. The stream which is in this case continually running out from its coffers is necessarily much larger than that which is continually running in; so that, unless they are replenished by some great and continual effort of expense, those coffers must soon be exhausted altogether.

The banking companies of Scotland, accordingly, were for a long time very careful to require frequent and regular repayments from all their customers, and did not care to deal with any person, whatever might be his fortune or credit, who did not make, what they called, frequent and regular operations with them. By this attention, besides saving almost entirely the extraordinary expense of replenishing their coffers, they gained two other very considerable advantages.

First, by this attention they were enabled to make some tolerable judgement concerning the thriving or declining circumstances of their debtors, without being obliged to look out for any other evidence besides what their own books afforded them; men being for the most part either regular or irregular in their repayments, according as their circumstances are either thriving or declining. A private man who lends out his money to perhaps half a dozen or a dozen of debtors, may, either by himself or his agents, observe and inquire both constantly and carefully into the conduct and situation of each of them. But a banking company, which lends money to perhaps five hundred different people, and of which the attention is continually occupied by objects of a very different kind, can have no regular information concerning the conduct and circumstances of the greater part of its debtors beyond what its own books afford it. In requiring frequent and regular repayments from all their customers, the banking companies of Scotland had probably this advantage in view.

Secondly, by this attention they secured themselves from the possibility of issuing more paper money than what the circulation of the country could easily absorb and employ. When they observed that within moderate periods of time the repayments of a particular customer were upon most occasions fully equal to the advances which they had made to him, they might be assured that the paper money which they had advanced to him had not at any time exceeded the quantity of gold and silver which he would otherwise have been obliged to keep by him for answering occasional demands; and that, consequently, the paper money, which they had circulated by his means, had not at any time exceeded the quantity of gold and silver which would have circulated in the country had there been no paper money. The frequency, regularity, and amount of his repayments would sufficiently demonstrate that the amount of their advances had at no time exceeded that part of his capital which he would otherwise have been obliged to keep by him unemployed and in ready money for answering occasional demands; that is, for the purpose of keeping the rest of his capital in constant employment. It is this part of his capital only which, within moderate periods of time, is continually returning to every dealer in the shape of money, whether paper or coin, and continually going from him in the same shape. If the advances of the bank had commonly exceeded this part of his capital, the ordinary amount of his repayments could not, within moderate periods of time, have equalled the ordinary amount of its advances. The stream which, by means of his dealings, was continually running into the coffers of the bank, could not have been equal to the stream which, by means of the same dealings, was continually running out. The advances of the bank paper, by exceeding the quantity of gold and silver which, had there been no such advances, he would have been obliged to keep by him for answering occasional demands, might soon come to exceed the whole quantity of gold and silver which (the commerce being supposed the same) would have circulated in the country had there been no paper money; and consequently to exceed the quantity which the circulation of the country could easily absorb and employ; and the excess of this paper money would immediately have returned upon the bank in order to be exchanged for gold and silver. This second advantage, though equally real, was not perhaps so well understood by all the different banking companies of Scotland as the first.

When, partly by the conveniency of discounting bills, and partly by that of cash accounts, the creditable traders of any country can be dispensed from the necessity of keeping any part of their stock by them unemployed and in ready money for answering occasional demands, they can reasonably expect no farther assistance from banks and bankers, who, when they have gone thus far, cannot, consistently with their own interest and safety, go farther. A bank cannot, consistently with its own interest, advance to a trader the whole or even the greater part of the circulating capital with which he trades; because, though that capital is continually returning to him in the shape of money, and going from him in the same shape, yet the whole of the returns is too distant from the whole of the outgoings, and the sum of his repayments could not equal the sum of its advances within such moderate periods of time as suit the conveniency of a bank. Still less could a bank afford to advance him any considerable part of his fixed capital; of the capital which the undertaker of an iron forge, for example, employs in erecting his forge and smelting-house, his workhouses and warehouses, the dwelling-houses of his workmen, etc.; of the capital which the undertaker of a mine employs in sinking his shafts, in erecting engines for drawing out the water, in making roads and waggon-ways, etc.; of the capital which the person who undertakes to improve land employs in clearing, draining, enclosing, manuring, and ploughing waste and uncultivated fields, in building farm-houses, with all their necessary appendages of stables, granaries, etc. The returns of the fixed capital are in almost all cases much slower than those of the circulating capital; and such expenses, even when laid out with the greatest prudence and judgement, very seldom return to the undertaker till after a period of many years, a period by far too distant to suit the conveniency of a bank. Traders and other undertakers may, no doubt, with great propriety, carry on a very considerable part of their projects with borrowed money. In justice to their creditors, however, their own capital ought, in this case, to be sufficient to ensure, if I may say so, the capital of those creditors; or to render it extremely improbable that those creditors should incur any loss, even though the success of the project should fall very much short of the expectation of the projectors. Even with this precaution too, the money which is borrowed, and which it is meant should not be repaid till after a period of several years, ought not to be borrowed of a bank, but ought to be borrowed upon bond or mortgage of such private people as propose to live upon the interest of their money without taking the trouble themselves to employ the capital, and who are upon that account willing to lend that capital to such people of good credit as are likely to keep it for several years. A bank, indeed, which lends its money without the expense of stamped paper, or of attorneys' fees for drawing bonds and mortgages, and which accepts of repayment upon the easy terms of the banking companies of Scotland, would, no doubt, be a very convenient creditor to such traders and undertakers. But such traders and undertakers would, surely, be most inconvenient debtors to such a bank.

It is now more than five-and-twenty years since the paper money issued by the different banking companies of Scotland was fully equal, or rather was somewhat more than fully equal, to what the circulation of the country could easily absorb and employ. Those companies, therefore, had so long ago given all the assistance to the traders and other undertakers of Scotland which it is possible for banks and bankers, consistently with their own interest, to give. They had even done somewhat more. They had over-traded a little, and had brought upon themselves that loss, or at least that diminution of profit, which in this particular business never fails to attend the smallest degree of over-trading. Those traders and other undertakers, having got so much assistance from banks and bankers, wished to get still more. The banks, they seem to have thought, could extend their credits to whatever sum might be wanted, without incurring any other expense besides that of a few reams of paper. They complained of the contracted views and dastardly spririt of the directors of those banks, which did not, they said, extend their credits in proportion to the extension of the trade of the country; meaning, no doubt, by the extension of that trade the extension of their own projects beyond what they could carry on, either with their own capital, or with what they had credit to borrow of private people in the usual way of bond or mortgage. The banks, they seem to have thought, were in honour bound to supply the deficiency, and to provide them with all the capital which they wanted to trade with. The banks, however, were of a different opinion, and upon their refusing to extend their credits, some of those traders had recourse to an expedient which, for a time, served their purpose, though at a much greater expense, yet as effectually as the utmost extension of bank credits could have done. This expedient was no other than the well-known shift of drawing and redrawing; the shift to which unfortunate traders have sometimes recourse when they are upon the brink of bankruptcy. The practice of raising money in this manner had been long known in England, and during the course of the late war, when the high profits of trade afforded a great temptation to over-trading, is said to have been carried on to a very great extent. From England it was brought into Scotland, where, in proportion to the very limited commerce, and to the very moderate capital of the country, it was soon carried on to a much greater extent than it ever had been in England.

The practice of drawing and re-drawing is so well known to all men of business that it may perhaps be thought unnecessary to give an account of it. But as this book may come into the hands of many people who are not men of business, and as the effects of this practice upon the banking trade are not perhaps generally understood even by men of business themselves, I shall endeavour to explain it as distinctly as I can.

The customs of merchants, which were established when the barbarous laws of Europe did not enforce the performance of their contracts, and which during the course of the two last centuries have been adopted into the laws of all European nations, have given such extraordinary privileges to bills of exchange that money is more readily advanced upon them than upon any other species of obligation, especially when they are made payable within so short a period as two or three months after their date. If, when the bill becomes due, the acceptor does not pay it as soon as it is presented, he becomes from that moment a bankrupt. The bill is protested, and returns upon the drawer, who, if he does not immediately pay it, becomes likewise a bankrupt. If, before it came to the person who presents it to the acceptor for payment, it had passed through the hands of several other persons, who had successively advanced to one another the contents of it either in money or goods, and who to express that each of them had in his turn received those contents, had all of them in their order endorsed, that is, written their names upon the back of the bill; each endorser becomes in his turn liable to the owner of the bill for those contents, and, if he fails to pay, he comes too from that moment a bankrupt. Though the drawer, acceptor, and endorsers of the bill should, all of them, be persons of doubtful credit; yet still the shortness of the date gives some security to the owner of the bill. Though all of them may be very likely to become bankrupts, it is a chance if they all become so in so short a time. The house is crazy, says a weary traveller to himself, and will not stand very long; but it is a chance if it falls tonight, and I will venture, therefore, to sleep in it tonight.

The trader A in Edinburgh, we shall suppose, draws a bill upon B in London, payable two months after date. In reality B in London owes nothing to A in Edinburgh; but he agrees to accept of A's bill, upon condition that before the term of payment he shall redraw upon A in Edinburgh for the same sum, together with the interest and a commission, another bill, payable likewise two months after date. B accordingly, before the expiration of the first two months, redraws this bill upon A in Edinburgh; who again, before the expiration of the second two months, draws a second bill upon B in London, payable likewise two months after date; and before the expiration of the third two months, B in London re-draws upon A in Edinburgh another bill, payable also two months after date. This practice has sometimes gone on, not only for several months, but for several years together, the bill always returning upon A in Edinburgh, with the accumulated interest and commission of all the former bills. The interest was five per cent in the year, and the commission was never less than one half per cent on each draft. This commission being repeated more than six times in the year, whatever money A might raise by this expedient must necessarily have cost him something more than eight per cent in the year, and sometimes a great deal more; when either the price of the commission happened to rise, or when he was obliged to pay compound interest upon the interest and commission of former bills. This practice was called raising money by circulation.

In a country where the ordinary profits of stock in the greater part of mercantile projects are supposed to run between six and ten per cent, it must have been a very fortunate speculation of which the returns could not only repay the enormous expense at which the money was thus borrowed for carrying it on; but afford, besides, a good surplus profit to the projector. Many vast and extensive projects, however, were undertaken, and for several years carried on without any other fund to support them besides what was raised at this enormous expense. The projectors, no doubt, had in their golden dreams the most distinct vision of this great profit. Upon their awaking, however, either at the end of their projects, or when they were no longer able to carry them on, they very seldom, I believe, had the good fortune to find it.[1]

1. The method described in the text was by no means either the most common or the most expensive one in which those adventurers sometimes raised money by circulation. It frequently happened that A in Edinburgh would enable B in London to pay the first bill of exchange by drawing, a few days before it became due, a second bill at three months' date upon the same B in London. This bill, being payable to his own order, A sold in Edinburgh at par; and with its contents purchased bills upon London payable at sight to the order of B, to whom he sent them by post. Towards the end of the late war, the exchange between Edinburgh and London was frequently three per cent against Edinburgh, and those bills at sight must frequently have cost A that premium. This transaction therefore being repeated at least four times in the year, and being loaded with a commission of at least one half per cent upon each repetition, must at that period have cost A at least fourteen per cent in the year. At other times A would enable B to discharge the first bill of exchange by drawing, a few days before it became due, a second bill at two months date; not upon B, but upon some third person, C, for example, in London. This other bill was made payable to the order of B, who, upon its being accepted by C, discounted it with some banker in London; and A enabled C to discharge it by drawing, a few

The bills which A in Edinburgh drew upon B in London, he regularly discounted two months before they were due with some bank or banker in Edinburgh; and the bills which B in London re-drew upon A in Edinburgh, he as regularly discounted either with the Bank of England, or with some other bankers in London. Whatever was advanced upon such circulating bills, was, in Edinburgh, advanced in the paper of the Scotch banks, and in London, when they were discounted at the Bank of England, in the paper of that bank. Though the bills upon which this paper had been advanced were all of them repaid in their turn as soon as they became due; yet the value which had been really advanced upon the first bill, was never really returned to the banks which advanced it; because, before each bill became due, another bill was always drawn to somewhat a greater amount than the bill which was soon to be paid; and the discounting of this other bill was essentially necessary towards the payment of that which was soon to be due. This payment, therefore, was altogether fictitious. The stream, which, by means of those circulating bills of exchange, had once been made to run out from the coffers of the banks, was never replaced by any stream which really run into them.

The paper which was issued upon those circulating bills of exchange, amounted, upon many occasions, to the whole fund destined for carrying on some vast and extensive project of agriculture, commerce, or manufactures; and not merely to that part of it which, had there been no paper money, the projector would have been obliged to keep by him, unemployed and in

days before it became due, a third bill, likewise at two months' date, sometimes upon his first correspondent B, and sometimes upon some fourth or fifth person, D or E, for example. This third bill was made payable to the order of C; who, as soon as it was accepted, discounted it in the same manner with some banker in London. Such operations being repeated at least six times in the year, and being loaded with a commission of at least one-half per cent upon each repetition, together with the legal interest of five per cent, this method of raising money, in the same manner as that described in the text, must have cost A something more than eight per cent. By saving, however, the exchange between Edinburgh and London, it was less expensive than that mentioned in the foregoing part of this note; but then it required an established credit with more houses than one in London, an advantage which many of these adventurers could not always find it easy to procure.

ready money for answering occasional demands. The greater part of this paper was, consequently, over and above the value of the gold and silver which would have circulated in the country, had there been no paper money. It was over and above, therefore, what the circulation of the country could easily absorb and employ, and upon that account, immediately returned upon the banks in order to be exchanged for gold and silver, which they were to find as they could. It was a capital which those projectors had very artfully contrived to draw from those banks, not only without their knowledge or deliberate consent, but for some time, perhaps, without their having the most distant suspicion that they had really advanced it.

When two people, who are continually drawing and re-drawing upon one another, discount their bills always with the same banker, he must immediately discover what they are about, and see clearly that they are trading, not with any capital of their own, but with the capital which he advances to them. But this discovery is not altogether so easy when they discount their bills sometimes with one banker, and sometimes with another, and when the same two persons do not constantly draw and re-draw upon one another, but occasionally run the round of a great circle of projectors, who find it for their interest to assist one another in this method of raising money, and to render it, upon that account, as difficult as possible to distinguish between a real and fictitious bill of exchange; between a bill drawn by a real creditor upon a real debtor, and a bill for which there was properly no real creditor but the bank which discounted it, nor any real debtor but the projector who made use of the money. When a banker had even made this discovery, he might sometimes make it too late, and might find that he had already discounted the bills of those projectors to so great an extent that, by refusing to discount any more, he would necessarily make them all bankrupts, and thus, by ruining them, might perhaps ruin himself. For his own interest and safety, therefore, he might find it necessary, in this very perilous situation, to go on for some time, endeavouring, however, to withdraw gradually, and upon that account making every day greater and greater difficulties about discounting, in order to force those projectors by degrees to have recourse, either to other bankers, or to other methods of raising money; so that he himself might, as soon as possible, get out of the circle. The difficulties, accordingly, which the Bank of England, which the principal bankers in London, and which even the more prudent Scotch banks began, after a certain time, and when all of them had already gone too far, to make about discounting, not only alarmed, but enraged in the highest degree those projectors. Their own distress, of which this prudent and necessary reserve of the banks was, no doubt, the immediate occasion, they called the distress of the country; and this distress of the country, they said, was altogether owing to the ignorance, pusillanimity, and bad conduct of the banks, which did not give a sufficiently liberal aid to the spirited undertakings of those who exerted themselves in order to beautify, improve, and enrich the country. It was the duty of the banks, they seemed to think, to lend for as long a time, and to as great an extent as they might wish to borrow. The banks, however, by refusing in this manner to give more credit to those to whom they had already given a great deal too much, took the only method by which it was now possible to save either their own credit or the public credit of the country.

In the midst of this clamour and distress, a new bank was established in Scotland for the express purpose of relieving the distress of the country. The design was generous; but the execution was imprudent, and the nature and causes of the distress which it meant to relieve were not, perhaps, well understood. This bank was more liberal than any other had ever been, both in granting cash accounts, and in discounting bills of exchange. With regard to the latter, it seems to have made scarce any distinction between real and circulating bills, but to have discounted all equally. It was the avowed principle of this bank to advance, upon any reasonable security, the whole capital which was to be employed in those improvements of which the returns are the most slow and distant, such as the improvements of land. To promote such improvements was even said to be the chief of the public-spirited purposes for which it was instituted. By its liberality in granting cash accounts, and in discounting bills of exchange, it, no doubt, issued great quantities of its bank notes. But those bank notes being, the greater part of them, over and above what the circulation of the country could easily absorb

and employ, returned upon it, in order to be exchanged for gold
and silver as fast as they were issued. Its coffers were never well
filled. The capital which had been subscribed to this bank at
two different subscriptions, amounted to one hundred and sixty
thousand pounds, of which eighty per cent only was paid up.
This sum ought to have been paid in at several different in-
stalments. A great part of the proprietors, when they paid in
their first instalment, opened a cash account with the bank; and
the directors, thinking themselves obliged to treat their own
proprietors with the same liberality with which they treated all
other men, allowed many of them to borrow upon this cash
account what they paid in upon all their subsequent instal-
ments. Such payments, therefore, only put into one coffer what
had the moment before been taken out of another. But had the
coffers of this bank been filled ever so well, its excessive circulation must have emptied them faster than they could have been
replenished by any other expedient but the ruinous one of drawing upon London, and when the bill became due, paying it,
together with interest and commission, by another draft upon
the same place. Its coffers having been filled so very ill, it is said
to have been driven to this resource within a very few months
after it began to do business. The estates of the proprietors of
this bank were worth several millions, and by their subscription
to the original bond or contract of the bank, were really pledged
for answering all its engagements. By means of the great credit
which so great a pledge necessarily gave it, it was, notwithstanding its too liberal conduct, enabled to carry on business for
more than two years. When it was obliged to stop, it had in the
circulation about two hundred thousand pounds in bank notes.
In order to support the circulation of those notes which were
continually returning upon it as fast as they were issued, it had
been constantly in the practice of drawing bills of exchange upon
London, of which the number and value were continually
increasing, and, when it stopped, amounted to upwards of six
hundred thousand pounds. This bank, therefore, had, in little
more than the course of two years, advanced to different people
upwards of eight hundred thousand pounds at five per cent.
Upon the two hundred thousand pounds which it circulated in
bank notes, this five per cent might, perhaps, be considered as

clear gain, without any other deduction besides the expense of management. But upon upwards of six hundred thousand pounds, for which it was continually drawing bills of exchange upon London, it was paying, in the way of interest and commission, upwards of eight per cent, and was consequently losing more than three per cent upon more than three-fourths of all its dealings.

The operations of this bank seem to have produced effects quite opposite to those which were intended by the particular persons who planned and directed it. They seem to have intended to support the spirited undertakings, for as such they considered them, which were at that time carrying on in different parts of the country; and at the same time, by drawing the whole banking business to themselves, to supplant all the other Scotch banks, particularly those established in Edinburgh, whose backwardness in discounting bills of exchange had given some offence. This bank, no doubt, gave some temporary relief to those projectors, and enabled them to carry on their projects for about two years longer than they could otherwise have done. But it thereby only enabled them to get so much deeper into debt, so that, when ruin came, it fell so much the heavier both upon them and upon their creditors. The operations of this bank, therefore, instead of relieving, in reality aggravated in the long-run the distress which those projectors had brought both upon themselves and upon their country. It would have been much better for themselves, their creditors, and their country, had the greater part of them been obliged to stop two years sooner than they actually did. The temporary relief, however, which this bank afforded to those projectors, proved a real and permanent relief to the other Scotch banks. All the dealers in circulating bills of exchange, which those other banks had become so backward in discounting, had recourse to this new bank, where they were received with open arms. Those other banks, therefore, were enabled to get very easily out of that fatal circle, from which they could not otherwise have disengaged themselves without incurring a considerable loss, and perhaps too even some degree of discredit.

In the long-run, therefore, the operations of this bank increased the real distress of the country which it meant to relieve; and effectually relieved from a very great distress those rivals whom it meant to supplant.

At the first setting out of this bank, it was the opinion of some people that how fast soever its coffers might be emptied, it mighty easily replenish them by raising money upon the securities of those to whom it had advanced its paper. Experience, I believe, soon convinced them that this method of raising money was by much too slow to answer their purpose; and that coffers which originally were so ill filled, and which emptied themselves so very fast, could be replenished by no other expedient but the ruinous one of drawing bills upon London, and when they became due, paying them by other drafts upon the same place with accumulated interest and commission. But though they had been able by this method to raise money as fast as they wanted it, yet, instead of making a profit, they must have suffered a loss by every such operation; so that in the long-run they must have ruined themselves as a mercantile company, though, perhaps, not so soon as by the more expensive practice of drawing and re-drawing. They could still have made nothing by the interest of the paper, which, being over and above what the circulation of the country could absorb and employ, returned upon them, in order to be exchanged for gold and silver, as fast as they issued it; and for the payment of which they were themselves continually obliged to borrow money. On the contrary, the whole expense of this borrowing, of employing agents to look out for people who had money to lend, of negotiating with those people, and of drawing the proper bond or assignment, must have fallen upon them, and have been so much clear loss upon the balance of their accounts. The project of replenishing their coffers in this manner may be compared to that of a man who had a water-pond from which a stream was continually running out, and into which no stream was continually running, but who proposed to keep it always equally full by employing a number of people to go continually with buckets to a well at some miles distance in order to bring water to replenish it.

But though this operation had proved not only practicable but profitable to the bank as a mercantile company, yet the country could have derived no benefit from it; but, on the contrary, must have suffered a very considerable loss by it. This operation could not augment in the smallest degree the quantity of money to be lent. It could only have erected this bank into a sort of general loan office for the whole country. Those who wanted to borrow must have applied to this bank instead of applying to the private persons who had lent it their money. But a bank which lends money perhaps to five hundred different people, the greater part of whom its directors can know very little about, is not likely to be more judicious in the choice of its debtors than a private person who lends out his money among a few people whom he knows, and in whose sober and frugal conduct he thinks he has good reason to confide. The debtors of such a bank as that whose conduct I have been giving some account of were likely, the greater part of them, to be chimerical projectors, the drawers and re-drawers of circulating bills of exchange, who would employ the money in extravagant undertakings, which, with all the assistance that could be given them, they would probably never be able to complete, and which, if they should be completed, would never repay the expense which they had really cost, would never afford a fund capable of maintaining a quantity of labour equal to that which had been employed about them. The sober and frugal debtors of private persons, on the contrary, would be more likely to employ the money borrowed in sober undertakings which were proportioned to their capitals, and which, though they might have less of the grand and the marvellous, would have more of the solid and the profitable, which would repay with a large profit whatever had been laid out upon them, and which would thus afford a fund capable of maintaining a much greater quantity of labour than that which had been employed about them. The success of this operation, therefore, without increasing in the smallest degree the capital of the country, would only have transferred a great part of it from prudent and profitable to imprudent and unprofitable undertakings.

That the industry of Scotland languished for want of money to employ it was the opinion of the famous Mr Law. By establishing a bank of a particular kind, which he seems to have imagined might issue paper to the amount of the whole value of all the lands in the country, he proposed to remedy this want of money. The parliament of Scotland, when he first proposed his project, did not think proper to adopt it. It was afterwards adopted, with some variations, by the Duke of Orleans, at that time Regent of France. The idea of the possibility of multiplying paper money to almost any extent was the real foundation of what is called the Mississippi scheme, the most extravagant project both of banking and stock-jobbing that, perhaps, the world ever saw. The different operations of this scheme are explained so fully, so clearly, and with so much order and distinctness, by Mr Du Verney, in his examination of the Political Reflections upon Commerce and Finances of Mr Du Tot, that I shall not give any account of them. The principles upon which it was founded are explained by Mr Law himself, in a discourse concerning money and trade, which he published in Scotland when he first proposed his project. The splendid but visionary ideas which are set forth in that and some other works upon the same principles still continue to make an impression upon many people, and have, perhaps, in part, contributed to that excess of banking which has of late been complained of both in Scotland and in other places.

The Bank of England is the greatest bank of circulation in Europe. It was incorporated, in pursuance of an act of parliament, by a charter under the great seal, dated 27 July 1694. It at that time advanced to government the sum of £1,200,000, for an annuity of one hundred thousand pounds; or for £96,000 a year interest, at the rate of eight per cent, and £4,000 a year for the expense of management. The credit of the new government, established by the Revolution, we may believe, must have been very low, when it was obliged to borrow at so high an interest.

In 1697 the bank was allowed to enlarge its capital stock by an engraftment of £1,001,171 10s. Its whole capital stock, therefore, amounted at this time to £2,201,171 10s. This engraftment is said to have been for the support of public credit. In 1696, tallies had been at 40, and 50, and 60 per cent discount, and bank notes at twenty per cent.[1] During the great recoinage of the silver, which was going on at this time, the bank had thought proper to discontinue the payment of its notes, which necessarily occasioned their discredit.

1. James Postlethwaite's *History of the Public Revenue*, page 301.

In pursuance of the 7th Anne, c. vii, the bank advanced and paid into the exchequer the sum of £400,000; making in all the sum of £1,600,000 which it had advanced upon its original annuity of £96,000 interest and £4,000 for expense of management. In 1708, therefore, the credit of government was as good as that of private persons, since it could borrow at six per cent interest the common legal and market rate of those times. In pursuance of the same act, the bank cancelled exchequer bills to the amount of £1,775,027 17s. 10½d. at 6 per cent interest, and was at the same time allowed to take in subscriptions for doubling its capital. In 1708, therefore, the capital of the bank amounted to £4,402,343; and it had advanced to government the sum of £3,375,027 17s. 10½d.

By a call of 15 per cent in 1709, there was paid in and made stock £656,204 1s. 9d.; and by another of 10 per cent in 1710, £501,448 12s. 11d. In consequence of those two calls, therefore, the bank capital amounted to £5,559,995 14s. 8d.

In pursuance of the 3rd George I c. 8, the bank delivered up two millions of exchequer bills to be cancelled. It had at this time, therefore, advanced to government £5,375,027 17s. 10d. In pursuance of the 8th George I c. 21, the bank purchased of the South Sea Company stock to the amount of £4,000,000; and in 1722, in consequence of the subscriptions which it had taken in for enabling it to make this purchase, its capital stock was increased by £3,400,000. At this time, therefore, the bank had advanced to the public £9,375,027 17s. 10½d.; and its capital stock amounted only to £8,959,995 14s. 8d. It was upon this occasion that the sum which the bank had advanced to the public, and for which it received interest, began first to exceed its capital stock, or the sum for which it paid a dividend to the proprietors of bank stock; or, in other words, that the bank began to have an undivided capital, over and above its divided one. It has continued to have an undivided capital of the same kind ever since. In 1746, the bank had, upon different occasions, advanced to the public £11,686,800 and its divided capital had been raised by different calls and subscriptions to £10,780,000. The state of those two sums has continued to be the same ever since. In pursuance of the 4th of George III c. 25, the bank agreed to pay to government for the renewal of its charter

£110,000 without interest or repayment. This sum, therefore, did not increase either of those two other sums.

The dividend of the bank has varied according to the variations in the rate of the interest which it has, at different times, received for the money it had advanced to the public, as well as according to other circumstances. This rate of interest has gradually been reduced from 8 to 3 per cent. For some years past the bank dividend has been at 5½ per cent.

The stability of the Bank of England is equal to that of the British government. All that it has advanced to the public must be lost before its creditors can sustain any loss. No other banking company in England can be established by act of parliament, or can consist of more than six members. It acts, not only as an ordinary bank, but as a great engine of state. It receives and pays the greater part of the annuities which are due to the creditors of the public, it circulates exchequer bills, and it advances to government the annual amount of the land and malt taxes, which are frequently not paid up till some years thereafter. In those different operations, its duty to the public may sometimes have obliged it, without any fault of its directors, to overstock the circulation with paper money. It likewise discounts merchants' bills, and has, upon several different occasions, supported the credit of the principal houses, not only of England, but of Hamburgh and Holland. Upon one occasion, in 1763, it is said to have advanced for this purpose, in one week, about £1,600,000, a great part of it in bullion. I do not, however, pretend to warrant either the greatness of the sum, or the shortness of the time. Upon other occasions, this great company has been reduced to the necessity of paying in sixpences.

It is not by augmenting the capital of the country, but by rendering a greater part of that capital active and productive than would otherwise be so, that the most judicious operations of banking can increase the industry of the country. That part of his capital which a dealer is obliged to keep by him unemployed, and in ready money, for answering occasional demands, is so much dead stock, which, so long as it remains in this situation, produces nothing either to him or to his country. The judicious operations of banking enable him to convert this dead stock into active and productive stock; into materials to work upon, into tools to work with, and into provisions and subsistence to work for; into stock which produces something both to himself and to his country. The gold and silver money which circulates in any country, and by means of which the produce of its land and labour is annually circulated and distributed to the proper consumers, is, in the same manner as the ready money of the dealer, all dead stock. It is a very valuable part of the capital of the country, which produces nothing to the country. The judicious operations of banking, by substituting paper in the room of a great part of this gold and silver, enables the country to convert a great part of this dead stock into active and productive stock; into stock which produces something to the country. The gold and silver money which circulates in any country may very properly be compared to a highway, which, while it circulates and carries to market all the grass and corn of the country, produces itself not a single pile of either. The judicious operations of banking, by providing, if I may be allowed so violent a metaphor, a sort of waggon-way through the air, enable the country to convert, as it were, a great part of its highways into good pastures and corn-fields, and thereby to increase very considerably the annual produce of its land and labour. The commerce and industry of the country, however, it must be acknowledged, though they may be somewhat augmented, cannot be altogether so secure when they are thus, as it were, suspended upon the Daedalian wings of paper money as when they travel about upon the solid ground of gold and silver. Over and above the accidents to which they are exposed from the unskilfulness of the conductors of this paper money, they are liable to several others, from which no prudence or skill of those conductors can guard them.

An unsuccessful war, for example, in which the enemy got possession of the capital, and consequently of that treasure which supported the credit of the paper money, would occasion a much greater confusion in a country where the whole circulation was carried on by paper, than in one where the greater part of it was carried on by gold and silver. The usual instrument of commerce having lost its value, no exchanges could be made but either by barter or upon credit. All taxes having been usually paid in paper money, the prince would not have wherewithal either to pay his troops, or to furnish his magazines; and the state of the country would be much more irretrievable than if the greater part of its circulation had consisted in gold and silver. A prince, anxious to maintain his dominions at all times in the state in which he can most easily defend them, ought, upon this account, to guard, not only against that excessive multiplication of paper money which ruins the very banks which issue it; but even against that multiplication of it which enables them to fill the greater part of the circulation of the country with it.

The circulation of every country may be considered as divided into two different branches: the circulation of the dealers with one another, and the circulation between the dealers and the consumers. Though the same pieces of money, whether paper or metal, may be employed sometimes in the one circulation and sometimes in the other, yet as both are constantly going on at the same time, each requires a certain stock of money of one kind or another to carry it on. The value of the goods circulated between the different dealers, never can exceed the value of those circulated between the dealers and the consumers; whatever is bought by the dealers, being ultimately destined to be sold to the consumers. The circulation between the dealers, as it is carried on by wholesale, requires generally a pretty large sum for every particular transaction. That between the dealers and the consumers, on the contrary, as it is generally carried on by retail, frequently requires but very small ones, a shilling, or even a halfpenny, being often sufficient. But small sums circulate much faster than large ones. A shilling changes masters more frequently than a guinea, and a halfpenny more frequently than a shilling. Though the annual purchases of all the consumers, therefore, are at least equal in value to those of all the dealers, they can generally be transacted with a much smaller quantity of money; the same pieces, by a more rapid circulation, serving as the instrument of many more purchases of the one kind than of the other.

Paper money may be so regulated as either to confine itself very much to the circulation between the different dealers, or to extend itself likewise to a great part of that between the dealers

and the consumers. Where no bank notes are circulated under
ten pounds' value, as in London, paper money confines itself
very much to the circulation between the dealers. When a ten
pound bank note comes into the hands of a consumer, he is
generally obliged to change it at the first shop where he has
occasion to purchase five shillings' worth of goods, so that it
often returns into the hands of a dealer before the consumer
has spent the fortieth part of the money. Where bank notes are
issued for so small sums as twenty shillings, as in Scotland, paper
money extends itself to a considerable part of the circulation
between dealers and consumers. Before the act of parliament,
which put a stop to the circulation of ten and five shilling notes,
it filled a still greater part of that circulation. In the currencies
of North America, paper was commonly issued for so small a
sum as a shilling, and filled almost the whole of that circulation. In some paper currencies of Yorkshire, it was issued even
for so small a sum as sixpence.

Where the issuing of bank notes for very small sums is allowed
and commonly practised, many mean people are both enabled
and encouraged to become bankers. A person whose promissory
note for five pounds, or even for twenty shillings, would be
rejected by everybody, will get it to be received without scruple
when it is issued for so small a sum as a sixpence. But the frequent bankruptcies to which such beggarly bankers must be
liable may occasion a very considerable inconveniency, and
sometimes even a very great calamity to many poor people who
had received their notes in payment.

It were better, perhaps, that no bank notes were issued in any
part of the kingdom for a smaller sum than five pounds. Paper
money would then, probably, confine itself, in every part of the
kingdom, to the circulation between the different dealers, as
much as it does at present in London, where no bank notes are
issued under ten pounds' value; five pounds being, in most
parts of the kingdom, a sum which, though it will purchase,
perhaps, little more than half the quantity of goods, is as much
considered, and is as seldom spent all at once, as ten pounds are
amidst the profuse expense of London.

Where paper money, it is to be observed, is pretty much confined to the circulation between dealers and dealers, as at Lon-

MONEY A BRANCH OF THE GENERAL STOCK 423

don, there is always plenty of gold and silver. Where it extends itself to a considerable part of the circulation between dealers and consumers, as in Scotland, and still more in North America, it banishes gold and silver almost entirely from the country; almost all the ordinary transactions of its interior commerce being thus carried on by paper. The suppression of ten and five shilling bank notes somewhat relieved the scarcity of gold and silver in Scotland; and the suppression of twenty shilling notes would probably relieve it still more. Those metals are said to have become more abundant in America since the suppression of some of their paper currencies. They are said, likewise, to have been more abundant before the institution of those currencies.

Though paper money should be pretty much confined to the circulation between dealers and dealers, yet banks and bankers might still be able to give nearly the same assistance to the industry and commerce of the country as they had done when paper money filled almost the whole circulation. The ready money which a dealer is obliged to keep by him, for answering occasional demands, is destined altogether for the circulation between himself and other dealers of whom he buys goods. He has no occasion to keep any by him for the circulation between himself and the consumers, who are his customers, and who bring ready money to him, instead of taking any from him. Though no paper money, therefore, was allowed to be issued but for such sums as would confine it pretty much to the circulation between dealers and dealers, yet, partly by discounting real bills of exchange, and partly by lending upon cash accounts, banks and bankers might still be able to relieve the greater part of those dealers from the necessity of keeping any considerable part of their stock by them, unemployed and in ready money, for answering occasional demands. They might still be able to give the utmost assistance which banks and bankers can, with propriety, give to traders of every kind.

To restrain private people, it may be said, from receiving in payment the promissory notes of a banker, for any sum whether great or small, when they themselves are willing to receive them, or to restrain a banker from issuing such notes, when all his neighbours are willing to accept them, is a manifest violation of that natural liberty which it is the proper business of law not to infringe, but to support. Such regulations may, no doubt, be considered as in some respects a violation of natural liberty. But those exertions of the natural liberty of a few individuals, which might endanger the security of the whole society, are, and ought to be, restrained by the laws of all governments, of the most free, as well as of the most despotical. The obligation of building party walls, in order to prevent the communication of fire, is a violation of natural liberty, exactly of the same kind with the regulations of the banking trade which are here proposed.

A paper money consisting in bank notes, issued by people of undoubted credit, payable upon demand without any condition, and in fact always readily paid as soon as presented, is, in every respect, equal in value to gold and silver money; since gold and silver money can at any time be had for it. Whatever is either bought or sold for such paper, must necessarily be bought or sold as cheap as it could have been for gold and silver.

The increase of paper money, it has been said, by augmenting the quantity, and consequently diminishing the value of the whole currency, necessarily augments the money price of commodities. But as the quantity of gold and silver, which is taken from the currency, is always equal to the quantity of paper which is added to it, paper money does not necessarily increase the quantity of the whole currency. From the beginning of the last century to the present time, provisions never were cheaper in Scotland than in 1759, though, from the circulation of ten and five shilling bank notes, there was then more paper money in the country than at present. The proportion between the price of provisions in Scotland and that in England is the same now as before the great multiplication of banking companies in Scotland. Corn is, upon most occasions, fully as cheap in England as in France; though there is a great deal of paper money in England, and scarce any in France. In 1751 and in 1752, when Mr Hume published his Political Discourses, and soon after the great multiplication of paper money in Scotland, there was a very sensible rise in the price of provisions, owing, probably, to the badness of the seasons, and not to the multiplication of paper money.

It would be otherwise, indeed, with a paper money consisting in promissory notes, of which the immediate payment depended, in any respect, either upon the good will of those who issued them, or upon a condition which the holder of the notes might not always have it in his power to fulfil; or of which the payment was not exigible till after a certain number of years, and which in the meantime bore no interest. Such a paper money would, no doubt, fall more or less below the value of gold and silver, according as the difficulty or uncertainty of obtaining immediate payment was supposed to be greater or less; or according to the greater or less distance of time at which payment was exigible.

Some years ago the different banking companies of Scotland were in the practice of inserting into their bank notes, what they called an Optional Clause, by which they promised payment to the bearer, either as soon as the note should be presented, or, in the option of the directors, six months after such presentment, together with the legal interest for the said six months. The directors of some of those banks sometimes took advantage of this optional clause, and sometimes threatened those who demanded gold and silver in exchange for a considerable number of their notes, that they would take advantage of it, unless such demanders would content themselves with a part of what they demanded. The promissory notes of those banking companies constituted at that time the far greater part of the currency of Scotland, which this uncertainty of payment necessarily degraded below the value of gold and silver money. During the continuance of this abuse (which prevailed chiefly in 1762, 1763, and 1764), while the exchange between London and Carlisle was at par, that between London and Dumfries would sometimes be four per cent against Dumfries, though this town is not thirty miles distant from Carlisle. But at Carlisle, bills were paid in gold and silver; whereas at Dumfries they were paid in Scotch bank notes, and the uncertainty of getting those bank notes exchanged for gold and silver coin had thus degraded them four per cent below the value of that coin. The same act of parliament which suppressed ten and five shilling bank notes suppressed likewise this optional clause, and thereby restored the exchange between England and Scotland to its natural rate, or to what the course of trade and remittances might happen to make it.

In the paper currencies of Yorkshire, the payment of so small a sum as a sixpence sometimes depended upon the condition that the holder of the note should bring the change of a guinea to the person who issued it; a condition which the holders of such notes might frequently find very difficult to fulfil, and which must have degraded this currency below the value of gold and silver money. An act of parliament accordingly declared all such clauses unlawful, and suppressed, in the same manner as in Scotland, all promissory notes, payable to the bearer, under twenty shillings value.

The paper currencies of North America consisted, not in bank notes payable to the bearer on demand, but in a government paper, of which the payment was not exigible till several years after it was issued; and though the colony governments paid no interest to the holders of this paper, they declared it to be, and in fact rendered it, a legal tender of payment for the full value for which it was issued. But allowing the colony security to be perfectly good, a hundred pounds payable fifteen years hence, for example, in a country where interest is at six per cent, is worth little more than forty pounds ready money. To oblige a creditor, therefore, to accept of this as full payment for a debt of a hundred pounds actually paid down in ready money was an act of such violent injustice as has scarce, perhaps, been attempted by the government of any other country which pretended to be free. It bears the evident marks of having originally been, what the honest and downright Doctor Douglas assures us it was, a scheme of fraudulent debtors to cheat their creditors. The government of Pennsylvania, indeed, pretended, upon their first emission of paper money, in 1722, to render their paper of equal value with gold and silver, by enacting penalties against all those who made any difference in the price of their goods when they sold them for a colony paper, and when they sold them for gold and silver; a regulation equally tyrannical, but much less effectual than that which it was meant to support. A positive law may render a shilling a legal tender for a guinea, because it may direct the courts of justice to discharge the debtor who has made that tender. But no positive law can oblige a person who sells goods, and who is at liberty to sell as he pleases, to accept of a shilling as equivalent to a guinea in the price of them. Notwithstanding any regulations of this kind, it appeared by the course of exchange with Great Britain, that a hundred pounds sterling was occasionally considered as equivalent, in some of the colonies, to a hundred and thirty pounds, and in others to so great a sum as eleven hundred pounds currency; this difference in the value arising from the difference in the quantity of paper emitted in the different colonies, and in the distance and probability of the term of its final discharge and redemption.

No law, therefore, could be more equitable than the act of parliament, so unjustly complained of in the colonies, which declared that no paper currency to be emitted there in time coming should be a legal tender of payment.

Pennsylvania was always more moderate in its emissions of paper money than any other of our colonies. Its paper currency, accordingly, is said never to have sunk below the value of the gold and silver which was currency in the colony before the first emission of its paper money. Before that emission, the colony had raised the denomination of its coin, and had, by act of assembly, ordered 5s. sterling to pass in the colony for 6s 3d., and afterwards for 6s. 8d. A pound colony currency, therefore, even when that currency was gold and silver, was more than 30 per cent below the value of a pound sterling, and when that currency was turned into paper it was seldom much more than 30 per cent below that value. The pretence for raising the denomination of the coin, was to prevent the exportation of gold and silver, by making equal quantities of those metals pass for greater sums in the colony than they did in the mother country. It was found, however, that the price of all goods from the mother country rose exactly in proportion as they raised the denomination of their coin, so that their gold and silver were exported as fast as ever.

The paper of each colony being received in the payment of the provincial taxes, for the full value for which it had been issued, it necessarily derived from this use some additional value over and above what it would have had from the real or supposed distance of the term of its final discharge and redemption.

This additional value was greater or less, according as the quantity of paper issued was more or less above what could be employed in the payment of the taxes of the particular colony which issued it. It was in all the colonies very much above what could be employed in this manner.

A prince who should enact that a certain proportion of his taxes should be paid in a paper money of a certain kind might thereby give a certain value to this paper money, even though the term of its final discharge and redemption should depend altogether upon the will of the prince. If the bank which issued this paper was careful to keep the quantity of it always some-what below what could easily be employed in this manner, the demand for it might be such as to make it even bear a premium, or sell for somewhat more in the market than the quantity of gold or silver currency for which it was issued. Some people account in this manner for what is called the Agio of the bank of Amsterdam, or for the superiority of bank money over current money; though this bank money, as they pretend, cannot be taken out of the bank at the will of the owner. The greater part of foreign bills of exchange must be paid in bank money, that is, by a transfer in the books of the bank; and the directors of the bank, they allege, are careful to keep the whole quantity of bank money always below what this use occasions a demand for. It is upon this account, they say, that bank money sells for a premium, or bears an agio of 4 or 5 per cent above the same nominal sum of the gold and silver currency of the country. This account of the bank of Amsterdam, however, it will appear hereafter, is in a great measure chimerical.

A paper currency which falls below the value of gold and silver coin does not thereby sink the value of those metals, or occasion equal quantities of them to exchange for a smaller quantity of goods of any other kind. The proportion between the value of gold and silver and that of goods of any other kind, depends in all cases not upon the nature or quantity of any particular paper money, which may be current in any particular country, but upon the richness or poverty of the mines, which happen at any particular time to supply the greater market of the commercial world with those metals. It depends upon the proportion between the quantity of labour which is necessary in order to bring a certain quantity of gold and silver to market, and that which is necessary in order to bring thither a certain quantity of any other sort of goods.

If bankers are restrained from issuing any circulating bank notes, or notes payable to the bearer, for less than a certain sum, and if they are subjected to the obligation of an immediate and unconditional payment of such bank notes as soon as presented, their trade may, with safety to the public, be rendered in all other respects perfectly free. The late multiplication of banking companies in both parts of the united kingdom, an event by which many people have been much alarmed, instead of diminishing, increases the security of the public. It obliges all of them to be more circumspect in their conduct, and, by not extending their currency beyond its due proportion to their cash, to guard themselves against those malicious runs which the rivalship of so many competitors is always ready to bring upon them. It restrains the circulation of each particular company within a narrower circle, and reduces their circulating notes to a smaller number. By dividing the whole circulation into a greater number of parts, the failure of any one company, an accident which, in the course of things, must sometimes happen, becomes of less consequence to the public. This free competition, too, obliges all bankers to be more liberal in their dealings with their customers, lest their rivals should carry them away. In general, if any branch of trade, or any division of labour, be advantageous to the public, the freer and more general the competition, it will always be the more so.

CHAPTER III

OF THE ACCUMULATION OF CAPITAL, OR OF
PRODUCTIVE AND UNPRODUCTIVE LABOUR

THERE is one sort of labour which adds to the value of the subject upon which it is bestowed: there is another which has no such effect. The former, as it produces a value, may be called productive; the latter, unproductive[1] labour. Thus the labour of a manufacturer adds, generally, to the value of the materials which he works upon, that of his own maintenance, and of his master's profit. The labour of a menial servant, on the contrary, adds to the value of nothing. Though the manufacturer has his wages advanced to him by his master, he, in reality, costs him no expense, the value of those wages being generally restored, together with a profit, in the improved value of the subject upon which his labour is bestowed. But the maintenance of a menial servant never is restored. A man grows rich by employing a multitude of manufacturers: he grows poor by maintaining a multitude of menial servants. The labour of the latter, however, has its value, and deserves its reward as well as that of the former. But the labour of the manufacturer fixes and realizes itself in some particular subject or vendible commodity, which lasts for some time at least after that labour is past. It is, as it were, a certain quantity of labour stocked and stored up to be employed, if necessary, upon some other occasion. That subject, or what is the same thing, the price of that subject, can afterwards, if necessary, put into motion a quantity of labour equal to that which had originally produced it. The labour of the menial servant, on the contrary, does not fix or realize itself in any particular subject or vendible commodity. His services generally perish in the very instant of their performance, and seldom leave any trace or value behind them for which an equal quantity of service could afterwards be procured.

The labour of some of the most respectable orders in the society is, like that of menial servants, unproductive of any value, and does not fix or realize itself in any permanent subject, or vendible commodity, which endures after that labour is past, and for which an equal quantity of labour could afterwards be procured. The sovereign, for example, with all the officers both of justice and war who serve under him, the whole army and navy, are unproductive labourers. They are the servants of the public, and are maintained by a part of the annual produce of the industry of other people. Their service, how honourable,

1. Some French authors of great learning and ingenuity have used those words in a different sense. In the last chapter of the fourth book I shall endeavour to show that their sense is an improper one.

how useful, or how necessary soever, produces nothing for which an equal quantity of service can afterwards be procured. The protection, security, and defence of the commonwealth, the effect of their labour this year, will not purchase its protection, security, and defence for the year to come. In the same class must be ranked, some of the gravest and most important, and some of the most frivolous professions: churchmen, lawyers, physicians, men of letters of all kinds; players, buffoons, musicians, opera-singers, opera-dancers, etc. The labour of the meanest of these has a certain value, regulated by the very same principles which regulate that of every other sort of labour; and that of the noblest and most useful, produces nothing which could afterwards purchase or procure an equal quantity of labour. Like the declamation of the actor, the harangue of the orator, or the tune of the musician, the work of all of them perishes in the very instant of its production.

Both productive and unproductive labourers, and those who do not labour at all, are all equally maintained by the annual produce of the land and labour of the country. This produce, how great soever, can never be infinite, but must have certain limits. According, therefore, as a smaller or greater proportion of it is any one year employed in maintaining unproductive hands, the more in the one case and the less in the other will remain for the productive, and the next year's produce will be greater or smaller accordingly; the whole annual produce, if we except the spontaneous productions of the earth, being the effect of productive labour.

Though the whole annual produce of the land and labour of every country is, no doubt, ultimately destined for supplying the consumption of its inhabitants, and for procuring a revenue to them, yet when it first comes either from the ground, or from the hands of the productive labourers, it naturally divides itself into two parts. One of them, and frequently the largest, is, in the first place, destined for replacing a capital, or for renewing the provisions, materials, and finished work, which had been withdrawn from a capital; the other for constituting a revenue either to the owner of this capital, as the profit of his stock, or to some other person, as the rent of his land. Thus, of the produce of land, one part replaces the capital of the farmer; the other

pays his profit and the rent of the landlord; and thus constitutes
a revenue both to the owner of this capital, as the profits of his
stock; and to some other person, as the rent of his land. Of the
produce of a great manufactory, in the same manner, one part,
and that always the largest, replaces the capital of the undertaker of the work; the other pays his profit, and thus constitutes
a revenue to the owner of this capital.

That part of the annual produce of the land and labour of any
country which replaces a capital, never is immediately employed
to maintain any but productive hands. It pays the wages of
productive labour only. That which is immediately destined for
constituting a revenue, either as profit or as rent, may maintain
indifferently either productive or unproductive hands.

Whatever part of this stock a man employs as a capital, he
always expects it to be replaced to him with a profit. He employs it, therefore, in maintaining productive hands only; and
after having served in the function of a capital to him, it constitutes a revenue to them. Whenever he employs any part of it
in maintaining unproductive hands of any kind, that part is,
from that moment, withdrawn from his capital, and placed in
his stock reserved for immediate consumption.

Unproductive labourers, and those who do not labour at all,
are all maintained by revenue; either, first, by that part of the
annual produce which is originally destined for constituting a
revenue to some particular persons, either as the rent of land or
as the profits of stock; or, secondly, by that part which, though
originally destined for replacing a capital and for maintaining
productive labourers only, yet when it comes into their hands
whatever part of it is over and above their necessary subsistence
may be employed in maintaining indifferently either productive
or unproductive hands. Thus, not only the great landlord or the
rich merchant, but even the common workman, if his wages are
considerable, may maintain a menial servant; or he may sometimes go to a play or a puppet-show, and so contribute his share
towards maintaining one set of unproductive labourers; or he
may pay some taxes, and thus help to maintain another set,
more honourable and useful, indeed, but equally unproductive.
No part of the annual produce, however, which had been originally destined to replace a capital, is ever directed towards

maintaining unproductive hands till after it has put into motion its full complement of productive labour, or all that it could put into motion in the way in which it was employed. The workman must have earned his wages by work done before he can employ any part of them in this manner. That part, too, is generally but a small one. It is his spare revenue only, of which productive labourers have seldom a great deal. They generally have some, however; and in the payment of taxes the greatness of their number may compensate, in some measure, the smallness of their contribution. The rent of land and the profits of stock are everywhere, therefore, the principal sources from which unproductive hands derive their subsistence. These are the two sorts of revenue of which the owners have generally most to spare. They might both maintain indifferently either productive or unproductive hands. They seem, however, to have some predilection for the latter. The expense of a great lord feeds generally more idle than industrious people. The rich merchant, though with his capital he maintains industrious people only, yet by his expense, that is, by the employment of his revenue, he feeds commonly the very same sort as the great lord.

The proportion, therefore, between the productive and unproductive hands, depends very much in every country upon the proportion between that part of the annual produce, which, as soon as it comes either from the ground or from the hands of the productive labourers, is destined for replacing a capital, and that which is destined for constituting a revenue, either as rent or as profit. This proportion is very different in rich from what it is in poor countries.

Thus, at present, in the opulent countries of Europe, a very large, frequently the largest portion of the produce of the land is destined for replacing the capital of the rich and independent farmer; the other for paying his profits and the rent of the landlord. But anciently, during the prevalency of the feudal government, a very small portion of the produce was sufficient to replace the capital employed in cultivation. It consisted commonly in a few wretched cattle, maintained altogether by the spontaneous produce of uncultivated land, and which might, therefore, be considered as part of that spontaneous produce. It generally, too, belonged to the landlord, and was by him advanced to the occupiers of the land. All the rest of the produce properly belonged to him too, either as rent for his land, or as profit upon this paltry capital. The occupiers of land were generally bondmen, whose persons and effects were equally his property. Those who were not bondmen were tenants at will, and though the rent which they paid was often nominally little more than a quit-rent, it really amounted to the whole produce of the land. Their lord could at all times command their labour in peace and their service in war. Though they lived at a distance from his house, they were equally dependent upon him as his retainers who lived in it. But the whole produce of the land undoubtedly belongs to him who can dispose of the labour and service of all those whom it maintains. In the present state of Europe, the share of the landlord seldom exceeds a third, sometimes not a fourth part of the whole produce of the land. The rent of land, however, in all the improved parts of the country, has been tripled and quadrupled since those ancient times; and this third or fourth part of the annual produce is, it seems, three or four times greater than the whole had been before. In the progress of improvement, rent, though it increases in proportion to the extent, diminishes in proportion to the produce of the land.

In the opulent countries of Europe, great capitals are at present employed in trade and manufactures. In the ancient state, the little trade that was stirring, and the few homely and coarse manufactures that were carried on, required but very small capitals. These, however, must have yielded very large profits. The rate of interest was nowhere less than ten per cent, and their profits must have been sufficient to afford this great interest. At present the rate of interest, in the improved parts of Europe, is nowhere higher than six per cent, and in some of the most improved it is so low as four, three and two per cent. Though that part of the revenue of the inhabitants which is derived from the profits of stock is always much greater in rich than in poor countries, it is because the stock is much greater: in proportion to the stock the profits are generally much less.

That part of the annual produce, therefore, which, as soon as it comes either from the ground or from the hands of the productive labourers, is destined for replacing a capital, is not only much greater in rich than in poor countries, but bears a much greater proportion to that which is immediately destined for constituting a revenue either as rent or as profit. The funds destined for the maintenance of productive labour are not only much greater in the former than in the latter, but bear a much greater proportion to those which, though they may be employed to maintain either productive or unproductive hands, have generally a predilection for the latter.

The proportion between those different funds necessarily determines in every country the general character of the inhabitants as to industry or idleness. We are more industrious than our forefathers; because in the present times the funds destined for the maintenance of industry, are much greater in proportion to those which are likely to be employed in the maintenance of idleness, than they were two or three centuries ago. Our ancestors were idle for want of a sufficient encouragement to industry. It is better, says the proverb, to play for nothing than to work for nothing. In mercantile and manufacturing towns, where the inferior ranks of people are chiefly maintained by the employment of capital, they are in general industrious, sober, and thriving; as in many English, and in most Dutch towns. In those towns which are principally supported by the constant or occasional residence of a court, and in which the inferior ranks of people are chiefly maintained by the spending of revenue, they are in general idle, dissolute, and poor; as at Rome, Versailles, Compiegne, and Fontainebleau. If you except Rouen and Bordeaux, there is little trade or industry in any of the parliament towns of France; and the inferior ranks of people, being chiefly maintained by the expense of the members of the courts of justice, and of those who come to plead before them, are in general idle and poor. The great trade of Rouen and Bordeaux seems to be altogether the effect of their situation. Rouen is necessarily the entrepôt of almost all the goods which are brought either from foreign countries, or from the maritime provinces of France, for the consumption of the great city of Paris. Bordeaux is in the same manner the entrepôt of the wines which grow upon the banks of the Garonne, and of the rivers which run into it, one of the richest wine countries in the world, and which seems to produce the wine fittest for exportation, or best suited to the taste of foreign nations. Such advantageous situations necessarily attract a great capital by the great employment which they afford it; and the employment of this capital is the cause of the industry of those two cities. In the other parliament towns of France, very little more capital seems to be employed than what is necessary for supplying their own consumption; that is, little more than the smallest capital which can be employed in them. The same thing may be said of Paris, Madrid, and Vienna. Of those three cities, Paris is by far the most industrious; but Paris itself is the principal market of all the manufactures established at Paris, and its own consumption is the principal object of all the trade which it carries on. London, Lisbon, and Copenhagen, are, perhaps, the only three cities in Europe which are both the constant residence of a court, and can at the same time be considered as trading cities, or as cities which trade not only for their own consumption, but for that of other cities and countries. The situation of all the three is extremely advantageous, and naturally fits them to be the entrepôts of a great part of the goods destined for the consumption of distant places. In a city where a great revenue is spent, to employ with advantage a capital for any other purpose than for supplying the consumption of that city is probably more difficult than in one in which the inferior ranks of people have no other maintenance but what they derive from the employment of such a capital. The idleness of the greater part of the people who are maintained by the expense of revenue corrupts, it is probable, the industry of those who ought to be maintained by the employment of capital, and renders it less advantageous to employ a capital there than in other places. There was little trade or industry in Edinburgh before the union. When the Scotch parliament was no longer to be assembled in it, when it ceased to be the necessary residence of the principal nobility and gentry of Scotland, it became a city of some trade and industry. It still continues, however, to be the residence of the principal courts of justice in Scotland, of the boards of customs and excise, etc. A considerable revenue, therefore, still continues to be spent in it. In trade and industry it is much inferior to Glasgow, of which the inhabitants are chiefly maintained by the employ-

ment of capital. The inhabitants of a large village, it has sometimes been observed, after having made considerable progress in
manufactures, have become idle and poor in consequence of a
great lord having taken up his residence in their neighbourhood.

The proportion between capital and revenue, therefore, seems
everywhere to regulate the proportion between industry and
idleness. Wherever capital predominates, industry prevails:
wherever revenue, idleness. Every increase or diminution of
capital, therefore, naturally tends to increase or diminish the
real quantity of industry, the number of productive hands, and
consequently the exchangeable value of the annual produce of
the land and labour of the country, the real wealth and revenue
of all its inhabitants.

Capitals are increased by parsimony, and diminished by
prodigality and misconduct.

Whatever a person saves from his revenue he adds to his
capital, and either employs it himself in maintaining an additional number of productive hands, or enables some other person to do so, by lending it to him for an interest, that is, for a
share of the profits. As the capital of an individual can be increased only by what he saves from his annual revenue or his
annual gains, so the capital of a society, which is the same with
that of all the individuals who compose it, can be increased only
in the same manner.

Parsimony, and not industry, is the immediate cause of the
increase of capital. Industry, indeed, provides the subject which
parsimony accumulates. But whatever industry might acquire,
if parsimony did not save and store up, the capital would never
be the greater.

Parsimony, by increasing the fund which is destined for the
maintenance of productive hands, tends to increase the number
of those hands whose labour adds to the value of the subject
upon which it is bestowed. It tends, therefore, to increase the
exchangeable value of the annual produce of the land and labour
of the country. It puts into motion an additional quantity
of industry, which gives an additional value to the annual
produce.

What is annually saved is as regularly consumed as what is

annually spent, and nearly in the same time too; but it is consumed by a different set of people. That portion of his revenue
which a rich man annually spends is in most cases consumed by
idle guests and menial servants, who leave nothing behind them
in return for their consumption. That portion which he annually saves, as for the sake of the profit it is immediately employed as a capital, is consumed in the same manner, and nearly
in the same time too, but by a different set of people, by
labourers, manufacturers, and artificers, who reproduce with a
profit the value of their annual consumption. His revenue, we
shall suppose, is paid him in money. Had he spent the whole,
the food, clothing, and lodging, which the whole could have
purchased, would have been distributed among the former set
of people. By saving a part of it, as that part is for the sake of
the profit immediately employed as a capital either by himself or
by some other person, the food, clothing, and lodging, which
may be purchased with it, are necessarily reserved for the latter.
The consumption is the same, but the consumers are different.

By what a frugal man annually saves, he not only affords
maintenance to an additional number of productive hands, for
that or the ensuing year, but, like the founder of a public
workhouse, he establishes as it were a perpetual fund for the
maintenance of an equal number in all times to come. The
perpetual allotment and destination of this fund, indeed, is not
always guarded by any positive law, by any trust-right or deed
of mortmain. It is always guarded, however, by a very powerful
principle, the plain and evident interest of every individual to
whom any share of it shall ever belong. No part of it can ever
afterwards be employed to maintain any but productive hands
without an evident loss to the person who thus perverts it from
its proper destination.

The prodigal perverts it in this manner. By not confining
his expense within his income, he encroaches upon his capital.
Like him who perverts the revenues of some pious foundation
to profane purposes, he pays the wages of idleness with those
funds which the frugality of his forefathers had, as it were,
consecrated to the maintenance of industry. By diminishing the
funds destined for the employment of productive labour, he
necessarily diminishes, so far as it depends upon him, the quan-

tity of that labour which adds a value to the subject upon which it is bestowed, and, consequently, the value of the annual produce of the land and labour of the whole country, the real wealth and revenue of its inhabitants. If the prodigality of some was not compensated by the frugality of others, the conduct of every prodigal, by feeding the idle with the bread of the industrious, tends not only to beggar himself, but to impoverish his country.

Though the expense of the prodigal should be altogether in home-made, and no part of it in foreign commodities, its effect upon the productive funds of the society would still be the same. Every year there would still be a certain quantity of food and clothing, which ought to have maintained productive, employed in maintaining unproductive hands. Every year, therefore, there would still be some diminution in what would otherwise have been the value of the annual produce of the land and labour of the country.

This expense, it may be said indeed, not being in foreign goods, and not occasioning any exportation of gold and silver, the same quantity of money would remain in the country as before. But if the quantity of food and clothing, which were thus consumed by unproductive, had been distributed among productive hands, they would have reproduced, together with a profit, the full value of their consumption. The same quantity of money would in this case equally have remained in the country, and there would besides have been a reproduction of an equal value of consumable goods. There would have been two values instead of one.

The same quantity of money, besides, cannot long remain in any country in which the value of the annual produce diminishes. The sole use of money is to circulate consumable goods. By means of it, provisions, materials, and finished work, are bought and sold, and distributed to their proper consumers. The quantity of money, therefore, which can be annually employed in any country must be determined by the value of the consumable goods annually circulated within it. These must consist either in the immediate produce of the land and labour of the country itself, or in something which had been purchased with some part of that produce. Their value, therefore, must

diminish as the value of that produce diminishes, and along
with it the quantity of money which can be employed in circulating them. But the money which by this annual diminution of
produce is annually thrown out of domestic circulation will not
be allowed to lie idle. The interest of whoever possesses it requires that it should be employed. But having no employment
at home, it will, in spite of all laws and prohibitions, be sent
abroad, and employed in purchasing consumable goods which
may be of some use at home. Its annual exportation will in this
manner continue for some time to add something to the annual
consumption of the country beyond the value of its own annual
produce. What in the days of its prosperity had been saved from
that annual produce, and employed in purchasing gold and
silver, will contribute for some little time to support its consumption in adversity. The exportation of gold and silver, is in this
case, not the cause, but the effect of its declension, and may
even, for some little time, alleviate the misery of that declension.

The quantity of money, on the contrary, must in every
country naturally increase as the value of the annual produce
increases. The value of the consumable goods annually circulated within the society being greater, will require a greater
quantity of money to circulate them. A part of the increased
produce, therefore, will naturally be employed in purchasing,
wherever it is to be had, the additional quantity of gold and
silver necessary for circulating the rest. The increase of those
metals will in this case be the effect, not the cause, of the public
prosperity. Gold and silver are purchased everywhere in the
same manner. The food, clothing, and lodging, the revenue and
maintenance of all those whose labour or stock is employed in
bringing them from the mine to the market, is the price paid for
them in Peru as well as in England. The country which has this
price to pay will never be long without the quantity of those
metals which it has occasion for; and no country will ever long
retain a quantity which it has no occasion for.

Whatever, therefore, we may imagine the real wealth and
revenue of a country to consist in, whether in the value of the
annual produce of its land and labour, as plain reason seems to
dictate; or in the quantity of the precious metals which circulate
within it, as vulgar prejudices suppose; in either view of the

matter, every prodigal appears to be a public enemy, and every frugal man a public benefactor.

The effects of misconduct are often the same as those of prodigality. Every injudicious and unsuccessful project in agriculture, mines, fisheries, trade, or manufactures, tends in the same manner to diminish the funds destined for the maintenance of productive labour. In every such project, though the capital is consumed by productive hands only, yet, as by the injudicious manner in which they are employed they do not reproduce the full value of their consumption, there must always be some diminution in what would otherwise have been the productive funds of the society.

It can seldom happen, indeed, that the circumstances of a great nation can be much affected either by the prodigality or misconduct of individuals; the profusion or imprudence of some being always more than compensated by the frugality and good conduct of others.

With regard to profusion, the principle which prompts to expense is the passion for present enjoyment; which, though sometimes violent and very difficult to be restrained, is in general only momentary and occasional. But the principle which prompts to save is the desire of bettering our condition, a desire which, though generally calm and dispassionate, comes with us from the womb, and never leaves us till we go into the grave. In the whole interval which separates those two moments, there is scarce perhaps a single instant in which any man is so perfectly and completely satisfied with his situation as to be without any wish of alteration or improvement of any kind. An augmentation of fortune is the means by which the greater part of men propose and wish to better their condition. It is the means the most vulgar and the most obvious; and the most likely way of augmenting their fortune is to save and accumulate some part of what they acquire, either regularly and annually, or upon some extraordinary occasions. Though the principle of expense, therefore, prevails in almost all men upon some occasions, and in some men upon almost all occasions, yet in the greater part of men, taking the whole course of their life at an average, the principle of frugality seems not only to predominate, but to predominate very greatly.

With regard to misconduct, the number of prudent and successful undertakings is everywhere much greater than that of injudicious and unsuccessful ones. After all our complaints of the frequency of bankruptcies, the unhappy men who fall into this misfortune make but a very small part of the whole number engaged in trade, and all other sorts of business; not much more perhaps than one in a thousand. Bankruptcy is perhaps the greatest and most humiliating calamity which can befall an innocent man. The greater part of men, therefore, are sufficiently careful to avoid it. Some, indeed, do not avoid it; as some do not avoid the gallows.

Great nations are never impoverished by private, though they sometimes are by public prodigality and misconduct. The whole, or almost the whole public revenue, is in most countries employed in maintaining unproductive hands. Such are the people who compose a numerous and splendid court, a great ecclesiastical establishment, great fleets and armies, who in time of peace produce nothing, and in time of war acquire nothing which can compensate the expense of maintaining them, even while the war lasts. Such people, as they themselves produce nothing, are all maintained by the produce of other men's labour. When multiplied, therefore, to an unnecessary number, they may in a particular year consume so great a share of this produce, as not to leave a sufficiency for maintaining the productive labourers, who should reproduce it next year. The next year's produce, therefore, will be less than that of the foregoing, and if the same disorder should continue, that of the third year will be still less than that of the second. Those unproductive hands, who should be maintained by a part only of the spare revenue of the people, may consume so great a share of their whole revenue, and thereby oblige so great a number to encroach upon their capitals, upon the funds destined for the maintenance of productive labour, that all the frugality and good conduct of individuals may not be able to compensate the waste and degradation of produce occasioned by this violent and forced encroachment.

This frugality and good conduct, however, is upon most occasions, it appears from experience, sufficient to compensate, not only the private prodigality and misconduct of individuals, but the public extravagance of government. The uniform, constant, and uninterrupted effort of every man to better his condition, the principle from which public and national, as well as private opulence is originally derived, is frequently powerful enough to maintain the natural progress of things toward improvement, in spite both of the extravagance of government and of the greatest errors of administration. Like the unknown principle of animal life, it frequently restores health and vigour to the constitution, in spite, not only of the disease, but of the absurd prescriptions of the doctor.

The annual produce of the land and labour of any nation can be increased in its value by no other means but by increasing either the number of productive labourers, or the productive powers of those labourers who had before been employed. The number of its productive labourers, it is evident, can never be much increased, but in consequence of an increase of capital, or of the funds destined for maintaining them. The productive powers of the same number of labourers cannot be increased, but in consequence either of some addition and improvement to those machines and instruments which facilitate and abridge labour; or of a more proper division and distribution of employment. In either case an additional capital is almost always required. It is by means of an additional capital only that the undertaker of any work can either provide his workmen with better machinery or make a more proper distribution of employment among them. When the work to be done consists of a number of parts, to keep every man constantly employed in one way requires a much greater capital than where every man is occasionally employed in every different part of the work. When we compare, therefore, the state of a nation at two different periods, and find, that the annual produce of its land and labour is evidently greater at the latter than at the former, that its lands are better cultivated, its manufactures more numerous and more flourishing, and its trade more extensive, we may be assured that its capital must have increased during the interval between those two periods, and that more must have been added to it by the good conduct of some, than had been taken from it either by the private misconduct of others or by the public extravagance of government. But we shall find this to

THE WEALTH OF NATIONS

have been the case of almost all nations, in all tolerably quiet and peaceable times, even of those who have not enjoyed the most prudent and parsimonious governments. To form a right judgement of it, indeed, we must compare the state of the country at periods somewhat distant from one another. The progress is frequently so gradual that, at near periods, the improvement is not only not sensible, but from the declension either of certain branches of industry, or of certain districts of the country, things which sometimes happen though the country in general be in great prosperity, there frequently arises a suspicion that the riches and industry of the whole are decaying.

The annual produce of the land and labour of England, for example, is certainly much greater than it was, a little more than a century ago, at the restoration of Charles II. Though, at present, few people, I believe, doubt of this, yet during this period, five years have seldom passed away in which some book or pamphlet has not been published, written, too, with such abilities as to gain some authority with the public, and pretending to demonstrate that the wealth of the nation was fast declining, that the country was depopulated, agriculture neglected, manufactures decaying, and trade undone. Nor have these publications been all party pamphlets, the wretched offspring of falsehood and venality. Many of them have been written by very candid and very intelligent people, who wrote nothing but what they believed, and for no other reason but because they believed it.

The annual produce of the land and labour of England, again, was certainly much greater at the restoration, than we can suppose it to have been about an hundred years before, at the accession of Elizabeth. At this period, too, we have all reason to believe, the country was much more advanced in improvement than it had been about a century before, towards the close of the dissensions between the houses of York and Lancaster. Even then it was, probably, in a better condition than it had been at the Norman conquest, and at the Norman conquest than during the confusion of the Saxon Heptarchy. Even at this early period, it was certainly a more improved country than at the invasion of Julius Caesar, when its inhabitants were nearly in the same state with the savages in North America.

In each of those periods, however, there was not only much private and public profusion, many expensive and unnecessary wars, great perversion of the annual produce from maintaining productive to maintaining unproductive hands; but sometimes, in the confusion of civil discord, such absolute waste and destruction of stock, as much be supposed, not only to retard, as it certainly did the natural accumulation of riches, but to have left the country, at the end of the period, poorer than at the beginning. Thus, in the happiest and most fortunate period of them all, that which has passed since the restoration, how many disorders and misfortunes have occurred, which, could they have been foreseen, not only the impoverishment, but the total ruin of the country would have been expected from them? The fire and the plague of London, the two Dutch wars, the disorders of the revolution, the war in Ireland, the four expensive French wars of 1688, 1702, 1742, and 1756, together with the two rebellions of 1715 and 1745. In the course of the four French wars, the nation has contracted more than a hundred and forty-five millions of debt, over and above all the other extraordinary annual expense which they occasioned, so that the whole cannot be computed at less than two hundred millions. So great a share of the annual produce of the land and labour of the country has, since the revolution, been employed upon different occasions in maintaining an extraordinary number of unproductive hands. But had not those wars given this particular direction to so large a capital, the greater part of it would naturally have been employed in maintaining productive hands, whose labour would have replaced, with a profit, the whole value of their consumption. The value of the annual produce of the land and labour of the country would have been considerably increased by it every year, and every year's increase would have augmented still more that of the following year. More houses would have been built, more lands would have been improved, and those which had been improved before would have been better cultivated, more manufactures would have been established, and those which had been established before would have been more extended; and to what height the real wealth and revenue of the country might, by this time, have been raised, it is not perhaps very easy even to imagine.

But though the profusion of government must, undoubtedly, have retarded the natural progress of England towards wealth and improvement, it has not been able to stop it. The annual produce of its land and labour is, undoubtedly, much greater at present than it was either at the restoration or at the revolution. The capital, therefore, annually employed in cultivating this land, and in maintaining this labour, must likewise be much greater. In the midst of all the exactions of government, this capital has been silently and gradually accumulated by the private frugality and good conduct of individuals, by their universal, continual, and uninterrupted effort to better their own condition. It is this effort, protected by law and allowed by liberty to exert itself in the manner that is most advantageous, which has maintained the progress of England towards opulence and improvement in almost all former times, and which, it is to be hoped, will do so in all future times. England, however, as it has never been blessed with a very parsimonious government, so parsimony has at no time been the characteristical virtue of its inhabitants. It is the highest impertinence and presumption, therefore, in kings and ministers, to pretend to watch over the economy of private people, and to restrain their expense, either by sumptuary laws, or by prohibiting the importation of foreign luxuries. They are themselves always, and without any exception, the greatest spendthrifts in the society. Let them look well after their own expense, and they may safely trust private people with theirs. If their own extravagance does not ruin the state, that of their subjects never will.

As frugality increases and prodigality diminishes the public capital, so the conduct of those whose expense just equals their revenue, without either accumulating or encroaching, neither increases nor diminishes it. Some modes of expense, however, seem to contribute more to the growth of public opulence than others.

The revenue of an individual may be spent either in things which are consumed immediately, and in which one day's expense can neither alleviate nor support that of another, or it may be spent in things more durable, which can therefore be accumulated, and in which every day's expense may, as he chooses, either alleviate or support and heighten the effect of that of the following day. A man of fortune, for example, may either spend his revenue in a profuse and sumptuous table, and in maintaining a great number of menial servants, and a multitude of dogs and horses; or contenting himself with a frugal table and few attendants, he may lay out the greater part of it in adorning his house or his country villa, in useful or ornamental buildings, in useful or ornamental furniture, in collecting books, statues, pictures; or in things more frivolous, jewels, baubles, ingenious trinkets of different kinds; or, what is most trifling of all, in amassing a great wardrobe of fine clothes, like the favourite and minister of a great prince who died a few years ago. Were two men of equal fortune to spend their revenue, the one chiefly in the one way, the other in the other, the magnificence of the person whose expense had been chiefly in durable commodities, would be continually increasing, every day's expense contributing something to support and heighten the effect of that of the following day: that of the other, on the contrary, would be no greater at the end of the period than at the beginning. The former, too, would, at the end of the period, be the richer man of the two. He would have a stock of goods of some kind or other, which, though it might not be worth all that it cost, would always be worth something. No trace or vestige of the expense of the latter would remain, and the effects of ten or twenty years profusion would be as completely annihilated as if they had never existed.

As the one mode of expense is more favourable than the other to the opulence of an individual, so is it likewise to that of a nation. The houses, the furniture, the clothing of the rich, in a little time, become useful to the inferior and middling ranks of people. They are able to purchase them when their superiors grow weary of them, and the general accommodation of the whole people is thus gradually improved, when this mode of expense becomes universal among men of fortune. In countries which have long been rich, you will frequently find the inferior ranks of people in possession both of houses and furniture perfectly good and entire, but of which neither the one could have been built, nor the other have been made for their use. What was formerly a seat of the family of Seymour is now an inn upon the Bath road. The marriage-bed of James the First of Great

Britain, which his queen brought with her from Denmark as a present fit for a sovereign to make to a sovereign, was, a few years ago, the ornament at an alehouse at Dunfermline. In some ancient cities, which either have been long stationary, or have gone somewhat to decay, you will sometimes scarce find a single house which could have been built for its present inhabitants. If you go into those houses too, you will frequently find many excellent, though antiquated pieces of furniture, which are still very fit for use, and which could as little have been made for them. Noble palaces, magnificent villas, great collections of books, statues, pictures, and other curiosities, are frequently both an ornament and an honour, not only to the neighbourhood, but to the whole country to which they belong. Versailles is an ornament and an honour to France, Stowe and Wilton to England. Italy still continues to command some sort of veneration by the number of monuments of this kind which it possesses, though the wealth which produced them has decayed, and though the genius which planned them seems to be extinguished, perhaps from not having the same employment.

The expense too, which is laid out in durable commodities, is favourable, not only to accumulation, but to frugality. If a person should at any time exceed in it, he can easily reform without exposing himself to the censure of the public. To reduce very much the number of his servants, to reform his table from great profusion to great frugality, to lay down his equipage after he has once set it up, are changes which cannot escape the observation of his neighbours, and which are supposed to imply some acknowledgment of preceding bad conduct. Few, therefore, of those who have once been so unfortunate as to launch out too far into this sort of expense, have afterwards the courage to reform, till ruin and bankruptcy oblige them. But if a person has, at any time, been at too great an expense in building, in furniture, in books or pictures, no imprudence can be inferred from his changing his conduct. These are things in which further expense is frequently rendered unnecessary by former expense; and when a person stops short, he appears to do so, not because he has exceeded his fortune, but because he has satisfied his fancy.

The expense, besides, that is laid out in durable commodities gives maintenance, commonly, to a greater number of people than that which is employed in the most profuse hospitality. Of two or three hundredweight of provisions, which may sometimes be served up at a great festival, one-half, perhaps, is thrown to the dunghill, and there is always a great deal wasted and abused. But if the expense of this entertainment had been employed in setting to work masons, carpenters, upholsterers, mechanics, etc., a quantity of provisions, of equal value, would have been distributed among a still greater number of people who would have bought them in pennyworths and pound weights, and not have lost or thrown away a single ounce of them. In the one way, besides, this expense maintains productive, in the other unproductive hands. In the one way, therefore, it increases, in the other, it does not increase, the exchangeable value of the annual produce of the land and labour of the country.

I would not, however, by all this be understood to mean that the one species of expense always betokens a more liberal or generous spirit than the other. When a man of fortune spends his revenue chiefly in hospitality, he shares the greater part of it with his friends and companions; but when he employs it in purchasing such durable commodities, he often spends the whole upon his own person, and gives nothing to anybody without an equivalent. The latter species of expense, therefore, especially when directed towards frivolous objects, the little ornaments of dress and furniture, jewels, trinkets, gewgaws, frequently indicates, not only a trifling, but a base and selfish disposition. All that I mean is, that the one sort of expense, as it always occasions some accumulation of valuable commodities, as it is more favourable to private frugality, and, consequently, to the increase of the public capital, and as it maintains productive, rather than unproductive hands, conduces more than the other to the growth of public opulence.

CHAPTER IV

OF STOCK LENT AT INTEREST

THE stock which is lent at interest is always considered as a capital by the lender. He expects that in due time it is to be restored to him, and that in the meantime the borrower is to pay him a certain annual rent for the use of it. The borrower may use it either as a capital, or as a stock reserved for immediate consumption. If he uses it as capital, he employs it in the maintenance of productive labourers, who reproduce the value with a profit. He can, in this case, both restore the capital and pay the interest without alienating or encroaching upon any other source of revenue. If he uses it as a stock reserved for immediate consumption, he acts the part of a prodigal, and dissipates in the maintenance of the idle what was destined for the support of the industrious. He can, in this case, neither restore the capital nor pay the interest without either alienating or encroaching upon some other source of revenue, such as the property or the rent of land.

The stock which is lent at interest is, no doubt, occasionally employed in both these ways, but in the former much more frequently than in the latter. The man who borrows in order to spend will soon be ruined, and he who lends to him will generally have occasion to repent of his folly. To borrow or to lend for such a purpose, therefore, is in all cases, where gross usury is out of the question, contrary to the interest of both parties; and though it no doubt happens sometimes that people do both the one and the other; yet, from the regard that all men have for their own interest, we may be assured that it cannot happen so very frequently as we are sometimes apt to imagine. Ask any rich man of common prudence to which of the two sorts of people he has lent the greater part of his stock, to those who, he thinks, will employ it profitably, or to those who will spend it idly, and he will laugh at you for proposing the question. Even among borrowers, therefore, not the people in the world most famous for frugality, the number of the frugal and

STOCK LENT AT INTEREST

industrious surpasses considerably that of the prodigal and idle.

The only people to whom stock is commonly lent, without their being expected to make any very profitable use of it, are country gentlemen who borrow upon mortgage. Even they scarce ever borrow merely to spend. What they borrow, one may say, is commonly spent before they borrow it. They have generally consumed so great a quantity of goods, advanced to them upon credit by shopkeepers and tradesmen, that they find it necessary to borrow at interest in order to pay the debt. The capital borrowed replaces the capitals of those shopkeepers and tradesmen, which the country gentlemen could not have replaced from the rents of their estates. It is not properly borrowed in order to be spent, but in order to replace a capital which had been spent before.

Almost all loans at interest are made in money, either of paper, or of gold and silver. But what the borrower really wants, and what the lender really supplies him with, is not the money, but the money's worth, or the goods which it can purchase. If he wants it as a stock for immediate consumption, it is those goods only which he can place in that stock. If he wants it as a capital for employing industry, it is from those goods only that the industrious can be furnished with the tools, materials, and maintenance necessary for carrying on their work. By means of the loan, the lender, as it were, assigns to the borrower his right to a certain portion of the annual produce of the land and labour of the country, to be employed as the borrower pleases.

The quantity of stock, therefore, or, as it is commonly expressed, of money which can be lent at interest in any country, is not regulated by the value of the money, whether paper or in coin, which serves as the instrument of the different loans made in that country, but by the value of that part of the annual produce which, as soon as it comes either from the ground, or from the hands of the productive labourers, is destined not only for replacing a capital, but such a capital as the owner does not care to be at the trouble of employing himself. As such capitals are commonly lent out and paid back in money, they constitute what is called the monied interest. It is distinct, not only from the landed, but from the trading and manufacturing interests, as in these last the owners themselves employ their own capitals. Even in the monied interest, however, the money is, as it were, but the deed of assignment, which conveys from one hand to another those capitals which the owners do not care to employ themselves. Those capitals may be greater in almost any proportion than the amount of the money which serves as the instrument of their conveyance; the same pieces of money succesively serving for many different loans, as well as for many different purchases. A, for example, lends to W a thousand pounds, with which W immediately purchases of B a thousand pounds' worth of goods. B having no occasion for the money himself, lends the identical pieces to X, with which X immediately purchases of C another thousand pounds' worth of goods. C in the same manner, and for the same reason, lends them to Y, who again purchases goods with them of D. In this manner the same pieces, either of coin or of paper, may, in the course of a few days, serve as the instrument of three different loans, and of three different purchases, each of which is, in value, equal to the whole amount of those pieces. What the three monied men A, B, and C assign to the three borrowers, W, X, Y, is the power of making those purchases. In this power consist both the value and the use of the loans. The stock lent by the three monied men is equal to the value of the goods which can be purchased with it, and is three times greater than that of the money with which the purchases are made. Those loans, however, may be all perfectly well secured, the goods purchased by the different debtors being so employed as, in due time, to bring back, with a profit, an equal value either of coin or of paper. And as the same pieces of money can thus serve as the instrument of different loans to three, or for the same reason, to thirty times their value, so they may likewise successively serve as the instrument of repayment.

A capital lent at interest may, in this manner, be considered as an assignment from the lender to the borrowers of a certain considerable portion of the annual produce; upon condition that the borrower in return shall, during the continuance of the loan, annually assign to the lender a smaller portion, called the interest; and at the end of it a portion equally considerable with that which had originally been asigned to him, called the re-payment. Though money, either coin or paper, serves generally as the deed of assignment both to the smaller and to the more considerable portion, it is itself altogether different from what is assigned by it.

In proportion as that share of the annual produce which, as soon as it comes either from the ground, or from the hands of the productive labourers, is destined for replacing a capital, increases in any country, what is called the monied interest naturally increases with it. The increase of those particular capitals from which the owners wish to derive a revenue, without being at the trouble of employing them themselves, naturally accompanies the general increase of capitals; or, in other words, as stock increases, the quantity of stock to be lent at interest grows gradually greater and greater.

As the quantity of stock to be lent at interest increases, the interest, or the price which must be paid for the use of that stock, necessarily diminishes, not only from those general causes which make the market price of things commonly diminish as their quantity increases, but from other causes which are peculiar to this particular case. As capitals increase in any country, the profits which can be made by employing them necessarily diminish. It becomes gradually more and more difficult to find within the country a profitable method of employing any new capital. There arises in consequence a competition between different capitals, the owner of one endeavouring to get possession of that employment which is occupied by another. But upon most occasions he can hope to justle that other out of this employment by no other means but by dealing upon more reasonable terms. He must not only sell what he deals in somewhat cheaper, but in order to get it to sell, he must sometimes, too, buy it dearer. The demand for productive labour, by the increase of the funds which are destined for maintaining it, grows every day greater and greater. Labourers easily find employment, but the owners of capitals find it difficult to get labourers to employ. Their competition raises the wages of labour and sinks the profits of stock. But when the profits which can be made by the use of a capital are in this manner diminished, as it were, at both ends, the price which can be paid for the use of it, that is, the rate of interest, must necessarily be diminished with them.

Mr Locke, Mr Law, and Mr Montesquieu, as well as many other writers, seem to have imagined that the increase of the quantity of gold and silver, in consequence of the discovery of the Spanish West Indies, was the real cause of the lowering of the rate of interest through the greater part of Europe. Those metals, they say, having become of less value themselves, the use of any particular portion of them necessarily became of less value too, and consequently the price which could be paid for it. This notion, which at first sight seems so plausible, has been so fully exposed by Mr Hume that it is, perhaps, unnecessary to say anything more about it. The following very short and plain argument, however, may serve to explain more distinctly the fallacy which seems to have misled those gentlemen.

Before the discovery of the Spanish West Indies, ten per cent seems to have been the common rate of interest through the greater part of Europe. It has since that time in different countries sunk to six, five, four, and three per cent. Let us suppose that in every particular country the value of silver has sunk precisely in the same proportion as the rate of interest; and that in those countries, for example, where interest has been reduced from ten to five per cent, the same quantity of silver can now purchase just half the quantity of goods which it could have purchased before. This supposition will not, I believe, be found anywhere agreeable to the truth, but it is the most favourable to the opinion which we are going to examine; and even upon this supposition it is utterly impossible that the lowering of the value of silver could have the smallest tendency to lower the rate of interest. If a hundred pounds are in those countries now of no more value than fifty pounds were then, ten pounds must now be of no more value than five pounds were then. Whatever were the causes which lowered the value of the capital, the same must necessarily have lowered that of the interest, and exactly in the same proportion. The proportion between the value of the capital and that of the interest must have remained the same, though the rate had never been altered. By altering the rate, on the contrary, the proportion between those two values is necessarily altered. If a hundred pounds now are worth no more than

STOCK LENT AT INTEREST

fifty were then, five pounds now can be worth no more than
two pounds ten shillings were then. By reducing the rate of
interest, therefore, from ten to five per cent, we give for the use
of a capital, which is supposed to be equal to one-half of its
former value, an interest which is equal to one-fourth only of
the value of the former interest.

Any increase in the quantity of silver, while that of the commodities circulated by means of it remained the same, could
have no other effect than to diminish the value of that metal.
The nominal value of all sorts of goods would be greater, but
their real value would be precisely the same as before. They
would be exchanged for a greater number of pieces of silver;
but the quantity of labour which they could command, the
number of people whom they could maintain and employ,
would be precisely the same. The capital of the country would
be the same, though a greater number of pieces might be requisite for conveying any equal portion of it from one hand to
another. The deeds of assignment, like the conveyances of a
verbose attorney would be more cumbersome, but the thing
assigned would be precisely the same as before, and could produce only the same effects. The funds for maintaining productive labour being the same, the demand for it would be the
same. Its price or wages, therefore, though nominally greater,
would really be the same. They would be paid in a greater
number of pieces of silver; but they would purchase only the
same quantity of goods. The profits of stock would be the same
both nominally and really. The wages of labour are commonly
computed by the quantity of silver which is paid to the labourer.
When that is increased, therefore, his wages appear to be increased, though they may sometimes be no greater than before.
But the profits of stock are not computed by the number of
pieces of silver with which they are paid, but by the proportion
which those pieces bear to the whole capital employed. Thus in
a particular country five shillings a week are said to be the
common wages of labour, and ten per cent the common profits
of stock. But the whole capital of the country being the same
as before, the competition between the different capitals of
individuals into which it was divided would likewise be the
same. They would all trade with the same advantages and dis-

THE WEALTH OF NATIONS

advantages. The common proportion between capital and profit, therefore, would be the same, and consequently the common interest of money; what can commonly be given for the use of money being necessarily regulated by what can commonly be made by the use of it.

Any increase in the quantity of commodities annually circulated within the country, while that of the money which circulated them remained the same, would, on the contrary, produce many other important effects, besides that of raising the value of the money. The capital of the country, though it might nominally be the same, would really be augmented. It might continue to be expressed by the same quantity of money, but it would command a greater quantity of labour. The quantity of productive labour which it could maintain and employ would be increased, and consequently the demand for that labour. Its wages would naturally rise with the demand, and yet might appear to sink. They might be paid with a smaller quantity of money, but that smaller quantity might purchase a greater quantity of goods than a greater had done before. The profits of stock would be diminished both really and in appearance. The whole capital of the country being augmented, the competition between the different capitals of which it was composed would naturally be augmented along with it. The owners of those particular capitals would be obliged to content themselves with a smaller proportion of the produce of that labour which their respective capitals employed. The interest of money, keeping pace always with the profits of stock, might, in this manner, be greatly diminished, though the value of money, or the quantity of goods which any particular sum could purchase, was greatly augmented.

In some countries the interest of money has been prohibited by law. But as something can everywhere be made by the use of money, something ought everywhere to be paid for the use of it. This regulation, instead of preventing, has been found from experience to increase the evil of usury; the debtor being obliged to pay, not only for the use of the money, but for the risk which his creditor runs by accepting a compensation for that use. He is obliged, if one may say so, to insure his creditor from the penalties of usury.

In countries where interest is permitted, the law, in order to prevent the extortion of usury, generally fixes the highest rate which can be taken without incurring a penalty. This rate ought always to be somewhat above the lowest market price, or the price which is commonly paid for the use of money by those who can give the most undoubted security. If this legal rate should be fixed below the lowest market rate, the effects of this fixation must be nearly the same as those of a total prohibition of interest. The creditor will not lend his money for less than the use of it is worth, and the debtor must pay him for the risk which he runs by accepting the full value of that use. If it is fixed precisely at the lowest market price, it ruins with honest people, who respect the laws of their country, the credit of all those who cannot give the very best security, and obliges them to have recourse to exorbitant usurers. In a country, such as Great Britain, where money is lent to government at three per cent and to private people upon a good security at four and four and a half, the present legal rate, five per cent, is perhaps as proper as any.

The legal rate, it is to be observed, though it ought to be somewhat above, ought not to be much above the lowest market rate. If the legal rate of interest in Great Britain, for example, was fixed so high as eight or ten per cent, the greater part of the money which was to be lent would be lent to prodigals and projectors, who alone would be willing to give this high interest. Sober people, who will give for the use of money no more than a part of what they are likely to make by the use of it, would not venture into the competition. A great part of the capital of the country would thus be kept out of the hands which were most likely to make a profitable and advantageous use of it, and thrown into those which were most likely to waste and destroy it. Where the legal rate of interest, on the contrary, is fixed but a very little above the lowest market rate, sober people are universally preferred, as borrowers, to prodigals and projectors. The person who lends money gets nearly as much interest from the former as he dares to take from the latter, and his money is much safer in the hands of the one set of people than in those of the other. A great part of the capital of the country is thus thrown into the hands in which it is most likely to be employed with advantage.

No law can reduce the common rate of interest below the lowest ordinary market rate at the time when that law is made. Notwithstanding the edict of 1766, by which the French king attempted to reduce the rate of interest from five to four per cent, money continued to be lent in France at five per cent, the law being evaded in several different ways.

The ordinary market price of land, it is to be observed, depends everywhere upon the ordinary market rate of interest. The person who has a capital from which he wishes to derive a revenue, without taking the trouble to employ it himself, deliberates whether he should buy land with it or lend it out at interest. The superior security of land, together with some other advantages which almost everywhere attend upon this species of property, will generally dispose him to content himself with a smaller revenue from land than what he might have by lending out his money at interest. These advantages are sufficient to compensate a certain difference of revenue; but they will compensate a certain difference only; and if the rent of land should fall short of the interest of money by a greater difference, nobody would buy land, which would soon reduce its ordinary price. On the contrary, if the advantages should much more than compensate the difference, everybody would buy land, which again would soon raise its ordinary price. When interest was at ten per cent, land was commonly sold for ten and twelve years' purchase. As interest sunk to six, five, and four per cent, the price of land rose to twenty, five-and-twenty, and thirty years' purchase. The market rate of interest is higher in France than in England; and the common price of land is lower. In England it commonly sells at thirty, in France at twenty years' purchase.

CHAPTER V

OF THE DIFFERENT EMPLOYMENT OF CAPITALS

THOUGH all capitals are destined for the maintenance of productive labour only, yet the quantity of that labour which equal capitals are capable of putting into motion varies extremely according to the diversity of their employment; as does likewise the value which that employment adds to the annual produce of the land and labour of the country.

A capital may be employed in four different ways: either, first, in procuring the rude produce annually required for the use and consumption of the society; or, secondly, in manufacturing and preparing that rude produce for immediate use and consumption; or, thirdly, in transporting either the rude or manufactured produce from the places where they abound to those where they are wanted; or, lastly, in dividing particular portions of either into such small parcels as suit the occasional demands of those who want them. In the first way are employed the capitals of all those who undertake the improvement or cultivation of lands, mines, or fisheries; in the second, those of all master manufacturers; in the third, those of all wholesale merchants; and in the fourth, those of all retailers. It is difficult to conceive that a capital should be employed in any way which may not be classed under some one or other of those four.

Each of those four methods of employing a capital is essentially necessary either to the existence or extension of the other three, or to the general conveniency of the society.

Unless a capital was employed in furnishing rude produce to a certain degree of abundance, neither manufactures nor trade of any kind could exist.

Unless a capital was employed in manufacturing that part of the rude produce which requires a good deal of preparation before it can be fit for use and consumption, it either would never be produced, because there could be no demand for it; or if it was produced spontaneously, it would be of no value in exchange, and could add nothing to the wealth of the society.

Unless a capital was employed in transporting either the rude or manufactured produce from the places where it abounds to those where it is wanted, no more of either could be produced than was necessary for the consumption of the neighbourhood. The capital of the merchant exchanges the surplus produce of one place for that of another, and thus encourages the industry and increases the enjoyments of both.

Unless a capital was employed in breaking and dividing certain portions either of the rude or manufactured produce into such small parcels as suit the occasional demands of those who want them, every man would be obliged to purchase a greater quantity of the goods he wanted than his immediate occasions required. If there was no such trade as a butcher, for example, every man would be obliged to purchase a whole ox or a whole sheep at a time. This would generally be inconvenient to the rich, and much more so to the poor. If a poor workman was obliged to purchase a month's or six months' provisions at a time, a great part of the stock which he employs as a capital in the instruments of his trade, or in the furniture of his shop, and which yields him a revenue, he would be forced to place in that part of his stock which is reserved for immediate consumption, and which yields him no revenue. Nothing can be more convenient for such a person than to be able to purchase his subsistence from day to day, or even from hour to hour, as he wants it. He is thereby enabled to employ almost his whole stock as a capital. He is thus enabled to furnish work to a greater value, and the profit, which he makes by it in this way, much more than compensates the additional price which the profit of the retailer imposes upon the goods. The prejudices of some political writers against shopkeepers and tradesmen are altogether without foundation. So far is it from being necessary either to tax them or to restrict their numbers that they can never be multiplied so as to hurt the public, though they may so as to hurt one another. The quantity of grocery goods, for example, which can be sold in a particular town is limited by the demand of that town and its neighbourhood. The capital, therefore, which can be employed in the grocery trade cannot exceed what is sufficient to purchase that quantity. If this capital is divided between two different grocers, their competition will tend to make both of them sell cheaper than if it were in the hands of one only; and if it were divided among twenty, their competition would be just so much the greater, and the chance of their combining together, in order to raise the price, just so much the less. Their competition might perhaps ruin some of themselves; but to take care of this is the business of the parties concerned, and it may safely be trusted to their discretion. It can never hurt either the consumer or the producer; on the contrary, it must tend to make the retailers both sell cheaper and buy dearer, than if the whole trade was monopolized by one or two persons. Some of them, perhaps, may sometimes decoy a weak customer to buy what he has no occasion for. This evil, however, is of too little importance to deserve the public attention, nor would it necessarily be prevented by restricting their number. It is not the multitude of ale-houses, to give the most suspicious example, that occasions a general disposition to drunkenness among the common people; but that disposition arising from other causes necessarily gives employment to a multitude of ale-houses.

The persons whose capitals are employed in any of those four ways are themselves productive labourers. Their labour, when properly directed, fixes and realizes itself in the subject or vendible commodity upon which it is bestowed, and generally adds to its price the value at least of their own maintenance and consumption. The profits of the farmer, of the manufacturer, of the merchant, and retailer, are all drawn from the price of the goods which the two first produce, and the two last buy and sell. Equal capitals, however, employed in each of those four different ways, will immediately put into motion very different quantities of productive labour, and augment, too, in very different proportions the value of the annual produce of the land and labour of the society to which they belong.

The capital of the retailer replaces, together with its profits, that of the merchant of whom he purchases goods, and thereby enables him to continue his business. The retailer himself is the only productive labourer whom it immediately employs. In his profits consists the whole value which its employment adds to the annual produce of the land and labour of the society.

The capital of the wholesale merchant replaces, together with their profits, the capitals of the farmers and manufacturers of whom he purchases the rude and manufactured produce which he deals in, and thereby enables them to continue their respective trades. It is by this service chiefly that he contributes indirectly to support the productive labour of the society, and to increase the value of its annual produce. His capital employs, too, the sailors and carriers who transport his goods from one place to another, and it augments the price of those goods by the value, not only of his profits, but of their wages. This is all the productive labour which it immediately puts into motion, and all the value which it immediately adds to the annual produce. Its operation in both these respects is a good deal superior to that of the capital of the retailer.

Part of the capital of the master manufacturer is employed as a fixed capital in the instruments of his trade, and replaces, together with its profits, that of some other artificer of whom he purchases them. Part of his circulating capital is employed in purchasing materials, and replaces, with their profits, the capitals of the farmers and miners of whom he purchases them. But a great part of it is always, either annually, or in a much shorter period, distributed among the different workmen whom he employs. It augments the value of those materials by their wages, and by their masters' profits upon the whole stock of wages, materials, and instruments of trade employed in the business. It puts immediately into motion, therefore, a much greater quantity of productive labour, and adds a much greater value to the annual produce of the land and labour of the society, than an equal capital in the hands of any wholesale merchant.

No equal capital puts into motion a greater quantity of productive labour than that of the farmer. Not only his labouring servants, but his labouring cattle, are productive labourers. In agriculture, too, nature labours along with man; and though her labour costs no expense, its produce has its value, as well as that of the most expensive workmen. The most important operations of agriculture seem intended not so much to increase, though they do that too, as to direct the fertility of nature towards the production of the plants most profitable to man. A field overgrown with briars and brambles may frequently produce as great a quantity of vegetables as the best cultivated vineyard or corn field. Planting and tillage frequently regulate more than they animate the active fertility of nature; and after all their labour, a great part of the work always remains to be done by her. The labourers and labouring cattle, therefore, employed in agriculture, not only occasion, like the workmen in manufacturers, the reproduction of a value equal to their own consumption, or to the capital which employs them, together with its owners' profits; but of a much greater value. Over and above the capital of the farmer and all its profits, they regularly occasion the reproduction of the rent of the landlord. This rent may be considered as the produce of those powers of nature, the use of which the landlord lends to the farmer. It is greater or smaller according to the supposed extent of those powers, or in other words, according to the supposed natural or improved fertility of the land. It is the work of nature which remains after deducting or compensating everything which can be regarded as the work of man. It is seldom less than a fourth, and frequently more than a third of the whole produce. No equal quantity of productive labour employed in manufactures can ever occasion so great a reproduction. In them nature does nothing; man does all; and the reproduction must always be in proportion to the strength of the agents that occasion it. The capital employed in agriculture, therefore, not only puts into motion a greater quantity of productive labour than any equal capital employed in manufactures, but in proportion, too, to the quantity of productive labour which it employs, it adds a much greater value to the annual produce of the land and labour of the country, to the real wealth and revenue of its inhabitants. Of all the ways in which a capital can be employed, it is by far the most advantageous to the society.

The capitals employed in the agriculture and in the retail trade of any society must always reside within that society. Their employment is confined almost to a precise spot, to the farm and to the shop of the retailer. They must generally, too, though there are some exceptions to this, belong to resident members of the society.

The capital of a wholesale merchant, on the contrary, seems to have no fixed or necessary residence anywhere, but may

wander about from place to place, according as it can either buy
cheap or sell dear.

The capital of the manufacturer must no doubt reside where
the manufacture is carried on; but where this shall be is not
always necessarily determined. It may frequently be at a great
distance both from the place where the materials grow, and
from that where the complete manufacture is consumed. Lyons
is very distant both from the places which afford the materials
of its manufactures, and from those which consume them. The
people of fashion in Sicily are clothed in silks made in other
countries, from the materials which their own produces. Part of
the wool of Spain is manufactured in Great Britain, and some
part of that cloth is afterwards sent back to Spain.

Whether the merchant whose capital exports the surplus produce of any society be a native or a foreigner is of very little
importance. If he is a foreigner, the number of their productive
labourers is necessarily less than if he had been a native by one
man only, and the value of their annual produce by the profits
of that one man. The sailors or carriers whom he employs may
still belong indifferently either to his country or to their
country, or to some third country, in the same manner as if he
had been a native. The capital of a foreigner gives a value to
their surplus produce equally with that of a native by exchanging it for something for which there is a demand at home. It as
effectually replaces the capital of the person who produces that
surplus, and as effectually enables him to continue his business;
the service by which the capital of a wholesale merchant chiefly
contributes to support the productive labour, and to augment
the value of the annual produce of the society to which he
belongs.

It is of more consequence that the capital of the manufacturer
should reside within the country. It necessarily puts into motion
a greater quantity of productive labour, and adds a greater
value to the annual produce of the land and labour of the
society. It may, however, be very useful to the country, though
it should not reside within it. The capitals of the British manufacturers who work up the flax and hemp annually imported
from the coasts of the Baltic are surely very useful to the countries which produce them. Those materials are a part of the

surplus produce of those countries which, unless it was annually exchanged for something which is in demand there, would be of no value, and would soon cease to be produced. The merchants who export it replace the capitals of the people who produce it, and thereby encourage them to continue the production; and the British manufacturers replace the capitals of those merchants.

A particular country, in the same manner as a particular person, may frequently not have capital sufficient both to improve and cultivate all its lands, to manufacture and prepare their whole rude produce for immediate use and consumption, and to transport the surplus part either of the rude or manufactured produce to those distant markets where it can be exchanged for something for which there is a demand at home. The inhabitants of many different parts of Great Britain have not capital sufficient to improve and cultivate all their lands. The wool of the southern counties of Scotland is, a great part of it, after a long land carriage through very bad roads, manufactured in Yorkshire, for want of capital to manufacture it at home. There are many little manufacturing towns in Great Britain, of which the inhabitants have not capital sufficient to transport the produce of their own industry to those distant markets where there is demand and consumption for it. If there are any merchants among them, they are properly only the agents of wealthier merchants who reside in some of the greater commercial cities.

When the capital of any country is not sufficient for all those three purposes, in proportion as a greater share of it is employed in agriculture, the greater will be the quantity of productive labour which it puts into motion within the country; as will likewise be the value which its employment adds to the annual produce of the land and labour of the society. After agriculture, the capital employed in manufactures puts into motion the greatest quantity of productive labour, and adds the greatest value to the annual produce. That which is employed in the trade of exportation has the least effect of any of the three.

The country, indeed, which has not capital sufficient for all those three purposes has not arrived at that degree of opulence for which it seems naturally destined. To attempt, however, prematurely and with an insufficient capital to do all the three, is certainly not the shortest way for a society, no more than it would be for an individual, to acquire a sufficient one. The capital of all the individuals of a nation has its limits in the same manner as that of a single individual, and is capable of executing only certain purposes. The capital of all the individuals of a nation is increased in the same manner as that of a single individual, by their continually accumulating and adding to it whatever they save out of their revenue. It is likely to increase the fastest, therefore, when it is employed in the way that affords the greatest revenue to all the inhabitants of the country, as they will thus be enabled to make the greatest savings. But the revenue of all the inhabitants of the country is necessarily in proportion to the value of the annual produce of their land and labour.

It has been the principal cause of the rapid progress of our American colonies towards wealth and greatness, that almost their whole capitals have hitherto been employed in agriculture. They have no manufactures, those household and coarser manufactures excepted which necessarily accompany the progress of agriculture, and which are the work of the women and children in every private family. The greater part both of the exportation and coasting trade of America is carried on by the capitals of merchants who reside in Great Britain. Even the stores and warehouses from which goods are retailed in some provinces, particularly in Virginia and Maryland, belong many of them to merchants who reside in the mother country, and afford one of the few instances of the retail trade of a society being carried on by the capitals of those who are not resident members of it. Were the Americans, either by combination or by any other sort of violence, to stop the importation of European manufactures, and, by thus giving a monopoly to such of their own countrymen as could manufacture the like goods, divert any considerable part of their capital into this employment, they would retard instead of accelerating the further increase in the value of their annual produce, and would obstruct instead of promoting the progress of their country towards real wealth and greatness. This would be still more the case were they to attempt, in the same manner, to monopolize to themselves their whole exportation trade.

The course of human prosperity, indeed, seems scarce ever to have been of so long continuance as to enable any great country to acquire capital sufficient for all those three purposes; unless perhaps, we give credit to the wonderful accounts of the wealth and cultivation of China, of those of ancient Egypt, and of the ancient state of Indostan. Even those three countries, the wealthiest, according to all accounts, that ever were in the world, are chiefly renowned for their superiority in agriculture and manufactures. They do not appear to have been eminent for foreign trade. The ancient Egyptians had a superstitious anti-pathy to the sea; a superstition nearly of the same kind pre-vails among the Indians; and the Chinese have never excelled in foreign commerce. The greater part of the surplus produce of all those three countries seems to have been always exported by foreigners, who gave in exchange for it something else for which they found a demand there, frequently gold and silver.

It is thus that the same capital will in any country put into motion a greater or smaller quantity of productive labour, and add a greater or smaller value to the annual produce of its land and labour, according to the different proportions in which it is employed in agriculture, manufactures, and the wholesale trade. The difference, too, is very great, according to the differ-ent sorts of wholesale trade in which any part of it is em-ployed.

All wholesale trade, all buying in order to sell again by wholesale, may be reduced to three different sorts. The home trade, the foreign trade of consumption, and the carrying trade. The home trade is employed in purchasing in one part of the same country, and selling in another, the produce of the in-dustry of that country. It comprehends both the inland and the coasting trade. The foreign trade of consumption is employed in purchasing foreign goods for home consumption. The carrying trade is employed in transacting the commerce of foreign coun-tries, or in carrying the surplus produce of one to another.

The capital which is employed in purchasing in one part of the country in order to sell in another the produce of the in-dustry of that country, generally replaces by every such opera-tion two distinct capitals that had both been employed in the agriculture or manufactures of that country, and thereby enables them to continue that employment. When it sends out from the residence of the merchant a certain value of commodities, it generally brings back in return at least an equal value of other commodities. When both are the produce of domestic industry, it necessarily replaces by every such operation two distinct capitals which had both been employed in supporting productive labour, and thereby enables them to continue that support. The capital which sends Scotch manufactures to London, and brings back English corn and manufactures to Edinburgh, necessarily replaces, by every such operation, two British capitals which had both been employed in the agriculture or manufactures of Great Britain.

The capital employed in purchasing foreign goods for home consumption, when this purchase is made with the produce of domestic industry, replaces too, by every such operation, two distinct capitals; but one of them only is employed in supporting domestic industry. The capital which sends British goods to Portugal, and brings back Portuguese goods to Great Britain, replaces by every such operation only one British capital. The other is a Portuguese one. Though the returns, therefore, of the foreign trade of consumption should be as quick as those of the home trade, the capital employed in it will give but one-half the encouragement to the industry of productive labour of the country.

But the returns of the foreign trade of consumption are very seldom so quick as those of the home trade. The returns of the home trade generally come in before the end of the year, and sometimes three or four times in the year. The returns of the foreign trade of consumption seldom come in before the end of the year, and sometimes not till after two or three years. A capital, therefore, employed in the home trade will sometimes make twelve operations, or be sent out and returned twelve times, before a capital employed in the foreign trade of consumption has made one. If the capitals are equal, therefore, the one will give four-and-twenty times more encouragement and support to the industry of the country than the other.

The foreign goods for home consumption may sometimes be purchased, not with the produce of domestic industry, but with some other foreign goods. These last, however, must have been purchased either immediately with the produce of domestic industry, or with something else that had been purchased with it; for, the case of war and conquest excepted, foreign goods can ever be acquired but in exchange for something that had been produced at home, either immediately, or after two or more different exchanges. The effects, therefore, of a capital employed in such a round-about foreign trade of consumption, are, in every respect, the same as those of one employed in the most direct trade of the same kind, except that the final returns are likely to be still more distant, as they must depend upon the returns of two or three distinct foreign trades. If the flax and hemp of Riga are purchased with the tobacco of Virginia, which had been purchased with British manufactures, the merchant must wait for the returns of two distinct foreign trades before he can employ the same capital in re-purchasing a like quantity of British manufactures. If the tobacco of Virginia had been purchased, not with British manufactures, but with the sugar and rum of Jamaica which had been purchased with those manufactures, he must wait for the returns of three. If those two or three distinct foreign trades should happen to be carried on by two or three distinct merchants, of whom the second buys the goods imported by the first, and the third buys those imported by the second, in order to export them again, each merchant indeed will in this case receive the returns of his own capital more quickly; but the final returns of the whole capital employed in the trade will be just as slow as ever. Whether the whole capital employed in such a round-about trade belong to one merchant or to three can make no difference with regard to the country, though it may with regard to the particular merchants. Three times a greater capital must in both cases be employed, in order to exchange a certain value of British manufactures for a certain quantity of flax and hemp, than would have been necessary had the manufactures and the flax and hemp been directly exchanged for one another. The whole capital employed, therefore, in such a round-about foreign trade of consumption will generally give less encouragement and support to the productive labour of the country, than an equal capital employed in a more direct trade of the same kind.

Whatever be the foreign commodity with which the foreign

goods for home consumption are purchased, it can occasion no essential difference either in the nature of the trade, or in the encouragement and support which it can give to the productive labour of the country from which it is carried on. If they are purchased with the gold of Brazil, for example, or with the silver of Peru, this gold and silver, like the tobacco of Virginia, must have been purchased with something that either was the produce of the industry of the country, or that had been purchased with something else that was so. So far, therefore, as the productive labour of the country is concerned, the foreign trade of consumption which is carried on by means of gold and silver has all the advantages and all the inconveniences of any other equally round-about foreign trade of consumption, and will replace just as fast or just as slow the capital which is immediately employed in supporting that productive labour. It seems even to have one advantage over any other equally round-about foreign trade. The transportation of those metals from one place to another, on account of their small bulk and great value, is less expensive than that of almost any other foreign goods of equal value. Their freight is much less, and their insurance not greater; and no goods, besides, are less liable to suffer by the carriage. An equal quantity of foreign goods, therefore, may frequently be purchased with a smaller quantity of the produce of domestic industry, by the intervention of gold and silver, than by that of any other foreign goods. The demand of the country may frequently, in this manner, be supplied more completely and at a smaller expense than in any other. Whether, by the continual exportation of those metals, a trade of this kind is likely to impoverish the country from which it is carried on, in any other way, I shall have occasion to examine at great length hereafter.

That part of the capital of any country which is employed in the carrying trade is altogether withdrawn from supporting the productive labour of that particular country, to support that of some foreign countries. Though it may replace by every operation two distinct capitals, yet neither of them belongs to that particular country. The capital of the Dutch merchant, which carries the corn of Poland to Portugal, and brings back the fruits and wines of Portugal to Poland, replaces by every such operation two capitals, neither of which had been employed in supporting the productive labour of Holland; but one of them in supporting that of Poland, and the other that of Portugal. The profits only return regularly to Holland, and constitute the whole addition which this trade necessarily makes to the annual produce of the land and labour of that country. When, indeed, the carrying trade of any particular country is carried on with the ships and sailors of that country, that part of the capital employed in it which pays the freight is distributed among, and puts into motion, a certain number of productive labourers of that country. Almost all nations that have had any considerable share of the carrying trade have, in fact, carried it on in this manner. The trade itself has probably derived its name from it, the people of such countries being the carriers to other countries. It does not, however, seem essential to the nature of the trade that it should be so. A Dutch merchant may, for example, employ his capital in transacting the commerce of Poland and Portugal, by carrying part of the surplus produce of the one to the other, not in Dutch, but in British bottoms. It may be presumed that he actually does so upon some particular occasions. It is upon this account, however, that the carrying trade has been supposed peculiarly advantageous to such a country as Great Britain, of which the defence and security depend upon the number of its sailors and shipping. But the same capital may employ as many sailors and shipping, either in the foreign trade of consumption, or even in the home trade, when carried on by coasting vessels, as it could in the carrying trade. The number of sailors and shipping which any particular capital can employ does not depend upon the nature of the trade, but partly upon the bulk of the goods in proportion to their value, and partly upon the distance of the ports between which they are to be carried; chiefly upon the former of those two circumstances. The coal-trade from Newcastle to London, for example, employs more shipping than all the carrying trade of England, though the ports are at no great distance. To force, therefore, by extraordinary encouragements, a larger share of the capital of any country into the carrying trade than what would naturally go to it, will not always necessarily increase the shipping of that country.

The capital, therefore, employed in the home trade of any country will generally give encouragement and support to a greater quantity of productive labour in that country, and increase the value of its annual produce more than an equal capital employed in the foreign trade of consumption: and the capital employed in this latter trade has in both these respects a still greater advantage over an equal capital employed in the carrying trade. The riches, and so far as power depends upon riches, the power of every country, must always be in proportion to the value of its annual produce, the fund from which all taxes must ultimately be paid. But the great object of the political economy of every country is to increase the riches and power of that country. It ought, therefore, to give no preference nor superior encouragement to the foreign trade of consumption above the home trade, nor to the carrying trade above either of the other two. It ought neither to force nor to allure into either of those two channels a greater share of the capital of the country than what would naturally flow into them of its own accord.

Each of these different branches of trade, however, is not only advantageous, but necessary and unavoidable, when the course of things, without any constraint or violence, naturally introduces it.

When the produce of any particular branch of industry exceeds what the demand of the country requires, the surplus must be sent abroad and exchanged for something for which there is a demand at home. Without such exportation a part of the productive labour of the country must cease, and the value of its annual produce diminish. The land and labour of Great Britain produce generally more corn, woollens, and hardware than the demand of the home market requires. The surplus part of them, therefore, must be sent abroad, and exchanged for something for which there is a demand at home. It is only by means of such exportation that this surplus can acquire a value sufficient to compensate the labour and expense of producing it. The neighbourhood of the sea-coast, and the banks of all navigable rivers, are advantageous situations for industry, only because they facilitate the exportation and exchange of such surplus produce for something else which is more in demand there.

When the foreign goods which are thus purchased with the surplus produce of domestic industry exceed the demand of the home market, the surplus part of them must be sent abroad again and exchanged for something more in demand at home. About ninety-six thousand hogsheads of tobacco are annually purchased in Virginia and Maryland with a part of the surplus produce of British industry. But the demand of Great Britain does not require, perhaps, more than fourteen thousand. If the remaining eighty-two thousand, therefore, could not be sent abroad and exchanged for something more in demand at home, the importation of them must cease immediately, and with it the productive labour of all those inhabitants of Great Britain, who are at present employed in preparing the goods with which these eighty-two thousand hogsheads are annually purchased. Those goods, which are part of the produce of the land and labour of Great Britain, having no market at home, and being deprived of that which they had abroad, must cease to be produced. The most round-about foreign trade of consumption, therefore, may, upon some occasions, be as necessary for supporting the productive labour of the country, and the value of its annual produce, as the most direct.

When the capital stock of any country is increased to such a degree that it cannot be all employed in supplying the consumption and supporting the productive labour of that particular country, the surplus part of it naturally disgorges itself into the carrying trade, and is employed in performing the same offices to other countries. The carrying trade is the natural effect and symptom of great national wealth; but it does not seem to be the natural cause of it. Those statesmen who have been disposed to favour it with particular encouragements, seem to have mistaken the effect and symptom for the cause. Holland, in proportion to the extent of the land and the number of its inhabitants, by far the richest country in Europe, has, accordingly, the greatest share of the carrying trade of Europe. England, perhaps the second richest country of Europe, is likewise supposed to have a considerable share of it; though what commonly passes for the carrying trade of England will frequently, perhaps, be found to be of no more than a round-about foreign trade of consumption. Such are, in a great measure, the trades which carry the goods of the East and West Indies, and of America, to different European markets. Those goods are generally purchased either immediately with the produce of British industry, or with something else which had been purchased with that produce, and the final returns of those trades are generally used or consumed in Great Britain. The trade which is carried on in British bottoms between the different ports of the Mediterranean, and some trade of the same kind carried on by British merchants between the different ports of India, make, perhaps, the principal branches of what is properly the carrying trade of Great Britain.

The extent of the home trade and of the capital which can be employed in it, is necessarily limited by the value of the surplus produce of all those distant places within the country which have occasion to exchange their respective productions with one another: that of the foreign trade of consumption, by the value of the surplus produce of the whole country and of what can be purchased with it: that of the carrying trade by the value of the surplus produce of all the different countries in the world. Its possible extent, therefore, is in a manner infinite in comparison of that of the other two, and is capable of absorbing the greatest capitals.

The consideration of his own private profit is the sole motive which determines the owner of any capital to employ it either in agriculture, in manufactures, or in some particular branch of the wholesale or retail trade. The different quantities of productive labour which it may put into motion, and the different values which it may add to the annual produce of the land and labour of the society, according as it is employed in one or other of those different ways, never enter into his thoughts. In countries, therefore, where agriculture is the most profitable of all employments, and farming and improving the most direct roads to a splendid fortune, the capitals of individuals will naturally be employed in the manner most advantageous to the whole society. The profits of agriculture, however, seem to have no superiority over those of other employments in any part of Europe. Projectors, indeed, in every corner of it, have within these few years amused the public with most magnificent accounts of the profits to be made by the cultivation and improvement of land. Without entering into any particular discussion of their calculations, a very simple observation may satisfy us that the result of them must be false. We see every day the most splendid fortunes that have been acquired in the course of a single life of trade and manufactures, frequently from a very small capital, sometimes from no capital. A single instance of such a fortune acquired by agriculture in the same time, and from such a capital, has not, perhaps, occurred in Europe during the course of the present century. In all the great countries of Europe, however, much good land still remains uncultivated, and the greater part of what is cultivated is far from being improved to the degree of which it is capable. Agriculture, therefore, is almost everywhere capable of absorbing a much greater capital than has ever yet been employed in it. What circumstances in the policy of Europe have given the trades which are carried on in towns so great an advantage over that which is carried on in the country, that private persons frequently find it more for their advantage to employ their capitals in the most distant carrying trades of Asia and America, than in the improvement and cultivation of the most fertile fields in their own neighbourhood, I shall endeavour to explain at full length in the two following books.

BOOK THREE

*Of the Different Progress of Opulence in
Different Nations*

CHAPTER I

OF THE NATURAL PROGRESS OF OPULENCE

THE great commerce of every civilized society is that carried on between the inhabitants of the town and those of the country. It consists in the exchange of rude for manufactured produce, either immediately, or by the intervention of money, or of some sort of paper which represents money. The country supplies the town with the means of subsistence and the materials of manufacture. The town repays this supply by sending back a part of the manufactured produce to the inhabitants of the country. The town, in which there neither is nor can be any reproduction of substances, may very properly be said to gain its whole wealth and subsistence from the country. We must not, however, upon this account, imagine that the gain of the town is the loss of the country. The gains of both are mutual and reciprocal, and the division of labour is in this, as in all other cases, advantageous to all the different persons employed in the various occupations into which it is subdivided. The inhabitants of the country purchase of the town a greater quantity of manufactured goods, with the produce of a much smaller quantity of their own labour, than they must have employed had they attempted to prepare them themselves. The town affords a market for the surplus produce of the country, or what is over and above the maintenance of the cultivators, and it is there that the inhabitants of the country exchange it for something else which is in demand among them. The greater the number and revenue of the inhabitants of the town, the more extensive is the market which it affords to those of the country; and the more extensive that market, it is always the more advantageous to a great number. The corn which grows within a mile of the town sells there for the same price with that which comes from twenty miles distance. But the price of the latter must generally not only pay the expense of raising and bringing it to market, but afford, too, the ordinary profits of agriculture to the farmer.

The proprietors and cultivators of the country, therefore, which lies in the neighbourhood of the town, over and above the ordinary profits of agriculture, gain, in the price of what they sell, the whole value of the carriage of the like produce that is brought from more distant parts, and they save, besides, the whole value of this carriage in the price of what they buy. Compare the cultivation of the lands in the neighbourhood of any considerable town with that of those which lie at some distance from it, and you will easily satisfy yourself how much the country is benefited by the commerce of the town. Among all the absurd speculations that have been propagated concerning the balance of trade, it has never been pretended that either the country loses by its commerce with the town, or the town by that with the country which maintains it.

As subsistence is, in the nature of things, prior to conveniency and luxury, so the industry which procures the former must necessarily be prior to that which ministers to the latter. The cultivation and improvement of the country, therefore, which affords subsistence, must, necessarily, be prior to the increase of the town, which furnishes only the means of conveniency and luxury. It is the surplus produce of the country only, or what is over and above the maintenance of the cultivators, that constitutes the subsistence of the town, which can therefore increase only with the increase of this surplus produce. The town, indeed, may not always derive its whole subsistence from the country in its neighbourhood, or even from the territory to which it belongs, but from very distant countries; and this, though it forms no exception from the general rule, has occasioned considerable variations in the progress of opulence in different ages and nations.

That order of things which necessity imposes in general, though not in every particular country, is, in every particular country, promoted by the natural inclinations of man. If human institutions had never thwarted those natural inclinations, the towns could nowhere have increased beyond what the improvement and cultivation of the territory in which they were situated could support; till such time, at least, as the whole of that territory was completely cultivated and improved. Upon equal, or nearly equal profits, most men will choose to employ

their capitals rather in the improvement and cultivation of land
than either in manufactures or in foreign trade. The man who
employs his capital in land has it more under his view and
command, and his fortune is much less liable to accidents than
that of the trader, who is obliged frequently to commit it, not
only to the winds and the waves, but to the more uncertain
elements of human folly and injustice, by giving great credits in
distant countries to men with whose character and situation he
can seldom be thoroughly acquainted. The capital of the landlord, on the contrary, which is fixed in the improvement of his
land, seems to be as well secured as the nature of human affairs
can admit of. The beauty of the country besides, the pleasures of
a country life, the tranquillity of mind which it promises, and
wherever the injustice of human laws does not disturb it, the
independency which it really affords, have charms that more or
less attract everybody; and as to cultivate the ground was the
original destination of man, so in every stage of his existence he
seems to retain a predilection for this primitive employment.

Without the assistance of some artificers, indeed, the cultivation of land cannot be carried on but with great inconveniency
and continual interruption. Smiths, carpenters, wheelwrights,
and ploughwrights, masons, and bricklayers, tanners, shoemakers, and tailors, are people whose service the farmer has
frequent occasion for. Such artificers, too, stand occasionally in
need of the assistance of one another; and as their residence is
not, like that of the farmer, necessarily tied down to a precise
spot, they naturally settle in the neighbourhood of one another,
and thus form a small town or village. The butcher, the brewer,
and the baker soon join them, together with many other
artificers and retailers, necessary or useful for supplying their
occasional wants, and who contribute still further to augment
the town. The inhabitants of the town and those of the country
are mutually the servants of one another. The town is a continual fair or market, to which the inhabitants of the country
resort in order to exchange their rude for manufactured produce. It is this commerce which supplies the inhabitants of the
town both with the materials of their work, and the means of
their subsistence. The quantity of the finished work which they
sell to the inhabitants of the country necessarily regulates the

quantity of the materials and provisions which they buy.
Neither their employment nor subsistence, therefore, can augment but in proportion to the augmentation of the demand
from the country for finished work; and this demand can
augment only in proportion to the extension of improvement
and cultivation. Had human institutions, therefore, never disturbed the natural course of things, the progressive wealth and
increase of the towns would, in every political society, be conse-
quential, and in proportion to the improvement and cultivation
of the territory or country.

In our North American colonies, where uncultivated land is
still to be had upon easy terms, no manufactures for distant sale
have ever yet been established in any of their towns. When an
artificer has acquired a little more stock than is necessary for
carrying on his own business in supplying the neighbouring
country, he does not, in North America, attempt to establish
with it a manufacture for more distant sale, but employs it in the
purchase and improvement of uncultivated land. From artificer
he becomes planter, and neither the large wages nor the easy
subsistence which that country affords to artificers can bribe him
rather to work for other people than for himself. He feels that an
artificer is the servant of his customers, from whom he derives
his subsistence; but that a planter who cultivates his own land,
and derives his necessary subsistence from the labour of his own
family, is really a master, and independent of all the world.

In countries, on the contrary, where there is either no uncultivated land, or none that can be had upon easy terms, every
artificer who has acquired more stock than he can employ in
the occasional jobs of the neighbourhood endeavours to prepare
work for more distant sale. The smith erects some sort of iron,
the weaver some sort of linen or woollen manufactory. Those
different manufactures come, in process of time, to be gradually
subdivided, and thereby improved and refined in a great
variety of ways, which may easily be conceived, and which it is
therefore unnecessary to explain any further.

In seeking for employment to a capital, manufactures are,
upon equal or nearly equal profits, naturally preferred to
foreign commerce, for the same reason that agriculture is naturally preferred to manufactures. As the capital of the landlord or

farmer is more secure than that of the manufacturer, so the capital of the manufacturer, being at all times more within his view and command, is more secure than that of the foreign merchant. In every period, indeed, of every society, the surplus part both of the rude and manufactured produce, or that for which there is no demand at home, must be sent abroad in order to be exchanged for something for which there is some demand at home. But whether the capital, which carries this surplus produce abroad, be a foreign or a domestic one is of very little importance. If the society has not acquired sufficient capital both to cultivate all its lands, and to manufacture in the completest manner the whole of its rude produce, there is even a considerable advantage that that rude produce should be exported by a foreign capital, in order that the whole stock of the society may be employed in more useful purposes. The wealth of ancient Egypt, that of China and Indostan, sufficiently demonstrate that a nation may attain a very high degree of opulence, though the greater part of its exportation trade be carried on by foreigners. The progress of our North American and West Indian colonies would have been much less rapid had no capital but what belonged to themselves been employed in exporting their surplus produce.

According to the natural course of things, therefore, the greater part of the capital of every growing society is, first, directed to agriculture, afterwards to manufactures, and last of all to foreign commerce. This order of things is so very natural that in every society that had any territory it has always, I believe, been in some degree observed. Some of their lands must have been cultivated before any considerable towns could be established, and some sort of coarse industry of the manufacturing kind must have been carried on in those towns, before they could well think of employing themselves in foreign commerce.

But though this natural order of things must have taken place in some degree in every such society, it has, in all the modern states of Europe, been, in many respects, entirely inverted. The foreign commerce of some of their cities has introduced all their finer manufactures, or such as were fit for distant sale; and manufactures and foreign commerce together have given birth to the principal improvements of agriculture. The manners and

customs which the nature of their original government introduced, and which remained after that government was greatly
altered, necessarily forced them into this unnatural and retro-
grade order.

CHAPTER II

OF THE DISCOURAGEMENT OF AGRICULTURE
IN THE ANCIENT STATE OF EUROPE
AFTER THE FALL OF THE ROMAN EMPIRE

WHEN the German and Scythian nations overran the western
provinces of the Roman empire, the confusions which followed
so great a revolution lasted for several centuries. The rapine and
violence which the barbarians exercised against the ancient inhabitants interrupted the commerce between the towns and the
country. The towns were deserted, and the country was left
uncultivated, and the western provinces of Europe, which had
enjoyed a considerable degree of opulence under the Roman
empire, sunk into the lowest state of poverty and barbarism.
During the continuance of those confusions, the chiefs and
principal leaders of those nations acquired or usurped to themselves the greater part of the lands of those countries. A great
part of them was uncultivated; but no part of them, whether
cultivated or uncultivated, was left without a proprietor. All of
them were engrossed, and the greater part by a few great proprietors.

This original engrossing of uncultivated lands, though a
great, might have been but a transitory evil. They might soon
have been divided again, and broke into small parcels either by
succession or by alienation. The law of primogeniture hindered
them from being divided by succession: the introduction of
entails prevented their being broke into small parcels by alienation.

When land, like movables, is considered as the means only of
subsistence and enjoyment, the natural law of succession divides
it, like them, among all the children of the family; of all of

whom the subsistence and enjoyment may be supposed equally
dear to the father. This natural law of succession accordingly
took place among the Romans, who made no more distinction
between elder and younger, between male and female, in the
inheritance of lands than we do in the distribution of movables.
But when land was considered as the means, not of subsistence
merely, but of power and protection, it was thought better that
it should descend undivided to one. In those disorderly times
every great landlord was a sort of petty prince. His tenants were
his subjects. He was their judge, and in some respects their
legislator in peace, and their leader in war. He made war
according to his own discretion, frequently against his neighbours, and sometimes against his sovereign. The security of a
landed estate, therefore, the protection which its owner could
afford to those who dwelt on it, depended upon its greatness.
To divide it was to ruin it, and to expose every part of it to be
oppressed and swallowed up by the incursions of its neighbours.
The law of primogeniture, therefore, came to take place, not
immediately, indeed, but in process of time, in the succession of
landed estates, for the same reason that it has generally taken
place in that of monarchies, though not always at their first
institution. That the power, and consequently the security of the
monarchy, may not be weakened by division, it must descend
entire to one of the children. To which of them so important a
preference shall be given must be determined by some general
rule, founded not upon the doubtful distinctions of personal
merit, but upon some plain and evident difference which can
admit of no dispute. Among the children of the same family,
there can be no indisputable difference but that of sex, and that
of age. The male sex is universally preferred to the female; and
when all other things are equal, the elder everywhere takes
place of the younger. Hence the origin of the right of primogeniture, and of what is called lineal succession.

Laws frequently continue in force long after the circumstances which first gave occasion to them, and which could
alone render them reasonable, are no more. In the present state
of Europe, the proprietor of a single acre of land is as perfectly
secure of his possession as the proprietor of a hundred thousand.
The right of primogeniture, however, still continues to be

respected, and as of all institutions it is the fittest to support the
pride of family distinctions, it is still likely to endure for many
centuries. In every other respect, nothing can be more contrary
to the real interest of a numerous family than a right which, in
order to enrich one, beggars all the rest of the children.

Entails are the natural consequences of the law of primogeniture. They were introduced to preserve a certain lineal succession, of which the law of primogeniture first gave the idea, and
to hinder any part of the original estate from being carried out
of the proposed line either by gift, or devise, or alienation;
either by the folly, or by the misfortune of any of its successive
owners. They were altogether unknown to the Romans.
Neither their substitutions nor fideicommisses bear any resemblance to entails, though some French lawyers have thought
proper to dress the modern institution in the language and garb
of those ancient ones.

When great landed estates were a sort of principalities, entails
might not be unreasonable. Like what are called the fundamental laws of some monarchies, they might frequently hinder
the security of thousands from being endangered by the caprice
or extravagance of one man. But in the present state of Europe,
when small as well as great estates derive their security from the
laws of their country, nothing can be more completely absurd.
They are founded upon the most absurd of all suppositions, the
supposition that every successive generation of men have not
an equal right to the earth, and to all that it possesses; but
that the property of the present generation should be restrained
and regulated according to the fancy of those who died perhaps
five hundred years ago. Entails, however, are still respected
through the greater part of Europe, in those countries particularly in which noble birth is a necessary qualification for the
enjoyment either of civil or military honours. Entails are
thought necessary for maintaining this exclusive privilege of the
nobility to the great offices and honours of their country; and
that order having usurped one unjust advantage over the rest of
their fellow-citizens, lest their poverty should render it ridiculous, it is thought reasonable that they should have another. The
common law of England, indeed, is said to abhor perpetuities,
and they are accordingly more restricted there than in any other

European monarchy; though even England is not altogether without them. In Scotland more than one-fifth, perhaps more than one-third, part of the whole lands of the country are at present supposed to be under strict entail.

Great tracts of uncultivated land were, in this manner, not only engrossed by particular families, but the possibility of their being divided again was as much as possible precluded for ever. It seldom happens, however, that a great proprietor is a great improver. In the disorderly times which gave birth to those barbarous institutions, the great proprietor was sufficiently employed in defending his own territories, or in extending his jurisdiction and authority over those of his neighbours. He had no leisure to attend to the cultivation and improvement of land. When the establishment of law and order afforded him this leisure, he often wanted the inclination, and almost always the requisite abilities. If the expense of his house and person either equalled or exceeded his revenue, as it did very frequently, he had no stock to employ in this manner. If he was an economist, he generally found it more profitable to employ his annual savings in new purchases than in the improvement of his old estate. To improve land with profit, like all other commercial projects, requires an exact attention to small savings and small gains, of which a man born to a great fortune, even though naturally frugal, is very seldom capable. The situation of such a person naturally disposes him to attend rather to ornament which pleases his fancy than to profit for which he has so little occasion. The elegance of his dress, of his equipage, of his house, and household furniture, are objects which from his fancy he had been accustomed to have some anxiety about. The turn of mind which this habit naturally forms follows him when he comes to think of the improvement of land. He embellishes perhaps four or five hundred acres in the neighbourhood of his house, at ten times the expense which the land is worth after all his improvements; and finds that if he was to improve his whole estate in the same manner, and he has little taste for any other, he would be a bankrupt before he had finished the tenth part of it. There still remain in both parts of the united kingdom some great estates which have continued without interruption in the hands of the same family since the times of feudal anarchy. Compare the present condition of those estates with the possessions of the small proprietors in their neighbourhood, and you will require no other argument to convince you how unfavourable such extensive property is to improvement.

If little improvement was to be expected from such great proprietors, still less was to be hoped for from those who occupied the land under them. In the ancient state of Europe, the occupiers of land were all tenants at will. They were all or almost all slaves; but their slavery was of a milder kind than that known among the ancient Greeks and Romans, or even in our West Indian colonies. They were supposed to belong more directly to the land than to their master. They could, therefore, be sold with it, but not separately. They could marry, provided it was with the consent of their master; and he could not afterwards dissolve the marriage by selling the man and wife to different persons. If he maimed or murdered any of them, he was liable to some penalty, though generally but to a small one. They were not, however, capable of acquiring property. Whatever they acquired was acquired to their master, and he could take it from them at pleasure. Whatever cultivation and improvement could be carried on by means of such slaves was properly carried on by their master. It was at his expense. The seed, the cattle, and the instruments of husbandry were all his. It was for his benefit. Such slaves could acquire nothing but their daily maintenance. It was properly the proprietor himself, therefore, that, in this case, occupied his own lands, and cultivated them by his own bondmen. This species of slavery still subsists in Russia, Poland, Hungary, Bohemia, Moravia, and other parts of Germany. It is only in the western and south-western provinces of Europe that it has gradually been abolished altogether.

But if great improvements are seldom to be expected from great proprietors, they are least of all to be expected when they employ slaves for their workmen. The experience of all ages and nations, I believe, demonstrates that the work done by slaves, though it appears to cost only their maintenance, is in the end the dearest of any. A person who can acquire no property, can have no other interest but to eat as much, and to labour as little

Slaves became unfeasible because they have no incentive

as possible. Whatever work he does beyond what is sufficient to
purchase his own maintenance can be squeezed out of him by
violence only, and not by any interest of his own. In ancient
Italy, how much the cultivation of corn degenerated, how unprofitable it became to the master when it fell under the
management of slaves, is remarked by both Pliny and
Columella. In the time of Aristotle it had not been much better
in ancient Greece. Speaking of the ideal republic described in
the laws of Plato, to maintain five thousand idle men (the
number of warriors supposed necessary for its defence) together
with their women and servants, would require, he says, a territory of boundless extent and fertility, like the plains of Babylon.

The pride of man makes him love to domineer, and nothing
mortifies him so much as to be obliged to condescend to persuade his inferiors. Wherever the law allows it, and the nature
of the work can afford it, therefore, he will generally prefer the
services of slaves to that of freemen. The planting of sugar and
tobacco can afford the expense of slave-cultivation. The raising
of corn, it seems, in the present times, cannot. In the English
colonies, of which the principal produce is corn, the far greater
part of the work is done by freemen. The late resolution of the
Quakers in Pennsylvania to set at liberty all their Negro slaves
may satisfy us that their number cannot be very great. Had they
made any considerable part of their property, such a resolution
could never have been agreed to. In our sugar colonies, on the
contrary, the whole work is done by slaves, and in our tobacco
colonies a very great part of it. The profits of a sugar-plantation
in any of our West Indian colonies are generally much greater
than those of any other cultivation that is known either in
Europe or America; and the profits of a tobacco plantation,
though inferior to those of sugar, are superior to those of corn,
as has already been observed. Both can afford the expense of
slave-cultivation, but sugar can afford it still better than tobacco.
The number of Negroes accordingly is much greater, in proportion to that of whites, in our sugar than in our tobacco colonies.

To the slave cultivators of ancient times gradually succeeded a
species of farmers known at present in France by the name of
Metayers. They are called in Latin, Coloni Partiarii. They have
been so long in disuse in England that at present I know no

English name for them. The proprietor furnished them with the seed, cattle, and instruments of husbandry, the whole stock, in short, necessary for cultivating the farm. The produce was divided equally between the proprietor and the farmer, after setting aside what was judged necessary for keeping up the stock, which was restored to the proprietor when the farmer either quitted, or was turned out of the farm.

Land occupied by such tenants is properly cultivated at the expense of the proprietor as much as that occupied by slaves. There is, however, one very essential difference between them. Such tenants, being freemen, are capable of acquiring property, and having a certain proportion of the produce of the land, they have a plain interest that the whole produce should be as great as possible, in order that their own proportion may be so. A slave, on the contrary, who can acquire nothing but his maintenance, consults his own ease by making the land produce as little as possible over and above that maintenance. It is probable that it was partly upon account of this advantage, and partly upon account of the encroachments which the sovereign, always jealous of the great lords, gradually encouraged their villains to make upon their authority, and which seem at last to have been such as rendered this species of servitude altogether inconvenient, that tenure in villanage gradually wore out through the greater part of Europe. The time and manner, however, in which so important a revolution was brought about, is one of the most obscure points in modern history. The church of Rome claims great merit in it; and it is certain that so early as the twelfth century, Alexander III published a bull for the general emancipation of slaves. It seems, however, to have been rather a pious exhortation than a law to which exact obedience was required from the faithful. Slavery continued to take place almost universally for several centuries afterwards, till it was gradually abolished by the joint operation of the two interests above mentioned, that of the proprietor on the one hand, and that of the sovereign on the other. A villain enfranchised, and at the same time allowed to continue in possession of the land, having no stock of his own, could cultivate it only by means of what the landlord advanced to him, and must, therefore, have been what the French called a metayer.

It could never, however, be in the interest even of this last species of cultivators to lay out, in the further improvement of the land, any part of the little stock which they might save from their own share of the produce, because the lord, who laid out nothing, was to get one-half of whatever it produced. The tithe, which is but a tenth of the produce, is found to be a very great hindrance to improvement. A tax, therefore, which amounted to one-half must have been an effectual bar to it. It might be the interest of a metayer to make the land produce as much as could be brought out of it by means of the stock furnished by the proprietor; but it could never be his interest to mix any part of his own with it. In France, where five parts out of six of the whole kingdom are said to be still occupied by this species of cultivators, the proprietors complain that their metayers take every opportunity of employing the master's cattle rather in carriage than in cultivation; because in the one case they get the whole profits to themselves, in the other they share them with their landlord. This species of tenants still subsists in some parts of Scotland. They are called steel-bow tenants. Those ancient English tenants, who are said by Chief Baron Gilbert and Doctor Blackstone to have been rather bailiffs of the landlord than farmers properly so called, were probably of the same kind.

To this species of tenancy succeeded, though by very slow degrees, farmers properly so called, who cultivated the land with their own stock, paying a rent certain to the landlord. When such farmers have a lease for a term of years, they may sometimes find it for their interest to lay out part of their capital in the further improvement of the farm; because they may sometimes expect to recover it, with a large profit, before the expiration of the lease. The possession even of such farmers, however, was long extremely precarious, and still is so in many parts of Europe. They could before the expiration of their term be legally outed of their lease by a new purchaser; in England, even by the fictitious action of a common recovery. If they were turned out illegally by the violence of their master, the action by which they obtained redress was extremely imperfect. It did not always reinstate them in the possession of the land, but gave them damages which never amounted to the real loss. Even in

THE WEALTH OF NATIONS

England, the country perhaps of Europe where the yeomanry has always been most respected, it was not till about the 14th of Henry VII that the action of ejectment was invented, by which the tenant recovers, not damages only but possession, and in which his claim is not necessarily concluded by the uncertain decision of a single assize. This action has been found so effectual a remedy that, in the modern practice, when the landlord has occasion to sue for the possession of the land, he seldom makes use of the actions which properly belong to him as landlord, the writ of right or the writ of entry, but sues in the name of his tenant by the writ of ejectment. In England, therefore, the security of the tenant is equal to that of the proprietor. In England, besides, a lease for life of forty shillings a year value is a freehold, and entitles the lessee to vote for a member of parliament; and as a great part of the yeomanry have freeholds of this kind, the whole order becomes respectable to their landlords on account of the political consideration which this gives them. There is, I believe, nowhere in Europe, except in England, any instance of the tenant building upon the land of which he had no lease, and trusting that the honour of his landlord would take no advantage of so important an improvement. Those laws and customs so favourable to the yeomanry have perhaps contributed more to the present grandeur of England than all their boasted regulations of commerce taken together.

The law which secures the longest leases against successors of every kind is, so far as I know, peculiar to Great Britain. It was introduced into Scotland so early as 1449, by a law of James II. Its beneficial influence, however, has been much obstructed by entails; the heirs of entail being generally restrained from letting leases for any long term of years, frequently for more than one year. A late act of parliament has, in this respect, somewhat slackened their fetters, though they are still by much too strait. In Scotland, besides, as no leasehold gives a vote for a member of parliament, the yeomanry are upon this account less respectable to their landlords than in England.

In other parts of Europe, after it was found convenient to secure tenants both against heirs and purchasers, the term of their security was still limited to a very short period; in France, for example, to nine years from the commencement of the lease.

It has in that country, indeed, been lately extended to twenty-seven, a period still too short to encourage the tenant to make the most important improvements. The proprietors of land were anciently the legislators of every part of Europe. The laws relating to land, therefore, were all calculated for what they supposed the interest of the proprietor. It was for his interest, they had imagined, that no lease granted by any of his predecessors should hinder him from enjoying, during a long term of years, the full value of his land. Avarice and injustice are always short-sighted, and they did not foresee how much this regulation must obstruct improvement, and thereby hurt in the long-run the real interest of the landlord.

The farmers too, besides paying the rent, were anciently, it was supposed, bound to perform a great number of services to the landlord, which were seldom either specified in the lease, or regulated by any precise rule, but by the use and wont of the manor or barony. These services, therefore, being almost entirely arbitrary, subjected the tenant to many vexations. In Scotland the abolition of all services not precisely stipulated in the lease has in the course of a few years very much altered for the better the condition of the yeomanry of that country.

The public services to which the yeomanry were bound were not less arbitrary than the private ones. To make and maintain the high roads, a servitude which still subsists, I believe, everywhere, though with different degrees of oppression in different countries, was not the only one. When the king's troops, when his household or his officers of any kind passed through any part of the country, the yeomanry were bound to provide them with horses, carriages, and provisions, at a price regulated by the purveyor. Great Britain is, I believe, the only monarchy in Europe where the oppression of purveyance has been entirely abolished. It still subsists in France and Germany.

The public taxes to which they were subject were as irregular and oppressive as the services. The ancient lords, though extremely unwilling to grant themselves any pecuniary aid to their sovereign, easily allowed him to tallage, as they called it, their tenants, and had not knowledge enough to foresee how much this must in the end affect their own revenue. The taille, as it still subsists in France, may serve as an example of those ancient tallages. It is a tax upon the supposed profits of the farmer, which they estimate by the stock that he has upon the farm. It is his interest, therefore, to appear to have as little as possible, and consequently to employ as little as possible in its cultivation, and none in its improvement. Should any stock happen to accumulate in the hands of a French farmer, the taille is almost equal to a prohibition of its ever being employed upon the land. This tax, besides, is supposed to dishonour whoever is subject to it, and to degrade him below, not only the rank of a gentleman, but that of a burgher, and whoever rents the lands of another becomes subject to it. No gentleman, nor even any burgher who has stock, will submit to this degradation. This tax, therefore, not only hinders the stock which accumulates upon the land from being employed in its improvement, but drives away all other stock from it. The ancient tenths and fifteenths, so usual in England in former times, seem, so far as they affected the land, to have been taxes of the same nature with the taille.

Under all these discouragements, little improvement could be expected from the occupiers of land. That order of people, with all the liberty and security which law can give, must always improve under great disadvantages. The farmer, compared with the proprietor, is as a merchant who trades with borrowed money compared with one who trades with his own. The stock of both may improve, but that of the one, with only equal good conduct, must always improve more slowly than that of the other, on account of the large share of the profits which is consumed by the interest of the loan. The lands cultivated by the farmer must, in the same manner, with only equal good conduct, be improved more slowly than those cultivated by the proprietor, on account of the large share of the produce which is consumed in the rent, and which, had the farmer been proprietor, he might have employed in the further improvement of the land. The station of a farmer besides is, from the nature of things, inferior to that of a proprietor. Through the greater part of Europe the yeomanry are regarded as an inferior rank of people, even to the better sort of tradesmen and mechanics, and in all parts of Europe to the great merchants and master manufacturers. It can seldom happen, therefore, that a man of any considerable stock should quit the superior in order to place himself in an inferior station. Even in the present state of Europe, therefore, little stock is likely to go from any other profession to the improvement of the land in the way of farming. More does perhaps in Great Britain than in any other country, though even there the great stocks which are, in some places, employed in farming have generally been acquired by farming, the trade, perhaps, in which of all others stock is commonly acquired most slowly. After small proprietors, however, rich and great farmers are, in every country, the principal improvers. There are more such perhaps in England than in any other European monarchy. In the republican governments of Holland and of Berne in Switzerland, the farmers are said to be not inferior to those of England.

The ancient policy of Europe was, over and above all this, unfavourable to the improvement and cultivation of land, whether carried on by the proprietor or by the farmer; first, by the general prohibition of the exportation of corn without a special licence, which seems to have been a very universal regulation; and secondly, by the restraints which were laid upon the inland commerce, not only of corn, but of almost every other part of the produce of the farm by the absurd laws against engrossers, regraters, and forestallers, and by the privileges of fairs and markets. It has already been observed in what manner the prohibition of the exportation of corn, together with some encouragement given to the importation of foreign corn, obstructed the cultivation of ancient Italy, naturally the most fertile country in Europe, and at that time the seat of the greatest empire in the world. To what degree such restraints upon the inland commerce of this commodity, joined to the general prohibition of exportation, must have discouraged the cultivation of countries less fertile, and less favourably circumstanced, it is not perhaps very easy to imagine.

CHAPTER III

OF THE RISE AND PROGRESS OF CITIES AND TOWNS AFTER THE FALL OF THE ROMAN EMPIRE

THE inhabitants of cities and towns were, after the fall of the Roman empire, not more favoured than those of the country. They consisted, indeed, of a very different order of people from the first inhabitants of the ancient republics of Greece and Italy. These last were composed chiefly of the proprietors of lands, among whom the public territory was originally divided, and who found it convenient to build their houses in the neighbourhood of one another, and to surround them with a wall, for the sake of common defence. After the fall of the Roman empire, on the contrary, the proprietors of land seem generally to have lived in fortified castles on their own estates, and in the midst of their own tenants and dependants. The towns were chiefly inhabited by tradesmen and mechanics, who seem in those days to have been of servile, or very nearly of servile condition. The privileges which we find granted by ancient charters to the inhabitants of some of the principal towns in Europe sufficiently show what they were before those grants. The people to whom it is granted as a privilege that they might give away their own daughters in marriage without the consent of their lord, that upon their death their own children, and not their lord, should succeed to their goods, and that they might dispose of their own effects by will, must, before those grants, have been either altogether or very nearly in the same state of villanage with the occupiers of land in the country.

They seem, indeed, to have been a very poor, mean set of people, who used to travel about with their goods from place to place, and from fair to fair, like the hawkers and pedlars of the present times. In all the different countries of Europe then, in the same manner as in several of the Tartar governments of Asia at present, taxes used to be levied upon the persons and goods of travellers when they passed through certain manors, when they went over certain bridges, when they carried about their goods from place to place in a fair, when they erected in it a booth or stall to sell them in. These different taxes were known in England by the names of passage, pontage, lastage, and stallage. Sometimes the king, sometimes a great lord, who had, it seems, upon some occasions, authority to do this, would grant to particular traders, to such particularly as lived in their own demesnes, a general exemption from such taxes. Such traders, though in other respects of servile, or very nearly of servile condition, were upon this account called Free-traders. They in return usually paid to their protector a sort of annual poll-tax. In those days protection was seldom granted without a valuable consideration, and this tax might, perhaps, be considered as compensation for what their patrons might lose by their exemption from other taxes. At first, both those poll-taxes and those exemptions seem to have been altogether personal, and to have affected only particular individuals during either their lives or the pleasure of their protectors. In the very imperfect accounts which have been published from Domesday-book, of several of the towns of England, mention is frequently made sometimes of the tax which particular burghers paid, each of them, either to the king or to some other great lord for this sort of protection; and sometimes of the general amount only of all those taxes.[1]

But how servile soever may have been originally the condition of the inhabitants of the towns, it appears evidently that they arrived at liberty and independency much earlier than the occupiers of land in the country. That part of the king's revenue which arose from such poll-taxes in any particular town used commonly to be let in farm during a term of years for a rent certain, sometimes to the sheriff of the county, and sometimes to other persons. The burghers themselves frequently got credit enough to be admitted to farm the revenues of this sort which arose out of their own town, they becoming jointly and severally answerable for the whole rent.[2] To let a farm in this manner was quite agreeable to the usual economy of, I believe, the sovereigns of all the different countries of Europe, who used frequently to let whole manors to all the tenants of those

1. See Brady's *Historical Treatise of Cities and Burroughs*, p. 3, etc.
2. See Madox, *Firma Burgi*, p. 18, also *History of the Exchequer*, chap. 10, sect. v. p. 223, first edition.

manors, they becoming jointly and severally answerable for the whole rent; but in return being allowed to collect it in their own way, and to pay it into the king's exchequer by the hands of their own bailiff, and being thus altogether freed from the insolence of the king's officers—a circumstance in those days regarded as of the greatest importance.

At first, the farm of the town was probably let to the burghers, in the same manner as it had been to other farmers, for a term of years only. In process of time, however, it seems to have become the general practice to grant it to them in fee, that is for ever, reserving a rent certain never afterwards to be augmented. The payment having thus become perpetual, the exemptions, in return for which it was made, naturally became perpetual too. Those exemptions, therefore, ceased to be personal, and could not afterwards be considered as belonging to individuals as individuals, but as burghers of a particular burgh, which, upon this account, was called a free burgh, for the same reason that they had been called free burghers or free traders.

Along with this grant, the important privileges above mentioned, that they might give away their own daughters in marriage, that their children should succeed to them, and that they might dispose of their own effects by will, were generally bestowed upon the burghers of the town to whom it was given. Whether such privileges had before been usually granted along with the freedom of trade to particular burghers, as individuals, I know not. I reckon it not improbable that they were, though I cannot produce any direct evidence of it. But however this may have been, the principal attributes of villanage and slavery being thus taken away from them, they now, at least, became really free in our present sense of the word Freedom.

Nor was this all. They were generally at the same time erected into a commonalty or corporation, with the privilege of having magistrates and a town council of their own, of making bye-laws for their own government, of building walls for their own defence, and of reducing all their inhabitants under a sort of military discipline by obliging them to watch and ward, that is, as anciently understood, to guard and defend those walls against all attacks and surprises by night as well as by day. In England they were generally exempted from suit to the hundred and county courts; and all such pleas as should arise among them, the pleas of the crown excepted, were left to the decision of their own magistrates. In other countries much greater and more extensive jurisdictions were frequently granted to them.[1]

It might, probably, be necessary to grant to such towns as were admitted to farm their own revenues some sort of compulsive jurisdiction to oblige their own citizens to make payment. In those disorderly times it might have been extremely inconvenient to have left them to seek this sort of justice from any other tribunal. But it must seem extraordinary that the sovereigns of all the different countries of Europe should have exchanged in this manner for a rent certain, never more to be augmented, that branch of their revenue which was, perhaps, of all others the most likely to be improved by the natural course of things, without either expense or attention of their own; and that they should, besides, have in this manner voluntarily erected a sort of independent republics in the heart of their own dominions.

In order to understand this, it must be remembered that in those days the sovereign of perhaps no country in Europe was able to protect, through the whole extent of his dominions, the weaker part of his subjects from the oppression of the great lords. Those whom the laws could not protect, and who were not strong enough to defend themselves, were obliged either to have recourse to the protection of some great lord, and in order to obtain it to become either his slaves or vassals; or to enter into a league of mutual defence for the common protection of one another. The inhabitants of cities and burghs, considered as single individuals, had no power to defend themselves; but by entering into a league of mutual defence with their neighbours, they were capable of making no contemptible resistance. The lords despised the burghers, whom they considered not only as of a different order, but as a parcel of emancipated slaves, almost of a different species from themselves. The wealth of the burghers never failed to provoke their envy and indignation, and they plundered them upon every occasion without mercy or remorse. The burghers naturally hated and feared the lords. The king hated and feared them too; but though perhaps he

1. See Madox, *Firma Burgi:* See also Pfeffel on the remarkable events under Frederic II and his successors of the house of Suabia.

might despise, he had no reason either to hate or fear the burghers. Mutual interest, therefore, disposed them to support the king, and the king to support them against the lords. They were the enemies of his enemies, and it was his interest to render them as secure and independent of those enemies as he could. By granting them magistrates of their own, the privilege of making bye-laws for their own government, that of building walls for their own defence, and that of reducing all their inhabitants under a sort of military discipline, he gave them all the means of security and independency of the barons which it was in his power to bestow. Without the establishment of some regular government of this kind, without some authority to compel their inhabitants to act according to some certain plan or system, no voluntary league of mutual defence could either have afforded them any permanent security, or have enabled them to give the king any considerable support. By granting them the farm of their town in fee, he took away from those whom he wished to have for his friends, and, if one may say so, for his allies, all ground of jealousy and suspicion that he was ever afterwards to oppress them, either by raising the farm rent of their town or by granting it to some other farmer.

The princes who lived upon the worst terms with their barons seem accordingly to have been the most liberal in grants of this kind to their burghs. King John of England, for example, appears to have been a most munificent benefactor to his towns.[1] Philip the First of France lost all authority over his barons. Towards the end of his reign, his son Lewis, known afterwards by the name of Lewis the Fat, consulted, according to Father Daniel, with the bishops of the royal demesnes concerning the most proper means of restraining the violence of the great lords. Their advice consisted of two different proposals. One was to erect a new order of jurisdiction, by establishing magistrates and a town council in every considerable town of his demesnes. The other was to form a new militia, by making the inhabitants of those towns, under the command of their own magistrates, march out upon proper occasions to the assistance of the king. It is from this period, according to the French antiquarians, that we are to date the institution of the magis-

1. See Madox.

trates and councils of cities in France. It was during the unprosperous reigns of the princes of the house of Suabia that the
greater part of the free towns of Germany received the first
grants of their privileges, and that the famous Hanseatic league
first became formidable.[1]

The militia of the cities seems, in those times, not to have
been inferior to that of the country, and as they could be more
readily assembled upon any sudden occasion, they frequently
had the advantage in their disputes with the neighbouring
lords. In countries, such as Italy and Switzerland, in which, on
account either of their distance from the principal seat of
government, of the natural strength of the country itself, or of
some other reason, the sovereign came to lose the whole of his
authority, the cities generally became independent republics,
and conquered all the nobility in their neighbourhood, obliging
them to pull down their castles in the country and to live, like
other peaceable inhabitants, in the city. This is the short history
of the republic of Berne as well as of several other cities in
Switzerland. If you except Venice, for of that city the history is
somewhat different, it is the history of all the considerable
Italian republics, of which so great a number arose and perished
between the end of the twelfth and the beginning of the sixteenth century.

In countries such as France or England, where the authority
of the sovereign, though frequently very low, never was destroyed altogether, the cities had no opportunity of becoming
entirely independent. They became, however, so considerable
that the sovereign could impose no tax upon them, besides the
stated farm-rent of the town, without their own consent. They
were, therefore, called upon to send deputies to the general
assembly of the states of the kingdom, where they might join
with the clergy and the barons in granting, upon urgent occasions, some extraordinary aid to the king. Being generally, too,
more favourable to his power, their deputies seem, sometimes,
to have been employed by him as a counterbalance in those
assemblies to the authority of the great lords. Hence the origin
of the representation of burghs in the states-general of all the
great monarchies in Europe.

1. See Pfeffel.

Order and good government, and along with them the liberty and security of individuals, were, in this manner, established in cities at a time when the occupiers of land in the country were exposed to every sort of violence. But men in this defenceless state naturally content themselves with their necessary subsistence, because to acquire more might only tempt the injustice of their oppressors. On the contrary, when they are secure of enjoying the fruits of their industry, they naturally exert it to better their condition, and to acquire not only the necessaries, but the conveniences and elegancies of life. That industry, therefore, which aims at something more than necessary subsistence, was established in cities long before it was commonly practised by the occupiers of land in the country. If in the hands of a poor cultivator, oppressed with the servitude of villanage, some little stock should accumulate, he would naturally conceal it with great care from his master, to whom it would otherwise have belonged, and take the first opportunity of running away to a town. The law was at that time so indulgent to the inhabitants of towns, and so desirous of diminishing the authority of the lords over those of the country, that if he could conceal himself there from the pursuit of his lord for a year, he was free for ever. Whatever stock, therefore, accumulated in the hands of the industrious part of the inhabitants of the country naturally took refuge in cities as the only sanctuaries in which it could be secure to the person that acquired it.

The inhabitants of a city, it is true, must always ultimately derive their subsistence, and the whole materials and means of their industry, from the country. But those of a city, situated near either the sea coast or the banks of a navigable river, are not necessarily confined to derive them from the country in their neighbourhood. They have a much wider range, and may draw them from the most remote corners of the world, either in exchange for the manufactured produce of their own industry, or by performing the office of carriers between distant countries and exchanging the produce of one for that of another. A city might in this manner grow up to great wealth and splendour, while not only the country in its neighbourhood, but all those to which it traded, were in poverty and wretchedness. Each of those countries, perhaps, taken singly, could afford it but a small part either of its subsistence or of its employment, but all of them taken together could afford it both a great subsistence and a great employment. There were, however, within the narrow circle of the commerce of those times, some countries that were opulent and industrious. Such was the Greek empire as long as it subsisted, and that of the Saracens during the reigns of the Abassides. Such too was Egypt till it was conquered by the Turks, some part of the coast of Barbary, and all those provinces of Spain which were under the government of the Moors.

The cities of Italy seem to have been the first in Europe which were raised by commerce to any considerable degree of opulence. Italy lay in the centre of what was at that time the improved and civilized part of the world. The crusades too, though by the great waste of stock and destruction of inhabitants which they occasioned they must necessarily have retarded the progress of the greater part of Europe, were extremely favourable to that of some Italian cities. The great armies which marched from all parts to the conquest of the Holy Land gave extraordinary encouragement to the shipping of Venice, Genoa, and Pisa, sometimes in transporting them thither, and always in supplying them with provisions. They were the commissaries, if one may say so, of those armies; and the most destructive frenzy that ever befell the European nations was a source of opulence to those republics.

The inhabitants of trading cities, by importing the improved manufacturers and expensive luxuries of richer countries, afforded some food to the vanity of the great proprietors, who eagerly purchased them with great quantities of the rude produce of their own lands. The commerce of a great part of Europe in those times, accordingly, consisted chiefly in the exchange of their own rude for the manufactured produce of more civilized nations. Thus the wool of England used to be exchanged for the wines of France and the fine cloths of Flanders, in the same manner as the corn in Poland is at this day exchanged for the wines and brandies of France and for the silks and velvets of France and Italy.

A taste for the finer and more improved manufactures was in this manner introduced by foreign commerce into countries where no such works were carried on. But when this taste became so general as to occasion a considerable demand, the merchants, in order to save the expense of carriage, naturally endeavoured to establish some manufactures of the same kind in their own country. Hence the origin of the first manufactures for distant sale that seem to have been established in the western provinces of Europe after the fall of the Roman empire. No large country, it must be observed, ever did or could subsist without some sort of manufactures being carried on in it; and when it is said of any such country that it has no manufactures, it must always be understood of the finer and more improved or of such as are fit for distant sale. In every large country both the clothing and household furniture of the far greater part of the people are the produce of their own industry. This is even more universally the case in those poor countries which are commonly said to have no manufactures than in those rich ones that are said to abound in them. In the latter, you will generally find, both in the clothes and household furniture of the lowest rank of people, a much greater proportion of foreign productions than in the former.

Those manufactures which are fit for distant sale seem to have been introduced into different countries in two different ways.

Sometimes they have been introduced, in the manner above mentioned, by the violent operation, if one may say so, of the stocks of particular merchants and undertakers, who established them in imitation of some foreign manufactures of the same kind. Such manufactures, therefore, are the offspring of foreign commerce, and such seem to have been the ancient manufactures of silks, velvets, and brocades, which flourished in Lucca during the thirteenth century. They were banished from thence by the tyranny of one of Machiavel's heroes, Castruccio Castracani. In 1310, nine hundred families were driven out of Lucca, of whom thirty-one retired to Venice and offered to introduce there the silk manufacture.[1] Their offer was accepted; many privileges were conferred upon them, and they began the manufacture with three hundred workmen. Such, too, seem to have been the manufactures of fine cloths that anciently flour-

1. See Sandi, *Istoria Civile de Vinezia*, part ii. vol. i. pages 247 and 256.

ished in Flanders, and which were introduced into England in the beginning of the reign of Elizabeth; and such are the present silk manufactures of Lyons and Spitalfields. Manufactures introduced in this manner are generally employed upon foreign materials, being imitations of foreign manufactures. When the Venetian manufacture was first established, the materials were all brought from Sicily and the Levant. The more ancient manufacture of Lucca was likewise carried on with foreign materials. The cultivation of mulberry trees and the breeding of silk-worms seem not to have been common in the northern parts of Italy before the sixteenth century. Those arts were not introduced into France till the reign of Charles IX. The manufactures of Flanders were carried on chiefly with Spanish and English wool. Spanish wool was the material, not of the first woollen manufacture of England, but of the first that was fit for distant sale. More than one half the materials of the Lyons manufacture is at this day foreign silk; when it was first established, the whole or very nearly the whole was so. No part of the materials of the Spitalfields manufacture is ever likely to be the produce of England. The seat of such manufactures, as they are generally introduced by the scheme and project of a few individuals, is sometimes established in a maritime city, and sometimes in an inland town, according as their interest, judgement, or caprice happen to determine.

At other times, manufactures for distant sale grow up naturally, and as it were of their own accord, by the gradual refinement of those household and coarser manufactures which must at all times be carried on even in the poorest and rudest countries. Such manufactures are generally employed upon the materials which the country produces, and they seem frequently to have been first refined and improved in such inland countries as were, not indeed at a very great, but at a considerable distance from the sea coast, and sometimes even from all water carriage. An inland country, naturally fertile and easily cultivated, produces a great surplus of provisions beyond what is necessary for maintaining the cultivators, and on account of the expense of land carriage, and inconveniency of river navigation, it may frequently be difficult to send this surplus abroad. Abundance, therefore, renders provisions cheap, and encourages

a great number of workmen to settle in the neighbourhood,
who find that their industry can there procure them more of the
necessaries and conveniencies of life than in other places. They
work up the materials of manufacture which the land produces,
and exchange their finished work, or what is the same thing the
price of it, for more materials and provisions. They give a new
value to the surplus part of the rude produce by saving the
expense of carrying it to the water side or to some distant
market; and they furnish the cultivators with something in exchange for it that is either useful or agreeable to them upon
easier terms than they could have obtained it before. The
cultivators get a better price for their surplus produce, and can
purchase cheaper other conveniences which they have occasion
for. They are thus both encouraged and enabled to increase this
surplus produce by a further improvement and better cultivation of the land; and as the fertility of the land had given birth
to the manufacture, so the progress of the manufacture re-acts
upon the land and increases still further its fertility. The manufacturers first supply the neighbourhood, and afterwards, as
their work improves and refines, more distant markets. For
though neither the rude produce nor even the coarse manufacture could, without the greatest difficulty, support the expense of a considerable land carriage, the refined and improved
manufacture easily may. In a small bulk it frequently contains
the price of a great quantity of rude produce. A piece of fine
cloth, for example, which weighs only eighty pounds, contains in
it, the price, not only of eighty pounds' weight of wool, but
sometimes of several thousand weight of corn, the maintenance
of the different working people and of their immediate employers. The corn, which could with difficulty have been carried
abroad in its own shape, is in this manner virtually exported in
that of the complete manufacture, and may easily be sent to the
remotest corners of the world. In this manner have grown up
naturally, and as it were of their own accord, the manufactures
of Leeds, Halifax, Sheffield, Birmingham, and Wolverhampton. Such manufactures are the offspring of agriculture. In the
modern history of Europe, their extension and improvement
have generally been posterior to those which were the offspring
of foreign commerce. England was noted for the manufacture

of fine cloths made of Spanish wool more than a century before any of those which now flourish in the places above mentioned were fit for foreign sale. The extension and improvement of these last could not take place but in consequence of the extension and improvement of agriculture, the last and greatest effect of foreign commerce, and of the manufactures immediately introduced by it, and which I shall now proceed to explain.

CHAPTER IV

HOW THE COMMERCE OF THE TOWNS CONTRIBUTED TO THE IMPROVEMENT OF THE COUNTRY

THE increase and riches of commercial and manufacturing towns, contributed to the improvement and cultivation of the countries to which they belonged in three different ways.

First, by affording a great and ready market for the rude produce of the country, they gave encouragement to its cultivation and further improvement. This benefit was not even confined to the countries in which they were situated, but extended more or less to all those with which they had any dealings. To all of them they afforded a market for some part either of their rude or manufactured produce, and consequently gave some encouragement to the industry and improvement of all. Their own country, however, on account of its neighbourhood, necessarily derived the greatest benefit from this market. Its rude produce being charged with less carriage, the traders could pay the growers a better price for it, and yet afford it as cheap to the consumers as that of more distant countries.

Secondly, the wealth acquired by the inhabitants of cities was frequently employed in purchasing such lands as were to be sold, of which a great part would frequently be uncultivated. Merchants are commonly ambitious of becoming country gentlemen, and when they do, they are generally the best of all improvers. A merchant is accustomed to employ his money chiefly in profitable projects, whereas a mere country gentleman is accustomed to employ it chiefly in expense. The one often sees his money go from him and return to him again with a profit; the other, when once he parts with it, very seldom expects to see any more of it. Those different habits naturally affect their temper and disposition in every sort of business. A merchant is commonly a bold, a country gentleman a timid undertaker. The one is not afraid to lay out at once a large capital upon the improvement of his land when he has a probable prospect of raising the value of it in proportion to the expense. The other, if he has any capital, which is not always the case, seldom ventures to employ it in this manner. If he improves at all, it is commonly not with a capital, but with what he can save out of his annual revenue. Whoever has had the fortune to live in a mercantile town situated in an unimproved country must have frequently observed how much more spirited the operations of merchants were in this way than those of mere country gentlemen. The habits, besides, of order, economy, and attention, to which mercantile business naturally forms a merchant, render him much fitter to execute, with profit and success, any project of improvement.

Thirdly, and lastly, commerce and manufactures gradually introduced order and good government, and with them, the liberty and security of individuals, among the inhabitants of the country, who had before lived almost in a continual state of war with their neighbours, and of servile dependency upon their superiors. This, though it has been the least observed, is by far the most important of all their effects. Mr Hume is the only writer who, so far as I know, has hitherto taken notice of it.

In a country which has neither foreign commerce, nor any of the finer manufactures, a great proprietor, having nothing for which he can exchange the greater part of the produce of his lands which is over and above the maintenance of the cultivators, consumes the whole in rustic hospitality at home. If this surplus produce is sufficient to maintain a hundred or a thousand men, he can make use of it in no other way than by maintaining a hundred or a thousand men. He is at all times, therefore, surrounded with a multitude of retainers and dependants, who, having no equivalent to give in return for their maintenance, but being fed entirely by his bounty, must obey him, for the same reason that soldiers must obey the prince

who pays them. Before the extension of commerce and manufacture in Europe, the hospitality of the rich and the great, from
the sovereign down to the smallest baron, exceeded everything
which in the present times we can easily form a notion of.
Westminster hall was the dining-room of William Rufus, and
might frequently, perhaps, not be too large for his company. It
was reckoned a piece of magnificence in Thomas Becket that he
strewed the floor of his hall with clean hay or rushes in the
season, in order that the knights and squires who could not get
seats might not spoil their fine clothes when they sat down on
the floor to eat their dinner. The great Earl of Warwick is said
to have entertained every day at his different manors thirty
thousand people, and though the number here may have been
exaggerated, it must, however, have been very great to admit of
such exaggeration. A hospitality nearly of the same kind was
exercised not many years ago in many different parts of the
highlands of Scotland. It seems to be common in all nations to
whom commerce and manufactures are little known. I have
seen, says Doctor Pocock, an Arabian chief dine in the streets of
a town where he had come to sell his cattle, and invite all
passengers, even common beggars, to sit down with him and
partake of his banquet.

The occupiers of land were in every respect as dependent
upon the great proprietor as his retainers. Even such of them as
were not in a state of villanage were tenants at will, who paid a
rent in no respect equivalent to the subsistence which the land
afforded them. A crown, half a crown, a sheep, a lamb, was
some years ago in the highlands of Scotland a common rent for
lands which maintained a family. In some places it is so at this
day; nor will money at present purchase a greater quantity of
commodities there than in other places. In a country where the
surplus produce of a large estate must be consumed upon the
estate itself, it will frequently be more convenient for the proprietor that part of it be consumed at a distance from his own
house, provided they who consume it are as dependent upon
him as either his retainers or his menial servants. He is thereby
saved from the embarrassment of either too large a company or
too large a family. A tenant at will, who possesses land sufficient
to maintain his family for little more than a quit-rent, is as

dependent upon the proprietor as any servant or retainer whatever, and must obey him with as little reserve. Such a proprietor, as he feeds his servants and retainers at his own house, so he feeds his tenants at their houses. The subsistence of both is derived from his bounty, and its continuance depends upon his good pleasure.

Upon the authority which the great proprietors necessarily had in such a state of things over their tenants and retainers was founded the power of the ancient barons. They necessarily became the judges in peace, and the leaders in war, of all who dwelt upon their estates. They could maintain order and execute the law within their respective demesnes, because each of them could there turn the whole force of all the inhabitants against the injustice of any one. No other person had sufficient authority to do this. The king in particular had not. In those ancient times he was little more than the greatest proprietor in his dominions, to whom, for the sake of common defence against their common enemies, the other great proprietors paid certain respects. To have enforced payment of a small debt within the lands of a great proprietor, where all the inhabitants were armed and accustomed to stand by one another, would have cost the king, had he attempted it by his own authority, almost the same effort as to extinguish a civil war. He was, therefore, obliged to abandon the administration of justice through the greater part of the country to those who were capable of administering it; and for the same reason to leave the command of the country militia to those whom that militia would obey.

It is a mistake to imagine that those territorial jurisdictions took their origin from the feudal law. Not only the highest jurisdictions both civil and criminal, but the power of levying troops, of coining money, and even that of making bye-laws for the government of their own people, were all rights possessed allodially by the great proprietors of land several centuries before even the name of the feudal law was known in Europe. The authority and jurisdiction of the Saxon lords in England appear to have been as great before the Conquest as that of any of the Norman lords after it. But the feudal law is not supposed to have become the common law of England till after the

Conquest. That the most extensive authority and jurisdictions were possessed by the great lords in France allodially, long before the feudal law was introduced into that country, is a matter of fact that admits of no doubt. That authority and those jurisdictions all necessarily flowed from the state of property and manners just now described. Without remounting to the remote antiquities of either the French or English monarchies, we may find in much later times many proofs that such effects must always flow from such causes. It is not thirty years ago since Mr Cameron of Lochiel, a gentleman of Lochabar in Scotland, without any legal warrant whatever, not being what was then called a lord of regality, nor even a tenant in chief, but a vassal of the Duke of Argyle, and without being so much as a justice of peace, used, notwithstanding, to exercise the highest criminal jurisdiction over his own people. He is said to have done so with great equity, though without any of the formalities of justice; and it is not improbable that the state of that part of the country at that time made it necessary for him to assume this authority in order to maintain the public peace. That gentleman, whose rent never exceeded five hundred pounds a year, carried, in 1745, eight hundred of his own people into the rebellion with him.

The introduction of the feudal law, so far from extending, may be regarded as an attempt to moderate the authority of the great allodial lords. It established a regular subordination, accompanied with a long train of services and duties, from the king down to the smallest proprietor. During the minority of the proprietor, the rent, together with the management of his lands, fell into the hands of his immediate superior, and consequently, those of all great proprietors into the hands of the king, who was charged with the maintenance and education of the pupil, and who, from his authority as guardian, was supposed to have a right of disposing of him in marriage, provided it was in a manner not unsuitable to his rank. But though this institution necessarily tended to strengthen the authority of the king, and to weaken that of the great proprietors, it could not do either sufficiently for establishing order and good government among the inhabitants of the country, because it could not alter sufficiently that state of property and manners from which

the disorders arose. The authority of government still continued
to be, as before, too weak in the head and too strong in the
inferior members, and the excessive strength of the inferior
members was the cause of the weakness of the head. After the
institution of feudal subordination, the king was as incapable
of restraining the violence of the great lords as before. They
still continued to make war according to their own discretion,
almost continually upon one another, and very frequently upon
the king; and the open country still continued to be a scene of
violence, rapine, and disorder.

But what all the violence of the feudal institutions could
never have effected, the silent and insensible operation of
foreign commerce and manufactures gradually brought about.
These gradually furnished the great proprietors with something
for which they could exchange the whole surplus produce of
their lands, and which they could consume themselves without
sharing it either with tenants or retainers. All for ourselves and
nothing for other people, seems, in every age of the world, to
have been the vile maxim of the masters of mankind. As soon,
therefore, as they could find a method of consuming the whole
value of their rents themselves, they had no disposition to share
them with any other persons. For a pair of diamond buckles
perhaps, or for something as frivolous and useless, they exchanged the maintenance, or what is the same thing, the price
of the maintenance of a thousand men for a year, and with it
the whole weight and authority which it could give them. The
buckles, however, were to be all their own, and no other human
creature was to have any share of them; whereas in the more
ancient method of expense they must have shared with at least a
thousand people. With the judges that were to determine the
preference, this difference was perfectly decisive; and thus, for
the gratification of the most childish, the meanest, and the most
sordid of all vanities, they gradually bartered their whole power
and authority.

In a country where there is no foreign commerce, nor any of
the finer manufactures, a man of ten thousand a year cannot
well employ his revenue in any other way than in maintaining,
perhaps, a thousand families, who are all of them necessarily at
his command. In the present state of Europe, a man of ten

thousand a year can spend his whole revenue, and he generally does so, without directly maintaining twenty people, or being able to command more than ten footmen not worth the commanding. Indirectly, perhaps, he maintains as great or even a greater number of people than he could have done by the ancient method of expense. For though the quantity of precious productions for which he exchanges his whole revenue be very small, the number of workmen employed in collecting and preparing it must necessarily have been very great. Its great price generally arises from the wages of their labour, and the profits of all their immediate employers. By paying that price he indirectly pays all those wages and profits, and thus indirectly contributes to the maintenance of all the workmen and their employers. He generally contributes, however, but a very small proportion to that of each, to very few perhaps a tenth, to many not a hundredth, and to some not a thousandth, nor even a ten-thousandth part of their whole annual maintenance. Though he contributes, therefore, to the maintenance of them all, they are all more or less independent of him, because generally they can all be maintained without him.

When the great proprietors of land spend their rents in maintaining their tenants and retainers, each of them maintains entirely all his own tenants and all his own retainers. But when they spend them in maintaining tradesmen and artificers, they may, all of them taken together, perhaps, maintain as great, or, on account of the waste which attends rustic hospitality, a greater number of people than before. Each of them, however, taken singly, contributes often but a very small share to the maintenance of any individual of this greater number. Each tradesman or artificer derives his subsistence from the employment, not of one, but of a hundred or a thousand different customers. Though in some measure obliged to them all, therefore, he is not absolutely dependent upon any one of them.

The personal expense of the great proprietors having in this manner gradually increased, it was impossible that the number of their retainers should not as gradually diminish, till they were at last dismissed altogether. The same cause gradually led them to dismiss the unnecessary part of their tenants. Farms were enlarged, and the occupiers of land, notwithstanding the complaints of depopulation, reduced to the number necessary for cultivating it, according to the imperfect state of cultivation and improvement in those times. By the removal of the unnecessary mouths, and by exacting from the farmer the full value of the farm, a greater surplus, or what is the same thing, the price of a greater surplus, was obtained for the proprietor, which the merchants and manufacturers soon furnished him with a method of spending upon his own person in the same manner as he had done the rest. The same cause continuing to operate, he was desirous to raise his rents above what his lands, in the actual state of their improvement, could afford. His tenants could agree to this upon one condition only, that they should be secured in their possession, for such a term of years as might give them time to recover with profit whatever they should lay out in the further improvement of their land. The expensive vanity of the landlord made him willing to accept of this condition; and hence the origin of long leases.

Even a tenant at will, who pays the full value of the land, is not altogether dependent upon the landlord. The pecuniary advantages which they receive from one another are mutual and equal, and such a tenant will expose neither his life nor his fortune in the service of the proprietor. But if he has a lease for a long term of years, he is altogether independent; and his landlord must not expect from him even the most trifling service beyond what is either expressly stipulated in the lease or imposed upon him by the common and known law of the country.

The tenants having in this manner become independent, and the retainers being dismissed, the great proprietors were no longer capable of interrupting the regular execution of justice or of disturbing the peace of the country. Having sold their birthright, not like Esau for a mess of pottage in time of hunger and necessity, but in the wantonness of plenty, for trinkets and baubles, fitter to be the playthings of children than the serious pursuits of men, they became as insignificant as any substantial burgher or tradesman in a city. A regular government was established in the country as well as in the city, nobody having sufficient power to disturb its operations in the one any more than in the other.

It does not, perhaps, relate to the present subject, but I cannot help remarking it, that very old families, such as have possessed some considerable estate from father to son for many successive generations are very rare in commercial countries. In countries which have little commerce, on the contrary, such as Wales or the highlands of Scotland, they are very common. The Arabian histories seem to be all full of genealogies, and there is a history written by a Tartar Khan, which has been translated into several European languages, and which contains scarce anything else; a proof that ancient families are very common among those nations. In countries where a rich man can spend his revenue in no other way than by maintaining as many people as it can maintain, he is not apt to run out, and his benevolence it seems is seldom so violent as to attempt to maintain more than he can afford. But where he can spend the greatest revenue upon his own person, he frequently has no bounds to his expense, because he frequently has no bounds to his vanity or to his affection for his own person. In commercial countries, therefore, riches, in spite of the most violent regulations of law to prevent their dissipation, very seldom remain long in the same family. Among simple nations, on the contrary, they frequently do without any regulations of law, for among nations of shepherds, such as the Tartars and Arabs, the consumable nature of their property necessarily renders all such regulations impossible.

A revolution of the greatest importance to the public happiness was in this manner brought about by two different orders of people who had not the least intention to serve the public. To gratify the most childish vanity was the sole motive of the great proprietors. The merchants and artificers, much less ridiculous, acted merely from a view to their own interest, and in pursuit of their own pedlar principle of turning a penny wherever a penny was to be got. Neither of them had either knowledge or foresight of that great revolution which the folly of the one, and the industry of the other, was gradually bringing about.

It is thus that through the greater part of Europe the commerce and manufactures of cities, instead of being the effect, have been the cause and occasion of the improvement and cultivation of the country.

This order, however, being contrary to the natural course of things, is necessarily both slow and uncertain. Compare the slow progress of those European countries of which the wealth depends very much upon their commerce and manufactures, with the rapid advances of our North American colonies, of which the wealth is founded altogether in agriculture. Through the greater part of Europe the number of inhabitants is not supposed to double in less than five hundred years. In several of our North American colonies, it is found to double in twenty or five-and-twenty years. In Europe, the law of primogeniture and perpetuities of different kinds, prevent the division of great estates, and thereby hinder the multiplication of small proprietors. A small proprietor, however, who knows every part of his little territory, who views it with all the affection which property, especially small property, naturally inspires, and who upon that account takes pleasure not only in cultivating but in adorning it, is generally of all improvers the most industrious, the most intelligent, and the most successful. The same regulations, besides, keep so much land out of the market that there are always more capitals to buy than there is land to sell, so that what is sold always sells at a monopoly price. The rent never pays the interest of the purchase money, and is, besides, burdened with repairs and other occasional charges to which the interest of money is not liable. To purchase land is everywhere in Europe a most unprofitable employment of a small capital. For the sake of the superior security, indeed, a man of moderate circumstances, when he retires from business, will sometimes choose to lay out his little capital in land. A man of profession too, whose revenue is derived from another source, often loves to secure his savings in the same way. But a young man, who instead of applying to trade or to some profession, should employ a capital of two or three thousand pounds in the purchase and cultivation of a small piece of land, might indeed expect to live very happily, and very independently, but must bid adieu for ever to all hope of either great fortune or great illustration, which by a different employment of his stock he might have had the same chance of acquiring with other people. Such a person too, though he cannot aspire at being a proprietor, will often disdain to be a farmer. The small quantity of land, therefore, which is brought to market, and the high price of what is brought thither, prevents a great number of capitals from being employed in its cultivation and improvement which would otherwise have taken that direction. In North America, on the contrary, fifty or sixty pounds is often found a sufficient stock to begin a plantation with. The purchase and improvement of uncultivated land is there the most profitable employment of the smallest as well as of the greatest capitals, and the most direct road to all the fortune and illustration which can be acquired in that country. Such land, indeed, is in North America to be had almost for nothing, or at a price much below the value of the natural produce – a thing impossible in Europe, or, indeed, in any country where all lands have long been private property. If landed estates, however, were divided equally among all the children upon the death of any proprietor who left a numerous family, the estate would generally be sold. So much land would come to market that it could no longer sell at a monopoly price. The free rent of the land would go nearer to pay the interest of the purchase-money, and a small capital might be employed in purchasing land as profitably as in any other way.

England, on account of the natural fertility of the soil, of the great extent of the sea-coast in proportion to that of the whole country, and of the many navigable rivers which run through it and afford the conveniency of water carriage to some of the most inland parts of it, is perhaps as well fitted by nature as any large country in Europe to be the seat of foreign commerce, of manufactures for distant sale, and of all the improvements which these can occasion. From the beginning of the reign of Elizabeth too, the English legislature has been peculiarly attentive to the interests of commerce and manufactures, and in reality there is no country in Europe, Holland itself not excepted, of which the law is, upon the whole, more favourable to this sort of industry. Commerce and manufactures have accordingly been continually advancing during all this period. The cultivation and improvement of the country has, no doubt, been gradually advancing too; but it seems to have followed slowly, and at a distance, the more rapid progress of commerce and manufactures. The greater part of the country must probably have been cultivated before the reign of Elizabeth; and a very great part of it still remains uncultivated, and the cultivation of the far greater part much inferior to what it might be. The law of England, however, favours agriculture not only indirectly by the protection of commerce, but by several direct encouragements. Except in times of scarcity, the exportation of corn is not only free, but encouraged by a bounty. In times of moderate plenty, the importation of foreign corn is loaded with duties that amount to a prohibition. The importation of live cattle, except from Ireland, is prohibited at all times, and it is but of late that it was permitted from thence. Those who cultivate the land, therefore, have a monopoly against their countrymen for the two greatest and most important articles of land produce, bread and butcher's meat. These encouragements, though at bottom, perhaps, as I shall endeavour to show hereafter, altogether illusory, sufficiently demonstrate at least the good intention of the legislature to favour agriculture. But what is of much more importance than all of them, the yeomanry of England are rendered as secure, as independent, and as respectable as law can make them. No country, therefore, in which the right of primogeniture takes place, which pays tithes, and where perpetuities, though contrary to the spirit of the law, are admitted in some cases, can give more encouragement to agriculture than England. Such, however, notwithstanding, is the state of its cultivation. What would it have been had the law given no direct encouragement to agriculture besides what arises indirectly from the progress of commerce, and had left the yeomanry in the same condition as in most other countries of Europe? It is now more than two hundred years since the beginning of the reign of Elizabeth, a period as long as the course of human prosperity usually endures.

France seems to have had a considerable share of foreign commerce near a century before England was distinguished as a commercial country. The marine of France was considerable, according to the notions of the times, before the expedition of Charles VIII to Naples. The cultivation and improvement of France, however, is, upon the whole, inferior to that of England. The law of the country has never given the same direct encouragement to agriculture.

The foreign commerce of Spain and Portugal to the other

parts of Europe, though chiefly carried on in foreign ships, is very considerable. That to their colonies is carried on in their own, and is much greater, on account of the great riches and extent of those colonies. But it has never introduced any considerable manufactures for distant sale into either of those countries, and the greater part of both still remains uncultivated. The foreign commerce of Portugal is of older standing than that of any great country in Europe, except Italy.

Italy is the only great country of Europe which seems to have been cultivated and improved in every part by means of foreign commerce and manufactures for distant sale. Before the invasion of Charles VIII, Italy, according to Guicciardin, was cultivated not less in the most mountainous and barren parts of the country, than in the plainest and most fertile. The advantageous situation of the country, and the great number of independent states which at that time subsisted in it, probably contributed not a little to this general cultivation. It is not impossible too, notwithstanding this general expression of one of the most judicious and reserved of modern historians, that Italy was not at that time better cultivated than England is at present.

The capital, however, that is acquired to any country by commerce and manufactures, is all a very precarious and uncertain possession till some part of it has been secured and realized in the cultivation and improvement of its lands. A merchant, it has been said very properly, is not necessarily the citizen of any particular country. It is in a great measure indifferent to him from what place he carries on his trade; and a very trifling disgust will make him remove his capital, and together with it all the industry which it supports, from one country to another. No part of it can be said to belong to any particular country, till it has been spread as it were over the face of that country, either in buildings or in the lasting improvement of lands. No vestige now remains of the great wealth said to have been possessed by the greater part of the Hans towns except in the obscure histories of the thirteenth and fourteenth centuries. It is even uncertain where some of them were situated or to what towns in Europe the Latin names given to some of them belong. But though the misfortunes of Italy in the end of the fifteenth and beginning of the sixteenth centuries greatly diminished the commerce and manufactures of the cities of Lombardy and Tuscany, those countries still continue to be among the most populous and best cultivated in Europe. The civil wars of Flanders, and the Spanish government which succeeded them, chased away the great commerce of Antwerp, Ghent, and Bruges. But Flanders still continues to be one of the richest, best cultivated, and most populous provinces of Europe. The ordinary revolutions of war and government easily dry up the sources of that wealth which arises from commerce only. That which arises from the more solid improvements of agriculture is much more durable, and cannot be destroyed but by those more violent convulsions occasioned by the depredations of hostile and barbarous nations continued for a century or two together, such as those that happened for some time before and after the fall of the Roman empire in the western provinces of Europe.

INDEXES

INDEX OF MODERN AUTHORITIES

Meggens, N., *Universal Merchant* (1753), 313

Messance, *Recherches sur la Population* . . . (1766), 187, 303, 347

Montesquieu, *Spirit of the Laws* (1748), 198, 454

Pfeffel, *Nouvel Abregé Chronologique de l'Histoire* . . . *d'Allemagne* (1776), 499 *n*.

Poivre, *Voyages d'un Philosophe* . . . (1768), 260

Pocock, R., *Description of the East* (1743), 509

Postlethwaite, James, *History of the Public Revenue* (1759), 417 *n*.

Ramazzini, *Treatise on the Diseases of Tradesmen* (1746), 185

Ruddiman, T., ed. Anderson's *Diplomata Scotiae* (1739), 289, 318 *n*, 394 *n*.

St Maur, Duprè de, *Essai sur les Nonnoies* (1746), 285, 290, 347

Sandi, V., *Istoria Civile de Venezia* (1755), 504 *n*.

Smith, J., *Memoirs of Wool* (1747), 337 ff.

Three Tracts on the Corn Trade by C. Smith (1766), 304 *n*.

Ulloa, *Voyage Historique* . . . (1752), 252, 274 ff.

The reader interested in Smith's authorities should consult H. Mizuta's *Adam Smith's Library* (1967).

INDEX

MORE ABOUT PENGUINS
AND PELICANS

Penguinews, which appears every month, contains details of all the new books issued by Penguins as they are published. From time to time it is supplemented by *Penguins in Print*, which is our complete list of almost 5,000 titles.

A specimen copy of *Penguinews* will be sent to you free on request. Please write to Dept EP, Penguin Books Ltd, Harmondsworth, Middlesex, for your copy.

In the U.S.A.: For a complete list of books available from Penguins in the United States write to Dept CS, Penguin Books, 625 Madison Avenue, New York, New York 10022.

In Canada: For a complete list of books available from Penguins in Canada write to Penguin Books Canada Ltd, 41 Steelcase Road West, Markham, Ontario.

REFORMATION TO INDUSTRIAL REVOLUTION

Christopher Hill

The period 1530–1780 witnessed the making of modern English society. Under the Tudors England was a society of subsistence agriculture in which it was taken for granted that a fully human existence was possible only for the landed ruling class. In 1780 England was a national market on the threshold of industrial revolution, and the ideology of self-help had permeated into the middle ranks. A universal belief in original sin had been supplanted by the romanticism of 'Man is good'. And the first British Empire had already been won and lost.

In this masterly study, one of the great historians of the seventeenth century analyses the transformation of British society and the complex interaction of economic, cultural and political change in the period. In particular he stresses the political ferment of the seventeenth century and its influence on the revolutions in trade and agriculture, which in their turn prepared English society for the take-off into the modern industrial world.

'This formidable little book – its range of information is remarkable and it is stuffed with fruitful hypotheses – is rather a commentary than an analysis' – Peter Laslett in the *Guardian*

'There is clearly no lack of controversial matter here: Mr Hill has fulfilled an important function of a good social history' – *The Times Literary Supplement*

The Pelican Economic History of Britain: 3

INDUSTRY AND EMPIRE

E. J. Hobsbawm

The industrial revolution marks the most fundamental transformation in the history of the world recorded in written documents. For a brief period it coincided with the history of a single country, Great Britain. This book describes and accounts for Britain's rise as the world's first industrial world power, its decline from the temporary dominance of the pioneer, its rather special relationship with the rest of the world (notably the underdeveloped countries), and the effects of all these on the life of the British people.

'When a brilliantly gifted and learned man impatiently sets about the lesser people who profess his subject, he writes a book that attracts and deserves attention. Eric Hobsbawm, by far the most gifted economic historian now writing, has done just this. Under the guise of a textbook he has produced an original and masterly reinterpretation of Western economic (not to speak of social and political) history' – John Vaizey in the *Listener*

'A masterly survey of the major economic developments and changes of the last 200 years, sharply and ironically observed, elegantly written and, for the statistically undernourished, illustrated by a host of excellent diagrams and maps' – *Guardian*

Pelican Classics

LEVIATHAN

HOBBES

Edited by C. B. Macpherson

From the turmoil of the English Civil War, when life was truly 'nasty, brutish, and short', Hobbes's *Leviathan* (1651) speaks directly to the twentieth century. In its over-riding concern for peace, its systematic analysis of power, and its elevation of politics to the status of a science, it mirrors much modern thinking. And despite its contemporary notoriety – Pepys called it 'a book the Bishops will not let be printed again' – it was also, as Dr Macpherson shows, a convincing apologia for the emergent seventeenth-century market society.

REFLECTIONS ON THE
REVOLUTION IN FRANCE

BURKE

Edited by Conor Cruise O'Brien

Burke's *Reflections* (1790) detonated the great debate on the French Revolution. But Burke's conservatism was more radical than is often admitted by those who see him as the father of modern conservatism. Traditionalism, for him, involved a return to an earlier humanity and even his counter-revolutionary prescriptions were revolutionary in their way. Added to this, Burke was an Irishman: and this fact, argues Dr O'Brien, entails a wholly new evaluation of the man.

ON WAR

CLAUSEWITZ

Edited by Anatol Rapoport

In his famous treatise *On War* (1832) Carl von Clausewitz may be said
to have distilled Napoleon into theory. He is best remembered for his
pronouncement that war is a continuation of politics by other means
and for his observation on total war: but modern strategists who profess
to apply his doctrines would do well to read him again. For Clausewitz,
as Professor Rapoport contends, made a distinction between judicious
and injudicious war, and the relationship he detected between war and
politics really means that war can only be waged in certain circumstances.

THE PELICAN CLASSICS

'A boon to students young and perennial ... the admirable introductions by reputable scholars are required reading' – *The Times Literary Supplement*